Praise for *Mashup Patterns*

"Enterprise architects think in high-level arch. .... this book cuts through the mashup marketing fluff and gets right down to presenting patterns as a way to analyze and solve enterprise problems using mashups."

—John Crupi, Chief Technology Officer of JackBe and Coauthor of *Core J2EE Patterns*

"Mashups offer an opportunity to rapidly deliver value to the business, either on top of an existing internal corporate SOA or on common freely available Internet services. In this work, Ogrinz guides the reader through frequently encountered scenarios in the mashup space. The examples alone will help you think laterally about the problems facing your business and new ways of solving them."

—Kevin P. Davis, Ph.D., Software Architect

"*Mashup Patterns* is an excellent, comprehensive treatment of a subject increasingly central to corporate IT management. With the benefit of his extensive software architecture experience, Michael is able to provide a wide array of mashup solutions to real world data wrangling problems. He clearly explains how to successfully apply mashup patterns and avoid going down anti-pattern rabbit holes. This book is a must-have for developers venturing into the vast and rapidly expanding enterprise mashup space."

—Daniel Leuck, CEO, Ooi

"Michael Ogrinz takes a broad view of mashups, focusing on their growing (and potentially revolutionary) role for harvesting and repurposing data within the modern information-driven enterprise. Don't look for code or programming tips here, because you won't find them. What you'll find instead are inspiring examples, clever ideas, and new ways to use the data already hiding in your business and in the Web around you."

—Rob Miller, Associate Professor of Computer Science, Massachusetts Institute of Technology

"To a user, a mashup has all the personal qualities of an advanced form of spreadsheet, except it's not limited only to figures; this is only a fraction of the value that enterprises can gain from deploying mashups as well-managed sophisticated tools. Michael has done us all a service by producing this book as a great step forward in helping IT and business managers to access this value."

—Andy Mulholland, Global Chief Technology Officer, Capgemini

"Mike Ogrinz has done an excellent job with thorough analysis of the various mashup patterns. What makes this book very exciting is the timing, when everyone wants to know more about mashups as well as the wide range of audience this book caters to. From director to engineer, everyone can find examples relevant to them. Congrats, Mike, on a job well done!"

—Sona Srinivasan, IT Engineer/ITG Architect, Cisco Systems

"Michael Ogrinz does for mashups what the illustrious Gang of Four (Gamma, Helm, Johnson, and Vlissides) did for object-oriented software design. He starts with a buzzword-free explanation of what mashups are and how they matter to the enterprise. He then presents a taxonomy of ready-to-implement design patterns, chock-full of concrete examples. Finally, he includes an appendix of real-world case studies, ranging from a Web 2.0 startup to the Defense Intelligence Agency. This clear, readable, no-nonsense book is a must-have for enterprise IT workers who are ready to embrace the brave new world of Enterprise 2.0."

—Daniel Tunkelang, Ph.D., Chief Scientist, Endeca

Mashup Patterns

Mashup Patterns

Designs and Examples for the
Modern Enterprise

Michael Ogrinz

Addison-Wesley

Upper Saddle River, NJ • Boston • Indianapols • San Francisco
New York • Toronto • Montreal • London • Munich • Paris • Madrid
Capetown • Sydney • Tokyo • Singapore • Mexico City

Many of the designations used by manufacturers and sellers to distinguish their products are claimed as trademarks. Where those designations appear in this book, and the publisher was aware of a trademark claim, the designations have been printed with initial capital letters or in all capitals.

The author and publisher have taken care in the preparation of this book, but make no expressed or implied warranty of any kind and assume no responsibility for errors or omissions. No liability is assumed for incidental or consequential damages in connection with or arising out of the use of the information or programs contained herein.

The publisher offers excellent discounts on this book when ordered in quantity for bulk purchases or special sales, which may include electronic versions and/or custom covers and content particular to your business, training goals, marketing focus, and branding interests. For more information, please contact:

U.S. Corporate and Government Sales
(800) 382-3419
corpsales@pearsontechgroup.com

For sales outside the United States please contact:

International Sales
international@pearsoned.com

Visit us on the Web: informit.com/aw

Library of Congress Cataloging-in-Publication Data

Ogrinz, Michael.
   Mashup patterns : designs and examples for the modern enterprise / Michael Ogrinz.
      p.   cm.
   Includes index.
   ISBN 978-0-321-57947-8 (pbk. : alk. paper)
   1. Web 2.0. 2. Mashups (World Wide Web) 3. Business enterprises—Technological innovations. 4. Application software—Development. I. Title.

TK5105.88817.O57 2009
005.7'2—dc22

                                                        2008053762

ISBN-13: 978-0-321-57947-8
ISBN-10:   0-321-57947-X
Text printed in the United States on recycled paper at R.R. Donnelley in Crawfordsville, Indiana.

First printing, March 2009

Editor-in-Chief
Mark Taub

Acquisitions Editor
Trina MacDonald

Development Editor
Songlin Qiu

Managing Editor
John Fuller

Project Editor
Anna V. Popick

Copy Editor
Jill Hobbs

Indexer
Michael Loo

Proofreader
Kelli Brooks

Cover Designer
Chuti Prasertsith

Composition
Rob Mauhar

To my wife, Monica,
and our two little mashups,
Meghan and Alexis

Contents

Preface

Once you understand the design patterns and have had an "Aha!" experience with them, you won't ever think about . . . design in the same way.[1]

The inspiration for writing this book came from my own "Aha!" moment. Initially I dismissed mashups as a hack best suited to consumer-focused sites that did things like combine craigslist and Google Maps[2] or merge local event calendars. I couldn't see how any public information on the Internet could benefit my employer. I laughed behind the backs of vendors who tried to demonstrate the promise of the technology based on examples that involved checking the weather or searching for a used car.

I had my epiphany when I was meeting with some frustrated business associates one afternoon. They were performing a series of tedious actions that seemed ripe for automation except for one problem: They had to repeatedly consult an outside vendor's Web site at each step of the process. The Web site didn't expose an application programming interface (API), so they mistakenly thought that some degree of human interaction was inevitable. After all, Web pages are just for people, right? It suddenly dawned on me that the mashup tools I had dismissed could get around this problem. I could automatically extract the data I needed from the site and write a small application to perform the rest of the process. In essence, I could create an API where none existed before. Once the "people requirement" was removed, the entire procedure was easily offloaded to a computer.

Traditional approaches to application reuse require that a system or its constituent parts be designed for inclusion in new solutions. While an admirable goal, one limitation of this architecture is that it's implemented "by developers, for developers." Mashups explode this narrow view of reuse. Mashups can certainly leverage open systems, but they can also reach deep into applications where no API currently exists to grab data or automate processing. In addition,

---

1. Gamma, Erich, Richard Helm, Ralph Johnson, and John M. Vlissides. *Design Patterns.* Addison-Wesley Professional, 1994.

2. Housingmap.com, created by Paul Rademacher, combined the craigslist.com and Google Maps Web sites in what is considered the Web's first mashup.

many mashup tools leverage the latest advances in user interface design to make the entire solution-building process accessible to the average user.

The goal of this book is to demonstrate situations where mashups can be used to solve what appear to be intractable problems outside the realm of traditional solutions. Once you have a breakthrough moment similar to mine, you'll never look at application development the same way again. In learning about how mashups foster efficiencies and inspire creativity, you may discover a path that will lead your business toward profitable new areas.

There are many meanings of "pattern" in the world of software engineering. In the classic text *Design Patterns,* the authors include the following disclaimer:

> Point of view affects one's interpretation of what is and isn't a pattern. One person's pattern can be another person's primitive building block.

In this book I am using a less rigorous interpretation of the term "pattern." I hope this will not prevent readers from exploring the text on mere ideological grounds. My goal is not to provide an academic treatise on the subject, but rather to provide a cookbook of ideas that will help you unlock the hidden potential in the resources that surround you. Enterprise mashups present exciting new opportunities for organizations to mine wikis, blogs, and other document-centric Web content as first-class data. Firms can combine these resources with others inside the corporation, such as databases and Web Services, in a near-endless series of permutations.

Not all of the patterns presented here will fit perfectly within your company—but ideally they will trigger fresh ways of thinking that will lead you to build exciting new solutions.

Who Should Read This Book

An understanding of mashup technology can spark new ideas for addressing old or dismissed problems. This book caters to the broad community of skills and abilities found within the next generation enterprise.

Software Developers

Each pattern is presented within a standard template that provides a technical summary (diagram, problem statement, and solution) of that pattern. This summary will resonate most with developers, who are often accustomed to dealing with abstractions as part of their normal course of work. Mashups can be a key tool for personnel in an organization's Information Technology (IT) department to address the backlog of unmet or unfulfilled end-user requirements.

Content Creators

Content creators should also familiarize themselves with the examples provided for each pattern, as these sections will provide insight into how their information is being consumed. In the era of mashups, anything placed on the Web is fair game not only for people, but also for software agents, automated bots, Web scrapers, and crawlers.

Business Users and Executive Management

Mashups are sometimes viewed as part of an egalitarian new world where information is freely shared. While that may be the case, they can also be used to flat-out make money. The examples given for each pattern provide the layperson with details about how mashups help a business be more productive and competitive.

The discussion of security in Chapter 10 is applicable to everyone. The rampant adoption of any technology without appropriate controls for managing its use is a recipe for failure. Almost every day a new headline cries out about how an employee accidentally mishandled or abused data. This behavior can lead to loss of trust or outright litigation between a company and its customers. Unless we want mashups to become the latest high-profile failure, we must work to supervise them correctly.

The organization of this book is designed to encourage browsing and self-discovery. I encourage you to skip around and explore the numerous feats of which mashups are capable. There is no "right way" to use them. When you apply a mashup to solve a particularly thorny problem, you've succeeded!

How Patterns Are Presented

Each pattern is presented by means of a standard template:

- *Name.* The name is the most succinct summary of what the pattern actually does. Once a pattern enters common usage, it's typically referenced in conversation only by its name.

- *Icon.* To facilitate use of the patterns in architectural diagrams, each one has been assigned a specific icon.

- *Diagram.* The diagram provides a visual representation of how the pattern is constructed. The diagrams are especially useful to demonstrate how multiple patterns interact (e.g., API Enabler and Competitive Analysis).

- *Core Activities.* Every mashup is associated with a set of highly generic capabilities (data extraction, transformation, and so on). Not all mashup products necessarily implement all of these features. Rather than redundantly list each requirement with each pattern, they have been abstracted into a set of core activities. When you attempt to use a pattern, you should verify that your selected toolset supports the functionality of the requisite core activities.

- *Problem.* This section explains the difficulty or opportunity that the pattern seeks to address; it offers a short summary that explains the value proposition of the pattern.

- *Solution.* This part addresses the problem identified earlier to show how mashups can be used to create a solution. Success in implementing a solution may depend on the toolset you are using, the sites participating in the mashup, and the pattern's fragility rating.

- *Related Patterns.* The context in which a pattern is applied can have a major impact on its description. This section references the use of similar mashup features in other patterns. If the pattern described is a composite of other patterns with new functionality, the leveraged patterns are listed here as well.

- *Fragility.* Mashups may contain elements of instability based on the resources they leverage. The degree of this fragility varies with each implementation. In essence, mashups allow some fragility for the benefit of agility. This section assigns a general risk rating to a particular pattern and provides a brief explanation of how it was derived.

- *Examples.* These short vignettes illustrate uses of the particular pattern in an enterprise context.

About the Pattern Examples

The most persuasive component of a pattern's detail is an example. To drive home the benefits regardless of the reader's background, this book typically presents more than one example of each pattern's use that spans different industries. It's my hope that as you peruse these examples some will resonate as potential opportunities within your organization. In addition, these sections should serve to expand your knowledge regarding the flexibility and capabilities of enterprise mashups.

In a divergence from some patterns books, *Mashup Patterns* does not supplement the formal definitions with sample code. At this early stage of evolution, no standard libraries or toolkits have been developed for mashups, and the capabilities of off-the-shelf products vary greatly. In place of code, examples are provided based on Web sites, applications, and other resources. Where an example relies on interactions with external data sources and third-party applications (e.g., API Enabler, Field Agent, Competitive Analysis, Usability Enhancer), sample products were constructed from scratch. Any resemblance to actual software or Web sites is purely coincidental.

The case studies presented in the book's appendix illustrate how leading organizations have used specific products to implement the patterns described in the text. This material should neither be interpreted as an endorsement of any particular product nor used as a substitute for conducting your own due-diligence analysis. Rather, the case studies are intended to underscore the practical nature of the technology and to encourage you to explore mashups further.

Mashups aren't just about Web sites, of course. Because the Internet is probably the richest source of raw material for their construction, however, I inevitably used it as a primary ingredient in many of the examples. Please excuse these momentary demonstrations of bias while I try and drive a larger point home. Don't forget that many mashup products support sources ranging from Web Services, XML feeds, and databases to email and binary formats (e.g., Excel and PDF).

What You Will Gain from Reading This Book

The information contained in this book will help you unleash the potential of enterprise mashups within your firm. The following topics are covered:

- An overview of Web 2.0 and Enterprise 2.0 and an exploration of how mashups fit into this framework

- Familiarity with the technology that makes mashups work

- Perspectives on how mashups coexist with other IT tools and initiatives

- A collection of patterns and practical examples that both explain and demonstrate the benefits of mashups in an enterprise context

Other Resources

This book has a companion Web site, http://mashuppatterns.com, where you can learn about new mashup patterns and contribute your own ideas and comments. You may contact the author at mike@mashuppatterns.com. The site also contains corrections to any errata discovered in this text. Please stop by and share your experiences with enterprise mashups!

Acknowledgments

The path that led me to write this book has been filled with interesting twists and turns. I must admit that when I encountered the notion of mashups within the enterprise, I greeted it with more than a little skepticism. It didn't help that my first exposure to the topic came as the result of a vendor's sales presentation. Luckily, I work in an environment that facilitates the open exchange of new ideas and solutions. I gradually came to see the promise of this new paradigm and to appreciate how it could help both my coworkers and my peers across different industries. After speaking at some conferences and surveying attendees, it was clear that the value of mashups needed to be broadcast to a wider audience. I am grateful that Mark Taub, Editor-in-Chief at Pearson, approached me with this opportunity.

Once my book-writing adventure was under way, I received the support of many individuals who I would like to publicly acknowledge for their assistance.

First and foremost I must thank my associates on the Global Markets Architecture team, led by B. J. Fesq. B. J. and I have been friends much longer than our tenure as coworkers. Besides suggesting an idea for one of the first enterprise mashups I ever created, B. J. has been extremely encouraging and flexible while I shifted around multiple priorities to finish this text. Rob Guild, another peer and friend, graciously read every word I put in front of him and offered his comments. Without Rob's feedback (and occasional YouTube comedic intervention), I am positive many of the patterns would not have had the impact I intended. Some of his "war stories" were the direct inspiration behind several of the examples. I must also thank my other teammates both for their direct support and for picking up the slack due to my preoccupation with mashups, especially Zo Obradovic and Sean Cody.

As a first-time author I had many (oh, so many) questions about the process. I must credit Trina MacDonald, my editor at Pearson, for her patience in enduring what must have sometimes seemed like an endless barrage of queries. I still recall our first conversation when I got on a rant about what the mashup community needed and Trina simply answered, "So, are you going to write it?"

Cire Gearhart of the design firm iOne Creative is a remarkable individual with whom I've had the satisfaction of working alongside for several years now. We share an uncommon notion that powerful applications can be easy (and fun!) to use. This attitude is reflected in my pursuit of mashups—but for Cire it's part of reimagining the entire user experience for his firm's customers. Cire donated a large portion of his personal time to provide nearly all of the screen renderings that accompany the pattern examples. Given that many of these images are reduced to small proportions, it would have been easy to turn out something quickly. Instead, he insisted on providing full-size mockups as evidence of his devotion to detail. Cire also provided the original cover design for this text, which I think is flat-out cool.

Membership in the New York CTO Club has been of special importance to me. First and foremost, the ability to converse with so many sharp-witted and talented individuals on a regular basis is a privilege. Mark Mathias sponsored my membership and has a preternatural ability to see what a person needs and the generosity to help them get it. Mark invited me into the Club just as "mashups" coincidentally became an almost regular part of any discussion. I'd also like to single out another member, John Musser. Many will recognize John as the founder of programmableweb.com. John invited me to blog on the subject of enterprise mashups at programmableweb and I am extraordinarily pleased to be able to use that forum to expand upon the conversation started in this book.

Stewart Mader, author of *Wikipatterns,* was kind enough to offer me space on wikipatterns.com while I was writing this text. Using a wiki was a natural approach for communicating with technical reviewers and vendors providing case studies. Thanks, Stewart, for alleviating any worries I might have had about setting up and managing this infrastructure myself.

I would like to thank my technical reviewers Anurag Prasad, Sona Srinivasan, and Kevin P. Davis for their thoughtful suggestions and feedback during the authoring process.

The vendor case studies are almost as important as the patterns themselves. The tangible successes they demonstrate should serve to further inspire the reader to look at mashups more seriously. Just as this book benefited from the input of many people, so the case studies leveraged the efforts of numerous individuals. I would like to recognize a few of the people with whom I had the pleasure of collaborating:

John Gerken from IBM's Emerging Technologies Software Group, along with coworkers Ed Elze, Sam Thompson, John Feller, and Vladimir Stemkovski, took time away from their work on IBM Mashup Center (the follow-up to the much-admired QEDWiki and Mashup Hub) to provide details on how this new platform extends the benefits of its predecessor deeper into the enterprise.

I'm grateful to Chris Warner and John Crupi of JackBe for their work on the Presto case studies. John is a noted figure in the patterns community and I'm flattered he chose to be associated with this work. Chris provided a novel structure where two different case studies were compared against each other to show how mashups' strengths are greater than the differences that separate different problem domains.

Stefan Andreasen, Michael Osowski, and Pete Melroy from Kapow Technologies—you guys have been so helpful and encouraging during this process that I can't thank you enough. Beyond the case studies, I appreciate your being a sounding board for many of my ideas and providing advice and support.

I first met Matt Jacobson of Connotate after a presentation where I had mentioned mashups were "almost" within the capabilities of a nondeveloper. Matt approached me because he thought I underestimated the current tools as well as the skill level of users. I thank him for correcting me on both counts.

René Bonvanie and his associates at Serena (including Kevin Parker, Tim Zonca, and Kathy Wells) have been leading a very public campaign to change the way we all think about mashups. Behind the interesting (and sometimes very funny) ads are some great stories, and I'm happy they shared a few for this book.

Joe McGonnell, Jesse Green, and Francis Carden of OpenSpan provided some great material on how mashups can be used to combine "thick-client" desktop applications with traditional Web-based resources. This is a powerful new area in which the patterns are being used; I'm sure many firms will want to explore this topic further.

Of course, "products" are only part of a successful case study. The real stars are the customers who used the tools and share their experiences with us. I'd like to thank the firms that allowed their stories to be told, especially Afni, the Associated Press, Audi, the Defense Intelligence Agency (DIA), MICROS Systems, Simply Hired, and Thomson Reuters.

I would be remiss in not thanking some other people who helped shape this text in some way: Mark Bolles, Tim W. Brown, John Cimral, Richard Eliano, Kurt Foeller, Ed Julson, Joe Keller, Amanda Leslie, Robert Lin, Brian Theodore, and Phillip Yang. Special thanks go out to Olivia Basegio, Songlin Qiu, and Anna Popick at Pearson, and copy editor Jill Hobbs.

Finally, and most importantly, I would like to thank my family. From a writer's perspective I can say the creation of this book has been a long and demanding process—but I can only imagine what it's been like for those around me. For your patience and understanding when I had to sequester myself away on holidays, weekends, or late at night (or ask you to drag the kids out for a few hours), you all have my deepest appreciation. I'm thankful to my parents, Dorothy and Emil, who bought me a Sinclair ZX81 computer (in kit form, no less!) more than 25 years ago and have supported my lifelong interest in science and technology, and to my Uncle Fred, who instilled both a respect for books and a voracious appetite for reading. And to my wife Monica—your support didn't just make this book possible; it was another reminder of how lucky I am to be your husband. Your help and encouragement kept my spirits lifted even when my personal reserves were running low.

About the Author

Michael Ogrinz is a principal architect at one of the world's largest financial institutions. His business focus is to identify and integrate emerging technologies into the enterprise and to create innovative and competitive solutions. A frequent industry speaker on various facets of Enterprise 2.0, Michael has been instrumental in enhancing the computing environment at his firm through his work on user interfaces and usability, wikis and blogs, and, most recently, mashups.

Michael cofounded localendar.com, a classic "garage start-up" that demonstrates how the "Long Tail" applies to online calendars as much as anything else. The niche site has provided more than 400,000 schools, churches, and clubs with simple online scheduling services since its inception more than eight years ago.

Michael lives with his wife, two daughters, a collection of classic pinball vector arcade machines, and a partially completed B9 Robot in wonderfully rural Easton, Connecticut.

About the Cover Picture

A common theme for patterns books is that they draw upon a large body of preexisting work in a specific discipline. Mashups are a relatively new technology, so they lack this long pedigree. The image on the front cover was selected for two reasons.

First, the pile of fortune cookies represents the multitude of potential implementations where this new paradigm will affect our lives and work. Each unopened cookie stands for our unfulfilled desire to know the future so that we can prepare for it.

Second, the open cookie with the message "Change is coming" is the single fortune capable of answering *all* of our questions and shocks us a little with its broad, yet unfocused prediction. Naturally, we already know that change—especially in the realm of technology—is inevitable, but sometimes we cling to old tools and techniques for too long out of fear or comfort. Mashups *are* change—a change to how solutions are built and who builds them. Once the reader embraces this vision, we can begin to explore the patterns that make it possible to leverage these changes to build creative new solutions.

Chapter 1

Understanding Mashup Patterns

Collaborators welcome![1]

Introduction

When the World Wide Web was first unveiled, "collaborators" referred to one small segment of the population: nerds.[2] The first browser ran on a computer that almost no one outside of a university or research lab used.[3] The Web itself consisted of a lone site[4] (WWW Growth, Figure 1.1). Yet from this singularity, a new universe would soon emerge.

The amount of content didn't grow much until two years later. That was when the first of several "Big Bangs" would occur. In 1993, the first PC-based program capable of browsing the Web was released.[5] Its introduction instantly put the Web within the reach of a far larger audience. Even so, Internet connectivity remained largely restricted to universities, research institutes, and corporations. Consumers enjoyed online communities, but generally did so via prepackaged, fenced-in services such as Compuserve, Prodigy, and America Online (AOL). Connectivity was achieved through slow "dial-up" connections over telephone lines. Access to content was typically billed at an hourly rate.

---

1. From Tim Berners-Lee's first public Usenet post announcing the public availability of the first Web server and browser in 1991.

2. A contingent of which I am proud to proclaim myself a member.

3. The NeXT workstation, conceived by computer luminary Steve Jobs.

4. Tim Berners-Lee invented the World Wide Web in 1989 while working at the CERN Particle Physics Laboratory.

5. NCSA Mosaic, released in 1993.

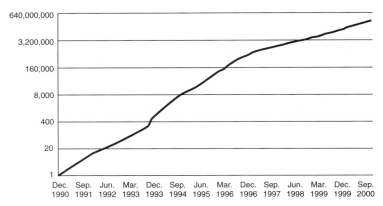

Figure 1.1 *The growth of the World Wide Web: number of Web sites, 1990–2000*

By 1994, the first independent Internet service providers (ISPs) had begun to pop up. By installing special software on their computers, consumers could access the entire content of the Web (almost 1,000 sites!). AOL began to open up Web access for its millions of subscribers. Prices universally moved to flat-rate monthly charges. WYSIWYG ("What you see is what you get") HTML editors appeared and made creating Web pages just a bit easier. In response, the second explosion in Web growth occurred. By 1996, corporations didn't see a Web presence as a luxury, but rather as a necessity. What better way to instantly push content to the consumer? The Web was viewed as a new media channel that offered endless opportunities for commercial success.

If the waning years of the past century had a motto, it certainly wasn't "Collaborators welcome"; "Venture capital welcome" is probably more accurate. Fueled by ill-conceived business plans and wild speculation, a worldwide expansion of the Web's underlying infrastructure took place. Meanwhile, the browser jumped from home computers to cell phones and mobile devices for the first time. High-speed cable and DSL "broadband" connectivity options became ubiquitous. The third explosion was the popping of the Web bubble, which saw these ventures implode en masse when they failed to turn a profit. This event marked the end of the first wave of the Web's evolution, which in hindsight we label Web 1.0.

Web 2.0

In the aftermath of the Web 1.0 crash, the glut of infrastructure kept the costs of going online low. That simple fact helped attract even more users to come online. A few companies began to figure out how to leverage the Web without going bankrupt. Collectively, their embrace of the Internet represented the slow expansion of the Web from that last primordial blast. New marketplaces evolved as sites like eBay linked buyers and sellers from around the globe. These online flea markets, in turn, spawned communities that helped pioneer the concepts behind new social networking sites like MySpace and Facebook.

By 2006, the firms that had simultaneously feared and tried to control Web 1.0 looked up from licking their wounds and saw the dawn of a new paradigm. In a symbolic changing of the guard, "old media" giant *Time* magazine announced the Person of the Year was "You."[6] There was no great single occurrence that made this milestone possible. Rather, the driving force was the confluence of many events: the spread of cheap broadband access, the Web-enabling of multiple devices, the arrival of new communication environments, and the emergence of cooperative environments for organizing information. Collaborators were finally running the show.

Industry figurehead Tim O'Reilly is credited with popularizing the term "Web 2.0" to define this new age:

> Web 2.0 is the business revolution in the computer industry caused by the move to the Internet as platform, and an attempt to understand the rules for success on that new platform.[7]

A simpler working definition is that Web 2.0 is a shift from *transaction-based* Web pages to *interaction-based* ones. This is how the power of "You" is mashed, mixed, and multiplied to create value. Social-networking sites, folksonomies (collaborative tagging, social bookmarking), wikis, blogs, and mashups are just some of the components that make this possible. The success of sites such as Facebook, wikipedia, flikr, and digg has demonstrated that democratization of content creation and manipulation is powering the latest wave of Internet growth.

The underlying driver of Web 2.0 is flexibility. The one trait technologies slapped with the Web 2.0 moniker share is that they are extremely (and perhaps sometimes unintentionally) malleable. The successful products don't break when a user tries to extend them beyond their original design; they bend to accept new uses. Two success stories of the new Web illustrate this principle:

> flickr was started by Caterina Fake and Stewart Butterfield as an add-on feature for a video game they were developing. The idea was to allow players to save and share photos during gameplay. When they realized that bloggers needed a convenient way to store and share photos, Fake and Butterfield started adding blog-friendly features.

---

6. *Time* magazine, December 13, 2006.

7. http://radar.oreilly.com/archives/2006/12/web-20-compact-definition-tryi.html

Opening up their architecture to allow users of the site to create custom enhancements fueled their viral spread. The original game was ultimately shelved and flickr was sold to Yahoo! a year later for an undisclosed sum.

Deli.cio.us grew from a simple text file that its founder, Joshua Schachter, used to keep track of his personal collection of tens of thousands of Web site links. When the site went public in 2003, it spawned a host of add-ons. The concept of associating data with simple keywords to aid in organization wasn't new, but the cooperative "social tagging" aspect of deli.cio.us resonated with the frustrations of other Internet users.

Enterprise 2.0

Inevitably, when people discover a useful tool outside the workplace, they want to use it at the office as well. This happened years earlier when employees began sneaking personal computers into their offices to make it easier to manage spreadsheets and documents. More recently, end users have imported instant messaging and unlimited email[8] services from external sources.

User demand for Web 2.0 technologies within existing corporate infrastructure is the catalyst for Enterprise 2.0.[9] The challenge for firms is to integrate these new peer-based collaboration models with legacy technologies and mindsets. Figure 1.2 illustrates three areas that established organizations have typically established to control how solutions are delivered.

Enterprise 2.0 breaks down traditional divisional barriers and encourages building bridges. The managerial structure does not change, but the ability to conceive solutions and access the technology to deliver them is available to everyone (as shown in Figure 1.3).

Changing the social structure of a firm is termed "soft reorganization." Its consequence is movement away from fixed roles and responsibilities and toward a more open and unrestricted workplace. The phrase "economies of scale" refers to the cost advantages associated with large-scale production. We term the benefits of Enterprise 2.0 the "economies of collaboration." How are they established?

---

8. When Gmail (Google Mail) was announced in April 2004, it offered 1 gigabyte of message storage. This was well beyond the storage limit most corporate mail systems impose on their employees.

9. McAfee, Andrew. "Enterprise 2.0: The Damn of Emergent Collaboration." *Sloan Management Review,* Vol. 47, Spring 2006.

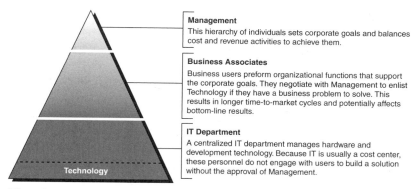

Management
This hierarchy of individuals sets corporate goals and balances cost and revenue activities to achieve them.

Business Associates
Business users preform organizational functions that support the corporate goals. They negotiate with Management to enlist Technology if they have a business problem to solve. This results in longer time-to-market cycles and potentially affects bottom-line results.

IT Department
A centralized IT department manages hardware and development technology. Because IT is usually a cost center, these personnel do not engage with users to build a solution without the approval of Management.

Different data security and information protection concerns are addressed by each particular tier. IT views security from a purely mechanical perspective (via the use of secure protocols, authentication, encryption, and so on). Business users depend on education (e.g., not writing down passwords, not emailing confidential documents, pursuing nondisclosure agreements). Management is concerned with making sure the firm is in conformance with any regulatory or industry-specific policies.

Figure 1.2   *Typical organizational hierarchy*

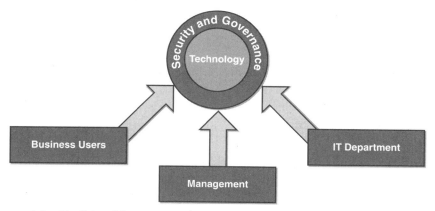

Figure 1.3   *Traditional barriers to solution delivery are removed in Enterprise 2.0. Each segment of an organization now has equal access to technology. To leverage this new environment, powerful (yet user-friendly) tools are introduced. These tools enable associates outside traditional IT to create their own solutions.*

- Nontechnical users are empowered to create application solutions without engaging management or IT personnel in the process. This agility leads to shorter time-to-market cycles.

- Folksonomies replace strict taxonomies (see the "Folksonomies versus Taxonomies" sidebar). Newly discovered connections between data and processes can be exploited to add business value.

- New communication tools mine "the wisdom of the crowd" to encourage collaboration and innovation, a technique known as crowdsourcing (see the "Crowdsourcing" sidebar).

Open interaction can help teams discover how the other lines of business operate. This knowledge, in turn, leads to changes that strengthen relationships across departments.

- IT must learn more about the business associates' goals, and create an environment that facilitates the rapid construction of products that they require.

- Members of the business team must participate more directly in the engineering process (either on their own or in partnership with IT), which requires some knowledge about development best practices.

- Management needs to cede some control to other teams and should work with all associates to encourage collaboration. This may entail:

  o Funding the necessary infrastructure.

  o Allowing cross-pollination between business teams.

  o Being open to ideas from nontraditional sources.

Security becomes a universal concern as the lines between teams vanish. The former "checks and balances" approach doesn't work when small teams are creating end-to-end solutions. In this collaborative milieu, firms have to strike a balance between technical controls[10] and education to mitigate risk.

▼
_____

Folksonomies versus Taxonomies

Taxonomies describe the organization of data within a strict hierarchy. In the business world, they are typically artifacts of established corporate structures. The managerial chain of command establishes processes for the composition, categorization, and flow of information. The structure of a rigid taxonomy may be nonintuitive to outsiders and consequently may restrict the sharing of useful information across the firm.

In a folksonomy, the community takes responsibility for collectively classifying and organizing information through a process known as "tagging." Tagging simply entails

_____

10. For example, putting a formal development process with relevant checkpoints and milestones in place.

labeling content with a few relevant keywords that describe the information or the ways in which it can be used. As more reviewers add and refine tags, it becomes easier to locate and navigate large amounts of information. The process of tagging creates a dynamic knowledge base of material that is not constrained by conventional organizational techniques.

Crowdsourcing

With crowdsourcing, a problem is framed so that it can be tackled by multiple teams or individuals, working either competitively or as a group effort. User-driven mashups can facilitate this type of mass collaboration in the enterprise, thereby resulting in far more resources contributing to solutions besides traditional IT.

A danger of this approach is that a "herd mentality" might develop that stifles creativity. Some degree of oversight can offset this risk, but care must be taken not to discourage participation.

Crowdsourcing success stories include the Ansari X-Prize, which was designed to encourage low-cost space travel, and Wikipedia, which benefits from the combined contributions of thousands of users.

The Birth of Mashups

You can have it "good," "fast," or "cheap." Pick any two of the three.
—Classic programmer's adage

Quick, easy, and affordable application development has always been a goal of software engineering. Reusing something that's already been built, tested, and paid for is one of the quickest ways to achieve this objective. From subroutines, to external libraries, to object orientation, to templates, to Web Services, each great advance in programming has been born from the desire to reuse material instead of starting from scratch. The limitation inherent in each of these milestones is that they were created by developers for the sole use by others in their profession.

It seemed inevitable that with the vast amount of new material being placed on the Web 2.0 every second, it could somehow evolve into raw material for software development. Tim Berners-Lee envisioned this leap in Web reusability in what he termed "the semantic Web," which describes a platform for the universal exchange of data, knowledge, and meaning.[11] And while work continues to define new languages and protocols to realize Sir Tim's dream, mashups are making this vision a reality now.

Mashups are an empowering technology. In the past, resources had to be designed for reuse. Application program interfaces (APIs) had to be created, packages compiled, documentation written. The application developers and solution architects who recycled resources were subject to the whims of the original designers. With mashups, you aren't limited to reusing an existing API; you can *impose* your own if none exists. So if an application or site offers no API, or if you don't like the access methods that are already in place, you can design and implement your own (see the API Enabler pattern in Chapter 4 for several examples). The promise of achieving programmatic access to almost unlimited data is intoxicating. Even more exciting is the notion that the tools for constructing mashups have begun to reach a level of usability where even nontechnical users can build their own solutions.

Many popular definitions of a mashup would have you believe the term is limited to a combination of Web-based artifacts: published APIs, RSS/Atom feeds (see the "RSS and Atom" sidebar), and HTML "screen scraping." Although there are certainly valuable solutions in that space, a broader world of data can be mashed up, including databases, binary formats (such as Excel and PDF), XML, delimited text files, and more. The rush of vendors attempting to capitalize on the burgeoning market for enterprise solutions hasn't helped bring clarity to the field. To turn a classic phrase on its head, we have a ton of nails out there, and everyone is trying to tell us that they have the best hammer.

RSS and Atom

RSS (also known as Rich Site Syndication or Real Simple Syndication) and Atom are formats for publishing Web-based content in a manner consumable by special applications termed "feed readers." Feed readers aggregate multiple feeds (or "subscriptions") so that a user can view updates to numerous Web pages from a single environment.

Before RSS and ATOM existed, users had to manually visit each site and check for any new updates. Feeds also serve as a popular method for allowing Web sites to dynamically incorporate content from external information providers. Regardless of their originally intended purpose, because feeds are created using a well-structured format (XML), mashups can easily consume them as a data source.

---

11. Berners-Lee, Tim, James Hendler, and Ora Lassila. "The Semantic Web." *Scientific American*, May 17, 2001.

Another common misconception is that mashups combine at least two disparate sites to form a brand-new "composite" application, complete with a neat new user interface. That's certainly possible, but mashups need not be an end in themselves. It is more accurate to say that all composite applications are mashups, but not all mashups are composite applications. The enterprise mashup creator can use the technology to transform the Web into his or her own private information source. This data can be used for strategic planning or analysis in systems like Excel or MATLAB. Mashups may also be used to access a single resource at superhuman levels to mine data or migrate content. Creating mashups is all about finding data, functionality, and services and using them to both solve problems and create opportunities.[12]

Types of Mashups

Mashups have several different colloquial interpretations, which has resulted in some confusion regarding the term and its use. The word originated in the music industry, where a mashup was a combination of two or more songs to create a new experience. Typically, the vocal track of one song was combined with the instrumental background of another in this process.

The technology industry extended this definition to encompass a new application genus that described the combination of two or more sources into an integrated site. This technique of development hybridization can be roughly split into two separate categories: consumer mashups and enterprise mashups.

Consumer mashups are generally associated with Web 2.0. They require a lesser amount of programming expertise because they rely on public Web sites that expose well-defined APIs and feeds (see Figure 1.4).

The output is usually created by one of the sites participating in the mashup. In the classic "show craigslist listings on a Google map,"[13] the API of Google Maps is used to plot and present the feed obtained from craigslist.com. The limitation of this approach was that resources had to be "mashup ready."

Enterprise 2.0 mashups (sometimes referred to as data mashups) are more complex. Depending on which solution a firm deploys, enterprise mashups can emerge in several ways:

- Mashups are used solely by IT to rapidly deliver products. Application developers use both internal and external sources to create data mashups

---

12. This naturally presents potential legal complications, as discussed in Chapter 10.

13. http://housingmaps.com

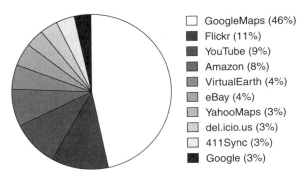

Figure 1.4 *A small number of sites with public APIs account for the majority of consumer-created mashups.* Source: *http://www.programmableweb.com/apis*

and employ traditional coding techniques to create the user interface around them. Users aren't directly involved in the construction process but they benefit from IT's ability to provide solutions more quickly.

- IT creates a set of "mashable" components and gives end users a sand-box environment where they can freely mix and match the pieces together themselves. If users need new components, they have to solicit IT help to create them.

- An organization deploys an environment that lets anyone create and combine his or her own mashups. This approach is the most difficult implementation to manage, but probably has the greatest impact. To understand the challenge of this approach, consider the use of Microsoft Excel in many firms. Users can create spreadsheet-based applications and pass them around without any central oversight of what exists, how it is used, or if it was tested. This friction-free creation and distribution model spreads good solutions as quickly as bad ones.

Whether mashups are used by IT, business associates, or both, their agile nature makes them a key enabler of Enterprise 2.0. Unfortunately, they are not without potential downsides. In an attempt to "deconstruct" the success of Google, the *Harvard Business Review* points out several pitfalls[14] that can hinder success in a culture of open development:

- As people spend more time experimenting, productivity in other areas can suffer.

---

14. Iyer, Bala, and Thomas H. Davenport. "Reverse Engineering Google's Innovation Machine." *Harvard Business Review,* April 2008.

- Poor coordination across groups can lead to duplication of efforts and repeated mistakes.

- A constant stream of new products may confuse the organization and its employees.

Despite these potential hazards, the authors indirectly identify the virtuous circle of Enterprise 2.0 (Figure 1.5). As diverse products are combined to create useful new resources, they themselves become fodder for the next generation of useful products. In principle, this process isn't very different from the long-standing goal of reusability that firms have strived for in their applications and architecture. Three important differences arise this time around, however:

1. In the age of mashups "reuse" is no longer an ivory-tower concept restricted to the purview of application architects. Because end users and developers alike will be creating solutions, *everyone* will engage in the practice of reuse.

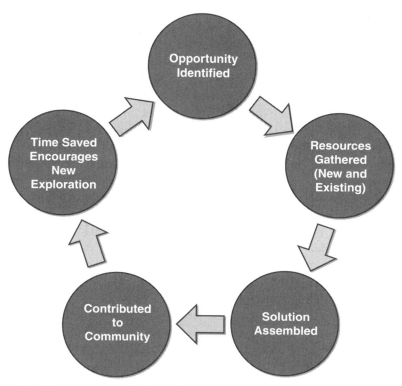

Figure 1.5 *The virtuous circle of mashups*

2. The existing approach to reuse front-loads development efforts with additional planning and coding to create open APIs and extra documentation that may never be used. Because mashups impose reusability "after the fact," their creators will build their own APIs and include only the minimum functionality needed.

3. Traditional reuse practices don't require that a system that leverages existing code or libraries is itself reusable. This leads to implementations that are essentially "dead ends." Mashups are implicitly reusable, which creates a never-ending cycle of potential associations and recombination.

Acquiring Data from the Web

> Need input, More Input, MORE INPUT!
> —Johnny Five, *Short Circuit*, 1986

As we saw in the last section, the majority of consumer mashups use the public APIs of a handful of Web sites. In the enterprise model, the best potential sources for mashup data may not be as forthcoming. In these situations, it becomes necessary to employ creative techniques to extract information. One of the most common and controversial techniques is often referred to as "screen scraping." This derogatory phrase carries a long sullied history and is thrown around by detractors seeking to undermine this approach.

Traditional "screen scraping" owes its origins to the early days of desktop computing, when IT departments developed various techniques to migrate "dumb terminal" mainframe applications to end-user computers. Rather than tackle the costly and time-consuming task of rewriting or replacing existing applications, many IT departments used special PC-based applications that emulated the original terminals.[15] These applications could receive the data from the mainframe and extract the contents of the forms presented on the old green-screen systems. User keystrokes were likewise emulated to send input back to the original application. This technique relied on developer-created templates and was both highly position-sensitive and extremely unforgiving. The smallest alteration in the mainframe display would break the predefined template and break the new application.

Because of these drawbacks, screen scraping was generally viewed as a hack and a last resort. The negative experiences associated with this approach continue to haunt any solution that promises to extract raw data from a user inter-

---

15. Such as an IBM 3270 or VT220.

face. Before organizations feel comfortable with mashups, users will need to understand how modern methods differ from the brittle approaches of the past.

Too many of us have forgotten that the "L" in HTML stands for "Language." In HTML, the *description* of the presentation and the *presentation itself* are inexorably bound in most people's minds. Many view HTML and what is displayed in their browser as two sides of the same coin.

In fact, it is the underlying Document Object Model (DOM) that makes mashup "screen scraping" something that should more appropriately be referred to as "Web harvesting" or "DOM parsing." When HTML is read by a browser, it is internally organized into a hierarchal structure. The underlying data structure is tree based and much more organized than what the user sees (see "The Structure of HTML" sidebar). HTML elements may contain additional nonvisual information such as the id and class attributes (see "The class and id Attributes" sidebar).

The Structure of HTML

Consider the following simple Web form:

User Name	
Password	
Logon	

This is the underlying HTML:

```
<form method="POST">
<table border="0" width="250">
    <tr>
        <td width="85">User Name</td>
        <td><input id="user1" type="text" name="user_field" size="20"></td>
    </tr>
    <tr>
        <td width="85">Password</td>
        <td><input id="pw" type="password" name="password_field" size="20"></td>
    </tr>
</table>
<input type="submit" value="Logon" name="B1">
</form>
```

When parsed by a browser, this HTML is internally organized into a hierarchical structure known as the Document Object Model (DOM). The DOM is more conducive to automated analysis than the presentation users receive.

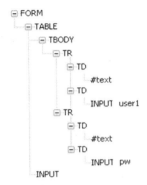

The `class` and `id` attributes

The ubiquitous use of `id` and `class` in HTML make them ideal markers for Web scrapers to identify document elements.

Uses of `id`:

A style sheet selector

```
<P id="bigheader">Important Update</P>
```

A target anchor for hypertext links:

```
<H1 id="news">Today's Top Stories</H1>
```

A means to identify an element in JavaScript:

```
document.getElementById("news");
```

Used to name a declared OBJECT element:

```
<OBJECT declare
        id="newyork.declaration"
        data="city.mpeg"
        type="application/mpeg">
        A tour of Manhattan.
</OBJECT>
```

Uses of `class`:

Assign one or more CSS styles to an element:

```
p.error {font-size: 18px; color: red;}
<p class="error">Incorrect Password</p>
```

Beyond their original intent within HTML, id and class attributes can also serve as "markers" for general-purpose processing by other applications/agents (e.g., mashups). Unlike the screen scrapers of the past that relied solely on positional information to parse screen content, mashups are able to examine the underlying attributes used to build the presentation. Although not a foolproof approach, this data changes much less frequently than the look and feel of a site, as demonstrated in the sidebar "Presentation Changes Don't Break Object Discovery." While consumer mashup builders queue up and wait for content providers to expose an API, enterprise teams are using Web harvesting to grab whatever data they want.

Presentation Changes Don't Break Object Discovery

This example shows a sample Web page before and after a radical redesign. Although a visitor might be disoriented by the drastic changes, similarities in the underlying HTML (and resulting DOM tree) will not slow down a mashup that examines the site.

Before

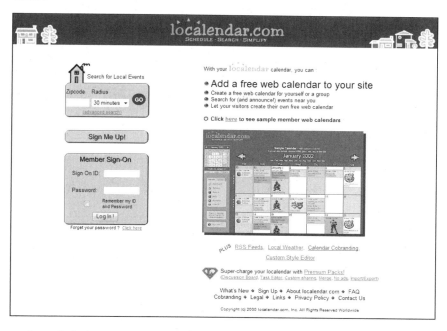

As part of a larger system, a mashup is created to sign in to a Web site by supplying a "Sign On ID" and a "Password." The form attributes and DOM information are displayed following the screenshot.

```
...
<td width="74" height="25"><div class="fixedfont">Sign On ID: </div></td>
<td width="89" height="25">
<p align="right"><input maxlength="20" name="username" size="10"
  style="font-family: courier"></p></td></tr>
<p align="center">
<tr>
<td width="74" height="5"><div class="fixedfont"> </div></td>
<td width="89" height="5"><div class="fixedfont"> </div></td></tr>
<tr>
<td width="74" height="25"><div class="fixedfont">Password:</div></td></p>
<td width="89" height="25">
<p align="right"><input maxlength="20" name="password" size="10"
  style="font-family: courier" type="password"></p></td></tr>
<tr>
...
```

After

Even though the site has been radically redesigned, it still contains form elements for "Sign On ID" and "Password." A peek at the underlying HTML and DOM shows that these fields retain the same attributes. A mashup most likely will not have a problem recognizing the new design, even though a human might take some time to become accustomed to the new interface.

```
...
<tr>
<td width="70" class="text_boxsubtitle">Sign-On ID:</td>
<td><input type="text" maxLength="20" name="username" size="10"
style='width:122px;FONT-FAMILY: Courier'/></td>
</tr>
<tr>
<td width="70" class="text_boxsubtitle">Password:</td>
<td><input maxLength="20" name="password" size="10" type="password"
style="width:122px;FONT-FAMILY: Courier"/></td>
</tr>
...
```

Enterprise mashups are not restricted to skimming content from HTML: They can leverage more structured formats such as XML (RSS, ATOM), Web Services, or even binary formats such as Excel and PDF (as shown in Figure 1.6). Nevertheless, the great promise of enterprise mashups derives from their ability to treat the entire World Wide Web as a first-class data source.

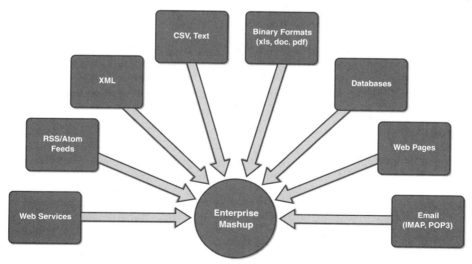

Figure 1.6 *Enterprise mashups can consume a variety of different data sources.*

The Long Tail

Although first coined to describe customers who purchase hard-to-find items,[16] the phrase "the Long Tail" has come to have a special meaning in the world of software. Traditionally, application development dollars are directed toward those projects and enhancements demanded by the largest group of users. This practice of catering to the masses doesn't necessarily lead to an outcome with the greatest positive impact on productivity. Unfortunately, because of the huge effort involved in developing applications, it is often impractical to provide custom solutions to a lone employee or a small team, even if it would greatly increase their efficiency (Figure 1.7). Thus only the "head" of the application demand curve is ever addressed. The exact cutoff point isn't fixed and will vary by organization, although the Pareto principle[17] or "80-20" rule suggests that 80% of application development efforts will benefit only 20% of your users.

IT focuses on the 20% of known problems that affect the most users (A).
The 80% of potential solutions (B) that serve a smaller audience are unaddressed.

Figure 1.7 *The Long Tail*

The cumulative potential of unfulfilled Long Tail opportunities exceeds that of the "head" of the curve. Alas, fulfilling the requirements of the remaining 80% of your staff might seem an impossible goal. Most technology departments do not have enough staff to meet the needs of each individual user. Unless there is a way for developers to become drastically more productive or for end users to solve their own problems, the prospects for meeting unmet demand seem bleak.

---

16. Anderson, Chris. "The Long Tail." *Wired*, October 2004.

17. The Pareto principle is based on empirical observation and isn't a mathematical certainty in all cases.

Meeting User Demand

Give me a place to stand on, and I will move the Earth.
—Archimedes

Enter the mashup. Armed with powerful new tools that leverage the resources of the Internet, developers and power users can quickly assemble products to target the Long Tail. We are witness to the dawn of a new era in technology. Mashups are making IT more agile and empowering individuals to create their own solutions.

The Long Tail is useful from an analysis standpoint only if it represents the universe of possible solutions that can be constructed. Consider the mashup example in "A Sample Mashup Use Case."

A Sample Mashup Use Case

There are countless examples where mashups can benefit an enterprise, and they needn't be complex. Consider the following example.

Every day, the employees of a firm have numerous conference calls to discuss project planning, resource management, and corporate strategy. Whenever someone new joins the conference, there is a "beep" that announces that individual's presence. The first ten minutes of every call go something like this:

"Beep."
"Hi, who's on the line?"
"It's me, Rob."
"Beep."
"Hi, who's on the line?"
"It's me, Maureen."

On each call, valuable time is wasted while the moderator takes attendance and furiously scribbles down names. Later on, he may try and match those (frequently misspelled) names to an email address or telephone number.

We can save time and expedite the meeting with a simple mashup. First, we visit the conference call Web site and grab the participant's caller ID directly from the Web page. Next, we look up those numbers in the firm's online corporate directory (where we also get the corresponding email addresses). Finally, in case someone is dialing in from his or her home telephone, we use the search form on a public Internet site (such as whitepages.com) to look up any unresolved numbers.

The entire process is hidden behind a simple Web front end with a single button, labeled "Get Attendees." No more misspelled names or missed participants. No more pausing to ask latecomers to introduce themselves. Meetings start on time and everyone is happy.

As if this capability wasn't enough of a breakthrough, it opens up new possibilities for behavior tracking (also known as reality mining). You can click the "Get Attendees" button multiple times during the call to see not only who is present, but *for how long.* Perhaps you can tie that "duration" data to other sources. You might find that callers drop off the line in coordination with weather, traffic patterns, or surf reports.

Although the "conference call attendance" issue was experienced by almost all employees of the firm, it was never identified as a business problem. This is because developers and business users are conditioned to view their actions in discrete, isolated chunks:

- First, I sign into Application A to locate a customer's account.

- Second, I sign into Application B to check item inventory.

- Third, I sign into Application C to create a purchase order for the client.

If you accept that Applications A, B, and C are immutable (perhaps because they were purchased from an external vendor), then you will never envision a solution where you can sign into Application D *once* and perform these three actions in a single step. The opportunity never appears on the Long Tail.

The greatest benefit of mashups may be their influence on our thought process. When we cast off our biases about the role of technology in the workplace, we discover the folly in applying IT to only the most obvious and well-understood problems. Once the blinders have been removed, you'll discover a world of missed and previously unknown challenges that you can tackle. Recognizing these opportunities is just the first stage. If you don't do something about them, then you've simply added to the tangle of unmet expectations. To achieve continuous innovation, it is essential to look outside the existing methods of measuring and meeting user demand.

Mashups and the Corporate Portal

The concept of aggregating data from multiple sites inside and outside the workplace isn't new. As companies struggled to share all of their disparate applications and information resources directly with their employees, many embarked upon a quest to create a single corporate portal. An organization's portal typically provides several features:

- Single sign-on (SSO), which allows users to authenticate only once to obtain access to multiple applications.

- Multiple "portlets" or "islands" that expose information and functionality from disparate systems.

- Interaction (or integration), which allows portals to influence one another's behavior. For example, a search portlet may cause the contents of other portlets to be filtered.

- Access control, which provides for the centralized administration of which information a user may access. A user's permissions on the portal are at least as restrictive as what the user would receive if he or she logged into the underlying application directly. Portals are unique in that they may bring content together from multiple sources wherein the user has varied entitlements.

- Personalization, which allows the user limited ability to customize the layout and presentation of the site to suit his or her own specific tastes and needs.

Of course, as our examination of the "80-20" rule suggests, portals will never meet the requirements of all users, all of the time. At best, they may meet the lowest set of common requirements across a broad audience (the 80%). The most specific requirements are typically the least general (the 20%), which explains why most corporate portals typically confine themselves to broadcasting company news, managing health and benefits information, and tracking the holiday calendar. Personalization, the latecomer to the portal infrastructure, was a desperate attempt to address this shortcoming. Unfortunately, users typically don't get a say in choosing *which* content can be personalized or *how* it can be manipulated.

At my daughters' nursery school, their teacher maintains order by telling the children, "You get what you get and you don't get upset." Those days in computing are passé. Whether we are talking about the corporate business user who wants to come to the office each day to a personalized workstation or a customer who wants to view your company's information in a certain fashion that suits his Web-based applications, this is the age of individualized construction.

When the popular social networking sites MySpace and Facebook published open APIs to leverage their data and create interfaces around it, thousands of users became bona fide developers. They quickly learned to build their own personal portals. This same demographic is just now beginning to enter the Enterprise 2.0 workforce. They won't be content to operate within the confines of a single, stoic portal that restricts how they consume and manipulate information.

A new metaphor for user interaction has recently emerged that, combined with mashups, threatens the relevance of the enterprise portal. Whether you know them as widgets, gadgets, or snippets, they are the small plug-in components that originated on the Web and have migrated to the desktop (e.g., Apple Dashboard, Yahoo Widgets, Google Gadgets, Microsoft Vista Desktop Widgets).

The tools for creating these "mini-applications" have become easier to use and more familiar to a much broader audience.

If enterprise mashups are the path to user-created data and widget platforms are the environment for presenting that information, the combination of the two represent the death knell for the corporate portal. At best, it will morph into a set of core services that provide information to mashup-powered personal environments.

Mashups and Service-Oriented Architecture

Service-oriented architecture (SOA) has come to be associated with Web Services, but at its core it is more mindset than methodology. The "service" in SOA shouldn't be thought of in terms of a particular technology, but rather as a *business task*. The tasks are implemented in an environment that facilitates loose coupling with other services. This combination, in turn, fosters an atmosphere where developers can create new applications that reuse and recombine existing functionality. Because the services are based on open standards, they can be consumed equally well across independent development platforms.

The promise of SOA is that it addresses the Sisyphean[18] labor of building duplicate, siloed functionality across the enterprise. Better yet, you don't have to build services yourself; you can discover and use third-party solutions. SOA is the equivalent of a home improvement store for application development. You simply fill up your shopping cart with all the raw materials and glue and nail them together in your basement to create a shiny new product. Using a traditional development mindset would place the burden on you to chop down trees for lumber or smelt the iron for nails.

The Common Object Request Broker Architecture (CORBA) was an early stab at implementing SOA—so early, in fact, that it predates the Internet explosion of the mid-1990s and even the SOA acronym itself. The level of complexity required to work with this technology was often found to outweigh its benefits, and while CORBA struggled to find its footing, newer technologies such as SOAP, XML, and Java (Enterprise Java Beans) arrived on the scene. They began to address the problems associated with CORBA's steep learning curve and security shortcomings.

---

18. Sisyphus was a Greek who was condemned by the gods to ceaselessly roll a rock to the top of a mountain, only to have it fall back of its own weight.

Web Services emerged as a technology-agnostic interoperable solution based on open standards such as XML, WSDL, UDDI, and SOAP. Although far from perfect,[19] SOAP-based Web Services have become the industry-preferred method for implementing SOA. The most popular method for exposing SOAP services across the enterprise is via a custom infrastructure known as an enterprise service bus (ESB). The ESB can provide additional data transformation capabilities, security, transaction support, and scalability, all while simultaneously reducing the degree of complexity exposed to service reusers. In an attempt at product differentiation, some ESB offerings service-enabled existing corporate resources (such as databases) and were themselves progenitors of the data mashup.

One point should be clear: SOA is not a revolutionary milestone but an evolutionary one. Open communication and technology standards, combined with the ubiquity of the protocols that power the Web, have finally helped SOA reach a level of maturity where its benefits exceed its costs.

Mashups represent the next leap in reuse. They initially came about when developers combined the published APIs of different Web applications to create interesting new content. The limitation of this approach was that resources had to be "mashup ready." Robust SOA environments were a hothouse for mashup growth, as they exposed componentized functionality that could be mixed together to provide new services.

You may be wondering if mashups are the latest harbinger of SOA, or the beneficiary of it. The answer is a resounding "Both!" With most vendors now using the terms "SOA" and "Web Services" interchangeably, it has become obvious that for most corporations, implementing a successful SOA will require the service-enablement of their existing applications. Mashups are a completely valid method of accomplishing this (see the "API Enabler" section in Chapter 4 and the discussion of the Quick Proof-of-Concept pattern in Chapter 7). Most mashup products allow you to create and publish Web Services either directly or via a third-party application container (e.g., WebSphere or JBoss). Likewise, mashups are voracious consumers of Web Services. Mashups gladly leverage the Web Services that SOA-centric organizations already have in place. Because mashups can produce services with the same agility that they consume them, they are a valuable addition to any service-oriented environment.

How do SOA patterns and mashup patterns relate to each other? SOA generally focuses on server-side architecture and internal corporate resources, whereas everything is fair game with mashups. Because of SOA's maturity and

---

19. Problems include interoperability issues and platform-specific implementation, testing, and security challenges.

association with Web Services, it has achieved greater clarity regarding its capabilities, protocols, implementation, and use. This allows SOA pattern discussions to focus on high-level abstractions. Indeed, several excellent Web sites and books[20] discuss the process of SOA-enabling the enterprise. Mashup patterns, which remain in a nascent stage of development, must focus on more practical examples. This will drive broader adoption, which in turn should to lead to consolidation and standardization similar to what SOA has achieved.

Mashups and EAI/EII

Enterprise application integration (EAI) is the practice of connecting corporate systems at the application level rather than at the data level. EAI solutions seek to streamline business processes and transactions, whereas mashups typically combine applications with the goal of providing new functionality. EAI tools rely on support for open standards such as Web Services or CORBA. If an application doesn't expose an API, one needs to be constructed programmatically. As systems and requirements evolve, there is an inevitably large carrying cost to maintain the custom integration code. When managed and funded correctly, EAI can provide the most rock-solid method of application integration. For business-critical solutions, EAI is recommended over mashups, which permit some fragility as a trade-off for the benefit of agility.

Enterprise information integration (EII) is a data management strategy for providing uniform access to all the data within an organization. The rise of "big box" stores that sell everything from baby clothing to car tires has demonstrated that patrons appreciate the convenience of one-stop shopping. Collecting data from multiple sources and providing a single point of access has similar appeal in the enterprise. EII is often easier to achieve than EAI because it simply attempts to unify information and not applications. If you think this approach sounds similar to a data mashup, you're correct. A mature EII implementation can provide new insights into data associations and facilitate rapid solution delivery. EII tools have historically focused only on back-end databases,[21] which limits the range of information that can be collected. By comparison, mashups surpass EII in their ability to obtain data from both structured and unstructured sources.

---

20. Author Thomas Erl has written several good books on this subject, including *SOA Design Patterns*.

21. These databases include relational databases, message queues, and data warehouses.

The knowledge requirement for successfully applying EII technology is higher than that for mashups, but as with EAI the advantage is stability. You can measure the benefits of a complex EAI/EII project empirically by developing a quick mashup-based prototype (see "Quick Proof-of-Concept," Chapter 7). This effort may help determine whether the potential benefits justify the considerable cost and time required to carry out a formal implementation.

Mashups and Software as a Service

In contrast to the architectural style and Web Service implementation strategy of SOA, software as a service (SaaS) is a business model. SaaS is the latest incarnation of the Internet-boom idea of an application service provider (ASP). Under the SaaS plan, businesses do not invest money to develop and host applications internally, but instead rent the functionality they need from an external service provider. End-user interaction with applications typically occurs via a prebuilt Web interface. The customer's business data is then fed into the system manually, using Web forms, or programmatically, using a Web Service API.

To appeal to as broad a market base as possible, most SaaS providers have focused on generic services and priced them competitively (a fee of less than $100 per service is not uncommon). Exposing macro capabilities and parameterizing functionality allows customers to achieve some degree of customization.

One of the most prominent success stories in SaaS is Salesforce.com. This "zero-infrastructure" customer relationship management (CRM) platform provides services to thousands of businesses worldwide. Small and large customers alike are able to start using the hosted service almost immediately without deploying custom hardware. The success of Salesforce.com has led many to assume SaaS is particularly well suited to CRM and sales force automation. In reality, this isn't the case. WebEx, a Web-based conference and collaboration solution, has achieved adoption on an even larger scale. Google Apps is an example of a viable alternative to traditional desktop software. It serves up a business-focused mail, spreadsheet, and word processing suite at a fraction of the cost of Microsoft Office. Many commercial vendors are exploring SaaS to create new revenue streams.

Assuming SaaS products can meet technical and functional user requirements, two key challenges must be overcome before SaaS can succeed as a general distribution model. First, firms must be comfortable with the notion that their data is housed externally to the organization. It seems that there's a new story almost every day in the press about missing hard drives or accidentally leaked personal information. SaaS providers may have better security than many of their clients, but the abdication of data management to a third party is still a tough pill for many corporations to swallow. The second obstacle for SaaS is availability. For mission-critical applications, the network remains a potentially dangerous point of failure.[22]

Mashups are a natural complement to SaaS. Perhaps there are SaaS solutions that appeal to your organization, but you have held back on implementing them because you couldn't get exactly the functionality you required from a single provider. Maybe the SaaS product is extensible, but you don't want to invest time and money in duplicating functionality you've already built internally. Mashup patterns such as Workflow (see Chapter 5) and Content Integration (see Chapter 6) can be used to link an external solution and internal products together. With SaaS and mashups, you may be able to maintain the bulk of your confidential data internally and send the hosted application only small subsets of data for processing. If the network link to the SaaS vendor fails, at least you will still have local access to your data.

If you're thinking about testing the SaaS waters as a *vendor*, then applying SOA via mashups can help you get started. The API Enabler (see Chapter 4) and Quick Proof-of-Concept (see Chapter 7) patterns are excellent means of creating a Web interface to your existing resources. You can use the Load Testing pattern (see Chapter 8) to see how your systems scale under heavy user activity.

SaaS shares another characteristic with mashups: It may already be in use in your company without your knowledge. Because this model requires only a Web browser and no special infrastructure, it is easy for end users to circumvent IT and obtain applications directly. It is crucial that an IT department doesn't have a monitoring and enforcement policy based solely on policing internal data centers. IT personnel need to engage with the business users and educate them about the risks and rewards of SaaS and the effects these decisions will have on future growth. Internal checkpoints with purchasing and legal departments are a necessity, too. All service level agreements (SLAs) should be reviewed and signed by appropriate parties, and attempts to expense software purchases that have not been vetted by IT should raise a warning flag. Otherwise, SaaS can sneak into your organization on a corporate credit card.

---

22. Service level agreements (SLAs) should be in place to ensure your applications are available when needed.

Mashups and the User

Make no mistake about it—despite the recent buzz around Enterprise 2.0, people have been creating mashups for many years. Of course, the process to this point has been overwhelmingly manual. Microsoft Excel is arguably the father of the corporate data mashup. For years, Excel end users have cut-and-pasted data to feed their calculation engines. Spreadsheet-based solutions have spread throughout the enterprise without the involvement of IT. Mashup tools enable the automation of this aggregation process, and a new clan of users is poised to run wild with the technology.

A culture of individualism is clearly emerging in today's world. People no longer plan their evenings around what TV networks schedule for them to watch, for example. Instead, they record their favorite shows onto digital video recorders (DVRs) or watch movies and shows on their computers and mobile devices. Similarly, the recording industry no longer has a stranglehold over music distribution. Newspaper readership is down, as more individuals choose to consult RSS feeds and blogs instead of purchasing the printed documents. People can even create personalized clothing and sneakers online.[23] Members of the public have evolved from docile consumers into "prosumers."[24] Products and services are moving away from mass markets and being shaped by the people who consume them. Likewise, a fundamental shift has occurred in software development. Armed with new tools and the skills to use them, users aren't waiting for IT to build solutions—they're doing it themselves.

Should organizations facilitate these individuals' efforts, or rein them in? For years, the mantra of professional software development was "Separate business logic from presentation logic." Programmers religiously structured their code around that principle but ignored the logical conclusion: *The best shepherd of business expertise is not the IT department, but the business users themselves.*

The inclination for IT departments to view user-led efforts in an adversarial light increases when IT experts believe that their "home turf"—application development—is threatened. IT needs the occasional reminder that in any development effort, it is the users who are the key to defining metrics for success. Besides, users are already creating mashups anyway, albeit human-powered ones.

---

23. Nike iD lets you design custom shoes and clothing (http://nikeid.nike.com).
24. Toffler, Alvin. *The Third Wave.* 1980.

Gartner has said mashups will make IT even more critical to business operations,[25] so a knee-jerk rejection to their emergence is not necessarily in the best interests of the firm. Rather than deny business users the tools that can increase their productivity, IT needs to embrace a new model. Besides, starting with a mashup product won't get you a business solution any more than staring at a word processor will get you the next great novel.[26] Because IT personnel clearly cannot scale to meet the requirements of each particular user, they should leverage the potential of mashups and work in partnership with the business associates to train a new class of self-serve builders. This effort is akin to adding hundreds of new developers at virtually no additional cost.

It's a common assumption that the latest generation of developers is intuitively suited to filling this role. Affectionately termed the "Millennials" or "Generation Y," these individuals came of age during the Internet boom of the last decade and are inherently comfortable with technology. Millennials, green with inexperience and giddy about tinkering, question everything. This behavior stands in stark contrast to that of the entrenched workforce, whose habits of working in a particular manner condition them to no longer question the "why."

Many companies are rushing to embrace Web 2.0 ideals such as mashups, social networks, wikis, and blogs not because they have inherent value, but rather because the firms think this practice will attract the "new thinkers." In reality, instead of abdicating responsibility for innovation to a younger generation or applying technology Band-Aids, firms need to cultivate an environment of creativity and collaboration for their employees regardless of their physical age. Any firm can realize the value of mashups and Enterprise 2.0 so long as its managers are capable of taking a critical look at their workplace and realizing they don't need to settle for "good enough" any more.

The "guerrilla-style" approach of mashup development is not without its drawbacks, of course. Most business users do not fully grasp the challenges in providing scalability, reliability, business continuity, disaster recovery, security, and fault tolerance. If users are permitted to develop ad hoc solutions, IT must provide an environment that cultivates these best practices.

A Patterns Primer

The benefits of enterprise mashups are communicated through a concept known as a *pattern*. If you've ever baked holiday cookies, then you already

---

25. David Cearley, Gartner analyst.

26. Or a *Mashup Patterns* book—trust me, I've tried.

have some idea of what a pattern is and how it works. Suppose you want to make a tray of chocolate-chip heart-shaped cookies. After you mix the dough, you roll it out and grab your cookie cutter. You use the cutter to press out a series of identical shapes. Afterward, you decide some oatmeal raisin hearts would be nice, so you mix a fresh batch of ingredients and cut out another series of hearts. The cookie cutter is a form of pattern. The different types of dough are the specific situations, or "use cases," where the pattern is applied. A pattern doesn't solve a problem in itself. It's just a general form that helps you think about the structure of the solution (what shaped cookie, in this example).

The remaining chapters of this book present a number of patterns, along with some examples to illustrate how they work in an enterprise context. Don't throw out the pattern if you don't like the dough! Every business has a different flavor, and the key to success with patterns is figuring out which one is yours. You can use the samples that fill out this book to help identify the mashup ingredients your organization already has. Apply the appropriate mashup pattern and you have a recipe for success.[27]

The Fragility Factor

It may seem that the title of this book is an oxymoron. How can something as ad hoc and unstructured as Web scraping be coupled with something so formal and structured as a pattern? Ideally, the previous discussion of how mashups work under the hood will have made you more comfortable with the technology.

If you think reverse-engineering Web pages still doesn't sound like the type of rock-solid approach that a professional developer should be using, I don't blame you. One of the core tenets of software engineering is that applications should behave in a reliable and predictable manner. Web harvesting—although a great deal more reliable than screen scraping—is inherently unstable if you don't control the Web sites from which you extract data. Because you can't determine when a scrape-based solution might break, you should never employ this approach on a mission-critical system.

If you have the chance to help your firm gain a competitive advantage or reduce costs—even if just for a limited time—you should explore the opportunity.

---

27. The classic reference for pattern-based design is Christopher Alexander's seminal text *The Timeless Way of Building* (Oxford Press, 1979). Buildings, like software components and cooking ingredients, can be combined in an almost endless variety. Nevertheless, certain basic concepts govern which elements work well together and which don't.

There is nothing wrong with an application that has a short lifespan, so long as you don't create a situation where the cost of remediating or retiring the solution exceeds the achieved benefit. The rapid speed with which mashups can be developed means occasional remediation isn't a time-consuming task. Plus, quick release cycles translate into more chances for exploratory development, which in turn can lead to the discovery of new uses or solutions.

The patterns in this book all adhere to this basic premise. You won't find examples of settling stock trades or sending online payments, even though mashups can facilitate those tasks. It's simply irresponsible to use the technology in this manner. Like any development effort, a mashup solution will require regular maintenance over its lifetime. Unlike with traditional applications, you may not be able to determine the time when this work will be required. Web Service APIs can change, RSS feeds can be restructured, or site redesigns may temporarily toss a monkey-wrench into your application's internal workings. Because of these possibilities, you should implement mashup-based solutions only where you can tolerate temporary downtime that may occur at unexpected intervals.

The fragility score is an ad hoc[28] rating based on a number of factors:

- A mashup pattern that relies on a single Web site (e.g., Infinite Monkeys, Time Series, Feed Factory, Accessibility, API Enabler, Filter, Field Medic) is less fragile because there is only a single point of potential failure.

- A multisite-based pattern (e.g., Workflow, Super Search, Location Mapping, Content Migration) is more fragile with each additional site that it leverages.

- Mashups that employ Web harvesting are generally more fragile than those that use feeds (RSS, Atom). Feeds are, in turn, more fragile than Web Service APIs. APIs are the most stable integration point because they reflect a site's commitment to expose data and functionality.

- Mashups that mine data from "hobby" sources have a greater risk of failing. For example, obtaining local weather data from the U.S. government-funded National Oceanic and Atmospheric Administration's (NOAA) weather site (http://www.nws.noaa.gov/) is probably a safer bet than obtaining the information from your local high school or radio station.

---

28. Translation: "Your mileage may vary." The fragility score is based on unpublished observations of the technology and will vary according to the resources you incorporate in your specific implementations.

For-profit sites may exert legal pressure to halt mashups (see the Sticky Fingers anti-pattern).

- Mashups that use boutique data not widely available on the Internet are at high risk. What are your alternatives if the site suddenly vanishes one day?

Each pattern template described in this book contains a fragility score ranging from 1 glass ♥♥♥♥♥ (the least fragile) to 5 glasses ♥♥♥♥♥ (the most fragile). No pattern receives a score of zero, because even the most rigorously tested mashup-backed application always has some degree of brittleness.

The fragility score is ultimately intended to encourage *thought* about mashup stability. It's possible to have five sites in a multisite pattern that change less frequently than an individual Web page used in a single-site pattern. This is particularly true when vendor products and internally created systems are involved. The user interfaces of commercial and in-house applications aren't frequently redesigned. Public Web sites, in contrast, must constantly reinvent themselves in the battle to attract eyeballs.

If you create a mashup-based solution and don't acknowledge that it encapsulates some degree of uncertainty, you are just kidding yourself. Worse, you are deceiving your users, who will not be pleased when the system "mysteriously" fails one day.

In case you think only mashups have this Achilles' heel, keep in mind that any distributed system (which is what a mashup is) contains an inherent level of risk. Each additional component and the infrastructure that connects it represent another potential point of failure. So before you think, "Why the heck would I build something that might break?" consider how you have handled similar situations in the past. You can address many of these fragility issues by thinking about redundancy, monitoring, and notification up front.

The Future of Mashups

Mashups aren't just about mixing Web sites together to create new solutions—
they're a tool for unlocking the treasure chest of data right under your nose.

The primary goal of this book is for the reader to scan at least one pattern and realize, "I never thought you could do that!" The examples that accompany the patterns are aimed at both the business end user and the technical user. When you understand how mashups can be used to mine new information or automate traditionally manual activities, you'll never look at your workplace in quite the same way. The morass of daily problems suddenly becomes visible—but now you'll have the inspiration and knowledge to tackle them. As with the classic *Design Patterns* text, *Mashup Patterns* is intended to provide a general language that developers and the business can use to succinctly communicate about a solution ("Oh, we can use a Time Series mashup here").

It's not every day that we witness a groundbreaking advancement in application development. Most improvements occur gradually and can take years to snowball into something useful. They may require costly new investments in infrastructure or reengineering of existing resources. Or they may be confined to a narrow niche in our industry. Only the naive overlook the dangers that come with any great leap; only the foolish cite those risks as reason enough to ignore the potential benefits.

Don't let the hype surrounding mashups cause you to abandon the best practices that guide good development. Likewise, be open to thinking creatively about the problems that exist around you. Employees who face seemingly intractable problems or whose careers have trained them to ignore the breakdowns in their organization will be delighted to discover that practical solutions are now available. The patterns in this book will help you get started by demonstrating how mashups can help you achieve the following goals:

- Make money for your organization

- Fill gaps not met by the existing IT infrastructure

- Create a quick proof-of-concept to explore new solutions

- Gain a competitive advantage

- Avoid "information overload"

- Expose your applications to a wider audience

and more!

Enterprise 2.0 is all about You. And the potential benefits from mashups are as big as anything you can imagine.

Chapter 2

Mashup Patterns Terminology

The only way to discover the limits of the possible is to go beyond them into the impossible.

—Arthur C. Clarke (1917–2008)

Introduction

In the previous chapter we examined the role of mashups within the modern enterprise. Before proceeding further, it's important to address the terminology of mashup patterns more closely. This slight diversion is important for the layperson who may still be somewhat unfamiliar with the singular concepts of both mashups and patterns, but will benefit the technical reader as well.

Readers who have read other patterns books should at least skim through the following sections. The emerging mashup ecosystem is rife with innovations that require a break from convention in some instances. Notably, mashups' appeal to nontechnically inclined users means this text must likewise eschew certain complexities to serve a broader audience.

Semantics

The term "mashup" intuitively implies the involvement of multiple participants. Yet certain patterns in this book will demonstrate that the same capabilities that allow more than one site to be combined are equally valuable when applied to a single resource. Because this book focuses on solutions, we will explore various uses for mashup concepts within the enterprise, whether or not they conform to the popular definition of the term. In some cases, a pattern involves several sites; in others, a resource may be "mashed" against itself. We'll take a more technical look at these features that make this possible in Chapter 3, Core Activities, before delving into the patterns themselves.

"Patterns" is another term that carries certain connotations. To begin with, it is almost never used outside of technical circles. If you aren't a developer and you've stuck with me this far, you have my admiration![1] Even if you haven't realized it yet, you are about to enter a new world. As author David Berlind writes regarding mashups within the modern enterprise, "The barrier to developing applications and turning creativity into innovation is so low that there's a vacuum into which an entire new class of developers will be sucked."[2]

Traditional patterns books document a series of challenges that their readers may have already encountered during their normal work. Many developers examine a pattern for the first time and exclaim, "I've solved that before!" This doesn't mean the time spent reading about the problem was in vain; rather, it validates that the pattern addresses a common issue. The accompanying solution is the second half of a pattern's value. Usually there are multiple ways to solve a problem, some better than others. A pattern attempts to describe the best practice (sometimes leveraging other patterns) to achieve resolution. Once a problem's description and solution have been paired and named, this label becomes a shorthand way of identifying other occurrences as well as implying how they should be handled. Many IT departments concern themselves with the reuse of physical assets like code and libraries; patterns complement these efforts by providing a format for converting good ideas into repeatable architectural designs.

Familiarity may lie at the heart of a traditional pattern discussion, but it is a luxury we must do without when venturing into the world of mashups. Enterprise use of the technology is still in its nascent stages of development, so a potential practitioner's first impression is likely to be surprise: "I never knew you could do that!" As previously discussed, that's not the way patterns are generally conceived. Ideally, they draw on a large body of existing work to arrive at a reusable solution. In fact, the subtitle to most patterns books could very well read, "Someone has already solved your problem." Many of the patterns we will explore in this text present ideas and tactics for realizing opportunities that firms may have already considered, yet dismissed as unattainable or prohibitively expensive. Revisiting these abandoned topics from the fresh perspective that mashups provide gives your organization a new chance to gain a competitive advantage or to become more productive.

Traditional patterns texts have a notorious tendency to unintentionally sabotage a good solution by presenting sample code. Although this approach is

---

1. If you need a break, I recommend you jump to Chapter 4 and start scanning the examples that accompany the individual patterns.

2. Berlind, David. "Mashup Ecosystem Poised to Explode." January 2006. http://blogs.zdnet.com/BTL/?p=2484

intended to provide clarity, readers often fall into the trap of following the implementation examples too closely and creating unwieldy solutions. The correctness of results is then undermined by unnecessarily complicated code that captures the structural notion of a pattern but ignores its spirit. *Mashup Patterns* dispenses with the risks of this practice by describing solutions without an accompanying implementation. I wish I could provide some grand explanation for this decision, but the simple truth is that this choice is unavoidable because the platforms for mashup development are still evolving. There are almost as many ways to construct mashups as there are ideas for mashups themselves. As the field inevitably consolidates, standards will likely arise that allow product-agnostic examples to be presented—at which time the "sample code" dilemma will have to be addressed. One thing is certain, however: When this additional level of detail is added, it should not come at the expense of isolating nontechnical users. As we have observed, the path to mashups is a journey that will be undertaken not just by developers, but also by users outside of traditional IT departments who are just now finding this subject approachable.

In lieu of code, this book provides numerous business-focused examples of how mashups can provide value to various industries. While some of these examples may be directly applicable to your organization, the real challenge is to see how the solutions can be applied outside the context in which they are presented here. The mashup patterns aren't mere solutions in themselves, but rather templates for solving many problems previously considered intractable or unsolvable.

Academics may argue that I have undermined both the terms "mashup" and "pattern." I've already alluded to the fact that many of the mashups examined in this book will use only a single site, which goes against common expectations. As for patterns, many of the ones examined here currently exist only in the ephemeral realm of Ideas, waiting for a motivated creator to summon them into existence. "A reusable solution based on a single-site mashup that no one has ever built before?" some might ask. "How can such a topic be allowed to desecrate the rich history of patterns or the fundamental notion of a mashup?"

I propose two counter-questions for these naysayers. How much value must a new technology demonstrate before it gains architectural acceptance? How many users need suffer unaided until their struggles are addressed?

Rather than cling to old terminology, we must expand our definitions beyond their original constraints if we are to educate and serve the builders of the next-generation enterprise. There is a point where new tools and old problems intersect that marks the genesis of a new development model. Having witnessed what mashups have achieved in the public sector, I propose the time for bringing this technology into the enterprise is now.

Structure

It's one thing to amass a collection of patterns; it's quite another thing altogether when that set can be combined and linked to create a whole greater than the sum of its parts. We will have then achieved what is known as a "pattern language" or, more simply, a mashup of different pattern concepts. Figure 2.1 illustrates the relationships between the mashup patterns we will examine in this book. The diagram is deceptively simple owing to mashups' unique ability to serve as the foundation for further work (see Figure 1.5, the virtuous circle of mashups, in Chapter 1). For example, the Splinter, Content Integration, and Filter patterns can be used in cyclical combinations to tap into and recombine existing source material for use by the other patterns. Likewise, Feed Factory and API Enabler can either expose new RSS feeds or Web Services interfaces where none previously existed or they can restructure present resources. Plus, given the continuous expansion of the Web (and associated resources), many of the patterns can tap a never-ending supply of raw materials. Although the most common connections are illustrated in this book, almost all of the patterns can interoperate to spur new creations.

The patterns presented in this book are organized into five main categories: Harvest, Enhance, Assemble, Manage, and Test. Each of these groups of patterns is the subject of its own chapter. Some of the patterns deal with creating or reducing content, while others focus on consuming it. There are also patterns that focus on application functionality or appearance alone. While the high-level groupings reflect a particular specialization, they do not preclude patterns from different chapters from working together. In fact, many of the examples rely on the coordination of multiple patterns to deliver a solution.

The **Harvest** patterns (Chapter 4) are a general class of solutions that lend themselves to obtaining data from sources outside the reach of traditional tools. The leading prospect is, of course, the World Wide Web, which, while programmatically accessible to custom crawlers or bots, is generally *not* leveraged as a first-class data source. The patterns in this section don't stop at the thin veneer of HTML that sites present to the public; instead, they show you how to automate online forms and reach into the *Deep Web* of data that sits behind the presentation layer. One study estimated the size of this information store to be nearly 500 times greater than what's available via the "surface" Web.[3]

---

3. Bergman, Michael K. "The Deep Web: Surfacing Hidden Value." September 2001. http://www.brightplanet.com/images/stories/pdf/deepwebwhitepaper.pdf

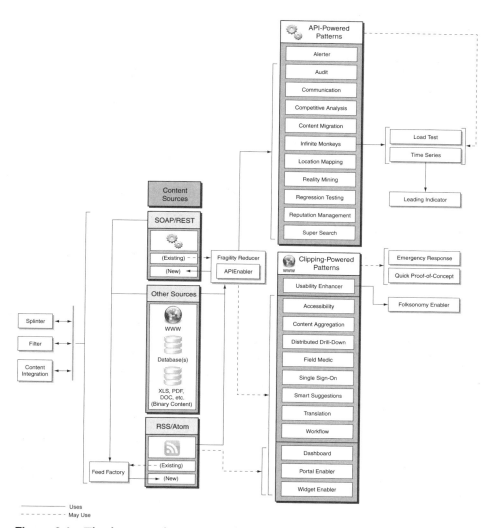

Figure 2.1 *The diversity of content sources belies the potential complexity of mashup relationships.*

Patterns in the **Enhance** category (Chapter 5) demonstrate how systems can be extended and improved. The exciting prospect is that these changes can be made without the assistance of the original developers. In fact, access to the source code isn't needed at all. Many of the solutions rely on mashups' ability to dynamically inject (or remove) presentation instructions from an existing user interface.

With new streams of data and new ways to present it, the next logical course of action is to mix everything together. The **Assemble** patterns (Chapter 6) show how fresh solutions can be minted by combining data and presentation from multiple sources.

It's been said that God was able to create the world in seven days only because He didn't have an installed base to contend with. For many firms, the greatest challenge lies not in building new solutions but in managing the ones they already have. Hence we have the **Manage** category (Chapter 7), which uses mashups as a vehicle for helping an organization leverage its existing assets more effectively.

The **Testing** category (Chapter 8) is a reflection of mashups' ties to the realm of traditional software development. As far as this new technology may take us, it must still adhere to the basic rules and requirements that form the foundation of any solution deployed within the modern enterprise. Among these building blocks are repeatability, scalability, and compatibility. Because mashups empower a new generation of builders, we must take special care not to abandon the practices that support the stability of operational infrastructure.

Not every mashup toolset will support every category or pattern, so this inventory should not be used as a "shopping list" for selecting a particular product. Issues of cost notwithstanding, there is no reason that multiple solutions cannot exist within one firm. Many organizations already manage more than one messaging platform or operating system as part of their core architecture and exploit their specialties as needed. As long as they adhere to open standards, it is completely appropriate to deploy various mashup tools to meet similar ends.

Where's the UML?

In this book, the discussion of each pattern is accompanied by a diagram that provides a high-level overview of its architecture. In another break from many traditional patterns texts, this image is *not* presented in the Unified Modeling Language (UML). Although I applaud UML's efforts to bring consistency to the discipline of modeling, nontechnical readers may have found its structures confusing. Because this demographic segment is important to the success of mashups, I chose not to entangle mashups' ease of use with diagramming techniques that might intimidate some individuals. If you're familiar with UML, you won't be completely disappointed. The pattern diagrams bear a striking similarity to a sequence diagram turned 90 degrees so that the progression of steps is vertical rather than horizontal. This arrangement accommodates the aspect ratio of the printed page more easily.

Summary

Strict compliance with legacy definitions is ultimately of minor concern. We have moved outside the confines of IT as a result of Enterprise 2.0, and we must adapt our language to embrace a wider audience. The goal of this book is to provide you with useful ideas; you are the ultimate judge of how practical the solutions will be for your firm. To this end, do not isolate yourself from your surroundings while reading this text. Think about the people and the systems that are part of your corporate environment while you explore the patterns. Engage in a mental game of "what if," where you randomly combine resources and gauge the business benefits of the outcome. Which barriers can be demolished? Which frustrations overcome?

The patterns in this book are meant for inspiration as much as for implementation. They describe what is *possible;* you must use your unique focus to shape them into what is *needed.* Above all, don't be afraid to experiment: Seed the tools across your enterprise and encourage creativity. The potential benefits are endless.

Chapter 3

Core Activities

Great things are not done by impulse, but by a series of small things brought together.

—Vincent van Gogh (1853–1890)

Introduction

Many of the patterns in this book can be broken apart into smaller sections for analysis, but ultimately we reach a point of irreducible functionality. At this level of detail we can observe the core activities that make the overall solution possible. *Core activities* describe the general capabilities that underlie most enterprise mashups. It is through a combination of these elements that the patterns in this book are realized. As new patterns are discovered, they will undoubtedly continue to make use of one or more of these capabilities.

It's a commonly held idea that patterns books shouldn't talk about toolsets. Any venture into a "feature set" discussion is fraught with challenges, as we run the risk of focusing on particular products rather than the general problems they were created to address. In this chapter we will navigate through these dangerous waters. The layperson who merely wishes to understand the business value of mashups may wish to return to this chapter after perusing the patterns themselves.

Whether a firm's decision to nurture an internal sandbox for mashups has its origins at the business, technical, or managerial level, the company must always understand its overall goals for the technology. Although Enterprise 2.0 certainly encourages experimentation, this doesn't mean that employees should start out empty-handed. It's been said that "A good carpenter doesn't blame his tools"—but have you ever seen a good carpenter who didn't have the proper tools to begin with? The core activities provide a framework for examining which resources should be available in your organization. To learn more about how firms are leveraging tools for specific implementations, consult the case studies in this book's appendix. These sections were produced in collaboration with the vendors whose tools are already helping organizations benefit from mashup technology.

Support for Open Standards

Open APIs form the backbone of consumer-focused Web 2.0 mashups. Every day more organizations are exposing functionality and data via publicly accessible Web Services and RSS feeds. A similar process has overtaken many enterprises, albeit with different motivations. Many firms have taken to adopting service-oriented architecture (SOA) to allow their internal resources to be easily leveraged across multiple projects. These services have increased in importance now that enterprise mashups have emerged as a new development paradigm.

IT can facilitate self-service application construction by exposing core services for internal consumption. Protocols and formats commonly used for this purpose include Web Services (SOAP, REST), LDAP, OpenID, RSS/Atom, XML, JSON, ODBC/JDBC, the Java Portlet Specification (JSR-168), and SMTP. These industry standards allow interaction between applications, authentication services, databases, email, news feeds, and portlets. As time passes, this collection of acronyms and their scope are likely to increase even more. Each standard carries with it the promises of being able to take advantage of those resources which it makes available. Because the raw material of mashups is preexisting data, support for open protocols is a fundamental element of most toolsets. This is not a "chicken and egg" proposition: Mashups currently do not play much of a part in the definition of new protocols, but rather play a critical role in driving widespread demand for open standards support across enterprise resources.

The standards that proliferate at a firm depend on the challenges faced by the organization. Pure data-driven mashups may require only tools that support XML and ODBC/JDBC, while RSS/Atom can power many content aggregation implementations. By contrast, interacting with the resources of an enterprise service bus (ESB) to leverage complex application functionality requires support for SOAP-based Web Services.

Despite the importance of ensuring support for open standards, you will not find this core capability specified for any of the patterns described in this book. The reason is that this functionality is too closely entwined with the implementation of a pattern and the particular resources that participate in it. For example, an instance of the Alerter pattern is much easier to build if the monitored resource exposes a Web Services interface or RSS feed. But if the pattern *required* either of these protocols, then the circumstances for its use would be severely limited. You would be able to apply this pattern only in cases where support for these standards was already available. The more general approach taken in this text is to rely on the API Enabler pattern, which describes using a separate mashup to create the necessary interfaces required for an Alerter implementation. Is this extra level of complexity necessary if an API that your toolset supports is already available? No. In fact, if it meets all of your functional requirements, this is the preferred approach for building the mashup. Nevertheless, issues involving construction are too closely associated with specific tools and resources to warrant their inclusion within a discussion of patterns.

From a nontechnical standpoint, the takeaway message from this section is this: You need to examine which resources will be participating in your mashups. Your firm may have already taken steps to formally support particular standards across its internal systems. If you want to mash up these resources in the most efficient manner possible, you need to ensure that the tools you obtain can take advantage of whatever open APIs are already in place.

If your toolset and mashup candidates do not already share a lingua franca, an alternative solution is to enlist IT to bridge this gap. If IT cannot be of assistance, or if external resources that you do not control are involved, you will need to rely on the API Enabler pattern from the Harvest category to cross the divide. API Enabler, in turn, depends on the core activities of data extraction and data entry, which are covered later in this chapter. Keep in mind that the raw ingredients for mashups are most commonly collected from systems outside your direct control. If they do not provide a conduit to their data and functionality—and if you don't have the tools to create one yourself—then your efforts to implement mashup patterns won't make much headway.

Once you have implemented a mashup, it may be equally important that your tools support the ability to *publish* content. Not all patterns describe solutions that are ends in themselves. In many cases (for example, in the Feed Factory and Content Integration patterns), the goal is to provide resources to downstream systems and potential new mashups. For example, the mashup-powered RSS feeds created by one employee may be recombined to create a personalized dashboard by another person. If the output cannot be exposed in a useful format, then the mashup is basically useless. As a general rule, make sure your toolset supports publishing data in compliance with the same standards it supports for consuming the data.

Data Extraction

Data extraction refers to a mashup platform's ability to obtain information from closed sources. In contrast to the previous section, where we examined how open APIs yield more mashup-friendly resources, here we are specifically concerned with content that is not exposed for programmatic access. As discussed in Chapter 1, the vast amount of publicly available information is presently presented in a manner that is useful to human beings but not to machines.

We have already discussed one form of data extraction known as Web harvesting. Our first look at the subject demonstrated how form fields and page elements could be located on a Web site even as the presentation format was regularly revised. This is a neat trick but it's only useful on a limited scale. It requires a person to manually preview a page and identify the specific sections that are of interest. But what if your intention is to build mashups that will automatically crawl through thousands of pages?

Data extraction builds on basic harvesting capabilities to provide more practical functionality. Many subtleties to the extraction process exist, and it's important to understand these nuances before you march headfirst into mashup development. Otherwise, you may find your pattern implementations still require a significant amount of human intervention.

Let's look at some of the major issues that surface during the planning process for data extraction.

Do You Know Exactly What You Are Looking For?

In some cases you will be able to look at a Web page or a spreadsheet, point to a specific spot, and say, "I want that!" The Web is chock full of discrete pieces of data that are ripe for the plucking. Company financial statements, addresses, weather forecasts, and catalog prices are a few simple examples. But sometimes useful information doesn't jump out and announce its presence. You have to be able to look deeper into the content to extract its true value. Examples include news stories, press releases, blogs, wikis, and online forums. Wherever a person is directly responsible for creating content, the job of teaching a computer to understand that content gets harder. A person may be able to examine these resources and uncover advantageous details, but the lack of formal structure often makes it a difficult process to automate.

A variety of methods for tackling this problem have been developed. Search engines already demonstrate that it is possible to index unstructured content and selectively return subsets based on simple keyword queries. Is this done with complete accuracy? No. That's because the search engine can only guess at the user's ultimate intention. A search engine is a single application designed to serve the ever-changing requirements of millions of users. In the case of mashups, you have a much clearer definition of the goal you wish to achieve. This foreknowledge enables a more focused interrogation of data because you can tune your techniques to the specific tasks and resources at hand.

One component of data extraction you should consider is how you will locate your source material. Will you require some type of embedded search mechanism? If you need to search, how will you specify your queries? Are exact keyword matches enough, or do you need to include synonyms and handle misspellings? Perhaps support for regular expressions[1] is sufficient. The out-of-the-box value of a mashup platform is diminished if you need features that are not natively supported. Although a skilled IT department can "bolt on" some of these functions afterward, that customization may come at the cost of increasing the complexity, timeline, or budget of mashup creation.

Will You Be Mining Dynamically Updated Pages?

The spread of AJAX (Asynchronous JavaScript and XML) programming has led to an explosion of Web sites that behave like interactive applications. Previously, actions on a Web site (e.g., clicking a link or submitting a form) initiated a new page load that displayed the results. With AJAX, a page can be updated outside the typical request/reload cycle. Many sites dynamically update their content with no user interaction whatsoever. For example, consider a financial site where the stocks in your portfolio blink every few seconds to reflect the latest market prices.

These interfaces pose a challenge for mashup developers. At what point is a continually changing page ready to be harvested? Periodic updates via AJAX (and other techniques such as Comet, which maintains an open HTTP connection) ensure there is no definitive point where a page's content is static. Suppose you were to grab and process data from the first half of page while the second half was being updated—you could easily wind up with conflicting or misleading results.

Other techniques for creating rich Internet applications (RIAs) include Adobe Flash and Microsoft Silverlight. Because these platforms rely on browser plugins to display their interface, data extraction from them might seem impossible. In many instances the underlying communication between the interface and the back-end server takes place via Web Services, however, so it is still possible to access the data if support for this standard is present within your tools.

---

1. Regular expressions (regex) are a powerful type of text string that specifies patterns to locate within a document.

Is Some of Your Content in Binary Format (e.g., Images, Spreadsheets, PDF Files)?

Web pages frequently contain links to download other forms of binary content such as Excel spreadsheets or Adobe PDF files. And images don't just contribute to the overall design of a Web page: They can provide maps, charts, product snapshots, employee photographs, or other useful content. If these details are important to your firm, you might consider selecting a mashup platform capable of dynamically pulling data from these resources. In Chapter 10, the section "Mashing Up Binary Types" discusses approaches for extracting data from application files even when a tool doesn't natively support this feature.

If you are collecting images or files, you will need some type of storage to retain this material until you are ready to use it. The type, size, and location of this repository directly impact its usefulness and the complexity of your mashup environment. An on-site database is the most flexible in terms of space but may not be easily manipulated by the layperson. In-memory solutions are more flexible but provide a finite amount of room. Storage solutions included with online mashup tools might not support successive manipulation of resources once they have been harvested.

Can You Access Alternative Views of the Data?

Although a mashup may be capable of collecting images, it cannot easily determine their content. In some cases optical character recognition (OCR) software can be used to convert graphical representations of letters into machine-readable text. Another option to consider is whether an alternative view of the data is available. Web sites designed to be accessible to users with visual limitations sometimes provide a text-only view that is easily consumed by a mashup. Wikis are another example of a case where a complicated display can be easily parsed if the underlying wiki markup is examined (see the "Extracting Hidden Data" sidebar). The need to navigate to different presentation formats is one reason why data extraction activities are frequently paired with data entry.

Extracting Hidden Data

In many cases alternative views are available that more easily lend themselves to data extraction. Wikis are an excellent example: They often expose a public "Edit" function that leads to the syntax responsible for a page's generated content.

Consider the following chart. A mashup that examined this image would find it impossible to recognize the columns, let alone obtain their exact values. But if the application could access the specific wiki markup behind the picture, then extracting the details becomes a simple task.

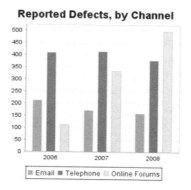

The preceding image was generated from the following wiki text:

```
{chart:type=bar|title=Reported Defects, by Channel}
|| 2006 || 2007 ||2008 ||
| Email| 212 | 170 | 158 |
| Telephone | 409 | 413 | 378 |
| Online Forums | 112 | 336 | 498 |
{chart}
```

There are other cases in which the displayed material can be extracted but contains information that is not as useful as the markup behind it. A perfect example is an HTML hyperlink. A link labeled "Quarterly report spreadsheet" is nowhere near as valuable as the underlying URL that specifies the location of the file. Or consider a drop-down list that displays a customer name but maps this name to a more relevant account number hidden underneath. Mashups that harvest Web sites should be capable of inspecting all aspects of a page for potentially valuable data.

Data extraction is not a trivial process. Before embarking on a quest to implement any of the patterns in this book, you should understand where the raw data you require ultimately resides. This knowledge will shape your design decisions and in some cases may advise against building a particular mashup until you obtain appropriate tools. Outlining your user interface is another good step toward understanding how the content will be displayed and used in its final environment.

Data Entry

Data entry is all about "faking it." Mashups don't only extract data; they can supply it as well. Reaching a mineable resource generally requires that a mashup mimic the steps a user would take to navigate to the same point. Data entry is the key capability involved in chaining multiple sites together. Additionally, it facilitates patterns such as Infinite Monkeys, which may involve only a single site but simulate user activity scaled to superhuman levels.

The process of surfing the Web has become so familiar to us that it is tempting to dismiss it as a series of simple "click and type" operations. The process is actually more complicated than we give ourselves credit for! In fact, plotting a mashup's course through the Web is as at least as difficult as automating data collection operations along the way. Consider the process outlined in the "Navigating the Web" sidebar.

▼_____

Navigating the Web

Traversing the Web is so easy that even your mother can do it—but don't take her intelligence for granted. Suppose you wanted to book a flight from New York to London. Here are the steps you might follow:

1. You begin by entering the Web address of an online travel service into your browser. When a pop-up for a Caribbean vacation appears, you click the Close button because you're not interested.

2. You notice options for car rentals, flights, and hotels. You click "Flights."

3. There are fields for "From" and "To." You enter "New York" and "London" and click "OK." Because there are multiple airports near New York, you are presented with a list that asks you to choose a specific one. You select "LaGuardia" and click "OK." Likewise, there are multiple airports near London. so you select "Heathrow" and click "OK."

4. You pick a departure date from a pop-up calendar and select "Afternoon" for the time. You also pick a return date and chose "4PM" for the return time.

5. You click the "Search for Flights" button. A list of flights appears. You click "Select" next to a departing flight. Another list of flights appears, and you click "Select" next to your preferred return trip.

6. You think you have a frequent flyer number for the selected airline. You enter it on the next screen and click "Submit." The page returns an error, so you guess you were mistaken. You clear the field and click "Next."

7. On the next two screens, you are presented with a seating diagram. You select your seats from the available options.

8. On the final screen, you are prompted for payment. You have an account with this travel service, so you supply your login credentials and pay using the credit card information you have on file.

This path seems like a straightforward process that could be easily automated. Closer examination, however, reveals that each step requires an intelligent action on the user's part. Let's examine the task from a mashup's perspective:

1. Who knew that a pop-up ad would appear when the page was loaded? What if it didn't appear every time? A mashup will need to know the difference between expected and unexpected windows and understand when to close them and when they merit further attention.

2. Suppose a new tab was added for cruises? Or the word "flights" was changed to "air travel"? Would the mashup still know which option to select?

3. Depending on the cities you selected, you might or might not receive a screen to choose a specific airport. A mashup would need to handle both cases.

4. The pop-up calendar makes date selection easy for a user, but a mashup would need to understand how to manipulate this control to navigate to the appropriate dates and select them.

5. Assuming the flight you wanted was on the first page, selecting it could be an easy step to perform. But what if you had to click through multiple results? A mashup would need to understand how to navigate across pages.

6. You supplied what you thought was a valid frequent flyer code but it was rejected. A mashup needs to recover from conditions where it provides incomplete or erroneous information. This may mean trying a different value or skipping a step.

7. Much like the challenge in picking dates, a mashup needs to understand how to operate the seat-selection control. Additionally, we need to imbue it with the intelligence to select preferred seats from those that are available.

8. The mashup concludes by signing in to an account. Where are the user's ID and password stored? How is it passed to the underlying Web site? Our data entry operations need to support secure authentication tasks when necessary.

From the user's standpoint, this is not a difficult transaction—but building an autonomous agent that can perform it flawlessly is a challenge. The Web is like an ocean without shores or lighthouses. Potential problems are ready to jump out at each step and introduce complications.

Data entry is no longer a simple process for man or machine. Rich new interface metaphors challenge our conventional notions about Web functionality. Data entry operations should be prepared to cope with an ever-increasing array of complex features, including input format masks, auto-completing fields, instant validations, and a host of robust new controls and widgets. Unexpected responses to input must be anticipated and accommodated. For example, a mashup needs to be prepared when a pop-up window randomly appears. Does the window contain information regarding content that is out-of-date or has moved, or it is just an advertisement? How will subsequent data entry activities be shaped by this event?

For these reasons, we rely on data extraction functionality to provide our mashups with clues about how they should behave. It's normal for data entry operations to be paired with data extraction ones. Each entry operation should be preceded and followed by an extraction. After all, the first step in providing some information is figuring out where to put it! The first extraction makes sure that the proper target for the simulated user activity has been identified. Otherwise, we run the risk of a mashup failing or, even worse, accidentally entering private information into inappropriate fields. The second check verifies that the input was interpreted correctly by the target.

Likewise, extraction operations cannot succeed without performing the input operations that lead to the resources to be harvested in the first place. Working in tandem, the two core activities can be used to collect content from one location and use it as input for another. This produces new output that can serve as input for another site, and so on. Ultimately, this progression of steps can be exposed as a single function that automates a series of operations; such a function is the foundation for many of the mashup patterns we will examine in this book. The proliferation of development languages and platforms across IT departments makes these paired activities even more useful as a lightweight bridging technology. Systems can be integrated "at the glass," meaning that they enter and exchange information via their user interfaces. This is a practical approach when an open API isn't available.

The input for data entry operations may also come from non-Web sources such as spreadsheets or databases. This latter is often the case when a mashup is used to "play back" a series of actions that were "recorded" earlier. Using mashups as supercharged macros allows complicated user activities to be scripted and scaled to new levels. For example, implementations of the Testing patterns rely heavily on this feature. Some mashup tools may require custom coding to perform these types of operations, whereas others provide direct support for this capability. The merits of either approach should be judged in relationship to the technical ability of your mashup developers.

Data Visualization

Although data validation and entry are systemic activities for most mashups, use of the remaining core activities in this chapter depends largely on the specific patterns you choose to implement. *Data visualization* describes a capability that is not provided by all the tools in this space but is nonetheless highly generic: It encompasses the ability to create user-friendly output based on data collected by the mashup.

The ability to convey the results of a mashup graphically is completely optional. In instances when a mashup performs strict data integration, it isn't even applicable. Likewise, it's not appropriate to consider visualizing a database update or a Web Service call. In other cases, visually presenting the information a mashup collects makes complete sense. Patterns such as Time Series (Chapter 4), which collects a sequence of values at regular intervals, can use a chart to illustrate trends in the data. A Reputation Management (Chapter 4) implementation could show a heat map with frequency and sentiment in relation to specific keywords. Instances of the Dashboard pattern (Chapter 7) often use bar and pie charts to provide a high-level summary of detailed metrics.

Visualization is also used to describe the rendering of user interface elements such as buttons, tables, and text-entry fields. A mashup may produce these constructs as output artifacts (see the Widget Enabler and Portal Enabler patterns in Chapter 7), or it may use them to collect input parameters that will be used during the course of its execution (see the Smart Suggestions pattern in Chapter 5).

Most visualization tasks can be delegated to external software and services if they are not supported by your tools. Numerous low-cost and open-source products can handle the most common requirements. These solutions can be roughly classified as belonging to one of two potential architectures: a self-hosted solution that runs on your own infrastructure or externally provided services.

Solutions available in-house suffer the same drawbacks we have encountered before. Namely, when functionality is managed and maintained internally, it requires that IT personnel be engaged in the process at some level. This approach creates a potential support and resource bottleneck that may limit both the flexibility and speed with which mashups can be constructed.

The downside of using external resources is that you have no guarantees of their reliability or availability. Your mashups may flawlessly collect troves of information, only to stop dead in their tracks when an online charting service is down for maintenance. Furthermore, you are providing potentially sensitive information to a third party. You should exercise this option only if you trust the service provider and can ensure that secure protocols are used.

A good example of a highly focused service that provides visualization capabilities is the Google Charts API.[2] A large collection of chart types (bar, line, radar, scatter, pie, gauge, Venn diagrams, and maps) can be created using custom URLs. Figure 3.1 provides some examples, along with their simple URL-based syntax. Usage guidelines were recently modified to remove previous restrictions on how often the service could be called,[3] which should make testing and tweaking charts easier. A mashup lacking native visualization features could easily rely on Google Charts to generate its output.

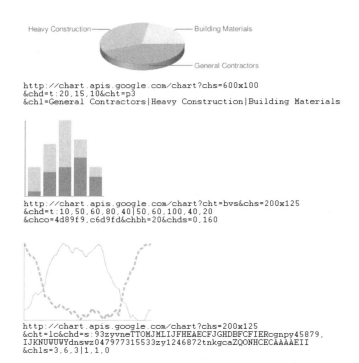

Figure 3.1   *Google Charts can add supplemental data visualization capabilities to mashups.*

2. http://code.google.com/apis/chart/

3. http://code.google.com/apis/chart/#usage

Scheduling and Surveillance

The advantage of automating a task is that afterward it can be performed repeatedly and with a high degree of consistency. As part of their design, many mashups are intended to perform repetitive tasks on an automated basis. As you investigate the patterns, it will become obvious that some fall into a category of "user-initiated" activities (see the Smart Suggestions pattern in Chapter 5), while others rely on "periodic execution" (see the Time Series and Infinite Monkeys patterns in Chapter 4). Although human intervention may be required to kick off regular activities, a core mashup goal is to eliminate this drudgery wherever possible.

Apart from determining when a task occurs, *scheduling* may also determine which resources are engaged for a mashup. Consider an organization that has branch offices in several countries and where those branches publish regular metrics on their internal operations. A mashup may be designed to run every hour and collect this information as part of building a global status report. It doesn't make sense to extract data from each individual site every time the mashup executes. When the U.S. office is open, its data will change frequently, but the Hong Kong branch will be closed and its statistics will remain static. Apart from controlling *when* the mashup runs, a scheduling facility might provide input as to *which* offices should be examined based on time and geography. Other options include identifying resources based on server utilization or network bandwidth. A scheduling component could even rely on mashups for input criteria to further coordinate processing tasks.

A robust scheduling facility can be a product unto itself, so it is not unusual for toolsets to omit this functionality. Luckily third-party resources are available for almost all platforms. The key criteria to consider before choosing a solution are highlighted here:

- Does the Scheduler support your usage model? Is your execution plan time based (e.g., hourly, daily, weekly) or is it controlled by other factors (e.g., when my computer is idle or when stock market volatility is high)?

- Does your toolset provide a method for mashups to be triggered externally? A third-party scheduler is useless if your mashups exist in an environment that prevents an outside application from setting them in motion. Purely Web-based tools can be controlled by pairing a scheduler with a desktop automation product (e.g., a user macro).

Surveillance is essentially a data extraction operation that executes on a periodic schedule. The results of each observation are compared according to predefined criteria. The output of a surveillance operation can be used to record baseline statistics, which can in turn answer questions such as these:

- With what frequency are different parts of a site updated?

- Did an *expected* change occur when it was planned?

- How do response times vary during different periods and with respect to different features?

- Does the site suffer any regular outages, and how long do they last?

To be an effective monitoring tool, a mashup must be as nonintrusive as possible. Otherwise, the act of measurement may affect the results that are obtained. For internally deployed resources, system-level logs may already be available. It's preferable to consume and analyze preexisting observations rather than add the strain of additional processing to an application. The Dashboard pattern provides more specific details about how this functionality can discover and report various metrics.

A toolset may offer the ability to "mark" sections of a site and target them for recurring analysis. Alternatively, a surveillance operation can be custom-coded, provided appropriate scheduling and extraction features are available. Variations from a predetermined baseline could be used to trigger subsequent mashup activities (see the "Action" section later in this chapter and the Alerter pattern in Chapter 4).

Clipping

Whereas data extraction describes mining discrete sections of a Web resource, *clipping* refers to the practice of grabbing a "chunk" of a Web site. The clipped region might be a subsection of a page or the page itself (see Figure 3.2). Clipping is generally used to create portlets from existing content. If you intend to select a toolset that supports this core ability, you should be familiar with JSR-168[4] (Java Portlets) and the WSRP[5] (Web Services for Remote Portlets). These

---

4. http://jcp.org/en/jsr/detail?id=168

5. http://www.oasis-open.org/committees/tc_home.php?wg_abbrev=wsrp

Figure 3.2 *Clipping harvests previously rendered content for reuse.*

specifications facilitate interoperability between portals and portlets. Most likely you will be incorporating clipped content into an existing portal framework, so you need to avoid creating an eyesore by ensuring your mashup toolset and portal environment follow a common set of visual standards.

Clipping allows you to repurpose Web content without requiring any changes to the underlying code base. How does this process differ from data extraction? In the case of extraction, we generally harvest discrete values from a page, absent of their presentation characteristics. This specific information is often the subject of further analysis. By contrast, clipping operations return information at a presentation level; this data cannot be broken down into its constituent parts. For example, if a Web page contained information on a company's stock and a historical performance chart, an "extract" might return only the text of the company name and the numeric value of the current price. A "clip" would return the complete page as a section of HTML that could be redisplayed in a different system.

It might seem that clipping would yield a portal with the aesthetic appeal of Frankenstein's monster. Stitching together pieces of different sites with varying font sizes, colors, layouts, and other styles could create a complete mess. First-class support for clipping includes the option to override existing Cascading Style Sheets (CSS) markup referenced on the pulled content. More sophisticated manipulations might require the ability to examine and change the structure of the extracted HTML.

What about any JavaScript associated with the harvested content? How is that functionality handled? There are three basic approaches, and a mashup tool might support any or all of them:

- Any JavaScript is completely removed from the clipped material, so that any interactive elements become static displays. This is akin to cutting an article out from a newspaper.

- The JavaScript remains and a transparent routing layer is added underneath to relay data to and from the original site. Clips of resources can be combined while retaining their native capabilities.

- JavaScript remains active and the mashup creator has the option to intercept, change, or cancel events before they are fed back to the source system. This capability is a key enabler of the Field Medic pattern.

Depending on the source of content for a clipping operation, use of the data entry ability to supply user credentials may be necessary. Republishing protected resources without taking measures to provide equal or greater security measures for them can have serious consequences. The Sticky Fingers and Open Kimono anti-patterns in Chapter 9 examine this risk in greater detail.

If you want to reassemble and reuse existing content, then clipping is a boon where internal assets are concerned and a necessity if third-party sites are involved. Caution must be exercised when clipping external resources. In the process of extracting an entire section of a page, it is possible to pick up some decidedly unfriendly hitchhikers. The Malicious Hitchhiker anti-pattern (see Chapter 9) discusses the potential downsides of this approach.

Transformation and Enrichment

When a mashup interacts with a collection of resources, it's unlikely that all of the constituents are going to expect or produce data in a common format. In fact, you should feel lucky if you observe any consistency across even two sites—internal or otherwise. These disparities can take the form of simple variations in presentation format (as shown in Figure 3.3), or they may be more

Black, Peter	Birch, Stephen	Carlos, Tim	Drum, Trevor

Name:	Black, Peter
Address:	600 South Lane
	Redding, CT 06896
Phone:	(203) 555-1212
Date of Hire:	12/28/2008

Name:	Peter Black
Address:	600 S. Lane
	Redding, CT 06896-2300
Phone:	+1 203.555.1212
Date of Hire:	28-December-2008

Figure 3.3 *Identical employee data may be presented differently depending on the application.*

complicated, such as when different measuring systems, currencies, or languages are involved. To be of any use, the data will need to be normalized so that it adheres to a uniform standard.

Transformation is an essential part of turning extracted data into a format where it can be useful. Remember that for a Web page there is no concept of a "data type." Numbers, words, dates, and dollar amounts all boil down to the same thing: simple text. As humans, our brains automatically translate from the representation of data to its underlying meaning and react accordingly; "Oh, that's an expensive item!" or "That date is only two weeks away!" are two examples. Mashups need to accomplish a similar feat to make any use of the material they collect.

As with several of the other core features, if transformation functionality is not present in a mashup product it can be included later with the assistance of developers (who will code custom transformation functions) or by adding another mashup step to the process (e.g., calling a Web Service that converts between various currencies). However, given the ubiquity of transformation work that mashups inevitably have to perform, it should be stressed that some level of support for this core function is practically a *requirement* when an organization chooses mashup-enabling technologies. Some of the more common transformation requirements include the following:

- *Explicit data casting.* A mashup that is supplying or receiving values needs to convert from one data type to another. A Web Service from one resource may return dates as text strings, while another mashup may return them as date objects. A third mashup might expect a date to be input as a numeric value.[6] Mashups that interact directly with Web forms require the ability to convert data types to plain text because that is how a user would enter a value.

- *Uppercase/lowercase.* A simple but important feature is the ability to change the case of text for comparison purposes. If one resource returns text in uppercase and another in lowercase, string comparisons will fail even if the data are identical.

- *Simple lookup tables.* As part of its internal data handling, a mashup frequently needs to be able to move between a presentation value and an identification code. For example, a Web site that displays a list of books for a user to choose from may translate these values to their ISBN codes before communicating the selection back to the server. A company name could be converted to its ticker symbol or CUSIP[7] without the user's knowledge.

- *Database lookups and enrichment.* The information a mashup captures does not always flow directly to other systems. Sometimes it is used to form a database query that retrieves the information that really matters first. Consider a mashup that shows a customer's location on a map given that individual's account number. The account number has no geographic significance but it is used to find the customer's street address and ZIP code from a database. These data are then passed to the map.

- *Mathematical formulas.* The ability to perform basic math is another important transformation capability. Each of the following is a method of expressing a value of fifty percent: 50, .50, or 5000bps (basis points). Simple multiplication can be used to express all of these forms in a common format. Converting from one currency to another is a simple calculation given the exchange rate. You may need to dynamically perform addition or subtraction during processing if you find that one system starts counting at 0 while another starts from 1.

- *Format masks.* A format mask is a template that specifies how a data value should be arranged for input, presentation, or storage. Format masks are commonly used to instruct users on providing input that an application will understand. In the request, "Please enter your birthday (MM/DD/YY)," "MM/DD/YY" is a format mask. Other masks may control the formatting

---

6. A common method of representing dates is the number of milliseconds elapsed since midnight, January 1, 1970.

7. CUSIP refers to a unique nine-character identification code given to securities traded in the United States.

of numbers or monetary values based on locale. Because mashups often receive data from multiple sources, it is frequently necessary to rearrange information to conform to a homogeneous style before additional processing can occur. Format masks provide a quick shorthand for specifying this common standard. If a tool does not offer native formatting support, then it can be achieved with custom-coded services.

- *HTML markup.* Text returned in HTML format will not necessarily wind up being displayed or stored by a component that supports HTML. In other cases it could be useful if objects such as email addresses are automatically converted into clickable links. The ability to either add or remove HTML markup handles these situations.

- *Transforming binary data.* One of the more sophisticated transformations involves converting binary data stored in a proprietary format (for example, an Excel spreadsheet) into an open standard such as XML. Conversion between different media formats for audio and visual files is another possible use. When a toolset does not natively support this ability, there are alternative approaches for accomplishing this task. See the section "Mashing Up Binary Types" in Chapter 10 for more information.

Chaining transform operations together is an important feature. If you convert a string value into a date, you'll want the ability to follow up by changing the date to a particular format. Basic filtering—which might be implemented as a regular expression parser or through some type of query builder—is another desirable feature. We will examine more sophisticated screening operations when we discuss the Filter pattern in Chapter 6.

Action

In our examination of data extraction, scheduling, and surveillance, we observed techniques for allowing mashups to dynamically react to changes in outside data sources. Ultimately these solutions entailed *polling*—that is, periodically checking a resource to see if further action was warranted. There are two downsides to this approach. First, it relies on having something to monitor in the first place. If an email is automatically sent to a customer, there may be no visual artifact that a mashup can examine to learn this has occurred. Second, polling can be inefficient. You will discover a change only when you specifically look for it. If response time is crucial, this approach requires you to frequently perform checks. This step can reduce the performance of the resource you are monitoring in addition to needlessly consuming network bandwidth.

In some circumstances it is more desirable to have specific events trigger a mashup. At first glance, this might seem to run counter to the general principles of mashup development. Wouldn't it require changes to the original systems to set the mashup in motion? Not necessarily, as we will discover.

For starters, many applications *already* broadcast their activities. A mashup just needs to know how and where to listen. The Simple Network Management Protocol (SNMP) is one example. It describes a mechanism for publishing health and status information for network-connected devices. SNMP agents can be queried for regular updates, or they may automatically broadcast an alert according to predefined settings. This data is commonly used by application and network monitoring tools to diagnose problems and plan for future infrastructure growth. A mashup platform capable of intercepting SNMP messages could extend the usefulness of these products. For example, a "low disk space" warning might trigger a mashup that collects release notes from the wikis of various teams. This activity might lead to the discovery that multiple groups compile their applications at the same time, which causes a temporary spike in storage consumption. Or perhaps a slowdown in network traffic might launch a mashup that temporarily paused the scheduled execution of other mashups until the situation improved. Thus SNMP messages could be used to set off any number of mashup actions that could remediate problems in addition to tracking down their cause.

Another commonly supported technique for event-based processing is message-oriented middleware (MOM). In a publish–subscribe (pub/sub) implementation, a publisher sends messages to a topic. Subscribers to that topic receive all the messages that are sent to it. There may be multiple subscribers per topic, but the publisher knows nothing about them; all it understands is how to communicate with the topic. With this approach, the message creator and any recipients are completely decoupled. Two common MOM standards are Java's JMS[8] and Microsoft's MSMQ.[9] A mashup platform capable of subscribing to topics based on these standards could dynamically extend systems in interesting new ways. For example, a "create new customer" message might trigger a mashup that goes out to the Internet and automatically sends a welcome card using one site and a bouquet of flowers using another.

---

8. http://java.sun.com/products/jms/

9. http://www.microsoft.com/windowsserver2003/technologies/msmq/default.mspx

A final example involves email—more specifically, the Simple Mail Transfer Protocol (SMTP). SMTP is the standard for mail transmission on the Internet. But email recipients don't need to be humans; they can be mashups as well. A mashup platform may provide a basic SMTP server that allows it to receive and react to incoming messages (and send mail as well, naturally).

Consider a firm that wants to handle customer support requests via email. It's not uncommon for an auto-generated reply to inform clients that "A representative will respond to your message shortly." Of course, in the meantime the customer is no closer to a resolution of the problem than when he or she started. A SMTP-aware mashup that pulls in other resources might respond with a more useful message. When an email is received, the mashup would swing into action. First, it might check the status of the network to see if any systems are overloaded. Next, it could scan the internal Help Desk knowledge base for summaries of the three most frequently encountered problems of the day and their solutions. Finally, the customer's account details would be retrieved and examined. Perhaps there is an opportunity to sell additional products or services to the customer. The contact information for his or her sales representative could be pulled as well. Figure 3.4 shows how this information is combined to create a customized email for the customer. If the email system had a Web interface, then similar results could be achieved (albeit more slowly) by creating a mashup to regularly poll the Web view of the account's inbox.

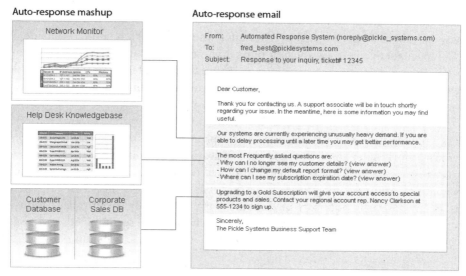

Figure 3.4 *Creating a mashup-powered email message*

Publication and Promotion

Only a few short years ago, it was difficult for ordinary people to share their thoughts and opinions with a large audience. Traditional media and publishing channels provided space for only a limited amount of content. Their focus on mass-market appeal and production values meant it was generally beyond the power of the individual to produce material of high enough quality to attract the attention of the media's gatekeepers. The explosion of the Web changed all that by democratizing the entire publishing process. An explosion of personal Web sites, blogs, and online videos provided a global soapbox for any individual who wished to be heard. But with more than 70 million blogs now in existence and more than 40 new blogs being created each minute,[10] their authors have become their own worst enemy. The challenge today is not getting the message out, it's getting it *noticed*.

Consumer mashups are currently in a state similar to where blogging was in its infancy. For example, the online directory ProgrammableWeb indexes slightly more than 3,500 mashups, with the list growing at the comparatively slow rate of about 3 per day.[11] In theory, you could examine each of these mashups in your spare time over the course of a few weeks—but thankfully the site is designed to support searching as well as browsing. Enterprise mashups are the even rarer animal. Although it's not unheard of for some firms to have created thousands of internal mashups, this behavior is the exception rather than the rule. Most companies are just beginning to recognize the value of this new paradigm as mashups slowly manifest themselves from sources outside of IT. The challenge is to establish a publishing infrastructure so that anyone can easily find and use these new solutions before they proliferate to unmanageable levels. Failure to put controls in place now could result in a mashup cacophony that parallels the current state of the blogosphere.

Why not just "let a thousand flowers bloom"? There are several reasons. First, having a centralized mashup "hub" promotes the technology by demonstrating working examples. These success stories then encourage would-be creators to explore how mashups can be applied to other problems they encounter. Second, creating an inventory of internal mashups avoids the situation where users unnecessarily duplicate one another's efforts. Finally, a centralized repository provides a source of raw materials that may be recombined and used beyond the vision of their creators to create *new* mashups. Mashup publication

---

10. http://www.sifry.com/alerts/archives/000493.html

11. http://www.programmableweb.com/mashups

isn't important when implementing a pattern, but it will help you leverage the economies of collaboration across your organization.

Some mashup products include a built-in publishing component. These range in scope from simple online directories to slick registries that allow mashups to be tagged and rated. Some type of search capability, version control, and documentation tools are highly recommended. Just because a mashup creator isn't necessarily a trained software developer doesn't mean that decades of "best practices" developed in this field should be thrown out the window.

If you are trying to foster a corporate culture of "self-service"—where non-developers are empowered to solve their own problems—you shouldn't underestimate the importance of this core feature. Most IT departments are organized so that a set of IT personnel serve a corresponding set of business users. Mashups democratize the process. Anyone can build a product that can be used by anyone else. The usefulness of something created by a small group of developers doesn't stop with their "assigned" business clients anymore: It could be mashed up and mixed in with the work other teams are doing. End users can share their mashups between themselves and across departments without IT ever having been involved. Of course, this requires a level of awareness that only a community platform for mashup promotion can provide. You might consider supplementing a central repository with other methods for marketing mashups to your users. For instance, once you have metrics for highly rated or frequently used mashups, you could publicly recognize or reward their authors. Highlighting mashup success stories can prompt additional users to explore building their own solutions.

Assembly Canvas

The *assembly canvas* is closely related to the data visualization and clipping core activities. With regard to mashup creation, a canvas is the least crucial of the features, yet is nonetheless an important component of how mashups are leveraged by your organization.

Consider the following example. A basic mashup is created to plot an employee's address given the person's name. This process could entail several steps but yields a single output—a map. Another simple mashup finds a person's name based on his or her cell phone number. A third determines the cheapest source of gas near a given address. Each one of these mashups could exist as an individual widget and provide a useful service in and of itself. But what if they were somehow linked together? Entering a cell number could drive the other mashups to display location along with nearby gas stations. At first this just seems like a mashup of other mashups, right? It certainly could be built that way—but there's an alternative approach.

The new version starts with a toolset that allows you to add metadata to a mashup's input and output. This mashup tags particular data so that it can be associated with other mashups that require or produce similar information. Next, the mashups are placed on a single screen (the canvas) using some basic design tools. Within this common environment, there is a layer of unseen functionality that supports intercommunication among mashups. The artifacts on the canvas recognize the metadata they have in common and "wire" themselves together as if a user had mashed them together manually. Now, when an individual mashup is triggered, the results will have a cascade effect and automatically update the other items on the canvas. Returning to our example, when a cell number is provided, the map and list of gas stations are automatically updated. Entering an employee's name could automatically display that person's cell number and nearby service stations. Clearly, the combinatorial effect provided by a canvas surpasses the effectiveness of combining mashups manually.

Canvases are not restricted to mashups that produce visual output. It is equally appropriate to mix and match data-centric mashups using this approach. Continuing with our example, a fourth mashup could be included that automatically sends an SMS message back to the employee containing local weather information. An RSS feed might be concurrently updated so the firm can track this mashup's use. Support for basic data entry features is another desired feature of a canvas. It should be possible to create simple input fields that will, in turn, drive the execution of mashups. This is a necessity when the canvas is populated with nonvisual services.

Three important issues must be addressed when considering the use of an assembly canvas. The first issue concerns adding mashups to the canvas palette. Ideally, this catalog will be a derivation of the central directory described in the previous section. However, publishing mashups is an easier task than preparing them to automatically connect with other components. You should understand the technical skills that your users must have to perform this feat and proceed accordingly.

The second issue concerns usability. A mashup such as the map in our example may produce output that commands a large portion of the canvas. Users might want to include more content than would fit on a single page. How is this scenario handled by a particular tool? Can the canvas communicate presentation details to its mashups? For example, if a map is resized on the canvas, can the underlying mashup be instructed to generate a less-detailed rendering or perhaps automatically add zoom-in and zoom-out controls?

The third issue relates to the fact that many firms have invested significant resources to ensure their applications adhere to a common presentation format. When IT personnel were solely responsible for creating applications, these style guidelines stood a good chance of being followed. Does the assembly canvas provide support for corporate branding or interface standards? If not, a firm may produce technically useful solutions that are hampered by poor design principles. Creating developers from end users is one of the remarkable achievements of mashup technology, but most of these individuals will lack the skills to address the overall user experience. Furthermore, the lack of a polished interface can lead to increased support costs and even put a firm's reputation at risk. If clients are exposed to amateurish products, they may develop doubts about an organization's overall capabilities. This can happen even if customers aren't interacting with the mashups directly. They might glance over an employee's shoulder and see the tools they're using. Clunky or awkward products—regardless of their effectiveness—could lead to a negative impression.

The assembly canvas is a powerful metaphor that realizes many of the promises of componentized application assembly. Users who are intimidated by the prospect of creating individual mashups may find it easier to combine existing products from the canvas palette. IT can be engaged to populate this resource with mashups, feeds, Web Services, and whatever other assets a particular toolset supports. As with any tool, make sure you understand the potential limitations as well as the advantages when you pursue a solution.

Summary

The responsibilities of IT may change significantly depending on which core functions an organization requires and whether the firm is committed to supporting business-wide mashup creation. The traditional job of managing the delivery of specific technology solutions to the business usually falls to an organization's chief technology officer (CTO) or chief information officer (CIO). The changes brought about by Enterprise 2.0 can shift their focus at a fundamental level. Rather than concentrate on managing specific business-aligned products, the CTO/CIO may choose to provide a suite of clean data sources and an open environment for mashing them together. This approach shifts IT away from project management and toward the role of a service provider. SOA and SaaS initiatives may coalesce nicely with this approach.

Ultimately, all mashups builders—be they technical or not—will need some familiarity with the information provided in this chapter. As part of establishing an environment for mashup creation, an IT department should understand which types of solutions its end users are likely to create. This knowledge instructs IT regarding the core activities that need to be supported. On the flip side, newly self-empowered business associates need to articulate the basic features they require so that they will receive a proper set of tools.

Chapter 4

Harvest Patterns

> As a general rule the most successful man in life is the man who has the best information.
> —Benjamin Disraeli (1804–1881)

Introduction

All too often the data required to solve thorny problems or unlock new business opportunities is trapped inside a proprietary system. The Harvest patterns describe methods for extracting information from resources previously viewed as closed. The basic premise of these patterns is a simple yet powerful one: *Mine existing assets for unique data.*

Outside the enterprise, user-created mashups typically do not utilize any Harvest patterns. Instead, they rely on data and functionality that is made publicly available via well-defined interfaces. Even with only a relatively small number of Web sites offering public APIs, thousands of unique applications have emerged.[1] As more sites begin to open their resources in the spirit of Web 2.0, it seems unavoidable that new mashups will continue to materialize.

Within the enterprise, the potential value of mashups is just as great, but the obstacles to their adoption may be even higher. IT departments and vendors design systems to solve specific business problems—not to be extensible. Even within the corridors of IT, existing assets frequently aren't reused. The technology workforce contains such a variety of skills and disciplines that the proverbial wheel is frequently reinvented using different tools.

New development, enhancements, and bug fixes are constrained to follow a formal approval process. But while this approach has yielded many useful solutions, it has done little to empower the business. As we saw when we examined

---

1. ProgrammableWeb tracks an average of more than three new mashups per day. The majority leverage the published APIs of only ten Web sites (see Figure 1.4 in Chapter 1).

the "Long Tail" in Chapter 1, only the changes demanded by the majority of users are likely to be tackled. That leaves a large minority of requirements unaddressed. End users aren't permitted to create tactical solutions or make changes themselves.

Certainly, it's possible to require IT build systems with open, well-documented interfaces. Firms implementing a SOA strategy may already have such requirements in place. Of course, this doesn't help extract data from vendor systems or resources on the Internet. The vast majority of applications used by the average businessperson remain closed.

The Harvest patterns are perhaps the most empowering ones, because they represent the first cracks in a dam holding back an ocean of useful data. The information they provide can turn the trickle of available resources into a flood. Whether employed by IT or end users, fresh sources of data encourage us to develop new ways to think about old or abandoned problems. They can also spark ideas for creating new tools to benefit the business.

Harvesting is used to retrieve data from both structured and unstructured sources. Structured sources may consist of databases, RSS feeds, XML, and tabular data streams. Functionality for extracting data from these resources already exists, but knowledge of a particular product or programming language is typically a prerequisite. The Harvest patterns circumvent this requirement by superimposing a consistent method for access on top of the underlying implementation.

Unstructured sources can be Web sites, binary files (e.g., Excel or PDF), or free-form text. The key to turning the Web into a first-class source of information is to abandon preconceived notions about how data needs to be organized. It's easy to view online reports and tabular data as good candidates for harvesting because their information is already arranged according to a formal structure. But recall from our examination of Web harvesting in Chapter 1 that underneath the presentation layer, almost all data conform to some type of rational definition. Even plain text documents can be analyzed to uncover useful patterns in their content. Skeptical? Every time you enter a few words on Google and find what you're looking for, you've proven that fact. Implementing Harvest patterns on unstructured material is the first step in enabling objective analysis of previously vague information.

Data extraction and data entry are core functions of all the Harvest patterns. Together, the two provide a mechanism to navigate to important information and then retrieve it. Surveillance functionality is used when the goal is to monitor a change in condition, rather than obtain specific figures.

Two of the Harvest patterns are of principal importance:

- API Enabler is used to create REST or Web Service interfaces that tap into previously closed resources. Some of these interfaces can then be used to power implementations of the Alerter, Leading Indicator, and Time Series patterns.

- Infinite Monkeys may rely on API Enabler implementations to extract still larger quantities of data (e.g., blogs, wikis, customer surveys, and press releases), which can then be used in conjunction with the Reputation Management, Competitive Analysis, and Reality Mining patterns covered in this chapter.

API Enabler and Infinite Monkeys will frequently be chained together or execute in parallel as part of a larger mashup implementation

In addition to retrieving facts and figures, it's possible to harvest the outcome of certain requests or interactions. For example:

- An unsuccessful search for a product with particular specifications may indicate a market opportunity.

- Periodically checking for traffic delays in the vicinity of client visits may allow you to preemptively reschedule meetings.

- The ability to regularly reserve meeting rooms on short notice may indicate there is an oversupply of office space.

Alerter

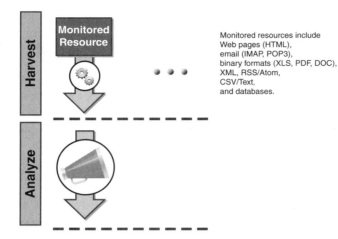

Monitored resources include
Web pages (HTML),
email (IMAP, POP3),
binary formats (XLS, PDF, DOC),
XML, RSS/Atom,
CSV/Text,
and databases.

Core Activities: Data extraction, surveillance

Problem

Business is a moving target. Prices fluctuate, dates slip, new products are released, and employees come and go. Management cannot afford to make decisions based on stale information, so keeping up with all of these changes is critical. Unfortunately the range of data that could potentially be monitored is typically enormous. Given the scale of the problem, firms must limit the areas where they focus their attention. It's the Long Tail in yet another circumstance: The 20% of items most subject to change will receive the most scrutiny. The remaining 80% of material—which might not change as often, yet will still be important when it does—will be neglected.

Solution

Mashups do not need to regularly interact with an end user to add value. Intelligent agents can be scheduled to automatically monitor conditions and announce sudden shifts instantly via email, SMS, or other channels. These "virtual observers" are created by API-enabling the desired resources and creating a process to examine the content periodically for any changes. Alerters can be implemented across thousands of resources to address the 20/80 problem of the Long Tail without requiring a dramatic increase in human capital.

An Alerter usually tracks only two data points: a current reading and the most recent historical reading (which may be absent, indicating the lack of any previous condition or state). Deviation in these two values outside a predefined setting will set off the alert. The Alerter can be chained with many of the other patterns to add a monitoring and notification service. For example, changes in the contents of a particular resource can trigger the execution of other mashups.

Related Patterns: API Enabler, Time Series

Fragility

The Alerter Pattern has the lowest fragility score of any pattern in the text. Should the monitored resource change significantly enough to induce failure, this occurrence is essentially an alert in itself. "Failure" is not the ideal notification approach, however: Remediation will still be necessary. Even so, the fact that some change has occurred will not go unnoticed.

The Alerter pattern can be used in conjunction with many of the other patterns as an "advance warning" detector for remediation. Knowing a resource that participates in a mashup has changed may be preferable to finding out later when the mashup is executed and fails.

Care must be taken with Alerter implementations not to affect the stability or availability of the systems being monitored. An Alerter instance is usually implemented to perform regularly scheduled data queries against the monitored resource, a technique also known as "polling." Unfortunately polling a resource at frequent intervals may overwhelm its ability to respond to normal usage requests. When this technique is used maliciously, it is known as a denial of service (DoS) attack. DoS attacks can encumber a computer or network. Depending on the nature of your enterprise, they can effectively immobilize your organization. If you are the publisher of a resource and believe you are (or may be) an intentional or accidental target of a DoS attack, you can find tips for prevention and response at the Computer Emergency Response Team (CERT) Web site: http://www.cert.org/tech_tips/denial_of_service.html.

Example: *Stay Informed about New Software Releases*

No matter the business in which a firm specializes, it most likely depends heavily on different software applications. Although we would all wish otherwise, software inevitably contains bugs. The severity of these annoyances can manifest themselves along a continuum ranging from minor inconveniences to substantial problems. It's to a company's advantage to stay up-to-date regarding any new releases, patches, or bug fixes that a software vendor releases. Unfortunately the amount of products in use at a firm can number in the thousands—simply too many for the staff to regularly check for updates. As we have observed, IT personnel will most likely monitor only the applications used by the largest number of employees.

Even if a product works correctly today, failure to move to a more current release can result in problems as other parts of a firm's IT infrastructure are upgraded. For example, an older application that runs perfectly under a particular operating system or virtual machine may fail when that computer is upgraded to a newer version. Figure 4.1 shows a sample Alerter implementation that monitors three separate open-source Web sites.

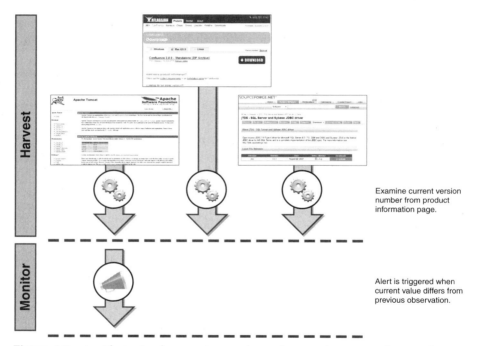

Examine current version number from product information page.

Alert is triggered when current value differs from previous observation.

Figure 4.1 *An Alerter implementation can be used to monitor new software releases.*

Example: *Receive Notification of Changes in Governance or Management*

Changes in a governing board can cause a sea change in how that body reacts or makes decisions. One highly visible example is the United States Supreme Court. An examination of historical judgments (along with the party affiliation of the nominating President) can provide clear insight into whether a particular judge will sympathize with Republican or Democratic views on an issue. When the balance shifts between liberal and conservative on the Court, the lives of countless individuals may be affected. Because new appointments to the Supreme Court occur very rarely and receive a great deal of press coverage, they are not good candidates for automated monitoring.

Changes to smaller entities such as federal subcommittees, local planning and zoning boards, and unions can also have a significant impact on a firm's business development plans:

- New members of an alumni board or board of trustees may open up new business opportunities.

- Sudden departures of board members may indicate internal troubles at an organization.

- A call for board nominations is an opportunity to present or support a preferred candidate.

It is to a firm's advantage to keep abreast of any organizational change in the agencies that govern it, the corporations with which it does business, and the institutions in which it invests. Individual contacts and clients who establish new affiliations or lose existing ones may merit additional attention.

Alerter implementations can leverage existing corporate supplier and customer directories or other internal databases to monitor persons and firms of interest. Organizations typically maintain "About Us," "Our Team," or "Management" pages on their Web sites; these pages are excellent candidates for periodic scrutiny. Changes to "Investor Relations" or "Corporate Partners" data may be a sign of new allegiances or sources of funding that signal new growth.

Example: *Monitor Corporate Earnings Calendars*

A public company is obligated to report its earnings once per fiscal quarter. For large corporations, this data can serve as a bellwether for an entire industry. Besides stating earnings for the prior period, this kind of report offers a chance to gauge the success or failure of the firm's corporate strategy and serves as an indicator of its overall economic health. It may contain information on new initiatives that will affect future performance.

The exact date on which this information will be released is typically published on a company's Web site, but it can be legally rescheduled without notice. Traders, investors, and analysts are acutely aware that any changes to a previously provided date—especially a postponement—may be advanced warning of bad news. Those who are aware of the change the soonest will have the most time to consider adjusting their positions or strategies in advance of the final earnings announcement. A suite of calendar-monitors based on the Alerter pattern can meet this need. In addition to regularly checking for changed reporting dates and sending alerts, these agents can fire off mashups to check the historical performance of the stock or to investigate the health of the industry as a whole.

Example: *Use Price Fluctuations to Locate Buying Opportunities*

Alerts can signal both opportunities and risks. For a business that maintains a regular stock of inventory or supplies, detecting changes in the prices of particular items can influence purchasing decisions. A sudden increase from a regular provider might be a reason to delay pending orders or begin searching for alternate suppliers. A decrease may indicate it's a good time to "stock up." Any change may signal an underlying shift in the market that belies the short-term price fluctuations. Changes to catalog pricing are an example of when an Alerter implementation may trigger another pattern instance (e.g., Competitive Advantage). Monitoring nonmaterial goods is also valuable. A favorable shift in advertising rates (especially combined with a price drop for materials) can be a chance to try a new marketing campaign.

Example: *Recognize Product Recalls Promptly and Engage Customers*

A firm ignores consumer alerts or recall notices at its peril. The U.S. Consumer Product Safety Commission is charged with protecting the public from unreasonable risks of serious injury or death from more than 15,000 types of consumer products.[2] Data can be monitored by manufacturer, product, and hazard. Tying this resource to an internal sales database can help a reseller quickly notify its customers. This type of company/customer interaction—known as a "touch"—is crucial to creating and maintaining loyalty.

---

2. A searchable index CPSC recalls is available at http://www.cpsc.gov/cpscpub/prerel/prerel.html

Every time a customer comes in direct contact with a company, a customer touch is created. This event represents an opportunity for a company to enhance or erode its relationship with that customer. A customer touch is an opportunity to make a good impression and to build upon the relationship. You can have the best products available, but if you fail to supplement them with a positive service experience, few people will notice the difference between you and your competition. Service success is a matter of setting yourself apart from other sources of products through unexpected excellence. [3]

Although a safety recall might seem to be an unfavorable circumstance for interaction, handling it swiftly and professionally can increase customers' trust in your firm. In the world outside Enterprise 2.0, today's consumer has more choices than ever before. A commitment to inform your clients of events that affect them is an essential skill for maintaining competitive advantage.

---

3. Timm, Paul R. *Customer Service: Career Success Through Customer Satisfaction.* Prentice Hall 2007

API Enabler

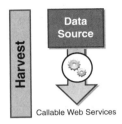

Data sources referred to in the diagram include Web pages (HTML), email (IMAP, POP3), binary formats (XLS, PDF, DOC), XML, RSS/Atom, and CSV/Text. These sources do not natively support a Web Services interface.

Core Activities: Data entry, data extraction, transformation

Problem

By definition, mashups combine data from multiple sources. If these resources natively expose an application programming interface (API), then leveraging their information is a matter of basic software development. However, it is often the case that the most valuable content is locked away in closed or proprietary formats. While it's possible to open a spreadsheet and copy and paste data, this procedure does not facilitate automation. RSS feeds can be examined via a feed reader, but the process is highly labor-intensive. The only interaction you may have with a vendor product is via a Web interface. Perhaps you want to regularly obtain data on your competitors. The information may be published on the Web, but the only way to collect it is by navigating a series of Web pages. In short, the usefulness of non-API-enabled resources is constrained to what can be manually accomplished by a human operator.

Solution

There are three steps in the API-enabling process: navigation (data entry), harvesting (data extraction), and transformation.

1. *Navigation.* The first step in extracting data involves locating it. If the information is located on a Web page, then the mashup will have to impersonate a person using a browser. All of the clicks, inputs, searches, and form submissions normally performed by a human are instead executed by

the system. This information can be hard-wired into the mashup (see the Open Kimono anti-pattern in Chapter 9 for a discussion of the risks inherent in this approach) or passed as parameters to the API for maximum flexibility and security. Sites such as Google follow a similar—albeit far less robust—approach when they crawl the Web to add pages to their searchable index.

2. *Harvesting.* Once the information has been located, the next step is to retrieve it. In the enterprise mashup tool-space, products generally support harvesting information from a variety of data sources. An explanation of the various techniques is provided in Table 4.1.

Table 4.1 *APIs Can Be Created Against Various Resources*

When the Data Source Is...	It Can Be API-Enabled by...
Web page	Web harvesting (see Chapter 1 for more information). This technique involves navigating the structure of the underlying HTML to supply and remove information.
RSS/Atom feed	Parsing the underlying text of the feed. Although feeds do not natively expose an API, because they are constructed of well-formed XML it is a straightforward process for a tool to create an interface to their content.
Email (IMAP/POP3)	Constructing a WS-proxy layer that calls the underlying protocol. IMAP and POP3 *do* expose an API but not one that is based on Web Services.
Proprietary binary format	Using one of several approaches. A tool may include a native ability to read these formats, or it need only be able to convert them to HTML so that they can be parsed by Web harvesting. (See the section titled "Mashing Up Binary Types" in Chapter 10 for further information.)
XML, CSV, plain text, or other open formats	Parsing the text. The extent to which the information can be service enabled depends on the structure of the format. XML is the most structured, CSV the least. Plain text may have no discernable structure but it can still be valuable. A block of text returned in its entirety can be handed off to another product that searches for particular word occurrences (see the Reputation Management pattern later in this chapter).

3. *Transformation.* The final step in the API-enabling process involves converting the data to a common format for subsequent analysis or processing. When multiple API-enabled data sources are combined to supply information a pattern, some transformation is almost inevitable. Cultural, conventional, and geographic traditions inevitably result in multiple methods for formatting the same information. A few common examples are illustrated in Table 4.2.

Table 4.2   *Common Data Transformations in Mashups*

Pre-transformation	A Possible Post-transformation Result
12/1/2009, Aug 31, 2008, 13/12/04	12/01/2009, 08/31/2008, 12/13/2004
12%, .065, 55 percent	.12, .065, .55
10 USD, $10.00, 30 EUR	10.00, 10.00, 41.42

For more details about the steps that power the API Enabler pattern, see the sections on data extraction, data entry, and support for open standards in Chapter 3.

API Enabler can be used in a near-endless variety of situations to impose an interface on structured or ad hoc data. Several examples follow the "Fragility" section for this pattern, and numerous other patterns in this text leverage API Enabler as part of their structure. The key to leveraging this pattern starts with identifying one or more possible resources that contain useful information and determining the desired inputs and outputs.

Related Patterns: Infinite Monkeys, Feed Factory

The flexible nature of the API Enabler pattern means that it is can be used to construct data sources for supplying almost all of the other patterns. This makes API Enabler one of the most important patterns we will examine.

Fragility

It is particularly difficult to assign a fragility rating to this pattern because it interacts with a variety of data sources, each having their own relative vulnerabilities.

Changes to a Web site's look-and-feel may break an API Enabler. Nevertheless, as was observed in Chapter 1, Web harvesting can handle drastic redesigns of a page. As long as information has not been removed or relocated, it can be relatively easy to fix a Web harvesting issue. RSS/Atom feeds follow a defined XML format and are extremely stable. Plain XML is also very stable, albeit subject to ad hoc redesign and reorganization. Email protocols are necessarily static to ensure the successful delivery of messages. Closed binary formats typically change only during a major product upgrade (e.g., Microsoft Excel 2003 to Microsoft Excel 2007). However fixing problems with binary formats is typically outside the user's control and must be handled by the toolset provider.

Example: *Convert Product Reviews into Sales Opportunities*

AutoMammoth is a manufacturer and retailer of high-performance automotive parts. Renowned for its quality and craftsmanship, the company's products are often reviewed in industry-related blogs. But AutoMammoth doesn't effectively leverage this press coverage to drive sales. The company would like to take its existing Web store and expose it as an API that external sites can use to place a "Buy it now" link alongside a product review. In exchange for this service, AutoMammoth will offer a commission on any sales to the referring site.

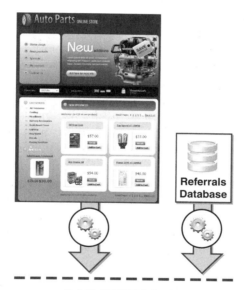

Callable REST Web Services

Figure 4.2 *The AutoMammoth Web store is API-enabled by using the data extraction and data entry core functions.*

The AutoMammoth online store is harvested to create an API (as shown in Figure 4.2) for performing the following tasks:

- Adding an item (supplied as an input parameter) to a shopping cart

- Identifying the site the request originated from (determined by examining the browser's HTTP request)

- Automatically forwarding the customer to the checkout page.

- Upon successful completion of a transaction, adding a commission to the referrer's account

The API is exposed as a REST-based Web Service.[4] Because blogs are created as simple HTML, this approach allows authors to easily link to the new functionality from their postings.

Example: *Leverage External Resources to Provide Better Customer Support*

As a boutique U.S.-based travel agency, Zoom Travel specializes in planning exciting journeys to exotic and remote locations. Because its travel packages are so unique, the company receives a lot of customer inquiries about the safety of the location, the weather, and any immunizations that might be required for a particular trip. The staff is happy to provide this information, but they must manually pull together multiple resources to obtain it. They have decided to automate the process and create a self-serve Web page for their clients.

Figure 4.3 shows chaining of one API to supply data to another. Because the Zoom Travel booking site is built on an off-the-shelf product, the first step is to API-enable it to allow for easy extraction of the destination countries within a selected adventure package. To determine if there is political unrest in the area, the country is passed to an API created against the U.S. Department of State's travel advisory site[5]; this check may result in a recommendation for trip insurance. The country name is also supplied to an internal database that identifies the surrounding region. The region code is passed to an API created on the Centers for Disease Control and Prevention's "Traveler's Health" page[6] to determine which vaccinations are suggested. One final external site is consulted to obtain a weather forecast for the area.[7] The entire collection of APIs is exposed as a single REST Web Service that is invoked by clicking a new "Current Conditions" link next to each travel package.

Once clients have booked a trip, this functionality can be combined with the Feed Factory pattern to ensure that customers receive up-to-date RSS notifications of any changes in their vacation plans. This mashup can be further

---

4. A REST (Representation State Transfer) service can be invoked using basic HTML.

5. http://travel.state.gov/

6. http://wwwn.cdc.gov/travel/

7. http://www.worldweather.org/

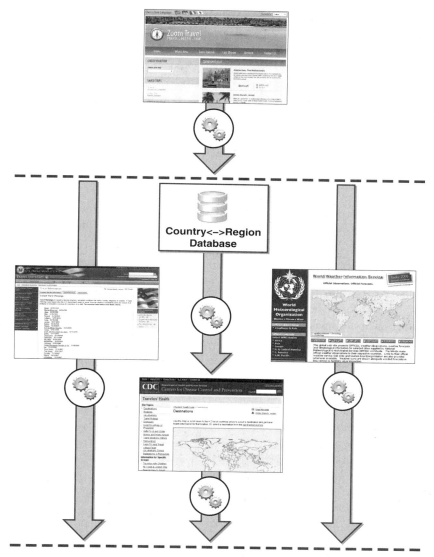

Figure 4.3 *Zoom Travel uses the API Enabler pattern to enhance its Web site's functionality.*

extended to harvest local airport and train station sites for information regarding possible delays.

Example: *Manage Risk*

Risk management is a key component of many business activities. Risk comes in many forms—for example, financial risk, political risk, location risk, environmental risk, and operational risk.

The U.S. Environmental Protection Agency's (EPA's) Toxics Release Inventory (TRI) program publishes information on more than 650 chemicals and chemical categories whose disposal or release is managed by over 23,000 industrial and federal facilities. In a single year, it is not uncommon for billions of pounds of chemicals to be disposed of by factories both on and off site. The EPA explains the rationale for the TRI program this way:

> Armed with TRI data, communities have more power to hold companies accountable and make informed decisions about how toxic chemicals are to be managed. The data often spurs companies to focus on their chemical management practices since they are being measured and made public. In addition, the data serves as a rough indicator of environmental progress over time.[8]

The EPA program is designed to work in the public interest but can also serve the interests of firms seeking to monitor the environmental impact (and resulting consumer backlash) of their competitors. Trends in the mishandling of particular materials can also give a firm early warning to investigate its own waste management process. The information is accessible through both an online search form and published PDF-based reports. API-enabling these resources (as shown in Figure 4.4) can then make it easy to construct surveillance applications (Reputation Management), early warning systems (Alerter), and competitor monitoring applications (Competitive Analysis).

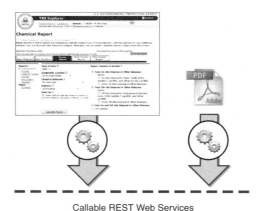

Callable REST Web Services

Figure 4.4   *Constructing a chemical warning system using EPA data*

---

8. http://www.epa.gov/trITriprogram/whatis.htm

Competitive Analysis

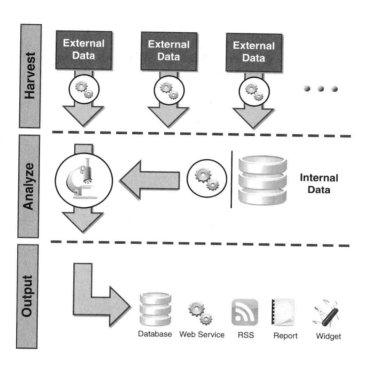

Core Activities: Data visualization, surveillance

Problem

You've probably noticed how all the gas stations on the same street advertise an identical price. Obviously, the operators just have to look out the window to see what their competitors are charging. They then adjust their prices so that no station has a definitive advantage over another. Under this system, where a customer chooses to fill up becomes a combination of other issues such as brand loyalty, location, and service. In today's global marketplace, it's obviously impossible to look down the block to see what your rivals are charging. Your competition can be halfway around the world! On top of that, your firm may not be selling a single commodity such as gasoline: You might stock thousands of items, as may your competition. How can you compare the prices on them all?

Other factors besides cost often influence a customer's decision to patronize a rival: How much advertising is the competitor doing, and where? Are its products more environmentally friendly? Can the rival deliver its items faster? Management needs answers to these questions to develop business strategies as well as anticipate the tactics of their opponents.

Solution

Competitive analysis (CA) may be defined as "the process by which organizations gather actionable information about competitors and the competitive environment and, ideally, apply it to their planning processes and decision-making in order to improve their enterprise's performance."[9] Skillful business and competitive analysis (BCA) is critically important in determining how an enterprise can compete and deliver value to its stakeholders.[10]

The practice is not illegal or unethical, as it relies on the examination of *public* material regarding competitors, their marketplace, and their operating environment. For example, as part of its CA process, a petroleum company may regularly monitor seismic activity in the vicinity of its competitors' pipelines to gain advance knowledge of possible service interruptions. A textile manufacturer may keep an eye on the political climate in countries where other firms outsource production. Planning a strategic CA strategy is beyond the scope of this text, but there are many resources available on the subject. The key to performing useful CA is to determine which information is available and to systematically go about acquiring it. Traditional approaches to this task have not been successful:

> What surprises us about competitive and strategic analysis is the relatively limited number of tools and techniques used by most practitioners and how little genuine insight emanates from them![11]

Mashups can close this gap. The first step in crafting an automated solution is to identify those aspects of your competition that you wish to profile—for example, its financial information, product data (e.g., price, energy efficiency, weight, storage capacity), marketing strategy, delivery times, or intellectual property (e.g., monitoring for patent filings). It's doubtful that your rivals will hand over any of this data willingly, so the next step is to identify alternative sources for this material.

For product data, you can scan the catalogs of online retailers. The U.S. Patent and Trademark Office[12] and the European Patent Office[13] are the de facto sources

---

9. Fleisher, Craig S., and Babette E. Bensoussan. *Business and Competitive Analysis: Effective Application of New and Classic Methods.* FT Press, 2007.

10. Fleisher and Bensoussan, *Business and Competitive Analysis.*

11. Fleisher and Bensoussan, *Business and Competitive Analysis.*

12. http://www.uspto.gov/

13. http://www.epo.org/

for patent applications. Advertisements blanket the Internet so your biggest challenge will be determining where *not* to look. In short, any Web site where your industry peers file public disclosures or sell and promote their merchandise is fair game.

Once you've decided which data is important, the next step is to create an interface to extract it programmatically (see the discussion of the API Enabler pattern earlier in this chapter). At this point you'll have a steady supply of raw data on your competitors, so your next task is to turn these observations into meaningful statistics. At this step in the pattern you'll probably want to pull in data about your own products, budgets, and strategies to compare it to the corresponding data of your competitors. You may need to API-enable some of your internal resources to accomplish this goal. The exact analysis required will vary depending on the key success factors for your industry. The resulting examination of this data can be entered into a database to test alternative business scenarios, generate strategic reports, or monitor market trends.

Related Patterns: API Enabler, Sentiment Analysis, Leading Indicator, Time Series

Fragility

The fragility of a CA solution is low because the sites that expose relevant data are typically very stable. For example:

- Many documents on firms are obtainable via online access to government and regulatory filings (including the U.S. Patent and Trademark Office, U.S. Securities and Exchange Commission,[14] and public court documents). These forms are standardized and not subject to frequent or drastic changes.

- Sites that monitor disease, weather, and political climate are typically run by government agencies. Empirical observation has shown that most government-operated Web sites rarely modify their user interfaces.

- A competitor's online catalog can be a useful means of monitoring price, variety, and stock levels. Catalogs are generally displayed in some form of paginated grid. As discussed in Chapter 1, Web harvesting is resilient enough to handle most redesigns a firm may make.

---

14. http://www.sec.gov/edgar.shtml

Example: *Competitive Price Analysis*

Paperclips is an office supply company that sells pens, paper, ink, and (of course) paperclips. It wants make sure that it is remaining price-competitive in its industry. Paperclips has identified two competitors with a significant online presence: Thumbtacks and WorkplaceWorld. Although Paperclips' managers are confident that they can meet anyone's price, the only way they find out when someone is charging less is by checking a random selection of products from the opposition's Web site. Unfortunately this time-consuming process addresses only a fraction of the thousands of products that its competitors sell.

To keep a closer eye on its competitors, Paperclips implements the mashup shown in Figure 4.5.

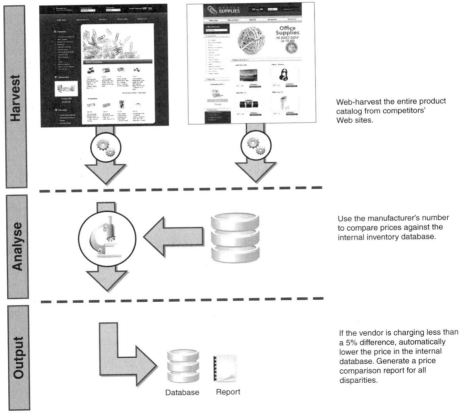

Web-harvest the entire product catalog from competitors' Web sites.

Use the manufacturer's number to compare prices against the internal inventory database.

If the vendor is charging less than a 5% difference, automatically lower the price in the internal database. Generate a price comparison report for all disparities.

Figure 4.5   *Paperclips' implementation of a Competitive Analysis mashup*

By monitoring the competition's catalogs and automatically adjusting prices, Paperclips is able to stay on top of its market. Further analysis of the Comparison report might lead to the discovery that WorkplaceWorld cyclically lowers the prices on certain items to increase its sales. Armed with this knowledge, Paperclips can lower its prices in anticipation of WorkplaceWorld's markdowns and put an advanced advertising campaign in place. This strategy would completely undermine WorkplaceWorld's own marketing strategy and cost the company numerous sales. The inventories of Paperclips, Thumbtacks, and WorkplaceWorld are basically identical, but having consistently lower prices can help Paperclips attract and keep more customers.

▼

Example: *Educate Potential Customers at the Point of Sale*

Willmark is a manufacturer of household appliances. Even though its products are well known for their high reliability and affordable prices, the company's sales have been down in the last four quarters. Company managers have conducted market surveys and learned that some buyers believe Willmark products are not the most energy efficient. Willmark wants to know if this perception is affecting its overall sales. If so, the company will have to redesign many of its models and phase out the current inventory—an expensive and time-consuming process. Willmark will also have to completely change its advertising strategy to announce the new products.

To determine the best course of action to address the lagging sales, Willmark creates APIs to mine the online catalogs of several big-box retailers, home improvement centers, and other resellers. These mashup agents not only extract the price of the item, but also determine the Energy Star rating (a measure of energy efficiency) and the quantity in stock (if applicable). Willmark compares the appliance data for its rivals to its own database of products to find similar items. Analysis of the data reveals that Willmark's appliances actually are *more* efficient than its rivals' equivalents, but that retailers have not been positioning various models correctly.

As a result of this analysis, the mashup output is used to power an online widget that is deployed to a point-of-purchase kiosk. The widget helps consumers compare the proper models across different brands, resulting in increased sales.

Example: *Track the Performance of an Advertising Campaign*

Trades4Less is an online brokerage that offers discount trading services to its customers. It has several competitors that it typically advertises against on the same handful of news and financial Web sites. Trades4Less has tried several different types of ads and tracked the performance of each in relation to how many new customers it receives. What the company has been unable to determine is how changes in a competitor's advertising strategy affect the performance of Trades4Less ads.

Trades4Less has decided to capture the size, position on the page, and underlying URL (so it can identify the advertiser) for all of the ads on the sites where it advertises. It will also record an image of the ad. The company knows from its own research that the ads are not billed on a "cost per view" basis but rather "cost per click," so this process will not cause competitors to be unfairly charged. On sites where the ads are text based, they will record that data for further examination. Trades4Less hopes that by studying this data it will be able to determine the most effective means of countering its rivals' ad campaigns.

Example: *Monitor How a Competitor's Actions Affect a Company's Sales*

A hotel chain in a highly competitive market regularly harvests data from the online reservation systems of its competitors. This step allows the company to monitor price changes and track which types of rooms (e.g., single, double, nonsmoking) sell out the quickest. When a rival rolls out a new perk such as free Internet access or a continental breakfast, the hotel chain can automatically track what effect this lure has on room availability.

Example: *Advance Notice of Competing Products or Competitive Strategies*

A Silicon Valley company is determined to maintain its status as an industry leader. Management isn't content with surveying competitors' products after they are on the market—they want to know what the competition is building *before* the item reaches store shelves. Regularly searching the data of the U.S. Patent and Trademark Office[15] and the European Patent Office[16] is a good

15. http://uspto.gov
16. http://ops.espacenet.com

start. In addition, methodically combing online job postings can unearth the technical and marketing skills firms are seeking to bring onboard. Combined with the frequency of recruitment postings, this information can provide valuable insight into a competitor's product or marketing strategy.

Infinite Monkeys

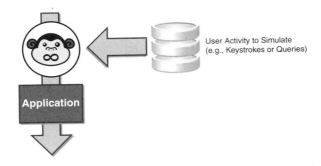

Core Activities: Data entry, data extraction

Problem

The Internet is rife with potentially useful data. The API Enabler pattern has demonstrated how this material can be accessed, but that still leaves the problem of how to determine which information to request. When the amount of available data increases to immense proportions, it may no longer be possible for a user to manage it effectively.

In other instances there may be series of dull, recurring tasks that yield value in only a small fraction of cases. Because these tasks are so mind-numbingly monotonous, however, no one bothers to perform them. The API Enabler demonstrates how to provide hooks into such a process, but not how to automate it.

Solution

It has been theorized somewhat humorously that given an infinite number of monkeys tapping away at typewriters, they will eventually produce the complete works of Shakespeare.[17] The premise is that a mundane task may eventually yield value if scaled to large proportions. Infinite Monkeys may also be used to automate a repetitive task that is too tedious and boring for human agents to complete.

The Infinite Monkeys pattern relies on instructions concerning user interests and actions. This information can be supplied via an internal database, a

---

17. Fortunately, this book contains diagrams, which I trust will take the monkeys more time to reproduce.

mashup, or both. The implementation uses this data to replicate simple tasks normally performed by a person. The emulated activity is then scalable to a level unachievable by even the largest collection of users.

This pattern can be an effective element of a data mining strategy. Data mining is the practice of mechanically searching large quantities of information with the goal of locating hidden relationships and trends. Structured content that a firm collects is valuable for mining purposes, but free-form text may be even more useful:

> Mining a wide spectrum of publicly available unstructured information sources over time can help the business spot important product and technology trends as they emerge. It can also help in gaining time to react to emerging external events before they become major business catastrophes.[18]

Unstructured content is particularly tiresome for a human operator to examine. Combining Infinite Monkeys with other techniques[19] in this problem space can yield significant business benefits.

Infinite Monkeys may also be applied to the task of business process automation (BPA). BPA is a technique for reducing costs and labor by delegating manual work to an automatic process. When a series of labor-intensive operations has been identified, it may be possible to service-enable the various steps with API Enabler and simulate the user's interactions with Infinite Monkeys.

Related Patterns: API Enabler

Fragility

This pattern is intended to address mundane tasks that by nature do not often change. As a consequence, the systems with which this mashup interacts are typically very stable.

Example: *Uncover New Sales Leads*

UniversalFinance (UF) is a corporation that specializes in financial management for educational institutions. The company's regional sales force regularly markets its services to colleges and universities across the country. Although those sales representatives are always on the lookout for new accounts, they can't

---

18. Spangler, Scott, and Jeffrey Kreulen. *Mining the Talk: Unlocking the Business Value in Unstructured Information.* July 2007.

19. Spangler and Kreulen, *Mining the Talk.*

keep in close contact with every school in their respective territories. Sometimes a rival firm may beat UF to the punch when new opportunities arise.

One thing experience has taught the sales team is that when a school initiates a fundraising campaign, it may indicate the institution will be kicking off a major new project such as construction of a building or stadium. Such a move may mean that some type of short-term financing will be required, which can be a great chance for UF to get new business. Unfortunately monitoring the Web pages for all of the schools in the country is a boring, time-consuming task that would distract UF sales representatives from managing the relationships the company already has.

To notify regional salespeople about possible new business prospects, UF uses the Infinite Monkeys pattern to guide the implementation of the mashup in Figure 4.6.

The mashup begins with the first instance of Infinite Monkeys (IM) being supplied with the territories that are of interest to the sales force. This information is contained in an internal corporate database. IM uses this information to search an API-enabled online directory of colleges and obtain the schools' Web site addresses. Another IM instance receives this list of Web pages and accesses a database of "campaign-related" keywords that the salespeople have supplied (e.g., "campaign," "contribution," "donation," "grant"). The Web pages are retrieved[20] and scanned for keyword hits. When potential new clients are located, the school location is matched to the appropriate salesperson via the API-enabled corporate directory. Regional reports are assembled and automatically emailed for further follow-up by UF staff.

Besides searching for campaign-related keywords, this mashup could scan public documents for recorded land purchases, which might indicate potential development projects. This example could also provide potential leads to corporations in the construction or insurance industries.

▼

Example: *Proactively Contact Customers and Maximize Profits*

A chain of automotive service centers collects a wide range of data on thousands of customers' vehicles. Manufacturer's make and model, service dates, mileage, and worked performed are stored in one system. Customer satisfaction surveys are recorded in another database. Price and availability of replacement

---

20. An instance of the Filter pattern could be used here to weed out smaller schools based on enrollment size or other criteria.

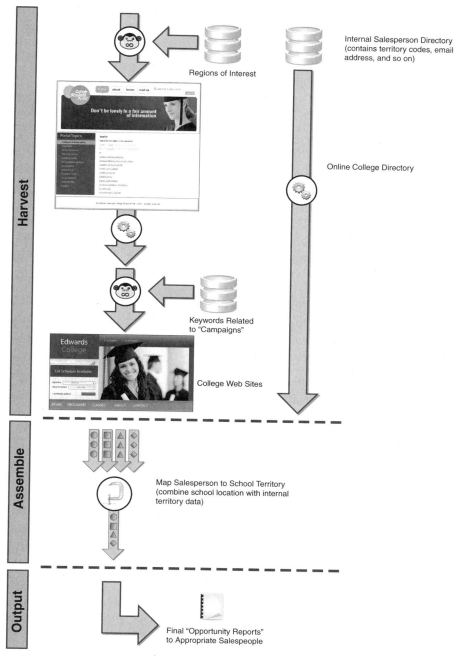

Figure 4.6 *An Infinite Monkeys implementation is used to uncover sales leads.*

parts are available from the suppliers' Web sites. Infinite Monkeys can be used to repeatedly scan this data in search of important research and opportunities:

- Does a particular type of repair (e.g., power train) generally receive a lower score on customer satisfaction? At all locations or at specific centers? If so, the firm may want to investigate its repair guidelines or employee qualifications.

- When the price drops on a particular item (e.g., brakes) for a given make/model, are customers within the recommended maintenance window for the part notified? The cost reduction can be passed along to the consumer to increase sales, or withheld to increase profits.

The National Highway Traffic Safety Administration (NHTSA) maintains an online database of recalls, customer complaints, and defect investigations.[21] Combining regular scans of this resource with existing data yields additional leads:

- NHTSA complaints plus price changes from a supplier may indicate a low-quality item is being "dumped." Analysis of satisfaction surveys can either refute or back up this contention. This effort may identify manufacturers or products to avoid in the future.

- Defect investigations into a particular part (e.g., tires) can be linked to vehicle models and maintenance frequency. This information can be used to encourage customers to replace the part before problems arise.

▼

Example: *More Thorough Fiscal Analysis*

The U.S. Securities and Exchange Commission's (SEC) EDGAR[22] database contains a searchable index of foreign and domestic filings for all companies doing business within the United States. Locating a specific set of filings is not a difficult task, but analyzing them for useful information can be. The footnotes that accompany a business's financials are often ignored, yet they can divulge useful information about the true state of the firm.

---

21. http://www.safercar.gov/
22. http://www.sec.gov/edgar.shtml

- There is no standard form for supplying information in the footnotes, so an implementation of Infinite Monkeys will rely on "words or phrases of interest" determined by a subject-matter expert. This may reveal valuable data:

- Details on the calculations used to compute the company's financial statements

- Disclosure of employee stock options

- Corrections of errors on previous reporting statements

- Changes in accounting methodologies from prior reports

Combined with other analysis methods, regularly scanning the details of filings can create a better understanding of an organization's true state. This technique can also be part of a larger strategy for identifying distressed debt or potential corporate misconduct.

▼
_____

Example: *Discover Hidden Corporate and Social Connections*

Knowing when a person sits on multiple boards (e.g., board of governors, trustees, directors, local government) can be valuable information for many purposes. From a sales and marketing perspective, it can highlight particularly useful contacts and serve as a path to establishing new relationships. Where corporate risk and governance are concerned, it can shed light on potential conflicts of interest or suggest how a scandal at one firm may spread to another. An individual who serves on several boards may be unable to give each one the attention it deserves. This may have been a factor in the collapse of Bear Stearns, for example. An investigation into that investment firm revealed that three members of its twelve-member board were busy serving on the boards of four other public companies. Two of these three individuals were in charge of Bear Stearns' risk committee.[23]

Board membership is a matter of public record, but it can be time-consuming to collect and collate. Most institutions publish this data right on their own Web sites. The Infinite Monkeys pattern can be applied to regularly visit these locations and collect the names of directors. This data can be assembled into a report or social network graph to highlight the "most connected" individuals and reveal previously obscure relationships.

_____

23. Nash, Jeff. "Bear's Board Was Busy Elsewhere." *Financial Week*, March 31, 2008.

Leading Indicator

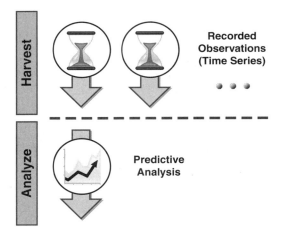

Core Activities: Data extraction, data entry, transformation

Problem

Time Series (TS) data are typically used for auditing purposes or to predict future values. For example:

- "Who was using the system when it crashed?"

- "The price of homes in the past five months has declined 18%; how much more will it drop in the next five months?"

While this is a valuable use of information, it is completely introspective. The unaddressed opportunity is to detect how different series affect one another as leading or coincident indicators.[24]

Changes in a leading indicator may foretell downstream impact in other areas. Some, like the measurement of new home sales or bankruptcy filings, have an obvious effect on many businesses. Well-known leading indicators do not offer any particular competitive advantage. Finding previously unknown relationships that predict business cycles and trends can be extremely useful.

---

24. A leading indicator changes before a related series. A coincident indicator varies in conjunction with another series.

The key to uncovering these hidden links begins with collecting TS data from multiple locations. Of course, with each additional source that is surveyed, the complexity of the data-gathering process increases.

Solution

The Leading Indicator (LI) pattern relies on the collection and examination of TS data from multiple sources to expose unapparent associations. When the TS pattern is implemented as a stand-alone solution, the value of its data is self-evident. It can prove useful as a forecast tool unto itself. In contrast, a leading indicator relies on TS sets that may exhibit little value until they are examined as part of a broader picture.

For example, knowledge of the week's upcoming television schedule might not seem useful for a chain of pet stores. But when matched against a set of keywords, a time series of "pet-themed" broadcasts can be assembled. Mashed up against a database of customer purchases, a leading indicator might emerge between dog (conformation) shows and increased sales. The retailer now has a mechanism for advance inventory and advertising planning.

Public shopping and travel sites are just two of the many treasure troves for discovering leading indicators. The key challenge is to stop thinking about these sites from a consumer's perspective and instead view them as databases to be mined via periodic data extraction.[25]

Related Patterns: Infinite Monkeys, Time Series

Fragility

The fragility of the LI pattern depends on the amount of TS collections and internal systems used in the mashup. Although no single component has a particularly high fragility, the fact that this pattern relies on a potentially large number of them explains why it merits a slightly higher rating.

▼———————————————————————————————

Example: *Advanced Knowledge of an Industry's Performance*

Suppose a firm tracks the performance of the airline industry. A number of well-documented public techniques for researching the major players and evaluating their fiscal health have been developed, most of which rely on backward

---

25. Make sure to obey these sites' terms of use, of course. Consult Chapter 9, Anti-patterns, for further discussion on this topic.

examination of public filings from the carriers themselves. What was net income for the quarter? What is the profit margin on seat sales? In traditional time series modeling, this information is directly used to predict future values. Because everyone has access to the same source material, the chance of gaining an advantage on competitors is small.

Now consider the value of building a mashup against popular online travel sites. Each day an automated agent could book multiple flights between New York and London and from Boston to San Francisco. The mashup would emulate the customer booking experience all the way up through seat selection, at which point it would record the number of seats available and the ticket price. Naturally the mashup wouldn't complete the process of paying for the trip.

This information can be used to extrapolate the performance of the sector in advance of quarterly reports. Are lots of seats are available even as ticket prices decline? That's probably not a sign of good earnings. Regularly filled seats at soaring prices might seem like good news until a time series of fuel prices hitting historical highs is added.

Example: *Spot the Underlying Causes of Trends in the Housing Market*

Are more homeowners losing their residences to foreclosure? The ripple effects on the economy can be devastating. Job losses and reduced consumer spending are two obvious outcomes that in turn affect almost every other industry. A variety of key economic indicators and national reports give some shape to a potential crisis, but by the time they are published it may be too late to take defensive action. Fortunately, TS and LI mashups can be used to provide early warning.

In the United States, public court filings are available from a variety of online sources. This data can be regularly culled for cases involving key phrases related to "mortgage" and "foreclosure." An increase in the number of matches might indicate potential trouble. Mash in the geographic location of the records and the forecast can be broken down by area. If you are interested in predicting the performance of local industries, then a regional housing crisis might be indicative of trouble. The localized decline may be the result of pay cuts and layoffs at area firms.

Working from the opposite direction, examining the results of other LI mashups (as in the airlines example) might expose a correlation between industry performance and its effect on individuals. An anticipated drop in sales or profits might lead to cutbacks, which in turn could set off a localized housing collapse.

The dollar amounts of foreclosures can show the impact on demographic segments (e.g., low income, middle income, high net worth). Knowing the portion of consumers who are affected lets you scope the impact to specific industries. When individuals with a high net worth are in trouble, the sale of luxury items will decrease. Middle-income earners are more likely to cut back on optional expenses such as dining out. This in turn implies an increase in sales at grocery stores.

Even more information can be collected to add value to these investigations. Online job sites can be monitored to collect postings and categorize them by specific keywords and ZIP code. Trend data can be collected for the number and type of positions employers seek to fill. Résumés may be scanned to uncover the skill sets of available candidates.

Let's examine all of the information we have been able to collect before any official announcement from corporations or government agencies:

- The number of foreclosures for a given region

- Social demographics about the homeowner

- Trends in consumer spending

- The fiscal health of local employers

- The state of the local job market

This information is speculative but nonetheless potentially very valuable to the firm that takes the time to collect it and dig deeper into its meaning. The fascinating property of this data is that it's completely proprietary to the firm that obtains it, even though it was collected from public sources.

▼

Example: *Create a "Shadow" Copy of Private Inventory Data*

Monitoring the performance of retail firms is another example where the Leading Indicator pattern shows its muscle. Whether this pattern is used for investment research or competitive purposes, it's possible to uncover some interesting data:

- How fast is a particular item selling?

- Are there problems with either insufficient or surplus inventory?

- Is the release of a new product imminent?

- Are competitors' products selling better?

- Are customers happy with their purchases?

Figure 4.7 depicts a potential implementation. The first step is to identify a set of online stores that sell the items of interest. At regular intervals, a Time Series mashup will visit these sites, attempt to add products to a shopping cart, and then check out. The purchase won't be completed of course, but the type, specifications, price, and quantity in stock are all recorded. Later this information can be analyzed by a Leading Indicator implementation.

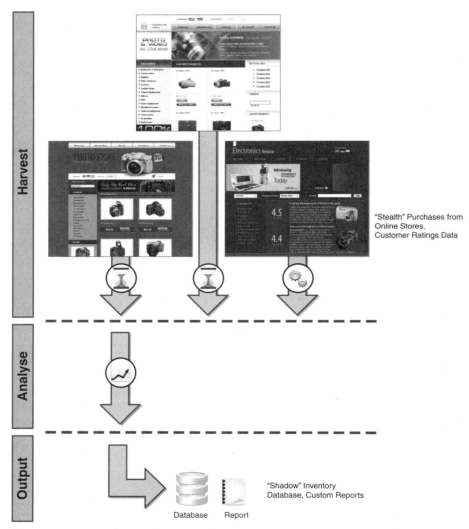

Figure 4.7 *A Leading Indicator implementation is used to monitor retail sales.*

Inventory levels over time will show which items are selling better (comparing the item type and other details assures corresponding products from different vendors are matched correctly). Items that are frequently out of stock may be either very popular or the victim of inventory shortages; mashing in ratings data from online reviews can help decide which interpretation is correct. An item that is never restocked may be on the verge of being discontinued or replaced by a newer model.

Retailers are prone to cutting costs or adding features in an effort to boost sales. A consistent inventory monitoring mashup can see if this decision has a positive outcome. If dropping a product's retail price does not lead to any increase in sales volume (as measured by the pace of inventory decline), then the firm is simply losing money at a faster rate.

The vendors naturally have all of this information privately maintained in their internal databases but until now there was no way to get to it. Regular "stealth" purchases are a unique forensic tool for approximating this data.

Reality Mining

Core Activities: Data extraction, data entry, transformation, surveillance

Problem

People are creatures of habit. We're prone to creating a daily routine that forms a rough organizational outline for our lives. Some of these habits are involuntary, such as reporting for work at a certain time or attending a regularly scheduled meeting. Others are purely a personal preference, such as which way to drive to work, where to eat lunch, and how often to check for new mail or chat with a coworker.

All of these human activities have a degree of randomness. They won't occur at exactly the same time or under the same circumstances every day—but they will happen. And each transaction, interaction, and reaction is a data point that may ultimately define a pattern. When the patterns of individuals take a parallel path or intersect, they form trends and connections that bubble up to affect the organization more visibly. Failure to comprehend the underlying relationships that exist in a company is a little bit like being an airline passenger: You think you know where you're going and how you're going to get there—but in reality you have no idea about what's happening in the cockpit until something unusual occurs. And the last time you want to acquire new intelligence is when there's a problem!

Behavioral modeling relies on identifying the undercurrent of activity that forms the patterns of our daily lives. Understanding where, when, and for how long regular activities take place can produce new ideas and insights:

- Who are the key information sources within an organization?

- Which systems do users have the most difficulty using?

- Are internal software release schedules having a measurable impact on user productivity?

- Which external conditions are affecting the business?

- Which factors affect employee performance, and how often do they occur?

Although a firm's organizational chart provides information regarding managerial responsibility, it provides virtually no insight into the underlying social structure. This data is where the true points of value can be found. Seasoned employees often build complex internal maps of who to talk to in a given situation. The importance of these individuals often goes unrecognized, however. It follows that the potential impact of their reassignment or departure won't be identified until after the fact. As with so many problems, the key to creating accurate models relies on obtaining useful observations.

Solution

Researchers at the Massachusetts Institute of Technology (MIT) define reality mining as "the collection of machine-sensed environmental data pertaining to human social behavior."[26] Early research in this field focused largely on work with mobile phones. That makes sense because cell phones are ubiquitous and capable of communicating their proximity to similar hardware as well as their location.[27] In an enterprise setting there are many more opportunities for capturing social and individual behavior patterns.

Many types of overt and veiled sensors can be mined to track users (see the "Resources for Reality Mining" sidebar). This data can provide information that is immediately useful (such as employee names and departments) or that can be used to model future behavior and system usage demands.

▼ ───────────────────────────────────

Resources for Reality Mining

Access badge logs
Application usage logs
Bluetooth scanning
Environmental data (e.g., temperature, decibel levels)
Facilities (e.g., conference room) availability
Market activity (e.g., trading volume)
Medical alerts
Moisture sensors

───────────────────────

26. MIT Media Lab. "Reality Mining." http://reality.media.mit.edu/
27. The Bluetooth protocol, which has been implemented in many modern phones, allows automatic discovery of other nearby devices.

Motion sensors
Network logins/logouts
Phone and fax logs
Police reports/crime data
Political alerts
Purchasing activity
Printer logs
Radiation detectors
RFID-embedded materials
Security cameras (when combined with facial recognition software)
Seismic activity
Smoke detectors
Tidal/surf reports
Traffic congestion
Weather reports and alerts

Related Patterns: Time Series

Fragility

A Reality Mining mashup depends on the recorded observations of external systems and sensors for input. The original purpose for logging this data is usually to diagnose problems, observe trends, or audit user activity. These uses demand a searchable repository with a consistent format. Data records are therefore not generally subject to significant alteration. By extension, that makes these logs a dependable resource for mashups. The greatest potential for breakdown occurs when the system being used as a sensor does not record historical observations. Weather and traffic reports, for example, focus on current conditions rather than prior ones. Because no allegiance is owed to previous reporting formats, sudden shifts in presentation are more likely—and these changes can potentially disrupt a mashup.

Example: *Save Time on Conference Calls and Monitor Their Usefulness*

Consider the example presented in the Chapter 1 sidebar, "A Sample Mashup Use Case." A firm has frequent conference calls but each attendee must vocally announce their presence. Linking the conference administration Web site's ANI[28]

---

28. Automatic number identification, also known as caller ID.

information with the firm's corporate directory provides push-button access to the name of everyone on the line and his or her location. When a number cannot be found in the corporate file (because the participant is dialing in from home), it is looked up on a public Web directory. Once identified, that caller's name can be fed back to the corporate directory to find that person's work number, manager, and department. Executing this mashup multiple times over the course of the call will determine how long each individual stays on the line.

This simple example depicted in Figure 4.8 shows how the Reality Mining pattern can be used to determine the approximate location of the callers, their line of business, contact information, and duration of participation.

Going further, we can use this general information to uncover possibly more useful information about the firm:

- Do particular departments interact more frequently than others?

- Suppose the information is linked to the corporate calendar. When multiple conference calls conflict, which person's line typically wins the most attendees?

- Do some individuals habitually join calls late or leave early? Do they dial into to private calls without verbally announcing themselves?

Reality Mining needn't focus on social interaction. Pull in the application logs for software used in the firm and other inquires can be made:

- Prior to, during, or after a call, does usage of any of these programs increase?

- Suppose a stock trading package is present. Is there an increase in buy or sell activity in conjunction with a particular call?

- Monitoring the flow of trades against conference-call statistics might show which meetings result in increased activity. This data could provide insight into which discussions (and participants) hold more sway over an organization's actions.

- Does the conclusion of one call precipitate other phone calls from the original attendees, which in turn lead to other patterns of application usage?

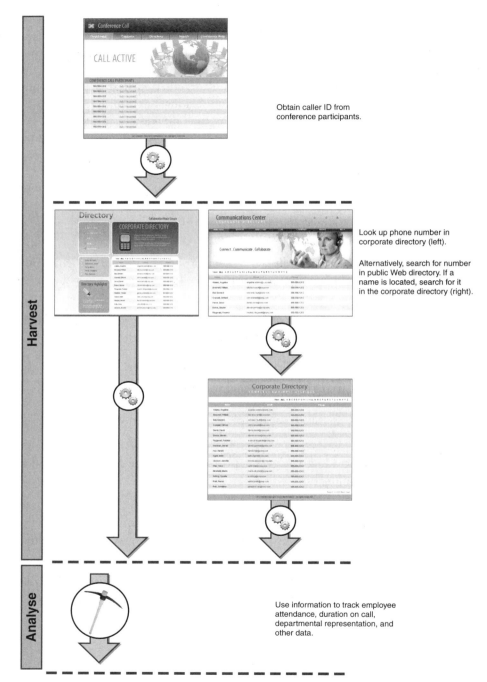

Obtain caller ID from conference participants.

Look up phone number in corporate directory (left).

Alternatively, search for number in public Web directory. If a name is located, search for it in the corporate directory (right).

Use information to track employee attendance, duration on call, departmental representation, and other data.

Figure 4.8 *Using Reality Mining to unlock data hidden in employee behavior*

Example: *Monitor Issues Affecting Employee Productivity*

A firm has four currently unconnected resources that can be linked together to provide more insight into factors that affect productivity:

1. A dedicated Help Desk exists to support IT infrastructure. Each call to the support line is treated as a new case and assigned a unique identifier ("ticket number"). Free-form text on the problem is captured as well as the following formal data:

   - Status (open, in progress, closed)

   - User name and location

   - Time of day

   - User type (employee or contractor)

   - Problem type (e.g., computer, application, phone, printer)

   - Operating system and version number

   - Associate assigned to the issue

   - Priority

   Once a case is closed, information on the resolution is captured in a searchable database that will help diagnose future problems.

2. A Release Management (RM) system is used to promote new application versions from development to production. The system connects to an internal bug database to log which issues are fixed in the latest package. The RM application also manages the schedule for when the package will be pushed to end users' desktops.

3. A Centralized Application Inventory (CAI) tracks the resources allocated to each internal development project. Its data include the number of developers and testers, the annual budget allocation, and the technology used by the solution.

4. The firm's Time Management system contains information on the names and locations of all employees and the projects to which they book their time. It also records absences due to holidays or vacation.

Table 4.3 shows the real-world events implicitly tracked by each of these products.

Table 4.3 *Combination of Four Separate Systems to Achieve Greater Insight into Internal Processes*

Application Category	Activity Monitored
Help Desk	User problem reports; their causes and resolutions
Release Management	Software release schedule, number of bugs fixed
Centralized Application Inventory	Budgets, personnel, and technology assigned to an application
Time Management	Employee location, hours billed across projects, out-of-office time

To make the example more interesting, let's also include data on trade volume from the major financial exchanges.

The information in these systems can be combined to provide insight into the real-world patterns and activities that shape the course of corporate productivity:

- Do the applications released on a specific platform result in fewer subsequent calls to the Help Desk?

- Do smaller teams produce higher-quality code? This trend might be demonstrated by fewer support calls, lower counts of bug fixes, and less frequent releases. Are particular locations more productive than others?

- Does increased trading volume result in more support incidents? If so, in which category? Is the firm's infrastructure equipped to support increased usage?

- Are new releases dispatched before or after holidays? Does that affect the number of calls to the Help Desk? When a user returns from vacation, is he or she more likely to experience problems?

- Does the geographic location of users experiencing problems with a particular application indicate problems with its underlying architecture? For example, perhaps the database and Web servers are located in different regions.

Instead of waiting for a support ticket to be created, some of these questions can be answered preemptively by pulling in application-specific usage logs.

Many organizations have developed systems similar to the ones in this example but treat their information as separate, discrete collections of historical activity. Linking these databases together lets you uncover how user actions and activities "bubble up" to create chains of events. Studying these interactions can suggest changes to financial and technological strategies.

Reputation Management

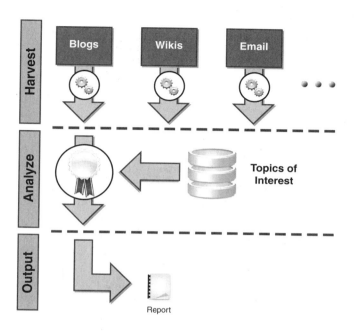

Core Activities: Data extraction, data entry, transformation

Also Known As: Sentiment Analysis

Problem

In the past, the publication of news (good or bad) was limited to a few information outlets with a handful of distribution channels. Monitoring events that affected a firm's public standing was a more manageable task in this era. But in the world of Web 2.0, everyone is a potential publisher. An employee who feels mistreated has a global forum for embarrassing his or her employer. An unhappy consumer can blast your product's shoddy workmanship in a public blog.

Reputation management is the process of identifying how a company is perceived and establishing an action plan to correct, maintain, or enhance the company's reputation.[29] Combined with a strong brand, a good reputation helps attract and retain customers. Conversely, a poor public image can drive away existing clients and send prospects looking elsewhere. Every action a company takes has

---

29. Harris, Elaine K. *Customer Service: A Practical Approach.* 2002.

a ripple effect on its reputation. New products may be met with praise or disgust. Response to a rumor or scandal may engender respect or promote outrage.

Corporations with spotless public records can still suffer as a result of their peers' actions. The collective reputation of an industry can be damaged by the failures of one "bad apple." When faced with this prospect, firms must act quickly and decisively to distinguish themselves before they become the target of negative public opinion.

Solution

The collaborative nature of Web 2.0 encourages the sharing of opinions. The exponential growth of blogs and wikis has empowered a small number of consumers to sway the opinions of an entire market.

According to a recent survey by Deloitte's Consumer Products group, almost two-thirds (62%) of consumers read consumer-written product reviews on the Internet. Of these people, more than 8 in 10 (82%) say their purchase decisions have been directly influenced by the reviews.[30]

"Word of mouth" is the practice of consumers providing information to other potential customers. As the Deloitte survey shows, it has evolved from conversations with friends and family to become a global phenomenon.

Sentiment analysis (SA) techniques allow text to be scanned for words that connote emotion and to rank how a document "feels" about a particular subject. By accessing thousands of blogs and other public postings collected by mashups, a firm can use SA to monitor its overall reputation as well as public opinion on specific products or industries. SA products exist as open-source and prepackaged solutions; alternatively, they can be built from scratch.

Identifying when people are talking about your products or brand in a negative manner gives you an opportunity to post a rebuttal or challenge the poster's facts. Multiple messages in a common forum can be a sign of an ongoing conversation. A favorable discussion can be a great opportunity to inject brand-specific advertising or announce new products. The firm that shows it listens to its customers and values their opinions will ultimately strengthen its reputation.

Related Patterns: Infinite Monkeys, Time Series

Fragility

The harvesting of content for Reputation Management purposes is straightforward—hence the low fragility rating for this pattern. Because machine-based

---

30. Deloitte LLP. October 1, 2007. http://www.deloitte.com/dtt/press_release/0,1014,
   sid%3D2283&cid%3D173666,00.html

analysis of this material is not yet as flexible as a human analyst (for example, sarcasm may be difficult to detect), there is a chance that some statements will be misclassified. If you choose to implement a packaged solution, ask for comparison statistics against a human evaluator.

Example: *How Does the Internet "Feel" Today?*

We Feel Fine[31] demonstrates the power of SA not for a particular product, but rather for the entire Internet community. Creators Jonathan Harris and Sep Kamvar created an application that obtains thousands of blog posts each day. Each post is scanned for the phrases "I feel" and "I am feeling." Once located, the sentence is compared against a database of more than 5,000 words that have emotional connotations. A successful match is recorded as a chronological instance of an emotion. Viewed over time, this data provides interesting insight into the Web's mood (Figure 4.9)

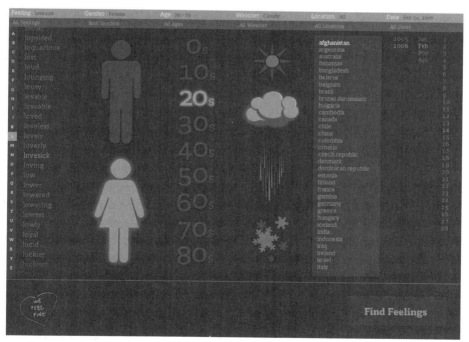

Figure 4.9   *One of several visualizations from wefeelfine.org*

---

31. http://weefeelfine.org

Jonathan and Sep took the further step of mining the blog owner's profile page to establish his or her age, gender, and location. That led to a mashup to obtain local weather data. This additional detail gives the emotional analysis several other dimensions and allows interesting new questions to be asked:

- How does the weather affect peoples' moods?

- Is a particular gender generally more or less happy?

- Are some cities angrier or sadder than others?

From a SA perspective, the approach is fairly basic because it relies on an explicit declaration of feeling. The phrase "I feel wonderful" is captured and cataloged, but the equally emotional "It sucks here" is not. Even so, the data is fascinating—and the accompanying user interface is a masterpiece of data visualization. This site is an excellent introduction to the SA field.

Example: *Gauge the Emotional Impact of Outsourcing*

Megalex Industries has decided to send some of its internal operations off-shore to an outside firm based in India. In the aftermath of this decision, some managers have begun to voice concerns about employee morale and lower productivity at the home office. There seems to be general discomfort under the new arrangement, though no one is quite sure why. Besides saving the firm significant money, only the most tedious tasks are being shipped overseas. One of the goals was to raise employee spirit but that seems to have backfired.

Sentiment analysis needn't be restricted to public postings made outside a firm. Monitoring internal blog and wiki postings (and possibly email) may provide the desired answers. By examining these conversations, Megalex is able to determine that employee perception of the new outsourcing arrangement is, in fact, unfavorable. For starters, the quality of workmanship is generally deemed poor by the more experienced staff—something management was unaware of until they double-checked Help Desk activity and see that it has increased. Employee postings generally indicate anger and fear, which suggests employees feel their job security is threatened—which is not the case.

Management decides to act on this data by conducting a quality audit of the outside firm. This move engenders the trust of associates who questioned the value of the new partnership. A series of information sessions is conducted to inform teams that the new relationship is not part of any headcount reduction strategy, but rather is intended to support more research and development efforts at headquarters. As the staff obtains more insight into the outsourcing measure, the tenor of internal discussion turns more productive.

▼

Example: *Detect How Price Changes Are Received by Consumers*

A major electronics manufacturer, Amazing Media Players (AMP), announces a revolutionary new portable media player (PMP). The device is praised in the press and the firm's loyal fans line up to purchase the item before it has even been shipped to retail outlets. The blogosphere[32] is abuzz with anticipation over the new gadget. The AMP marketing department, which is harvesting and analyzing thousands of new comments per day, is thrilled to proclaim the attention is almost universally positive.

The first day the new PMP is available, it flies off store shelves. Early adopters unwrap it and discover it meets their heightened expectations. There is another flood of positive comments and much celebration at AMP headquarters. The rapid pace of sales and heightened demand push AMP to further increase the pace of its manufacturing, which in turn creates an interesting new benefit. Because the company will be ordering larger quantities of the parts required to assemble its player, AMP is able to get additional breaks on the cost of components. AMP decides to pass a portion of this discount along to its customers and reduces the price of the PMP by 30%.

What was intended to help promote the PMP beyond the early adopters and further elevate AMP's positive image completely backfires. Sentiment analysis reveals that AMP's most loyal bloggers are outraged to have paid a higher price only weeks earlier. Many begin to rail against the company for "ripping them off" and "dishonest business practices." Sales across AMP's entire product line are in jeopardy of slowing as consumers wait to see when prices might fall next.

SA allows the firm to gauge the backlash and take measured action. Although AMP did not make a greater profit on the original players, its analysis shows that the sudden price drop is negatively affecting its brand. A decision is swiftly made to credit early purchasers the difference in price toward purchases of future products. Because AMP enjoys a 50% retail markup and these new sales will be spread out over time, the overall financial impact on the company will be minimal.

In the days after the rebate program is announced, SA shows that some detractors are still upset by the company's actions but the vast majority are

---

32. A buzzword for the totality of blogs hosted on the Internet

pleased with the rapid response from AMP. They complained and the company listened. A potentially disastrous affair has been manipulated to increase the bond between the firm and its customers.

▼

Example: *Uncover Public Relations Problems in Their Early Stages*

Consider the recent incidents of public failures and missteps in several industries. The following public blogs and wiki comments were chosen to demonstrate how customers voice their feedback in Web 2.0.[33]

> We've been posting the details about the revelations relating to Sony's DRM systems, which show jaw-dropping contempt for their customers, for copyright law, for fair trading and for the public interest.[34]

The discovery that Sony copy prevention software secretly installed a rootkit on users' computers led to a number of lawsuits being filed against Sony BMG.

> China Exports Lead Poisoning[35]

When high levels of lead were found in imported toys, toothpaste, and pet food, manufacturers with production facilities in China were suddenly thrust under a spotlight of scrutiny.

> Why was that not the first thing listed on their web site? I'll tell you why: because companies like HP think they can pull one over on consumers by making it more difficult than it should be in getting the appropriate information.[36]

Hewlett-Packard's recall of more than 135,000 notebook batteries wasn't handled smoothly enough for this particular poster.

Reputation Management (and SA) isn't a time machine that allows poor judgment to be erased or inaccurate posts to be corrected, but it can be a vital tool for shaping a firm's strategy in times of crisis.

---

33. I'm not a lawyer, but it seems prudent to state that these quotes represent the opinions of their authors and are not evidence of any corporate wrongdoings.

34. http://www.boingboing.net/2005/11/14/sony-anticustomer-te.html

35. http://www.worldnetdaily.com/news/article.asp?ARTICLE_ID=56056

36. http://arcware.net/archive/2005/10/15/5282.aspx

Time Series

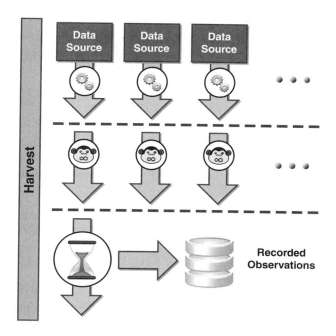

Recorded Observations

Core Activities: Data extraction, data entry, transformation

Problem

A time series (TS) is a sequence of data observed across a regular interval. Assuming some internal organization of the data exists, the measurements can be used to forecast new points in the series before they occur. TS analysis can also be backward looking. In circumstances where conducting a real-world test is too impractical or expensive, analysis of historical trends can serve as a potential substitute.

The output of TS analysis is an important asset in a corporation's decision-making process. The successful firm keeps an eye on current market conditions while positioning itself for the future. For example, studying past conditions can provide answers to the following questions:

- Which drug will most effectively combat the spread of a particular disease?

- How much gas should be refined for the upcoming holiday weekend?

- When will a particular assembly-line robot need to be replaced?

- Which food items sell best under particular weather conditions?

A firm can build a database of TS-powered models based solely on internal findings, but that ignores thousands of external observations that might prove very useful. Tracking in-house data can be difficult enough—how can reliable recordings from multiple sources outside the corporate walls be obtained?

Solution

The process of harvesting TS data can be broken down into four distinct steps: identification, collection, transformation, and scheduling and storage.

- *Identification.* The resources that contain the desired information are identified and API enabled.

- *Collection.* As shown by the Infinite Monkeys pattern, data-collection mashups can be scaled to a superhuman level of activity. In this instance the pattern is applied to the mundane task of assembling facts and figures from the API-enabled data sources.

- *Transformation.* The collected material may pass through a transformation function to ensure a common format. Examples include converting Fahrenheit values to Celsius temperatures, various currencies to euros or dollars, and dates to DD/MM/YYYY format.

- *Scheduling and Storage.* The mashup is scheduled to execute at regular intervals and records its output in a TS database. Later work with this data can focus on predicting forthcoming values or trying to establish relationships between independently measured series (see the discussion of the Leading Indicator pattern).

Most firms already collect some level of chronological data for auditing and forecast purposes. For example, utility companies use historical usage to anticipate future demand. Government agencies monitor traffic patterns so they can plan road and bridge maintenance. Drug companies record the results of clinical trials. Tracking information outside the corporate walls is not a straightforward process, but the results can be tremendously valuable. A TS mashup may be used to mine data from publicly available data sources, and the results can then be used to predict a competitor's actions.

Related Patterns: Infinite Monkeys, Leading Indicator

Fragility

The fragility of the Time Series pattern is directly determined by the API Enabler and Infinite Monkey instances that support it.

▼

Example: *Manage Over-purchased and Under-utilized Hardware and Software*

The effects of having too much or too little hardware can have a significant impact on a company's operating costs and productivity. If there is a shortage of computing horsepower, systems can't keep up with processing demand. At best this results in frustrated users; at worst it leads to missed opportunities. A surplus of hardware consumes extra cooling and electrical resources, takes up extra space, and requires additional staff to support it.

To address the problem of over- or under-utilized hardware, a firm can monitor several activities over time. Items to watch include CPU utilization, free memory, available disk space, and network I/O. Each of these items plays a part in determining how the system performs. Two common metrics that are recorded are peak usage and average usage. Peak usage is the highest value a given measurement achieved over a specific time period, whereas average usage reflects the most common level. The data must be collected over a long enough period so that accurate business usage is reflected. For example, in the financial industry the tracking process should include busy times such as month-end, quarter-end, and year-end.

Measuring this data isn't the responsibility of a mashup. A wealth of monitoring packages specialize in recording various statistics over time. Alas, most firms have several of them, which makes the process of gathering and normalizing the metrics a huge undertaking. A Time Series mashup can regularly visit each of the different products to collect and organize their findings under a common format.

A Time Series mashup can also visit other systems to enrich the monitoring results. Pulling in the Help Desk system can associate heavy call volume with server load. Application logs can be combed to identify variations in application response time.

One possible result of collecting this data is the justification of a move to a grid or utility computing (UC) environment. In a UC topology, applications aren't associated with dedicated servers, but rather are dynamically assigned resources as they require them. Spreading demand across multiple servers means average usage increases, so less hardware is required. Ultimately, this results in lower costs. If management decides to target IT for an optimization project (e.g., a 5% increase in utilization, a 10% decrease in support costs), a Time Series mashup can collect the data to track its progress.

A firm may also have an excess of software. Multiple systems that perform essentially identical tasks may then result in surplus hardware, extra licensing and maintenance charges, and heightened support costs. Most corporations don't consciously go down this path. Instead, growth from mergers and acquisitions often has the side effect of broadening infrastructure diversity. A firm can set policies about which software packages, libraries, and tools are not permitted, but regular monitoring for compliance is another burdensome task. IT generally retains a central inventory of all applications in use along with supplemental information for each product. A Time Series mashup can regularly scan this data to determine how many systems are using unapproved technology. Over time, this data can be used to pressure teams to create remediation plans, track progress, and shape budgets. When paired with a hardware monitoring TS, this information may demonstrate the advantages or drawbacks of particular architectures.

▼

Example: *Collect Data for Business Strategy Planning*

Six Sigma is the overarching name for a series of disciplines that seek to create continuous improvement within a firm. This approach was originally developed by Motorola but was perhaps most famously and universally applied by General Electric when Jack Welch was at its helm. In a Six Sigma-governed project, a defined process is measured over time followed by a formal analysis of the results.

For example, if the process being analyzed consists of the steps that customer support agent takes to handle a call, the following items might be measured:

- The type of problem reported by the customer.

- The duration of the call (with a note being made if the customer hangs up during the process).

- The outcome of the call. (Was the customer satisfied?)

While Six Sigma provides guidance in determining which information should be collected and suggests statistical techniques for evaluating data, it does nothing to recommend specific technical solutions for gathering the required observations.

If your organization has adopted Six Sigma, Time Series mashups can reduce the cost and complexity of monitoring internal processes. In this particular case the phone logs, corporate knowledge base, and employee schedules can all be connected to record Help Desk activity. Post-analysis recommendations might include installing a new phone system, hiring additional personnel, or providing better training for the support team.

Example: *Uncover Hidden Behavioral Trends*

Time Series mashups are a valuable tool when leveraged to record observations unrelated to a firm's core competency. Facebook's Insights platform is a good example. A popular social networking destination, Facebook created an entirely new advertising platform based historical user activity:

> Facebook Insights gives access to data on activity, fan demographics, ad performance and trends that better equip marketers to improve custom content on Facebook and adjust ad targeting.[37]

By monitoring the actions of its users, Facebook was able to learn more about their underlying behavior. This information could then be shared with advertisers to enable *situational marketing*:

> Facebook's ad system serves Social Ads that combine social actions from your friends—such as a purchase of a product or review of a restaurant—with an advertiser's message. This enables advertisers to deliver more tailored and relevant ads to Facebook users that now include information from their friends so they can make more informed decisions.[38]

Another use for TS activity is to anticipate the overall task the user is trying to complete. With this information it becomes possible to create a *situational interface*. A user interface that dynamically adapts itself to the job at hand can increase productivity and reduce the risk of errors (see the Usability Enhancer and Smart Suggestions patterns in Chapter 5).

---

37. "Facebook Unveils Facebook Ads." November 6, 2007. http://www.facebook.com/press/releases.php?p=9176

38. "Facebook Unveils Facebook Ads."

Chapter 5

Enhance Patterns

We cannot deny the facts of nature, but we should certainly try to improve on them.[1]
—Mihaly Csikszentmihalyi

Introduction

Computer applications are a snapshot in time. Just as counting rings on a stump can tell you how old a tree was when it was cut down, a close look at a piece of software uncovers a wealth of information. You can discover what the user's requirements were when it was written, which development tools and architectural strategies were in vogue, and how the application was intended to perform.

As time passes and the world changes, software becomes dated. Without regular attention the fate of many applications is inevitable replacement or retirement. This is a sobering fact given the amount of care and effort that goes into obtaining a solution in the first place. Countless books and articles have been written that prescribe methods for creating adaptable architectures that stretch a system's usable lifetime—yet none of these methods yields software that can thrive in the complete absence of attention.

There are countless reasons why applications fade into obsolescence. Time or budget constraints can preempt necessary maintenance and cause systems to fall into disrepair. New laws and industry regulations may mandate particular changes. Sometimes the prevailing business climate favors short-term design decisions over ones that would increase an application's longevity. Or perhaps a firm relies on an external vendor to provide solutions: When a vendor cannot keep pace with its customers' evolving requirements, then its products will fall into disuse.

---

1. Csikszentmihalyi, Mihaly. *Flow: The Psychology of Optimal Experience.* Harper Perennial, 1990.

121

Every organization has faced the challenge of enhancing its existing systems to get the most value from its investment. All too often the solution requires a substantial investment of time and money. If the work comes at the expense of other initiatives, the difficult problem of choosing which users' requirements are more important than others' is presented.

This chapter describes a collection of patterns where mashups make the process simpler and less expensive. Among the topics we will examine are these:

- Extending applications to a wider audience (Accessibility, Feed Factory, Translation)

- Fixing bugs without touching the underlying code (Field Medic)

- Making software more user-friendly (Usability, Smart Suggestions)

- Improving the "findability" of data (Super Search)

- Incorporating changing business rules (Workflow)

With the exception of the second item, these issues were not unsolvable in the enterprise before mashups emerged. However, existing approaches generally require skilled technical resources. Usually this means the original developers must alter an application's source code. If they are unavailable, then additional time is required to acquire and train new talent. Whether the team consists of rookies or seasoned veterans, any circumstance that entails touching the original code can introduce new bugs.

Mashups allow systems to be improved and updated with considerably less effort and risk. Much of the work requires no more than basic familiarity with the application. Likewise, programming skills are not a requirement. This is not a reflection of specific toolsets but rather an observation about mashups themselves. In Chapter 1, we examined how mashups allow nontechnical users to construct their own solutions. The Enhance patterns represent a slight twist on that proposition; users may just as easily correct existing products as create new ones.

Like the Harvest patterns, most Enhance implementations depend on the data extraction and data entry core functions. Action, clipping, and transformation are the core features that lay beneath most Enhance implementations. The Action capability allows an Enhance mashup to chain separate processes together. Clipping facilitates interface modification without requiring changes to the original source code. The Transformation operation allows data to be translated between steps when necessary.

Whereas the patterns presented in Chapter 4 showed the benefits of harvesting information, the Enhance patterns show the value of data left in place. Sometimes changing the interaction model is all an application needs to reinvigorate its usefulness.

Accessibility

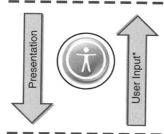

* Implementations may be presentation only
and not pass user input from the alternative
interface back to the existing application.

Core Activities: Data extraction, data entry

Problem

The process of software development is often compared to building a house, though usually this is a flawed metaphor. Home building has undergone centuries of evolution to produce numerous standards for making it a quick, safe, and efficient process. Software development, by contrast, is a relatively new activity.

One thing the two disciplines share is the need for continuous improvement. Changes come in two forms. The first type seeks to address issues of comfort. For a home this may mean rearranging the furniture, building an addition, or simply choosing an appealing color scheme. These modifications make the environment more livable. In the world of software, we face similar challenges and group them under the umbrella term "usability." The Usability Enhancer pattern examined later in this chapter explores this topic in greater detail.

The second form of home improvement is probably the more important of the two. Imagine you couldn't even get inside your house or that you couldn't get upstairs. These are issues of accessibility. It's a common misconception that accessibility issues pertain only to individuals with physical challenges. Anyone who buys a Hummer and can't fit it in the garage will tell you otherwise. Although it is certainly a more trivial example, this situation demonstrates that accessibility encompasses the task of ensuring existing resources remain compatible with advances in other fields.

For a house, addressing accessibility concerns might range from drastic measures such as completely tearing down the structure to simpler solutions such as adding an access ramp. We face greater challenges with code. A house usually serves a small family of occupants but a software application may be shared by thousands of end users. Maintaining unique interface environments for multiple users and devices is expensive and time-consuming. If the software is provided by an external party, it may not be possible to make changes at all.

Solution

When the methods we use to interact with existing applications don't keep pace with real-world requirements or technological advances, we need the ability to build on the underlying structure and extend it to serve new areas. Mashups enable the construction of an alternative application interface with no effect on the original code. If the software has a solid foundation, then it can be extended to meet users' evolving needs—much like a home improvement project. Moreover, programs can be enhanced even if they were created outside your team or firm. It's like remodeling a house you don't own!

The examples given here focus on two main accessibility challenges: increasing human accessibility and increasing device accessibility. In an effort to make applications available to all potential users many firms spend considerable time defining, testing, and maintaining duplicate application interfaces that are friendly to assistive software products (e.g., screen readers). Maintaining this additional code dilutes development resources and increases complexity. With the Accessibility pattern, a mashup is constructed to grab relevant portions of the application and present it in a format friendly to assistive software. The mashup may also be used to marshal user input and direct it back to the underlying application when necessary. Figure 5.1 presents a simple example in which an Accessibility mashup is used to provide an alternative visual representation.

As new platforms emerge for interacting with applications, another accessibility challenge arises. Consider the recent evolution of mobile phones. In the past decade, cell phones have evolved from supporting early Web access mechanisms like WAP and WML to include full-scale Web browsers. Who can predict what the next pervasive platform may be? Will it be networked home appliances? In-dash automotive systems? The Accessibility pattern lets you adapt your software to new environments instead of starting from scratch.

Related Patterns: Field Medic, Usability Enhancer, Widget Enabler

Fragility

The fragility of the Accessibility pattern is influenced by the portion of an existing system that is used under the new interface or protocol. Leveraging more features causes a corresponding increase in the potential number of places where changes to the original system may lead to failure.

Day	Mon	Tue	Wed	Thur	Fri
Outlook					
High (°F)	50°	55°	45°	50°	55°
Low (°F)	35°	40°	30°	35°	40°

Monday
Outlook: Partly Sunny
High (F): 50 Low: 35

Tuesday
Outlook: Partly Cloudy
High (F): 55 Low: 40

Wednesday
Outlook: Cloudy
High (F): 45 Low: 30

Thursday
Outlook: Rain
High (F): 50 Low: 35

Friday
Outlook: Thunderstorms
High (F): 55 Low: 40

Figure 5.1 *An Accessibility mashup is used to provide a weather forecast without relying on images.*

Example: *Make Your Applications Accessible*

In 1998, U.S. President Bill Clinton signed an amendment to the Workforce Rehabilitation Act into law. Section 508, as it is popularly known, requires that technology developed or procured by the federal government be accessible to persons with disabilities. There are ways around this requirement—for example, when providing accessibility creates an "undue burden"—but the intent of the legislation is clear: Where possible the government should use its influence to provide accessible content.

In 1990, the Americans with Disabilities Act (ADA) was signed into law. The ADA prohibits discrimination against people with disabilities in places of "public accommodation." If you've noticed a ramp alongside a staircase or seen Braille markings on an elevator panel, then you have most likely encountered the effects of the ADA. This piece of legislation could not anticipate the rise of the World Wide Web, however. Although there are no explicit provisions for providing accessible online content, several groups have proclaimed the Web to be "an open public space." The National Federation for the Blind (NFB) sued AOL in 1999, claiming that it did not meet the provisions of the ADA. The case was ultimately settled out of court. In 2007, the NFB sued Oracle over similar accessibility concerns.[2]

---

2. http://sev.prnewswire.com/computer-electronics/20070205/UNM00605022007-1.html

Defeats have been suffered by both pro- and anti-ADA forces. In October 2002, a Federal District Court judge ruled in favor of Southwest Airlines,[3] stating that the existing ADA language was too explicit to be applied to Web sites. The NFB sued click-and-mortar retailer Target on the grounds that the firm's Web site was not accessible as required by the ADA; this time a Federal District Court judge concluded that the case could proceed. The court further stated that California law required Web sites to be accessible.[4] A final ruling is pending.

Clearly accessibility is a hot issue, and not just in the United States. Many other countries have similar laws that encourage or require similar provisions for ensuring access to resources regardless of physical capability.[5]

Legal issues aside, what would motivate a company to intentionally isolate itself or its products from potential customers? Convenience and competitiveness are two common culprits. Many firms insist that providing alternative interfaces is an expensive and time-consuming process that detracts from their core business objectives. This is a false premise for two reasons. First, assistive software on the user's computer can often perform much of the "heavy lifting" for making content accessible; only minor work by the provider is required to ensure these enabling applications can operate correctly. Second, it's a mistake to assume that disabled consumers represent a small portion of the marketplace and can be safely dismissed.

> The Census Bureau reports that 7.7 million Americans have difficulty hearing what is said in normal conversations, while more than 13 million have impaired eyesight . . . More than 1.7 million are deaf in both ears.[6]

A company ignores this large pool of potential customers only out of ignorance or foolishness. Yet a majority of firms still do not implement the World Wide Web Consortium's (W3C) Content Accessibility Guidelines.[7]

There is some legitimacy to the argument that ADA compliance could dampen competitiveness. Companies trying to create a compelling online experience are using cutting-edge techniques to create highly interactive environments. These sites are known as rich Internet applications (RIAs). Many firms set aside issues of accessibility in their pursuit of this goal. The technology behind RIAs is so diverse that until recently little information about how these systems could provide adaptive interfaces was available. The W3C has moved

---

3. http://www.news.com/2100-1023-962761.html?part=wht&tag=wtop

4. http://www.dralegal.org/cases/private_business/nfb_v_target.php

5. A compilation of accessibility policies organized by country is available at http://www.w3.org/WAI/Policy/

6. Pear, Robert. "U.S. Proposes Rules to Bar Obstacles for the Disabled." *The New York Times*, January 22, 1991.

7. The guidelines are available at http://www.w3.org/TR/WCAG20/

to address this issue with its "Accessible Rich Internet Applications" guidelines.[8] Going forward these standards—and the RIA libraries that support them—should make creating accessible RIA applications a more straightforward process.

Our examination of accessibility issues concludes with an important question: What can be done about the vast majority of existing applications that are inaccessible by some users? Mashups provide the answer. The Accessibility pattern describes two potential approaches.

- An Accessibility implementation can be leveraged as a variation on the Field Medic and Usability Enhancer patterns. In this case, the existing interface is mined via data extraction and data entry core functionality to provide an alternative interface that is either overtly accessible (or at least friendly) to assistive tools such as screen readers and magnifiers.

- An existing application can be API-enabled and this functionality connected to predefined components that natively support accessibility. The advantage of this method is that only a single interface needs to be maintained on an ongoing basis. It will dynamically adapt itself based on the capabilities of the browser client that accesses it. This technique is similar to that prescribed by the Widget Enabler pattern in Chapter 7.

As we have observed with other patterns in this text, neither of these solutions requires changes to a site's main code base, nor must the changes be performed by the original development team. The skills required to make a site accessible are considerably less complex than those needed to create the initial implementation. In fact, the work may occur outside an enterprise's control. Third parties might perform the task of creating accessible versions of public Web resources when content owners fail to do so. Of course, a firm then runs the risk of its customers interacting with its systems via mechanisms the company had no hand in shaping.

Example: *Extend Your Products to New Platforms*

Mobile Web browsing is poised to grow from 76 million browsers delivered in 2007 to nearly 700 million by 2013.[9] According to ABI research director

---

8. http://www.w3.org/WAI/intro/aria.php

9. "Mobile Browser Market Is Transforming and Will Grow to 1.5 Billion Units in 2013." April 2008. http://www.abiresearch.com/abiprdisplay.jsp?pressid=1103

Michael Wolf, "The focus today for mobile browser developers is to take advantage of the latest Web standards while also developing solutions tailored toward the unique experience of using a browser on a mobile phone."

A firm cannot have a corporate Web presence and expect mobile browser technology to deliver the same experience as a PC-based browser. Constraints imposed by the form factor of a mobile device inevitably require customization for this market segment. This is a case where accessibility is determined by technological limitations.

Corporations that recognize the value of this marketplace face the task of maintaining a separate code stream designated to support the mobile user. This challenging effort may draw resources away from other important initiatives. An Accessibility mashup allows a stand-alone team to reinterpret the desktop experience for alternative platforms. The accessibility team doesn't require in-depth knowledge of the technology that underpins the firm's site, nor does the Web development team need to master the nuances of mobile devices. Figure 5.2 shows how the Accessibility pattern can provide an alternative interface for a portable browser.

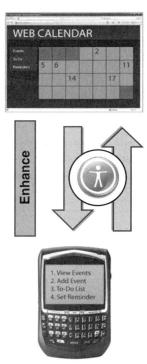

Figure 5.2   *An Accessibility implementation is used to provide an alternative presentation for mobile devices.*

Feed Factory

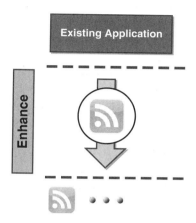

Core Activities: Data extraction, data entry, transformation

Also Known As: RSS Enabler

Problem

Keeping up-to-date with changing Web content can be a challenging task. The traditional approach is to regularly visit a site and inspect it for any new information. Multiply this activity across dozens of pages and the odds of staying informed drop dramatically. An early solution offered by many sites was the ability to sign up for an email newsletter. This practice required users to forego a small amount of privacy (their email address) and had the drawback of delivering updates only as frequently as the Webmaster decided to publish them.

RSS[10]—and later Atom—emerged as a means for sites to publish a feed of recently modified content. Feed readers (also known as aggregators) bring together content from multiple sources and assemble it under a common interface. Users view the collected material from a single location in a method not dissimilar from how newspapers present syndicated articles from multiple sources. Most feeds do not require authentication and may be accessed without exposing any personal information.

---

10. Originally defined as Rich Site Summary, but more popularly known as Real Simple Syndication.

As RSS and Atom became more widespread on the Internet, firms began to envision internal uses of this technology. Rather than forcing users to regularly check systems for important news or updates, this information could be published as a feed. Such feeds may be consumed by a desktop reader, by an internal portal, or by one of the many products available for mobile devices. This approach untethers users from their computers and allows them to stay informed wherever they're located.

Systems created *before* RSS/Atom became popular obviously have no support for these protocols. Even systems being created today may not support RSS if the developers have limited resources or fail to see any value in adding it.

How RSS is supported will be determined by who decides it is an important feature:

- If IT staff view RSS as a core requirement, then commercial and open-source products can be leveraged to speed development of RSS support. Staff must be allocated to determine what the feeds should contain and then implement them. Programmers familiar with the original code base or development platform will need to be enlisted.

- If business users want RSS capability, they need to convince IT personnel to marshal the necessary resources. It's possible that IT is already building feeds but some users want to change them (see the Filter pattern), combine them (see the Content Integration pattern), or create additional feeds. The Long Tail demonstrates that IT is usually unable to meet each user's specific requirements.

- Unless enhanced by the vendor, third-party applications would seem permanently closed to RSS.

Solution

The API Enabler pattern demonstrates how existing application functionality can be packaged and exposed as a developer-friendly interface. The Feed Factory pattern performs a similar task but produces output conforming to either the RSS or Atom standard. This pattern uses the data extraction and data entry core functions to navigate through the pages of interest and collect material to publish.

In traditional RSS/Atom feeds, content is derived from a single source. A mashup-powered feed doesn't have this limitation. The Content Integration pattern discusses how disparate sources can be combined using mashups. The information that underlies the feed can be obtained from any repository supported by the mashup toolset being used. Thus it is theoretically possible to

RSS-enable Web sites, binary files (e.g., spreadsheets), databases, and more. The Filter and Splitter patterns describe additional approaches that can be applied for feed manipulation. Moreover, some mashup products require only minimal technical skills so that even end users are capable of feed-enabling content that they find useful. This is another example of how the technologies of Enterprise 2.0 give consumers the power to craft their own solutions.

Another interesting use of the Feed Factory pattern is to create a syndicated query against an online search engine using particular keywords. Multiple feeds of this type can be combined with the Content Integration pattern and then cleaned up further (e.g., by removing duplicate results) using a Filter implementation.

Related Patterns: Filter, API Enabler, Widget Enabler

Fragility

Feed Factory is technically very similar to the API Enabler pattern. The main difference lies with how the mashup returns information. The reason the Feed Factory pattern receives a slightly higher fragility score relates to how failures with each pattern are detected. An API Enabler implementation usually participates in a larger process (e.g., Competitive Analysis) or is used interactively (e.g., Usability Enhancer). If it fails, the results are immediately obvious. Problems are less noticeable with RSS/Atom feeds even though they are checked periodically. Some feed readers will mistakenly interpret a broken feed as a sign that the source system has no new information. If a bad feed is not brought to the user's attention, some time may pass before the problem is noticed.

Example: *Personalized Notifications of Sales Opportunities*

UniversalFinance (UF) has implemented the sales-lead generation mashup discussed in Chapter 4 under the Infinite Monkeys pattern. Automatically receiving email reports of potential new clients has proved extremely useful but sometimes messages are accidentally ignored or miscategorized as spam. At the same time, UF employees have an internal corporate portal that they use heavily. This portal supports the display of personal RSS feeds—a feature usually used to display news stories related to existing customers. This stream of information helps the relationship managers keep abreast of events that affect their clients. If the sales-lead mashup was enhanced to support RSS, it could be integrated into the RSS portal. This solution would provide a unified dashboard for viewing information related to current and prospective clients.

Because the members of UF's IT department are already familiar with mashups, they decide to apply the technology to this latest challenge. A small amount of business analysis determines that users want to receive "prospect alerts" in any of three ways: email, online report, or corporate portal (RSS). Unfortunately the tools they are using are capable of supporting only one output type per mashup. The solution is straightforward, however: Deliver the data in one format and then apply additional mashups to provide it via the remaining two formats.

A Web-based report is selected as the primary output target. From there it is easily API-enabled to facilitate email alerts (see the Alerter and API Enabler patterns in Chapter 4). It is also used to provide data to a Feed Factory implementation that creates RSS for display within the internal portal.

What further differentiates a feed from basic email is the fact that it can be personalized by the user. An email recipient has no say whatsoever regarding the information received. In contrast, RSS and Atom feeds support input values encoded in their source URL, which allows the output to be constructed based on user-provided criteria. As it happens, support for custom queries was added when the "prospect alert" information was migrated to an online report. The Feed Factory implementation can leverage this feature by creating a feed that accepts incoming arguments. This data is passed to the reporting system and ultimately affects which data is included in the generated RSS. UF associates are now able to display personalized alerts on their client dashboard.

Example: *Market to a Broader Audience*

Skully Partners is a talent-management firm specializing in promoting hot new bands. Its goal is to grow a group's fan base until the band is noticed by a major recording label. Skully collects fees when a band it manages is signed to a recording contract. So far Skully has failed to capitalize on the World Wide Web as part of its promotional campaigns. Although a slick Web site is created for each client, little else is done to drive traffic to it.

Skully believes it can address this problem by RSS-enabling its sites using the Feed Factory pattern. The goal of the feeds is to publish concert schedules so fans can learn about bands' upcoming performances. The process of retrofitting hundreds of existing sites programmatically has been deemed too expensive—which is why mashups are used. The tools are straightforward enough that junior IT resources can quickly add RSS support without writing a single new line of code. To its dismay, however, Skully soon discovers that having a feed by itself doesn't guarantee visitors any more than a Web page. The time spent adding RSS support would seem to have been wasted.

Paul, a summer intern at Skully, makes an interesting observation. He knows that many of the people within the demographic group Skully seeks to attract maintain pages on the popular MySpace and Facebook social networking sites. When they attend a performance and like it, they sometimes write about the event on their personal blogs. Paul wonders if these fans can be leveraged as part of a viral marketing campaign. Then he remembers another Web site—Sprout[11]—that he recently discovered. Sprout is one of a handful of sites[12] that can convert an RSS feed into a widget suitable for use on a MySpace or Face-book page (see Figure 5.3). (This topic will be covered in greater detail when we examine the Widget Enabler pattern in Chapter 7.)

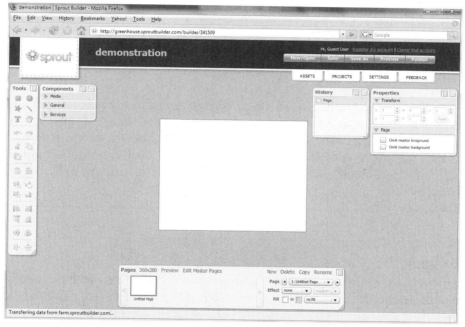

Figure 5.3 *Sites like Sprout allow you to create online components powered by RSS.*

This tool enables Skully Partners to offer widgets that automatically display a band's current tour schedule (see Figure 5.4). Although it's great when sup-porters blog about a performance they like, these entries eventually fade into the past and are forgotten. When a fan includes a widget for a favorite band,

---

11. http://sproutbuilder.com

12. http://widgetbox.com, http://www.springwidgets.com

however, it is regularly updated by the underlying feed. Fresh content tends to command greater attention on people's pages. This stream of new information might inspire visitors to check out future performances and ultimately add the widget to their sites, thereby spreading the publicity even further.

Figure 5.4   *A simple Web calendar is RSS-enabled with the Feed Factory pattern. This feed is then used to create a widget suitable for MySpace or Facebook using a third-party resource (http://www.sproutbuilder.com).*

Paul has not only discovered a new marketing channel, but has also vindicated the decision to create the feeds in the first place. This example demonstrates another use of the Feed Factory pattern: RSS/Atom content can be used as the basis for several types of widgets. The Widget Enabler pattern examines additional techniques that don't rely on RSS to make mashups and widgets work together.

Example: *Receive Alerts When Important Files Are Modified*

Applying the Alerter and Feed Factory patterns to binary file types allows unique new feeds to be created. For example, it is possible to receive automatic updates based on changes made to one or more spreadsheets. Documents posted to Web sites, placed on content management systems, and stored on network-accessible locations are eligible for monitoring using this technique. See the "Mashing Up Binary Types" section in Chapter 10 for further information.

Field Medic

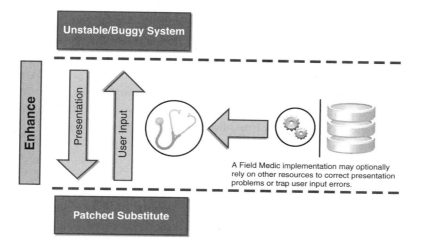

A Field Medic implementation may optionally rely on other resources to correct presentation problems or trap user input errors.

Core Activities: Data extraction, data entry, clipping, data transformation, action

Problem

It's an unfortunate state of affairs when software that isn't properly tested reaches the hands of end users. Delivering bug-free products is every developer's goal—but the complexity, schedule, and resources associated with a project are all too often at opposition with this desire. Sometimes a product is shipped with known issues already documented and scheduled for correction in a forthcoming release. At other times problems are not discovered until they are triggered by unsuspecting clients.

Once software is released "in the wild," limitations of the interface that prevent usage by certain users or devices can be corrected with the Accessibility pattern. Flaws of *design* (rather than construction) that decrease productivity are the concern of the Usability Enhancer pattern.

Certain issues are minor annoyances that can be suffered until the next version. Sometimes, however, software ships with a "showstopper"—a problem that prevents the application from working correctly under certain circumstances. When a critical bug is discovered in an essential system, the proper course of action is to fix the error and release a patch. In some cases this may not be possible. For example, if a flaw is discovered in a third-party software product, the client must wait until a patch is issued by the vendor. This presents two unappealing choices: (1) remove the system from production until the patch is issued or (2) leave the system in production with the bug waiting to be triggered.

Solution

If a problem is caused by user activity, the Field Medic pattern can be used to temporarily add checks to capture undesired input. A duplicate of the existing interface that acts as a facade to the existing system is created. A facade is a wrapper or shell that hides an existing system behind an alternative presentation. Data presented by the "real" application is harvested and presented on the facade. Any input the facade collects is fed back to the underlying program.

Traditionally, a facade's interface differs from the original product in that it attempts to reduce complexity. When the Field Medic pattern is applied, cosmetic differences are strictly avoided. The goal is to replicate the user's existing experience but without the bugs. If a bug is data entry based, then the new "application" is supplemented with additional code to trap error conditions before they reach the underlying system via the data entry function. The invalid input can then be corrected, discarded, or sent back to the user for changes. Presentation-based errors can be fixed after the data extraction activities are complete but before incorrect information is shown to the user. The temporary interface may be removed after the underlying software is patched.

Related Patterns: Accessibility, Usability Enhancer

Fragility

Field Medic has the highest possible fragility score. Like its battlefield counterpart, it should be deployed only in circumstances of utmost importance. Why is its fragility score so high? This pattern is used to correct problems with a system that is known to have bugs or be unstable, and these conditions can affect the reliability of the mashup. In addition, it is typically necessary to create a facade around the original system's *entire interface* (as described in the example, "Fix a Bad User Interface"). A sophisticated application can require numerous mashups, every one of which is a potential point of failure.

Example: *Fix a Bad User Interface*

The accounting office of Eaton and Eaton (E&E) depends on a document management system called Vindaloo to keep track of its clients' financial filings. The system is highly customized to meet the needs of financial planners. Vindaloo's vendor, ToffeeTech, is slow to offer new releases and bug fixes. The latest release of Vindaloo is crucial to E&E's business. It contains updated tax calculations and generates new reports required by the government. Unfortunately it contains some user interface changes that ToffeeTech programmers thought would be useful but are creating problems for E&E staff.

The most annoying "feature" ToffeeTech added was a new Delete button placed right next to the Save button on the Client Information screen (see Figure 5.5). The developers also added keyboard shortcuts: Alt-S can be used to save the current record; Alt-D can be used to delete the current record. The proximity of the "S" and "D" keys on the keyboard has led to a number of accidents—so many that E&E employees have been warned not to use the shortcuts. Users could still accidentally click the Delete button. E&E employees noticed another wonderful shortcoming of the latest Vindaloo release: The confirmation dialog no longer appears when the user removes customer information. One accidental click and the record is gone forever.

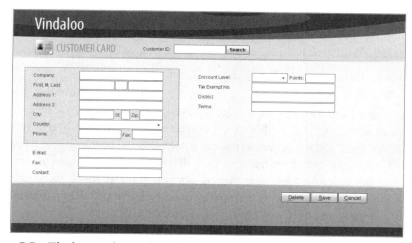

Figure 5.5   *The latest release of Vindaloo places the Save and Delete buttons dangerously close together and adds clumsy keyboard shortcuts.*

Figure 5.6 shows the new interface that corrects the button proximity issue and adds a new dialog to prevent unintended record deletion. The Alt-D "delete shortcut" is ignored by the Field Medic implementation.

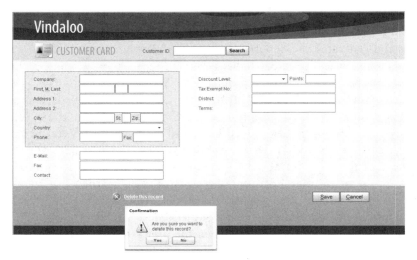

Figure 5.6   *A Field Medic implementation separates the Save and Delete buttons and adds a Delete Confirmation dialog.*

Example: *Eliminate Bugs That Ship with Commercial Software*

Barkley Heating and Plumbing is a regional distributor of plumbing, heating, and cooling equipment for the residential construction industry. The company has a complicated workflow that involves receiving orders for different job sites, aggregating those orders across suppliers to achieve the best possible price, and then optimizing shipping charges so that deliveries are made to customers as quickly as possible. Barkley's purchasing system, WhiteRush, connects directly to the inventory and routing systems used by its suppliers. Without WhiteRush, Barkley's employees could not perform their jobs efficiently.

It is not uncommon for Barkley's customers to be in the process of building multiple homes at various construction sites simultaneously. It is also an unfortunate occurrence that sometimes clients accidentally mix up delivery locations and request supplies to be sent to the wrong address. In the past, most mistakes could be corrected quickly. Making a change in WhiteRush immediately updated the routing information at the manufacturer. Unfortunately a recent new release of the software has introduced a critical bug. If an order is changed and resubmitted and the "Reason for Change" field is not completed, the update will not be sent to the supplier. Even worse, the WhiteRush system reports the order has been successfully changed and will not allow further edits to be made until the order is acknowledged on the manufacturer's side.

This behavior puts the order in a state of limbo: It won't be sent to the distributor until it is corrected, but it can't be corrected because the system believes it has already been sent. Barkley employees can reenter the order from scratch, but that places the order at the end of the queue and leads to delays—and unhappy customers.

Barkley cannot wait until the vendor responsible for WhiteRush issues a patch, so the company's personnel have decided to fix the issue themselves with a simple Field Medic solution. Because the problem affects only orders that already exist and just need to be changed, the IT staff will not have to duplicate the entire WhiteRush interface. Instead they can create a small new mashup that will be used in only in those situations where an order's destination details need to be modified.

The new interface provides fields for locating an order by customer ID or order number. The underlying mechanism uses the WhiteRush search functionality to retrieve the details. Once the original record is found, the Field Medic implementation displays a new screen for entering both the new address and the crucial "Reason for Change" field. When users click "Save," new code verifies that the Reason field has been populated. If not, the user receives an error message and must correct the input before continuing.

Once valid information has been supplied, the updated order details are sent to the WhiteRush system and the bug is avoided. What is unique about this example is that only a portion of the existing interface was replicated. This approach not only corrects a system defect, but also leads to increased usability. Barkley employees not familiar with the highly complicated WhiteRush system find the simple new method for changing order details more approachable.

Example: *Correct Calculation Errors on Reports Without Changing the Code*

Sometimes one mashup solution evolves into another out of necessity. Such was the case at Leslie Apparel. The firm has several systems for managing customer orders, scheduling regular deliveries, and tracking shipments. A third-party application, GarmentTrak, processes customer invoices. GarmentTrak contains an internal Web server that produces client-facing reports. The internal developers used a Content Aggregation mashup and Clipping (see core functionality: clipping) to capture these reports and expose them on a customer-facing portal.

Unfortunately the latest release of GarmentTrak produces reports that contain a nasty bug. Sales tax is incorrectly computed using the customer's billing address instead of delivery address. Two other patterns offer possible solutions:

- The purchasing system and customer database could be the target of API Enabler patterns that supply data to a separate reporting suite. Once the data was extracted, Leslie's internal development team would use additional tools to build a corrected report from scratch. The portal would need to be changed to integrate this new data. This would not be minor work and the revised report would most likely be jettisoned as soon as the next release of GarmentTrak became available.

- A Field Medic implementation could grab the existing flawed report and manipulate it directly by applying the clipping and transformation core functions. The inaccurate columns would either be stripped or replaced with correctly calculated values (which might still require API-enabling existing systems). The portal would be modified to point to the mashup instead of GarmentTrak to supply the report. This approach requires the lesser work of the two approaches.

This example demonstrates that Field Medic implementations are not limited to correcting usability or processing issues. Incorrect output can be processed and fixed before it leads to further problems.

Folksonomy Enabler

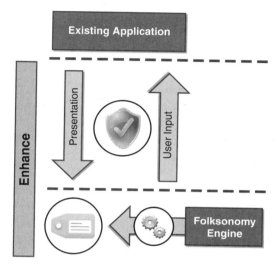

Core Activities: Clipping

Problem

Folksonomies have become a mainstay of the modern Web. With this organizational tool, content is associated with a particular name or label by multiple users, and labels are then aggregated together to create an ad hoc system of classification. The term *folksonomy* is a combination of the words *folk* (referring to the community aspect) and *taxonomy* (referring to classification). Folksonomies (also known as social tagging) are often visualized as a tag cloud—that is, a display of specific tag keywords in which their relative sizes are controlled by the frequency of their occurrence.

The practice of associating additional descriptive details (metadata) with existing sources is not new. Many systems already provide a controlled vocabulary from which users can choose particular keywords. What makes social tagging special is that it breaks through the narrowness of this approach and allows the wisdom of crowds to emerge. How often have you filled out a survey and chosen answers that were "close enough" because the options provided weren't suitable? Social tagging not only lets you provide your own input, but also lets you see which choices others have added and piggyback on their answers.

Most enterprise-class applications were not designed with this concept in mind. The assumption has historically been that if users are not presented with a finite set of selections, then the quality of information they contribute will vary widely. Although there is some truth to this assumption, it fails to consider the dilution of value that occurs when inaccurate labels are chosen from a fixed set that is incomplete or inadequate.

Systems that lack any sort of existing categorization rules might potentially benefit the most from applying folksonomy capabilities. Search tools will get you only so far when you are trying to navigate through unstructured content; their syntactic analysis barely begins to approximate the human mind's capacity for analyzing and summarizing information. Furthermore, most search products are limited to indexing textual resources. By contrast, tagging can be applied to documents, pictures, music, videos, and other artifacts.

Another benefit of tags is that they can supply supplemental information outside the context of the items to which they are attached. A jewelry store's inventory database likely contains the type and size of stone, metal purity, and a fixed category for the jewelry type (e.g., necklace, bracelet, earrings). If tagging features were available, salespeople who notice particular customer purchasing habits might tag specific items with labels such as "anniversary," "wedding," or "Sweet Sixteen." Not only would this data help streamline future in-store sales, but if the firm decided to create an online presence it would bring the benefits of an in-person consultation to the otherwise impersonal Web site.

Solution

It might be tempting to view tags as simply another user-specified field akin to "comment" or "notes" sections. Taking this overly simplified approach inevitably leads to problems. Collecting tags in this manner—with users unaware of each others' contributions—leads to only random or coincidental agreement on specific words. Once the size of a tag vocabulary grows too varied or loses relevancy, then its value is lost. It's insufficient to merely "collect" tags: Tagging behavior must be *managed* to reduce any potential messiness. In *Tagging: People-Powered Metadata for the Social Web*,[13] author Gene Smith suggests the following techniques:

- As a user types a tag, scan through the existing vocabulary to suggest appropriate words (also known as auto-completion).

---

13. Smith, Gene. *Tagging: People-Powered Metadata for the Social Web*. New Riders, December 2007.

- Establish conventions for tags such as using the singular form of a word instead of the plural.

- Connect synonyms inside the tag repository.

- Programmatically search for tag patterns around popular words and cluster the results together.

Associating tags with their contributors can prevent a small but "vocal" tagging minority from overwhelming the system with their particular vernacular. The contributions of some users may be weighted to counteract any counterproductive behavior.

Given these challenges as well as additional reporting or monitoring that may be desired, it is impractical to suggest a firm implement folksonomy features from scratch. A variety of open-source and commercial products already offer many of these features along with open APIs. The easiest way to incorporate social tagging features into an existing application is to inject one of these offerings into the system's user interface via the Usability Enhancer pattern (described later in this chapter).

Related Patterns: Field Medic, Usability Enhancer

Fragility

Due to its reliance on the Usability Enhancer pattern, Folksonomy Enabler receives an identical fragility score. The risks inherent in social tagging itself are actually relatively low owing to the recommendation that a third-party engine be used to power this feature. If a closed tagging product is API-enabled and bound to an existing system, then this step logically adds another potential point of failure.

This pattern describes adding tags to a system that was not originally designed to support them. Thus an obvious question to ask is, "How do tags know to which items they belong?" To associate tags with existing records it is necessary to extract some type of identifier from the source system's interface to serve as a unique key. If the application already has a field such as Order ID or Customer Number, the process is easy (and more reliable). If there is no obvious identification code, one must be created by combining whatever other values are available. For example, a customer's last name and phone number should form a unique combination; alternatively, a product's model number plus the manufacturer's name could be used. Because these "artificial" keys are not maintained by the source system they can potentially change, which would orphan any associated tags.

Example: *Supplement Inventory Data with Salesperson Knowledge*

Layers of paint that provide specific protective properties are known as "industrial coatings." These coatings can add a variety of industrial and consumer benefits to the paint:

- Fire resistance (building materials)

- Nonstick surfaces (cookware)

- Weather protection (outdoor furniture)

- Corrosion resistance (car undercarriages, fasteners)

- Friction reduction (fuel efficiency)

Splatter and Spray, Ltd. (Splat) produces a variety of industrial coatings that it both resells to third parties and applies directly in its on-site facility. Some products are air-dried; others must be baked on. Historically Splat's salespeople have taken a long time to acquire new customers. While they are experts on the properties of their chemicals, sales personnel need extra time to learn enough about their clients' products to recommend the best treatments. Conversely, customers know their products very well but may have trouble articulating the specific protections they hope to achieve via industrial coatings.

This situation is not unsolvable but it does waste valuable time, because Splat's sales staff must learn all about a new industry with each potential client they contact. An internal product database details the specific properties of the various coatings available but not how customers are currently using them. Some sales agents keep supplemental notes on this topic for themselves but they rarely share this information with other staff members because there is no convenient method for doing so.

Splat decides to capture the distributed knowledge of its salespeople by adding simple tagging capabilities to its product database. Staff members are encouraged to add multiple tags pertaining to the real-world applications of Splat's coatings. Tag clouds created from this information give salespeople visibility into this data, which in turn gives them a head start when visiting clients. For example, when meeting with a firm that makes kitchen supplies, the salesperson can quickly see which coatings are being used by other customers in the same industry.

Example: *Leveraging Crowdsourcing to Cross-sell Products*

Adding tagging to a customer-facing site can yield a variety of benefits to the consumer and ultimately to the site's owner. For retail sites, tags allow visitors to organize groups of otherwise unrelated merchandise into collections using specific keywords.

To understand how this ability can be useful, consider an online camping-supply store. Groundhog Gear sells a large collection of gear meant for a variety of locations and conditions. Because the company's customers generally make purchases in preparation for specific trips, item selection is closely related to the planned activity. A customer planning a climbing adventure might buy a lightweight stove and goose-down sleeping bag, whereas a family planning a weekend getaway might purchase a small grill, cast-iron cookware, and inflatable air mattresses.

In their retail store, Groundhog salespeople notice that customers' interactions frequently start with questions about a specific trip rather than about particular products. Groundhog reasons that customers on its website have similar issues that go unanswered and lead to lost sales. Appreciating the camaraderie among its clientele, Groundhog believes that if it adds a publicly searchable tagging mechanism to its online presence, it can apply the benefits of crowdsourcing to trip planning. Many customers will voluntarily tag their shopping carts' contents to share with their fellow adventurers. Customers could also use tags to mark items for "wish lists," track their cumulative purchases, and categorize gear expenses relative to specific treks.

The store can use this folksonomy to let Web shoppers explore recommended items based on destination, usage conditions, or customer rating. Even walk-in customers at the retail location can mine the wisdom of the much larger online community.

Fragility Reducer

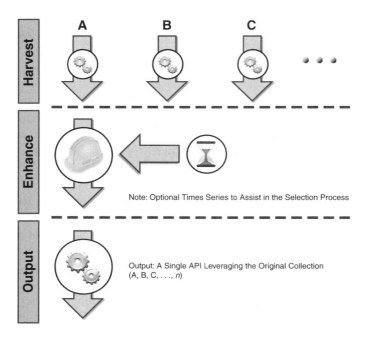

Core Activities: Data entry, data extraction, transformation

Also Known As: Load Balancer

Problem

Mashups are at risk of breaking when unanticipated changes are made to the systems they connect. This drawback is inherent in the technology and explains why each pattern presented in this book is accompanied by a fragility rating. Of course, the real risk of these potential outages must be weighed against the benefits that the mashup provides. So long as the business value of a mashup exceeds the cost and other effects of any downtime, it should not be eliminated from consideration as a possible means to achieve a solution.

Practically speaking, the more control a development team has over the resources involved in a project, the easier it is to coordinate any changes across systems or environments and avoid interruptions in service. This basic premise holds for traditional development approaches as well as mashups. Mashups often leverage resources outside the direct control of a team, department, or organization, however. Seasoned IT staff have lived with this problem for years and developed disciplined approaches for managing these challenges. As mashups spread beyond the confines of IT, they will inevitably be used by laypeople who lack the knowledge or experience to address issues of limited functionality, stability, or scalability (see the Drinking Seawater, Shadow Integration, and One-Hit Wonder anti-patterns in Chapter 9 for related discussions).

Solution

Users have always created ad hoc solutions without the involvement of IT personnel. These solutions may consist of a set of predefined manual processes, custom macros, or even small applications. If one stops working unexpectedly, the impact is typically compartmentalized to some degree. The inconvenience suffered might even engender some appreciation for the challenges IT departments face in creating stable products. Alas, mashups do not mesh well with such a cavalier approach. By nature, they lend themselves to be used as the foundation of other solutions (see Figure 1.5, which depicts the virtuous circle of mashups, in Chapter 1). Any interruption in service can lead to significant consequential damages—which is why it is crucial to reduce the chances of breakdowns.

The Fragility Reducer pattern addresses this issue by attempting to provide a level of internal redundancy for the most brittle stages of a mashup's operation. Namely, it addresses the touch points where external systems outside the implementer's control might suddenly slow down or become unavailable. With this pattern the preferred approach is to not rely on a single resource when more than one candidate is available. By creating an abstraction layer that surrounds a collection of products yet exposes only a single interface, the following benefits can be achieved:

- *Stability.* When one resource is not available, the mashup switches to the next operational replacement and keeps working uninterrupted. The mashup creator should add appropriate notifications and monitoring around these events as the fragility of the mashup increases when resources drop out.

- *Performance.* Simple load-balancing logic can be used to direct traffic to the resources that provide the quickest response.

- *Accuracy.* Comparing results from multiple sources provides a means for determining the precision of the data.

This approach is similar to the classic Facade pattern,[14] which may be used to wrap a collection of poorly designed APIs under a clean, unified interface. Many of the patterns in this text receive a high fragility score because of their dependency on underlying sources. Placing a Fragility Reducer between these sources and the remainder of the implementation can yield a more stable product.

Fragility

Unfortunately the Fragility Reducer cannot make its own fragility issues disappear completely. Addressing the stability or scalability of other pattern implementations comes at a price. If multiple sources are consulted to find the answer agreed upon by the majority, the possibility exists that individual results will be so varied that no consensus can be achieved. This leaves the mashup creator with the difficult task of implementing some logic to determine which answer to pick. Under such circumstances it may be appropriate to terminate further operations based on these disparities and signal an error condition.

If sources from a larger collection are used individually on a rotating basis according to some internal algorithm, the same inputs might potentially yield different results on subsequent invocations. This problem is discussed in conjunction with the One-Hit Wonder anti-pattern in Chapter 9.

In both of these cases, keeping a time series (see the discussion of the Time Series pattern in Chapter 4) of prior results can be a valuable tool for detecting answers that occurs outside the range of previously observed values.

Example: *Increasing Mashup Reliability and Usefulness*

Measure Twice (MT) is a regional firm employing local tradespeople for general repair and contracting services. Because its IT department is small, the company is very cautious about building internal systems that it is not staffed to adequately support. Its applications are generally purchased from third-party vendors. Recently MT staff discovered that mashups both provide unique solutions to a number of challenges faced by the organization and can be constructed with minimal effort. They have implemented a series of mashup-based solutions using internal and external sources that have quickly become an important part of MT's daily operations:

- To schedule appointments as efficiently as possible, customer addresses and contractor locations are geocoded and correlated according to the

---

14. Gamma et al. *Design Patterns*. 1995.

skills required for a particular job (see the Location Mapping pattern in Chapter 6).

- Contractors receive custom directions to each job site as well as the locations of the nearest home supply centers if they need to pick up any materials (also Location Mapping).

- Weather forecast information is added to each work order (see the Content Aggregation pattern in Chapter 6) so that outdoor jobs such as painting or roof maintenance are planned for when it's dry and indoor work is scheduled for rainy days.

- To allow operators at the main MT office to contact agents for status reports, the Communication and Collaboration pattern (see Chapter 6) is used to link the applications used by MT's dispatchers directly to the firm's email system.

- An implementation of the Smart Suggestions pattern (discussed later in this chapter) compares product energy usage statistics and has been deployed to staff members' laptops. It allows MT personnel to assist customers in deciding whether it makes sense to repair an item or whether replacing the item might yield more long-term savings.

At a recent staff meeting, MT's management highlighted the value of the new products but also voiced some questions. The new offerings had quickly spread throughout the company to become a crucial part of the firm's infrastructure but the size of the IT staff had remained constant. Concerns were raised about the reliability of the products and the ability of IT to address any issues given the limited staff.

IT managers responded to these issues by embarking on a mission to reinforce the existing mashups with backup resources integrated via the Fragility Reducer pattern. For each of the previously described systems, new sources were added to provide greater stability:

- Implementations that use geocoding now use multiple sites for resolving addresses and providing directions. Early feedback had suggested that the maps provided by the existing mashup were sometimes out-of-date or identified a less than optimal route. By applying separate sites to the same problem, not only could the most efficient route be suggested, but alternative directions could be provided in the event of traffic or construction delays.

- Weather forecasts are notoriously inaccurate. At first, pulling in different opinions seemed as if it would merely add to the confusion. MT's staff soon built up a time series database that showed which sites' weather models had the greatest accuracy. This information was invaluable when choosing which forecast to provide to contractors. If one site is temporarily slow or unavailable, the next most accurate one is selected.

- The communications mashup was useful but was hampered by its dependency on a single means of interaction (email). The inclusion of a Web site that sends SMS text messages means that agents can now choose their preferred means of contact.

- The Smart Suggestions mashup that compared product efficiency was a good first step, but it used only a single site for this information and didn't follow up with any cost comparison information. In the new implementation, multiple sites are used to increase reliability, and the data presented to the client include product price, availability, and location.

By shoring up their mashups with additional resources, MT's IT staff were able to provide greater reliability as well as increased performance and flexibility. When an underlying resource drops out unexpectedly, the solutions keep operating while developers investigate the problem.

Example: *Performing Ad Hoc Diagnostics from a Production Environment*

The Fragility Reducer pattern can play an important role in troubleshooting a mashup that suddenly stops working. Not every data source in an implementation needs to be a functional replacement for its peers. It is possible to include logic such that, for a given user or team (such as the mashup's creators), specific test resources will be used instead. These "mock services" mimic the expected behavior of the production resource while simultaneously recording the actions performed by the mashup. This approach provides the investigator with a means to swiftly confirm or disprove the mashup's role in the outage by verifying it against a "known working" source. If the mashup still fails, attention can quickly shift to examining other possible causes, including network maintenance or recent hardware upgrades.

Smart Suggestions

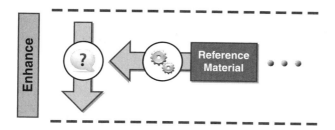

Output from a Smart Suggestions implementation is typically incorporated into an application via custom code. It can be added to existing systems by employing the Usability Enhancer pattern.

Core Activities: Data extraction, data entry, data visualization, transformation, action

Also Known As: Predictive Aiding, Recommendation Engine

Problem

Human–computer interaction (HCI) is the study of how people and programs work together. This field of research is important because software generally isn't "helpful" by nature. Rather than emulate the user's mental model of a task, most applications demand unconditional obedience for getting things done. HCI practitioners typically spend a great deal of time focusing on user interface design rather than user interface *adaptation*. To reach the next level in software usability, an application must be able to predict what the user wants to do and guide the user through the steps needed to accomplish that goal.

The late, unlamented Clippy was a notable early attempt at assistive software. Clippy first debuted with his animated cohorts in Microsoft Office 97. When a user started one of the programs in the Office suite, Clippy automatically appeared alongside the current work area. As the user typed, Clippy would attempt to figure out which task was being performed and offer suggestions for accomplishing it more quickly. For example, if you typed an address into a new Word document, Clippy might ask, "It looks like you're trying to type a letter. Would you like help?" Despite its groundbreaking nature, Clippy was universally reviled by users who despised his distractions and he was eventually removed.

It was almost seven years before the next high-profile "helpful" product debuted. Google Suggest[15] was released in 2004 as an improvement to the basic Google search. Rather than wait for a user to enter the entire query and click the Submit or famous "I'm Feeling Lucky" buttons, Suggest performs incremental background searches with each new keystroke. The results are displayed in a drop-down box underneath the user's input. Google Suggest became so popular that is was ultimately incorporated into the Google home page. This nonobtrusive technique found more friends than Clippy and has since been adopted by many other applications..

More recently Microsoft Office 2007 has made strides in software intuition. Its adaptive Ribbon control replaces traditional pull-down menus and changes its contents depending on actions the user performs. Another addition is the new floating toolbar that unobtrusively fades into view near text that is being manipulated. Many customers initially rejected the new interface, much as a dog will reject a new master even when it's regularly kicked by its current owner. However, after spending time with the suite and getting comfortable with this new approach, most cannot imagine ever switching back.

The HCI field still has a long way to go before the problems of usability and productivity are even partially resolved. Most applications make no attempt to aid the user but simply rely on training and documentation to explain their operation. In addition, users are often overburdened by the requirement to perform multiple actions to accomplish a single goal. The fact that it is now *possible* to perform a task is all too often viewed as synonymous with the work being *uncomplicated*. Sadly that's true only if the end user is willing to conform to the design of the system.

Solution

Software can be smarter, and mashups can help.

Users may think a system that enables them to perform a task is *helpful*—but it isn't. It's *useful*—which is a big difference. A useful application allows the work to be completed, though the user may still have to navigate a maze of irrelevant menus and forms. A helpful system recognizes specific behavior and adapts itself to help the user work as efficiently as possible.

Mashups can serve an important role in directly adding assistive functionality to a program. When a user provides input to a system, mashups can be used behind the scenes to pass this information to other applications and services, whose output is then rolled back into the original interface. An entire cast of supporting players can be pressed into service for each mouse click or keystroke.

---

15. http://www.google.com/webhp?complete=1&hl=en

Related Patterns: Usability Enhancer

Fragility

The key weakness of the Smart Suggestions pattern is not the failure to provide any assistance. Users are (unfortunately) already accustomed to forging ahead without help. The problem occurs when incorrect or irrelevant information is supplied. Technically this is not a failure of mashup technology but the user has a bad experience regardless. It may never be possible to entirely eliminate bad suggestions. Thus the key is to make them nonobtrusive yet still accessible. Failure to adopt this guideline can be partially blamed for the demise of Microsoft's Clippy.

Example: *Tailor Applications to Suit the User's Knowledge*

B9 Pharmaceuticals has decided to implement wikis and blogs as part of a new initiative to increase employee collaboration. Most of the products the company is considering lack key features such as a spelling checker and medical dictionary. It would also be beneficial to somehow include links to the Food and Drug Administration's (FDA) Drug Database[16] for users to reference while they compose messages that mention particular medicines.

B9 ultimately decides on an open-source wiki, which means users will have full access to the source code. It decides to use mashups to add some other features as well. While a user types into a text box, input is regularly passed to a custom module B9 has written. When the user presses the spacebar or a punctuation key, the new code assumes a complete word has just been entered. After a few more checks and basic cleanup, the text is passed through a Smart Suggestions implementation that connects to an online spelling checker, dictionary, and the FDA's Drug Database (as shown in Figure 5.7).

Now when a user is composing a post, he or she instantly sees details about a specific drug whenever the user types its name. Words that aren't located by the spelling checker are automatically highlighted. A small table on the right automatically includes appropriate definitions from the dictionary.

This information was always just a few clicks away, but integrating it more closely within the application has created a more helpful system and improved the quality of communication. Before-and-after screenshots of the system appear in Figure 5.8.

---

16. http://www.accessdata.fda.gov/scripts/cder/drugsatfda

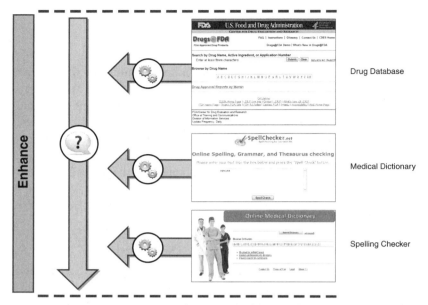

Figure 5.7   *A Smart Suggestions implementation for a medical application. Credit: SpellChecker.net screenshot used by permission*

Figure 5.8   *The existing interface (top) has a simple field for text entry. The new interface (bottom) helps the user by providing useful information.*

Example: *Automatically Pull Supplemental Data into a Sales Presentation*

As part of their regular work, agents at Sinkhole Realty frequently take potential home buyers on a tour of properties they may be interested in purchasing. The home details are usually available on a computerized listing service. Although this system provides many details about the home (e.g., square footage, number of bedrooms and bathrooms), it does not give any information about the surrounding neighborhood.

This supplemental material can have a strong influence on the client. A young couple may be more interested in property located in a highly regarded school district. Elderly buyers may want close proximity to a hospital. Nature lovers are likely to be wooed by access to parks or hiking trails. The realtors know this information is helpful but often can't spend the time researching it for every potential listing.

A Smart Suggestions mashup can address this problem. Incorporated into the system used to schedule appointments, the mashup can use the property location (see the Location Mapping pattern in Chapter 6) to collect relevant data about the area from dozens of online resources. This information is automatically included when the package of listings is created for the client. In addition to focusing on the size, price, or charm of a home, Sinkhole agents are now able to note its proximity to various amenities. Suggested details may also remove some properties from consideration. Armed with these additional facts an agent can let clients know they'll be living next door to a registered felon or near noisy air traffic.

Example: *Suggest Additional Items for Purchase*

Although aesthetic tastes vary from person to person, color theory teaches us that there are models for mathematically determining which colors naturally complement one another. To determine these pairings, we need to organize the range of possible colors into a structure known as a color wheel.[17] When working with visible light, the wheel is organized according to the primary colors red, yellow and blue. A simple color wheel is created by drawing a circle with an equilateral triangle inside, as shown in Figure 5.9. Place the three primary colors at the vertices of the triangle. The remaining spaces are filled in by mixing adjacent colors until the circle has no more available room.

---

17. The color wheel is a simple example. Colors can also be mapped to three-dimensional objects such as a cube.

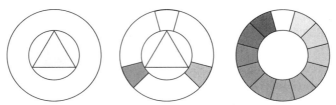

Figure 5.9   *Constructing a simple color wheel*

Given a single color, it's possible to locate its complementary color by selecting the value exactly opposite it on the color wheel. Overlaying an equilateral triangle on the wheel across any three colors creates a triadic palette (Figure 5.10), where the color at each vertex is part of a harmonious set. Other geometric shapes and formulas can be applied to derive other palettes. A complete discussion of color theory is beyond the scope of this text; suffice it to say that given a particular color or set of colors it is possible to calculate a range of color values that are either close matches to the initial value[18] or complementary to it.

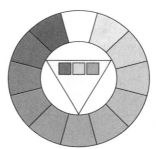

Figure 5.10   *A triadic palette on the color wheel*

Customer-facing applications can apply color theory to drive additional sales. Consider an online clothing retailer that sells products from multiple designers. When a customer adds an item to his or her shopping cart, automatically displaying other items that match the selected item might lead to further purchases on the same order. For example, when a blue dress from a particular designer is selected, displaying coordinating blouses, hats, shoes, and accessories from other lines could persuade the customer to buy additional products.

---

18. Given a point on the color wheel, the closest adjacent values to the left or right are approximately the same color. This correlation diminishes as you move farther away from the starting point.

Where do mashups figure into this discussion? A Smart Suggestions implementation crawls the product catalogs from individual brands. Along with the product prices and descriptions it grabs the *image* of each item. Popular graphic formats such as GIF are easily examined to determine the major colors[19] that make up each picture. The color values, along with the product category (e.g., hat, dress, shoes), are stored in an internal database. When the customer chooses an item, the item's category and major colors are then retrieved and color theory is used to suggest colors that complement the selected article. A query retrieves items from different categories that are a close match.

Because color perception varies from person to person, capturing the purchase frequency of "suggested items" in a Time Series is essential for gauging the appropriateness of recommendations. Algorithms might be automatically tailored to the individual based on prior effectiveness. Current or seasonal weather conditions could be mashed in to influence suggestions.

The same basic idea can be applied to any retail channel where color is a factor. Paint, furniture, window treatments, and makeup are other possibilities for applying this pattern.

---

19. GIF is a run-length encoded (RLE) format that helps with this process. Compressed image formats that approximate color values do not easily lend themselves to this task.

Super Search

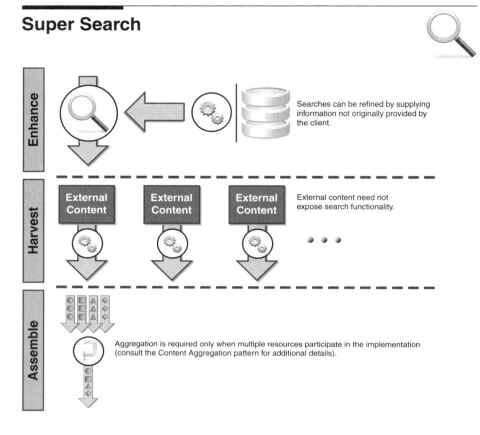

Core Activities: Data extraction, data entry, transformation

Problem

Popular sites such as Google and Yahoo are the Web surfer's first choice when searching for public content on the Internet. Nevertheless, situations frequently arise in which the process for locating data becomes less straightforward:

- You need to search across multiple internal systems, each with its own search capabilities. Results have to be manually aggregated.

- Your firm has adopted multiple SaaS vendors and you need a unified search function that works across all service providers.

- You have access to external services whose search functionality you want to extend or incorporate into internal applications (refer to the coverage of the Smart Suggestions pattern for a discussion of this particular requirement).

- You want to use search criteria that current tools do not support. For example, you want to search for an item by customer rating, but the existing functionality allows you to search only by product category.

- Your existing search product isn't very good at correcting spelling mistakes or automatically including synonyms. You want to add these features.

- You need to search for multiple disparate items simultaneously and bring back a single answer that represents the best hit for the entire set. For example, you have a purchase order for office supplies, and you want to know which vendor has the best price for the majority of items on your list.

You may even want to add search capabilities to an application that doesn't have any. Without access to the original developers or source code, however, this task might seem impossible.

In a world where information is being created at an ever-increasing rate, search capabilities are more important than ever. But we need more than tools that take a simple string of words and scan billions of documents. Search applications need to evolve to accept more complicated forms of input and produce results that are richer than a list of possible matches.

Solution

Generic search products are inherently limited because they serve the broadest possible audience. The Long Tail suggests that the vast majority of specialized search functionality is unmet by current tools.

But searching is not a typical Long Tail problem that can be divided into the "haves" and the "have nots." By definition searching is concerned with locating relevant information. To be effective one must search the entire universe of data that is created by applications at any point on the Long Tail. That does not mean the information from each system is applicable—but if you don't look for it, you'll never know.

Mashup-powered searches may be the key to bringing search functionality to the next level. A mashup can do more than simply unify existing search functionality; it can impose new search features on existing resources. How? As long as an application provides some method to navigate its content—even if it's a simple Next Record button—then a mashup can leverage the Infinite Monkeys pattern to visit every single item. Data extraction and transformation features can be used to extract details along the way. The entire process can be exposed as a callable service or even a regular feed based on predefined criteria (see the discussion of the Feed Factory pattern earlier in this chapter).

IT can use the Super Search pattern to do more than just enhance existing systems and processes. To achieve the real promise of this pattern, it should be implemented in a manner that makes it extendable by anyone. The results are revolutionary when end users are given the ability to create, combine, and chain[20] search tools that accept and produce highly specialized data. These new services can easily surpass the benefits offered by their constituent parts.

The usefulness of these implementations may impress users so much that they view the mashups as applications in their own right. In reality, all the interface does from a processing perspective is collect search criteria and display the results. It's not even necessary to perform any data validation at this layer because the underlying sites will automatically reject any invalid input (such as a start date that occurs after an end date). A collection of predefined APIs (to get results) and widgets (to display them) put the tools to create Super Searches directly into the hands of users.

Related Patterns: API Enabler, Infinite Monkeys, Smart Suggestions

Fragility

A Super Search implementation commonly includes interactions between multiple systems. As previously discussed, the more systems involved in a mashup, the greater the chance for potential failure. This outcome can occur when a site is radically redesigned or just temporarily offline. Implementations that crawl a single site to locate information that is not natively searchable (such as specific product details) are generally more reliable.

Example: *Find the Best . . .*

Dorothy is the office manager and an executive assistant at a law partnership. She wears many hats at the firm. She is responsible for booking corporate functions, arranging the travel schedules of the senior partners, and keeping the supply cabinets stacked with sundries such as pads, pens, ink, and toner. Once Dorothy was even asked to buy the top-of-the line microwave for the corporate cafeteria.

It seems that no matter what job she's performing at the moment, the mantra is consistent: "Find the best." Sometimes that means arranging for reservations at the best restaurant, purchasing tickets for the most popular show, and book-

---

20. In *chaining,* the results of one search are automatically sent as a query to a different search product.

ing a night at the finest hotel in a city she's never visited. When one of her firm's partners is involved, cost isn't a consideration. But "the best" means something else when Dorothy orders office supplies—the best price. She orders dozens of items at a time and can't spare the time to find the lowest price on everything.

Dorothy's professional life seems perpetually caught up with searching. The online travel agencies that offer preplanned packages are of little use because none combines travel, entertainment, and dining. Price comparison Web sites aren't of much assistance when you need to compare a hundred items at a time. Dorothy and her staff waste a large portion of their time jumping from one search site to another to collect the information she needs. When Dorothy shares her troubles with one of the developers in IT over lunch one day, he explains how a Super Search mashup can help.

Competition in specific industries has led to the emergence of many niche price or product comparison sites. It's now easy to find the best prices on airline flights and hotel accommodations from a single service. Likewise, it's possible to find recommended restaurants and Broadway shows from separate sources. A Super Search mashup can be constructed to unite each of these resources behind a single simple interface such as the one shown in Figure 5.11. When the user clicks the Plan it! button, a myriad of individual sites (travel agencies, restaurant guides, theater reviews, car rental agencies) are queried by the mashup and their results combined to create a comprehensive travel plan (Figure 5.12). Mashups could even be used to complete online bookings and reservations for the custom-built packages.

Figure 5.11 *A Super Search implementation capable of planning a complete trip*

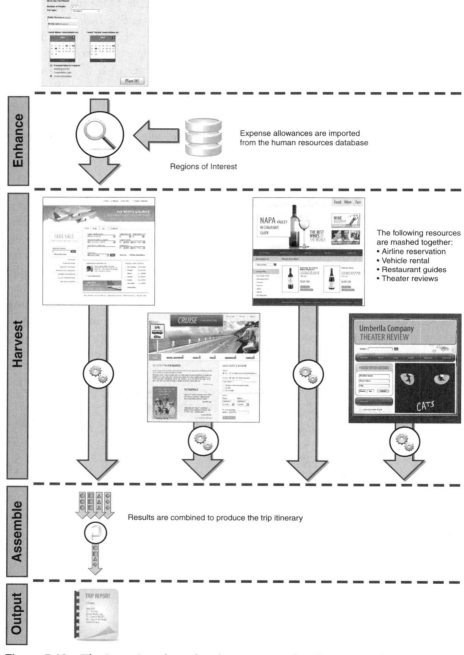

Figure 5.12   *The Super Search mashup leverages travel and recommendation sites to produce the itinerary.*

For those occasional times when Dorothy needs to purchase highly rated hardware or appliances, a Super Search mashup is also the answer. Consider the example where Dorothy needed to purchase a microwave. After a Super Search mashup is provided with the product category, it can visit the online sites of major retailers and obtain a list of the appropriate items. If customer feedback ratings are available from those sites, the mashup can examine which brand scored the highest. This data can be aggregated across multiple sellers and used to determine a clear winner.

The next step is to provide this data to a price comparison service. Dorothy has used these services in the past and noticed a major flaw. The vendor that has the lowest price usually has the highest shipping charges. She usually winds up visiting half a dozen sites before she finds the best *final* price. A mashup can handle this work as well. Armed with Dorothy's shipping address, it can pursue an order all the way up to checkout to determine the final cost. It can even search for online rebates that can save Dorothy additional money.

It's easy to find the best price on office supply orders, too. The trick is to give the entire order to a mashup and then let it place every item into online shopping carts at different suppliers. The mashup never completes the purchase; it just sends the lowest total price back to Dorothy. She can have one of her assistants place the real order later. This technique for determining the best price doesn't demonstrate the way most people envision a search, but it certainly provides Dorothy with the answer she needs.

▼

Example: *Create a Unified Search Across Multiple SaaS Products*

Software as a service (SaaS) has become an attractive method for companies to access business applications without the headaches of managing an IT department. The cost of licensing, desktop support, and on-site development can be greatly reduced by effectively "renting" software over the Internet. From the solution provider's perspective, the size of the market is enormous because anyone with a Web browser is a potential customer. The resulting economies of scale allow vendors to offer their services at bargain-basement prices.

Affordability and ease of use have hastened the adoption of SaaS at many organizations. But this situation has not been without its problems. When a firm outsources business functionality to multiple sites, it effectively fragments its most valuable asset: information. Reassembling this data can dilute the cost savings that prompted the switch to SaaS in the first place!

Consider the problem when Vendor A's application maintains an organization's customer records, Vendor B manages its technical support tickets, and

Vendor C manages its account contacts database. If all of these systems were managed internally or by a single vendor, it would be possible to quickly determine how the time spent consulting with a customer affects the frequency of calls to the technical support hotline.

SaaS providers typically incorporate search functionality into their own products—but this does nothing to alleviate the painful manual processing that's required to correlate results from different sites. A Super Search, by contrast, can address the lack of integration between Vendors A, B, and C. A single input field is provided to capture the customer ID and pass it to a mashup that will query each site individually. The results are then presented in a single comprehensive report.

This pattern should dispel any concerns about using multiple SaaS providers—at least from a data consolidation point of view. Other potential SaaS issues such as accessibility, usability, and workflow are addressed by their namesake patterns.

Translation

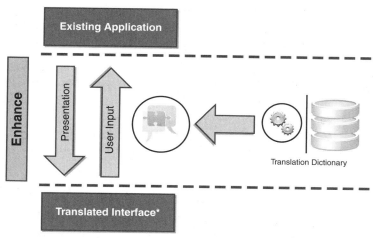

* Translation can occur in either or both directions (system to user, or user to system).

Core Activities: Data extraction, data visualization, transformation

Also Known As: Language Converter

Problem

The "World" in "World Wide Web" underscores the fact that online interaction is a global phenomenon. Yet many products of the information age remain confined to users in specific regions or of specific nationalities because they are isolated by the languages of their creators. People shy away from that which they cannot easily understand. A foreign language represents the ultimate user-unfriendly experience. When *citizens* receive information only from biased local sources, it can lead to unintentional nationalism or intolerance. When *employees* are isolated by language, it can affect both their productivity and their firm's local reputation.

A global corporation may handle the challenge of multilingual communication in several ways:

- *Do nothing.* Mandate that each employee be fluent in a standard language as well as his or her local tongue. This approach has the lowest impact on a firm's infrastructure but has severe consequences elsewhere. Valuable potential employees and customers may be overlooked because they are not bilingual. Non-native speakers are more apt to inadvertently supply incorrect data because they do not fully understand the systems they are using.

- *Support multiple interfaces.* Create a separate translation for each system that will be instantly familiar to each local audience. For simple applications (such as a bank ATM) this is a reasonable approach. However, more complicated systems present a more challenging task.

- *Provide for limited translation.* If many local dialects exist, then application release schedules may be affected by the time required to translate new phrases. When employees speak a variety of languages (the Long Tail appears again!), those users who share the most prevalent tongue will receive a custom interface and the remainder will face the bilingual requirement.

Internationalization and *localization*[21] are terms used to define the disciplines necessary to expose systems to a larger audience. Internationalization is the act of preparing an application to be customized for a different region. Localization is the process of applying region-specific translations to the program after it has been prepared to accept them.

Localization isn't restricted to language. Different countries use different formats for dates, currencies, punctuation, and more, even when they speak the same language! Two great challenges arise in supporting a multinational application. The first is obtaining a native's understanding of the local language and culture. The second is making the necessary application changes to apply this research.

Solution

The Translation pattern describes a lightweight technique for both enabling internationalization and performing dynamic localization. Two methods for using mashups may be applied to extend an application to a new audience:

- *Construct a new interface per language.* Adding internationalization features to an existing product typically requires the expertise of the original development team. Third-party products are enhanced at the discretion of the vendor. With mashups, however, a new lightweight interface can be constructed. It contains a dictionary for mapping user input and system responses against a pre-translated list of phrases and values. This new layer also transforms data and numeric formats across cultural equivalents. As with many mashup solutions this approach can be handled by a team separate from the initial developers.

---

21. Often referred to as i18n and L10n as a means of shorthand.

- *Use on-the-fly translation.* Language translation services are freely available[22] on the Internet; impressive commercial products are available for purchase as well. The accuracy of machine translation ranges from 50% to 85% depending on the languages and subject involved. If a system has already been internationalized, then a mashup can use a machine translation product behind the scenes. Once the user indicates a language preference, an "instantaneously localized" application is generated. For a nonlocalized system, a temporary facade can be created (as demonstrated earlier in this chapter by the Field Medic pattern) that provides the alternative interface and incorporates the translation functionality. The (obvious risks) in exposing a system with less than perfect accuracy are determined by the complexity of the user's interaction. Simple systems (such as the aforementioned ATM) are dynamically translated more accurately than complex ones. Care should be exercised when applying this method.

The Translation pattern can be paired with many other patterns to extend their usefulness beyond a single language. For example, Alerter, Competitive Analysis, and Reputation Management are good candidates for partnering with a Translation implementation.

Related Patterns: Accessibility, Field Medic, Usability Enhancer

Fragility

The Translation pattern utilizes the techniques underlying the Usability Enhancer and Field Medic patterns. As a consequence, it is susceptible to the same potential problems and likewise deserves the highest fragility rating. Translation uses additional mashups to dynamically access language translation resources. Should these services provide unacceptable or provide confusing data, a firm faces potential risk to its reputation. The Translation pattern is best suited for tactical internal solutions where a quick solution is required and quirky grammar will not create public embarrassment for the company.

▼―――――――――――――――――――――――――――――――――――――

Example: *Quick Localization of Applications*

Hasty Transport (HT) is a shipping and packaging firm with central facilities located across Europe and North America. As part of its efforts to expand into the Asian marketplace, the company has identified Kyoto, Japan, as the loca-

―――――――――――――

22. One example is the Google AJAX Language API available at http://code.google.com/apis/ajaxlanguage

tion for its first hub in Asia. HT has a number of systems for managing tasks such as tracking packages, scheduling vehicle maintenance, tracking employee time, and monitoring expenditures. As part of HT's expansion across Europe many of these systems are localization-ready. Because the company wants to enter the new territory rapidly, not every system will be able to receive a proper translation before Asia operations commence.

HT has decided that the bulk of translation resources will be allocated to business-critical systems such as package tracking and vehicle maintenance. The remaining language issues will be handled by a combination of Translation mashups and the hiring of additional bilingual staff. For systems that already have multiple localized vocabularies, some basic analysis will be performed to see which language yields the best translation to Japanese. This grammar will be used to dynamically build a localized dictionary using an API-enabled resource.

Handling applications that have not been localized requires slightly more effort. Most of these systems were created when HT strictly did business in the United Kingdom so their interfaces are English based. Field Medic mashups skin the interface from the underlying application. Translation mashups are used to convert field labels, buttons, online help, error messages, and other text to their local equivalents. A modicum of coding is required to translate different date and currency formats when required. The new interface is slightly rearranged to accommodate translations whose length exceeds the original English.

To aid the nonlocal Help Desk support personnel who are initially supporting the Kyoto office, HT implements a Translation mashup around its internal instant messaging platform. This allows non-English-speaking employees to converse in real-time with their U.K. counterparts regarding simple issues.

With the aid of local support personnel in Japan, HT is able to dynamically refine its translation dictionary; this effort results in progressively more useful applications. The dictionary data will give IT personnel a headstart in preparing for the day when resources are available for a proper localization effort.

Example: *Clarify Search Queries for Better Results*

Today more than two thirds (and growing) of Internet users originate from non-English-speaking countries.[23] Clearly it would be foolish to limit information searches to a particular grammar. Although some search engines already return results across multiple languages, unless the original query undergoes translation the quality of results is likely to be low. Pre-translating a search

---

23. Source: http://www.internetworldstats.com

string to a different language can have profound effects in improving these results. For example, a French user's search on "*devise*" ("currency") will probably not meet the user's expectations when passed to a multilingual search engine, owing to the different definitions the word has across multiple languages. By contrast, a pre-translation to "currency" can yield more appropriate results.

Why limit the context of this discussion to culture-specific examples? The field of technology is notorious for redefining words for its own purposes. *Mashups* is an obvious example. *Ubuntu* is another: This term refers to both a popular Linux distribution and African philosophical thinking (its original use).

A Translation mashup can add clarity to a search so that more usable results are obtained. When an unprocessed query having multiple meanings is provided to a search engine, the site must guess what the user intended. More often than not this leads to mixed or inaccurate hits. Consider the Google results for a query on "mashups" presented in Figure 5.13. Then consider how the results are clarified by adding either the term "music" or "web" as shown in Figure 5.14.

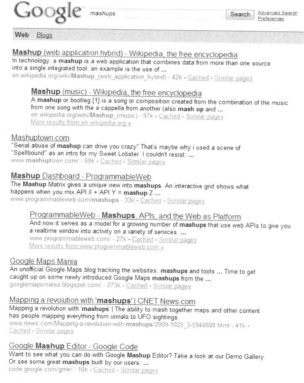

Figure 5.13 *A Google search on "mashups" yields mixed results.*

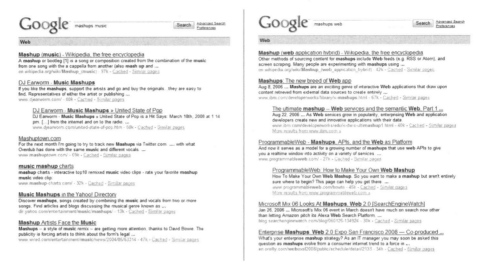

Figure 5.14 *Adding simple information we already possess can yield better search results.*

We know more about ourselves than we tell a search engine but we typically don't take the time to provide this information. There is only so much analysis that sites like Google and Yahoo can perform to guess what we want to see based on the handful of words that we provide to them. Future advances in searching will most likely come from user-specific clues that have nothing to do with the original query.

For example, a firm that builds an internal search product may want to use mashups to examine an employee's job code on the corporate organizational chart. This information would be used to clarify search queries by adding more details. If a trader at a financial firm specifies the text "options price," for example, his query may receive no special processing. But if a developer performs the same operation, the text "Java" or "C#" might be automatically appended to the search term. The results will be remarkably different. As another example, an appliance manufacturer that indexes its suppliers' Web sites could leverage a Translation mashup to transparently clarify queries for "green products" as relating to energy efficiency and not color.

Usability Enhancer

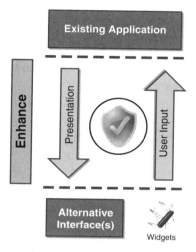

Core Activities: Data extraction, data entry, transformation

Problem

Software developers define usability as the measurement of how easy it is to use an application to complete a particular task. It's amusing and ironic that the term itself is largely unknown to end users—but that doesn't mean it isn't important to them. A customer or client readily provides feedback on a bad usability experience in a number of ways:

- Vocal complaints about how hard a product is to use

- Frequent calls to a technical support hotline

- Avoiding work that involves a complicated application

- Switching to a competitor's product

How did we get into this mess? Most software developers concentrate too much on the technical aspects of their profession and don't develop a good appreciation for the user's point of view.

Other factors come into play, of course. A vendor that is creating a product used by thousands of clients is unable to accommodate the desires of every customer. As Bill Cosby famously said, "I don't know the key to success, but the key to failure is trying to please everybody." In yet another manifestation of the Long Tail, application designers may focus on the usability of more popular features even if it means making sacrifices in other areas.

Internal development teams are frequently challenged by aggressive schedules and lack of resources. Under these circumstances the rallying cry is often "Solve the business problem first!" Usability takes a back-seat to the delivery of a working solution. Unfortunately, once the pressing deadlines have been met, the subject is rarely revisited. Just because users desperately need a product shouldn't mean they have to crawl over broken glass to use it.

Countless books, blogs, and articles have been written on the issue of usability. Entire businesses have sprung up to help you create a more pleasant application experience for users. Although they are certainly valuable, these resources all impose a giant precondition before they can be of any help: *You must have access to the original development team or source code.* For internal projects this is frequently impractical; for vendor products it is all but impossible.

Solution

The Usability Professionals Association (UPA) cites the following business benefits that are achieved when usability is addressed:[24]

- Increased productivity

- Decreased training and support costs

- Increased sales and revenues

- Reduced development time and costs

- Reduced maintenance costs

- Increased customer satisfaction

Given a system with a complicated interface, a mashup "wrapper" (or facade) can be constructed to tackle usability issues. Because the mashup will handle the communication between the existing system and the new interface, no remediation of the original application is required. Potential applications of this pattern to increase ease of use include the following examples:

- Change the data-entry order of fields so it matches the user's workflow

- Rename labels and other text to reflect an organization's particular vernacular

---

24. http://www.upassoc.org/usability_resources/usability_in_the_real_world/
    benefits_of_usability.html

- Add validations to prevent common mistakes (see the Field Medic pattern)

- Hide unnecessary features that merely cause confusion

- Automatically apply commonly used values and settings

- Expose a multistep process as a single task or, conversely, break a complicated process into smaller pieces

- Add corporate branding, change screen colors, and employ other design-oriented measures to repackage a set of disparate applications as a unified suite

- Accept additional input formats (e.g., Jan 15, 2008; 01/15/08; 15/01/08; 1/15/2008) and automatically translate them to a format the underlying application will recognize (see the Transformation and Enrichment core ability discussed in Chapter 3)

This pattern can be combined with other patterns (Smart Suggestions, Super Search, Workflow) to extend the original system in addition to enhancing its appearance.

Many applications permit the user to specify preferences that make the computing experience more enjoyable. Don't overlook these settings as a possible resource for a Usability Enhancer mashup. By examining customizations the user has already made to other systems, you may be able to dynamically tailor an application to suit an individual's tastes.

Related Patterns: Accessibility, Field Medic

Fragility

Like the Field Medic pattern, Usability Enhancer involves creating a facade that uses mashups to interact with an underlying application(s). The potential fragility is lower, however, because a system may be only partially wrapped in this manner. Certain system functions could be intentionally removed from the new interface as part of attaining increased usability.

Example: *Increase Application Usability*

Foreign exchange (Forex or FX) trading consists of trading one currency for another. It is the world's largest financial market and the average daily trade volume can be measured in terms of trillions of U.S. dollars. Applications similar to the one shown in Figure 5.15 have been created by many firms to capture and execute trades.

Figure 5.15   *A sample FX trading application*

As with many industries, participants in the Forex market have developed their own vernacular for quickly referring to currencies, financial instruments, and trade ideas. But applications still force the user to click from field to field and enter single discrete values. Why? Because it's simpler to build software that works the way a computer operates instead of how a business user thinks. Ultimately IT falls into the trap of delivering less usable software more quickly.

A system can be enhanced to accept a plain text description of a trade, break it into separate values, and pass the results through to the existing trade entry screen. This parsing is handled by custom code. A Usability Enhancer mashup is responsible for populating the required input fields (as shown in Figure 5.16).

In the mashup shown in Figure 5.16, entering "yen 3m f c 6" in the new Quick Text Entry field will be interpreted as a "6 million dollar call option on the USD/JPY currency pair in 3 months using the forward price." Previously, entering this transaction would have required multiple mouse clicks and user entries. Now a mashup is responsible for filling out the individual fields using data entry core functionality.

A form of shorthand in more widespread use concerns how people refer to dates. When an application requires a date it usually wants the date to appear in a specific format (such as MM/DD/YY). Most people do not handle dates so rigidly. "I'll see you next Friday" is generally preferred over "I'll see you March 29, 2009." Where does the work fall when someone says, "Set up a meeting two weeks from next Friday"? To the user, who must manually map real-world

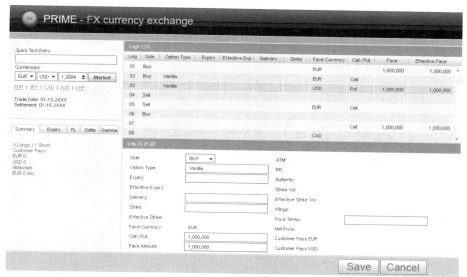

Figure 5.16 *Numerous usability enhancements have been made. The screen has been completely redesigned and pop-up help tips have been added for some fields. Note the new "Quick Text Entry" text field, which has been added in the upper-left corner.*

chronology to a form the computer will understand. The same approach demonstrated for handling plain text Forex trades can be used to allow an application to handle dates more flexibly: Custom code translates the date information into an explicit value, which a Usability Enhancer implementation then uses to populate a traditional input field.

▼ ───

Example: *Fix an Interface That No Longer Reflects the Business*

Slimline Shipping specializes in shipping and relocation services. The company has been trimming its internal software development staff for several years. Most of the systems used to support business functions either were purchased from vendors or were written by development teams no longer with the firm. A small group of programmers is available to fix bugs and make small changes but there aren't enough resources to build custom solutions.

One application that is subject to heavy use is the system that reserves moving vans for particular locations. It was built years earlier when Slimline served a much broader market. At that time Slimline maintained a fleet of trucks and vans of various models. It also covered the entire continental United States. Competition over the years has forced the company to scale back so that it now serves only the Northeast United States and offers a smaller selection of vehicles. The system was never updated to reflect the new business reality, which means it's possible to enter a reservation for vehicles that no longer exist at locations that aren't serviced. In addition, the Comments field has been repurposed to store requests for additional supplies like moving blankets or cardboard boxes. Figure 5.17 shows the interface with all its current irrelevancies.

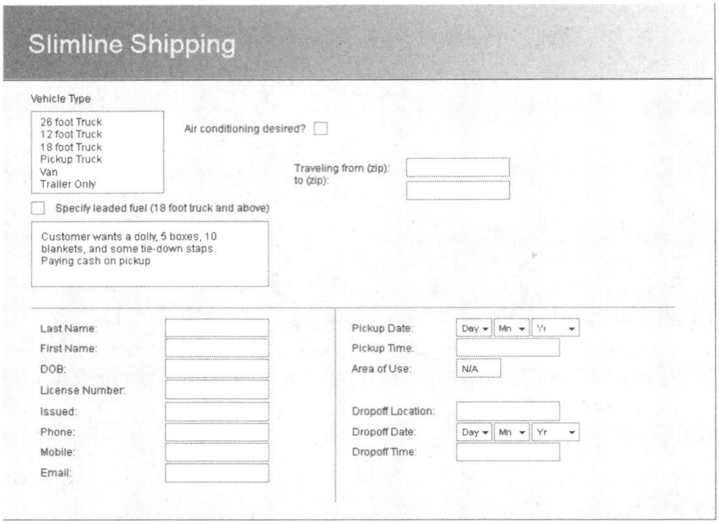

Figure 5.17   *The original reservation system contains options that are no longer valid.*

A mashup can not only increase the usability of this system, but also eliminate costly mistakes when obsolete values are specified. The skeleton IT crew is able to leverage the Usability Enhancer pattern to provide a new interface with minimal effort. Figure 5.18 shows the results of their work.

Several noticeable changes have been made:

- Invalid choices for vehicle type are no longer displayed.

- To and From ZIP codes are now validated against a list of acceptable values before the form can be submitted.

- Because most customers prefer vans with air conditioning, this choice is now selected by default.

- Several options that are no longer relevant have been removed. For example, all trucks now operate on unleaded fuel so the Fuel Type field is no

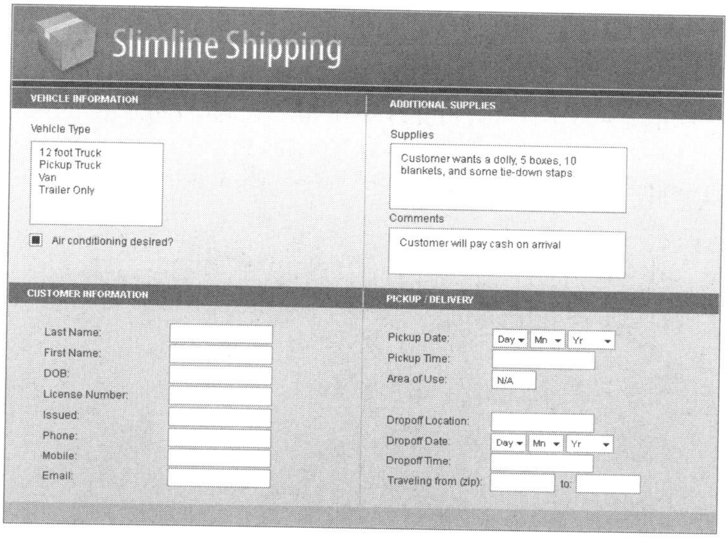

Figure 5.18 *The new interface contains updated branding and removes invalid options.*

longer displayed. The mashup will automatically select "Unleaded" when it interacts with the underlying system.

- The Comments field has been split in half and a new section for "Additional Supplies" has been added.

- Slimline changed its corporate branding after the original system was created, so the logo and screen colors have been updated.

The existing system still toils away under the covers but its outdated user interface no longer confuses users.

Example: *Add "Beginner" and "Expert" Interfaces to the Same Application*

Best Equity Investments (BEI) is an institutional investment firm that concentrates on buying and selling shares of public companies listed on the major financial exchanges. Its business model is fairly straightforward: Companies entrust their pension funds, endowments, and other investment capital with BEI, which manages the money in accordance with several strategies. As part of the company's pre-investment due diligence, BEI conducts custom risk analysis using proprietary mathematical models that its employees have created.

The internally developed risk modeling tool was initially designed solely with Quantitative Analysts (Quants) in mind. Screen real estate is a premium commodity on their desktops because they always have multiple applications open at once. Quants are extremely familiar with how to enter and manipulate financial data so they don't mind a form that lets them define and execute a ratings model in a single step. The result was the screen shown in Figure 5.19.

Figure 5.19   *A form for executing a custom Ratings Model*

The Research Assistants do not have the same level of knowledge possessed by the Quants. Their lower level of understanding makes it difficult for them to run models without sometimes making mistakes. New employees find the process particularly challenging. If a trade is placed based on incorrect ratings information, it may ultimately result in a loss of funds and erode client confidence in BEI.

Something needs to be done to accommodate both expert and novice users. BEI's IT department insists that writing and maintaining the code for two completely different interfaces will take at least a year, cost a significant amount, and potentially introduce unwanted bugs into the system.

With a Usability Enhancer mashup the existing system remains unchanged. In fact, it remains available for experienced users who are already comfortable with its functionality. New users receive access to a facade where the process of running a model has been split across several different screens (see Figure 5.20). An assistant can move backward and forward through the process using the navigation buttons. When the user reaches the last step and presses the Run Now button, the set of inputs is entered into the single screen of the original system.

Certain fields and labels are now accompanied by a small "question mark" icon that provides specific assistance for that item. A Help button displayed at the bottom of each dialog dynamically pulls additional information directly from BEI's corporate Help Desk knowledge base using another mashup. When a user is comfortable with the process for running a ratings model, he or she can switch back to the legacy interface if desired.

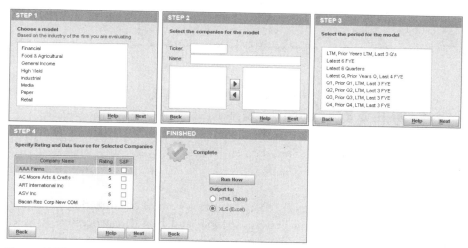

Figure 5.20   *A new "wizard-style" interface makes running a model a simple multistep process.*

Workflow

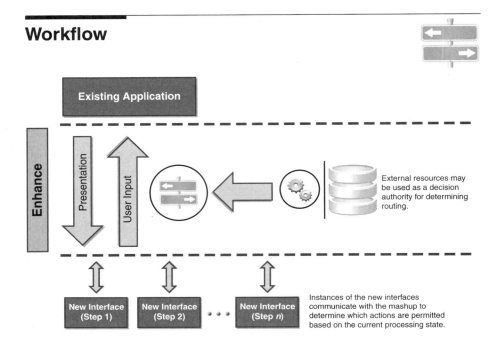

Core Activities: Data extraction, data entry, action

Problem

Workflow is a term that broadly describes the system of organization governing the exchange of information between people and business processes. It takes into account events that initiate a process (such as an application for a new account or a fiscal year-end reporting deadline) as well as the status of work and its influence on other resources. In many circles this discipline is known as business process management (BPM).

Almost all firms have some set of predefined procedures that frame the actions and responsibilities of its employees. These workflows allow tasks to be completed in an organized and repeatable manner. In many circumstances workflow is synonymous with accountability. When results are undesired or unsuccessful, a well-documented workflow allows a process to be traced backward to locate the point of failure.

In some cases industry regulations impose rules that can *only* be enforced via specific workflows. Irregular corporate reporting and failure to implement auditable processes are just two examples that can lead to fines and other penalties. Fines totaling more than $4.5 billion were leveled against Wall Street firms in

2004,[25] many for violations related to workflow. For example, Goldman Sachs was fined $2 million after the Securities and Exchange Commission (SEC) discovered that its sales traders had "violated the waiting period for marketing an IPO before a registration became effective. Additionally, the SEC alleged that a Goldman executive spoke to the media about an IPO before an initial registration was filed."[26] Goldman neither admitted nor denied the findings as part of the settlement.

Corporate responsibilities often change faster than existing processes can be amended. When the U.S. government passed the Sarbanes-Oxley Act, which established new and tougher reporting standards for public companies, the deadline for compliance was extended several times to allow businesses enough time to satisfy the new regulations.[27]

Applications inevitably participate in internal workflows because they play a crucial role in the day-to-day operation of most businesses. Unfortunately it's easier to change a business process than the software that underlies it. How can programs quickly adapt to new workflow requirements? What can be done when an application that was not originally designed to support workflow requirements must suddenly enforce them?

Solution

Many tools, techniques, and protocols for implementing and managing manual and automated processes have been developed. The Workflow pattern is not concerned with a particular discipline or product but rather with how mashups can address the challenge of creating or modifying workflows without enlisting the talents of the original developers or vendor. Mashups can also be used to add workflow capabilities to a system that does not natively support this functionality.

The first step is to define the process and determine which existing systems will participate in the solution. Individuals who serve a role in directing the flow of information should be identified as well. If an existing workflow is being modified, then the points where new activities are inserted or old ones removed need to be captured.

Earlier we used the API Enabler pattern to create functional interfaces into closed systems. In the Workflow pattern, API Enabler performs the additional role of exposing methods that allow the *status* of specific data to be monitored.

25. Weinberg, Ari. "Wall Street Fine Tracker." *Forbes.com.* http://www.forbes.com/2002/10/24/cx_aw_1024fine.html

26. Weinberg, "Wall Street Fine Tracker."

27. U.S. Securities and Exchange Commission. http://www.sec.gov/rules/final/33-8392.htm

The next step is to apply the techniques described in the Usability Enhancer pattern. A new interface is constructed that uses the status information obtained from API Enabler implementations to permit or restrict certain operations. Additional mashups (Alerter, Time Series) are then used to record audit information or create reports.

For a better understanding of the Workflow pattern, consider how an approval process might be added to an existing application. Suppose a sales agent for a regional beverage distributor enters his clients' orders using an in-house system. The application allows him to offer free shipping on any order although corporate guidelines suggest that this option should be restricted to customers who place at least a $10,000 order. With fuel costs reaching record levels, management decides that a new $25,000 minimum for free shipping must be strictly enforced. Any exceptions must be explicitly approved by a senior manager and must be summarized in a monthly report.

The IT department is caught completely flat-flooted: The sales application was built by a consultant three years ago and no one has access to the original code. How can the new requirements be implemented?

A new facade is created on top of the existing application by using the Usability Enhancer pattern to add functionality. When the "free shipping" box is checked and the "order amount" is less than $25,000, the application automatically hides the Submit button on the form. A new button, labeled "Request Approval," is shown instead. When the user clicks the Request Approval button, an email is sent to the agent's senior manager along with the customer information, order number, and amount. This action is possible because the firm's organizational chart and email system have been API-enabled to allow the manager to be automatically identified and contacted.

The manager replies to the email with a simple "Yes" or "No" message. Later, when the order is refreshed by the sales agent, the API-enabled mailbox is scanned for an email with a subject line matching the order number. If a match is found and if the message body contains a "Yes," the Submit button on the form is displayed. When the user clicks this button, another mashup enters a record in a reporting database from which the monthly exception report will be generated. At the same time the order is entered into the original system.

Related Patterns: API Enabler, Usability Enhancer, Field Medic

Fragility

The Workflow pattern rates the highest fragility score because a breakdown anywhere in the process can leave items in a state where they cannot proceed to the next stage of processing. This pattern should not be applied to add workflow capabilities to business-critical functions. At a minimum, alternative approval and routing procedures should be established in the event of an unexpected failure.

Example: *Add Enhanced Workflows Based on User Roles*

The trading system used by EFO Financial was purchased from a commercial vendor. The complete functionality EFO uses is incorporated on a single screen, as shown in Figure 5.21. There is no support whatsoever for the workflow. When the firm was small and everyone knew one another, this lack of support wasn't a major issue. Over time EFO has grown and taken on more staff and customers. The lack of enforced rules now exposes the firm to many risks.

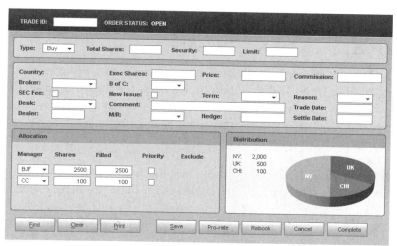

Figure 5.21   *The current trading system exposes all functionality on a single screen, regardless of a user's role.*

Four major job categories interact with EFO's trading platform:

- Fund Managers (FMs) meet promptly each morning to discuss the day's trading strategy. It wouldn't do to have one FM purchasing a stock while another sells it. Once the exchanges open, the FMs decide which specific stocks they will buy and sell and in what quantity. They allocate the orders across the accounts they manage. For example, if a FM decides to buy 1,000 shares of Mashups, Inc., and her fund has 10 clients, the FM may choose to direct 100 shares to each account. In some cases the size of the account or other factors may result in an unequal distribution.

- Sometimes an FM will want to change some particular aspect of the order—perhaps the price or the quantity. Such a request can be a minor request or a major headache depending on what state of processing the order is in.

- Portfolio Assistants (PAs) receive order details from FMs and fill out a subset of fields on a new record (also known as a "trading ticket"). In the interest of processing orders as quickly as possible, a PA enters only high-level information about a trade.

- The Trading Desk monitors the system for new orders. When a trader sees a new order appear, she starts working on it. She enters a comment so that no other trader accidentally picks the same order up and initiates a duplicate trade. The fact that the system does not natively support assigning and locking work-in-progress is a major weakness.

- The Desk Managers routinely monitor all the trades being worked on by the Trading Desk. If they see multiple trades for the same issue, they can instruct the traders working on them to pool their efforts. By combining several smaller orders into larger ones, EFO Financial may be able to get a better price for its clients.

Users are frequently stepping on one another's toes because of the lack of workflow support. Three traditional remedies for these problems exist:

- A new system could be purchased. This solution would require considerable investment for implementation and training.

- The original vendor could be hired to customize the system to EFO's needs. If additional changes were required at a later date EFO would have to pay for those as well. EFO would not be able to incorporate any new patches from the vendor until they were certified for the company's customized installation.

- The in-house development staff could write a new trading system from scratch. This would be a major effort and one that the firm is not sure it can justify financially.

A fourth—and more appealing—solution is to use mashups. The Workflow and Usability Enhancer patterns can be used to break down the monolithic trading screen into line-of-business screens that manage the flow of orders according to specific rules. How might this work? Refer again to the screen shown in Figure 5.21. The "Order Status" field near the top of the trade is a key part of the solution. The individual workflow steps will use this indicator to coordinate the overall process. Table 5.1 illustrates a few sample Order Status values and their effect on workflow. The "Comment" field is equally important. The first 20 characters of this field will be hidden and used to track the trader and trader assistant working on the order.

Table 5.1 *Sample Order Status Values and Their Consequences*

Order Status	Mashup Interpretation
Open	• Fund Managers (FMs) and Portfolio Assistants (PAs) are allowed to make changes to the quantity and limit price • Orders can be deleted • Traders can mark the order for themselves
In Progress	• FMs and PAs cannot change or delete an order, but they can send a cancellation request • Traders cannot reassign the order • Desk Managers can reassign the order to a different trader or combine similar orders
Partially Completed	• FMs can allocate shares across accounts • PAs cannot make any changes
Filled	• FMs can allocate shares and mark the order as complete • No other roles can make changes

The Usability Enhancer pattern is applied to the existing screen so that each business area receives only the portion of functionality that is appropriate to its role. Before this mashup is allowed to perform any function that will affect a trade's status, an underlying Workflow implementation retrieves the current state of the trade to determine which actions should be allowed.

The solution was not simple for EFO's IT department but it was nonetheless determined to be the quickest and most cost-effective approach. Each of the four areas that participate in the trading process receives a new screen that is based on the existing interface:

- The PAs use the simple Quick Order screen shown in Figure 5.22.

- The FMs receive the slightly more robust interface in Figure 5.23 because they will be entering allocations.

Figure 5.22 *A simple widget to allow Portfolio Assistants to quickly enter orders*

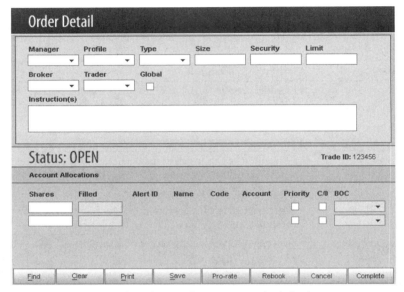

Figure 5.23 *The new interface for Fund Managers, which facilitates entering account allocations*

- The traders are able to view a list of orders similar to the one they saw with the original system but they now have the ability to "lock" a trade so that none of their coworkers accidentally starts working on it (see Figure 5.24). How was this new feature added? The original "Comment" field accepts 256 characters but the new interface exposes only the last 236 characters to the user. The first 20 characters invisibly store the code of the trader who initially grabbed the order (as well as the trader assistant's identification code). The user never sees this data but the mashups do. The "Comment" field still functions normally even though it accepts slightly less input.

- The Desk Managers receive a blotter similar to the traders, but related orders are now clearly marked. Figure 5.25 shows a new screen that appears when multiple similar trades for the same issue are identified.

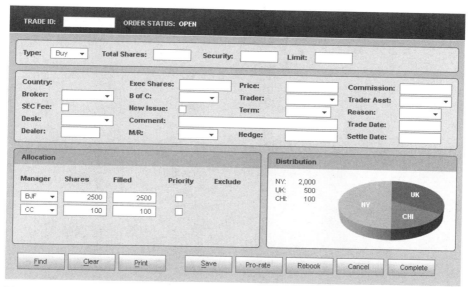

Figure 5.24 *The new Trader screen has drop-down fields for the trader and trader assistant that are used by the Workflow implementation to prevent other traders from working on this order.*

⚠ Similar Orders Exist

Multiple Open trades with matching criteria have been detected

(Type, Security, Limit, Broker, and Desk match exactly)

You may combine your order with an existing trade, or save it as a new order.

Trade ID	Manager	Type of Match
1234567890	McClintock, David	Buy, MASH
1342567855	Smith, Julia	
9343356213	Fearson, William	Sell, CHTP
8452277231	Geary, Peter	
1746844944	Southerland, Greg	

Combine Selected Orders | Save as a New Order

Figure 5.25 *Desk Managers are able to combine orders and resubmit them into EFO's trading workflow.*

Each of the new screens relies on a Workflow mashup to obtain a trade's Order Status. After comparing it to the operation flow shown in Table 5.1, certain functions are selectively allowed or prohibited by the interface. An implementation should maintain these rules separate from the presentation code so that the workflow can be modified without requiring a new release.

Chapter 6

Assemble Patterns

Coming together is a beginning; keeping together is progress; working together is success.

—Henry Ford

Introduction

In the previous chapters we examined patterns used to collect data from sources that have been traditionally closed to application developers. Ideally these investigations will have broken down any preconceived boundaries you may have placed around mashup technology. In this chapter we will return to the roots of mashups: assembling different material to create something entirely new.

The evolution of enterprise IT departments typically results in various core systems and vendor products being managed by different staff. Sometimes these systems are merged to support specific business goals. Other times, it takes a disruptive event (see the discussion of the Emergency Response pattern later in this chapter) to move integration efforts to the front of the queue. Wherever, whenever, and however it happens, integrating applications or data into a unified platform is a challenging effort. Everything about the systems—development language, database, Web and application servers, and operating system—may be different.

Within the modern enterprise, data flows across the corporate network in huge volumes every day. This information is the lifeblood of the company yet its exact course and structure are often known to relatively few individuals. Imagine if the data created by each system were freely available for examination, dissection, and recombination. What existing problems could be solved? What new uses might arise? IT personnel are typically trained to build applications "the right way" when sometimes all that users want is "right now." Rather than force an environment where requests for programs must go through formal design and specification phases, Assembly mashups provide relief. They

189

empower the layperson to quickly create ad hoc systems and data streams that can be used to test different theories or pioneer new solutions without incurring the burden of traditional IT processes.

What's the secret that makes it possible for nontechnical users to build these new tools? What allows them to be integrated on an ad hoc basis? The applications themselves! Everything about two applications can be completely different yet they will still share one special characteristic: the client. Of course, "the client" isn't necessarily a specific individual. Sometimes a *program* is a consumer of information directly provided by other systems. But the reality is that most applications ultimately serve some type of user, whether organic or electronic. If we can simulate these entities and their activities, then we can recombine functionality across systems at will. Assembly mashups make this feat possible. Using mimicry as the basis of a development methodology is not without potential problems, however. A number of the anti-patterns discussed in Chapter 9 (e.g., Conflicting SLAs and Drinking Seawater) examine the downsides of this approach.

Working with raw data can be a particular challenge for business professionals. Most have spent their careers insulated from the formats and protocols that are so familiar to IT personnel. The closest they have come to experiencing this world is through syndicated feeds such as RSS and Atom. Although email is a type of feed, people rarely view it as such, because they interact with it through individual messages and a friendly interface. Databases, messaging systems, enterprise service buses (ESBs), and other technically focused products form the bulk of a firm's remaining information infrastructure. At first only career programmers will be comfortable enough with these products to build mashups around them. But there's no reason these resources should remain closed to a select few. Providing a simple Web Services interface can make this material available to end users in a safe and secure manner. IT should consider the value in adopting a service-oriented architecture (SOA) to make the most complicated technologies accessible to everyone. Just because IT controls a firm's data doesn't mean that this division understands that data's intrinsic business value. Releasing the full breadth of a firm's stored knowledge back to the business can lead to new discoveries and products.

Let me stress one final point lest I mislead you into thinking mashups (in this category or any of the others) are targeted solely at end users. Mashups can provide laypeople with new pathways for exploration, but they can be just as valuable in accelerating the development curve within a traditional IT department. If the notion of openly sharing data across staff is simply too complicated to handle right now, mashups can still play an important role in increasing the productivity of your existing developers.

Communication and Collaboration

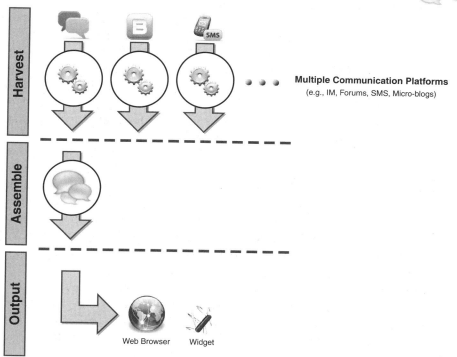

Multiple Communication Platforms
(e.g., IM, Forums, SMS, Micro-blogs)

Web Browser   Widget

Core Activities: Clipping, data entry, data extraction

Problem

Information overload (IO) means having access to so much material that it becomes burdensome rather than helpful. We will come across this topic frequently while examining the Assemble patterns. Many firms generate large amounts of useful knowledge. Perhaps that information is the natural product of their business or perhaps it arises from the actions of employees while they perform other tasks. When people freely exchange data, the general principles behind crowdsourcing help prevent useful material from being smothered by the sheer volume of communications. This isn't a revolutionary idea; various knowledge management (KM) tools and practices have been around for years. Nevertheless, problems commonly occur wherein a firm institutes *multiple* practices for KM. If there are too many options for collecting information, locating archived material down the road may prove much more difficult. Furthermore, any intrinsic value in the knowledge may be hidden if it's broken apart and spread across various systems. These situations lead to *information underload*—which can be just as detrimental as IO.

If information can't be found easily it might just as well not exist. Advances in search technology—and mashup patterns such as Super Search—have done much to address this issue. But the fact remains that the burden is still on the users to discover what is relevant to their needs. We might hope that a person working on a specific task who hits a roadblock will have a revelation and suddenly realize the need for some specific document. We can further trust that someone created this material and that it is findable. In other words, we can completely rely on people to surface solutions when they are needed. But how often do these assumptions actually come to fruition in practice? Instead most people wind up resorting to the "sneaker net": They get up from their desks and start walking around, asking coworkers for help. Likewise, they may pick up the phone, write emails, or send instant messages in search of an answer.

In the field of communication this problem is frequently described as *interruption overload*. As a consequence of the myriad of technologies that have arisen and allowed our personal networks to expand, we are often deluged with alerts from the multiple devices, products, and platforms to which we are all connected. An employee has numerous connections to coworkers on both organizational and social levels. But the communication channels that link people together have little or no way to discern the intrinsic value of the information they broadcast. As a result, all messages extract some measured amount of the recipient's attention regardless of their source or importance.

Solution

The key to unlocking problems of information underload and the subsequent interruption overloads it creates is to establish more refined communication and collaboration products. Mashups can be used to provide an environment where the person who needs information and the person (or persons) who holds that information are automatically connected through highly focused dynamic communities. This scheme minimizes those occasions where an employee in search of help broadcasts messages to a wide audience. Such an arrangement not only increases the likelihood that community members will be able to anticipate each other's requirements, but also ensures that they will help one another avoid rework or dead ends based on their collective experiences. This outcome is one of the chief differences between the Communication and Collaboration (C&C) pattern and the Portal Enabler pattern (see Chapter 7). Portals typically exist as a single, long-lived resource for accessing predefined sources of content; in contrast, the C&C pattern anticipates multiple instances regularly starting up to meet specific tactical requirements.

The C&C pattern does not seek to supplant existing communication tools. Unfortunately, email, instant messaging, and other services have become products unto themselves when in many cases they should revolve around specific projects. The C&C pattern describes methods for arranging these resources into subject-based channels on a situational basis. Because mashups make the creation of these ad hoc communities relatively easy, they should exist only for the duration of the task at hand; otherwise, they may be repurposed for other discussions and lose their relevancy. Once their usefulness is diminished they become contributors to the very problem they were designed to solve.

Related Patterns: Super Search

Fragility

The potential technical issues that may arise with implementations of the C&C pattern are obvious. Unintentional failure to surface important communications can have unfortunate consequences. So too can the propagation of unwanted messages to a wider audience. The challenge is to implement this pattern in a manner such that it governs its own growth; the goal is *not* to create connections between all possible recipients. The situation is analogous to how the human brain manages information. *Synapses* are the brain's mechanism of communication between neurons. Some theories describe the physical process of learning as the strengthening of these connections from repeated use. According to these hypotheses it is equally important that the brain sometimes *prune* infrequently used connections. The same idea applies to our personal connections: We strengthen ties on important subjects and weaken ones related to extraneous details. As the relevance of some topics waxes and wanes, our connections must change as well. A proper C&C implementation recognizes the necessity of regular adjustments and assists in making them happen.

Another challenge is that the C&C pattern can be applied to only a limited range of human interactions. History has shown that when new communication techniques emerge, the old ones don't go away. Most people still use postal mail, faxes, and the telephone—albeit less frequently now than when those means of communication were in their heyday. Implementations of this pattern are not very effective at managing "offline" communication.

Example: *Create Ad Hoc Communities for Support Issues, Research, and Customer Relations*

Phlegm Pharmaceuticals is a prominent healthcare company providing a broad range of medical solutions. The firm is actively involved in research and development of new drugs while at the same time monitoring the impact of its current products on the marketplace. Its IT department provides a rich internal suite of applications to support these endeavors. The array of business goals and their interactions with the company's products and technology provide numerous opportunities for implementations of the Communication and Collaboration pattern.

Consider the current situation when an end user experiences a problem with an application. He calls the support desk, describes the issue, and is issued a reference number. If this occasion is the first occurrence of the problem, someone may call back to get more information. If the issue is already widespread, the user may receive no further contact. To obtain the status of his issue, he must regularly call the support desk himself. Many coworkers will resort to interrupting one another to inquire if they are having similar problems. Multiplied across all users, this situation wastes everyone's time and leads to interruption overload.

Now suppose the C&C mashup was used to build the system depicted in Figure 6.1. The new dynamic support system mashes together the internal Help Desk application, change control database, and instant messaging (IM) products. When the mashup notices a new trouble ticket has been added, it instantly spins up custom IM channels for both user-centric and developer discussions. Email and SMS alerts are sent to appropriate resources within IT according to records maintained in the firm's application inventory database. Developers can use the user-based channel to ask questions that will help them debug the problem. Meanwhile, their internal IT channel can be used to collaborate with other programmers working to track down the root cause. Recent changes from the change control system are included because they may provide helpful clues. Meanwhile, the Help Desk personnel use the system to link similar items together and direct users to ongoing discussions.

All of this activity is monitored by the mashup, which uses this information to power the "Activity" gauge. This feedback device lets everyone have insight into the efforts being expended to address the issue at hand. The most important part of this mashup is that it knows when to remove one of these dynamic instances. Once the Help Desk closes the original issue, further collaboration on the subject is not allowed and the conversation history is archived.

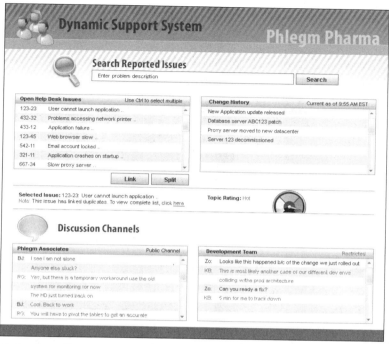

Figure 6.1 *An online support system dynamically creates communities around issues.*

The next area where Phlegm Pharmaceuticals can implement this pattern is in its R&D department. Researchers are actively involved in searching for new treatments and cures. Sometimes this work is conducted in cooperation with outside firms and universities. In fact, it was this basic cooperative model (albeit focused on issues of national defense) that led to the birth of the Internet's ancestor ARPANET and to the creation of email.[1] Of course, Phlegm Pharmaceuticals can do much more than rely on emails for exchanging data: An R&D "hub" mashup can link the disparate messaging products from different outside agencies together into one unified interface (see Figure 6.2).

Separate storage silos can be presented as a uniform repository to allow for an easier exchange of data. All of this material and its related communications can be tagged and organized by the contributing researchers. Applying a "folksonomy" (see Chapter 5), it is hoped, will lead teams working on seemingly nonrelated projects to discover and tap into one another's expertise (as shown

---

1. Internet Society. "A Brief History of the Internet." http://www.isoc.org/internet/history/brief.shtml

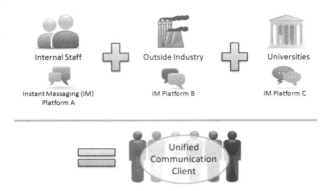

Figure 6.2 *Disparate communication products can be unified by a single mashup-powered client.*

in Figure 6.3). The C&C mashup itself could attempt to correlate the tags with the goal of suggesting possible synergies to the scientists.

The third area where Phlegm Pharmaceuticals could benefit from this pattern is in its Product Safety and Public Relations divisions. Although products undergo extensive private and government testing before being released to the public, new problems have been known to emerge after a drug becomes more widely available. These issues should be addressed as quickly as possible but the process for discovering problems is often painfully slow. Potential negative drug interactions might not be noticed until doctors and patients provide numerous empirical observations of these problems. Minor issues such as headaches or nausea that go underreported might never receive *any* attention.

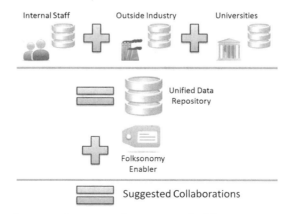

Figure 6.3 *Combining online research storage and adding tagging capabilities to connect researchers*

The solution is to provide an open environment for information reporting. Care must be taken in building this platform so that it doesn't undermine the advice of personal physicians or provide a forum that engenders unfounded concerns among patients. Phlegm Pharmaceuticals should consider establishing online communities based around each of its products. Visitors will be free to share their personal experiences with particular drugs. This information, along with similar data from forums outside the Phlegm network, can be mined and subjected to sentiment analysis (see the Reputation Management pattern in Chapter 4). This output can in turn be mashed together with a forum or IM product to create a "Doctors Only" area. Here physicians can find cases of patients following similar treatment plans who are exhibiting shared symptoms. This data may lead them to alter the medications being used. For its part Phlegm can monitor these activities so that the company becomes aware of issues before they escalate into major problems.

▼

Example: *Network Separate Suppliers to Form New Markets*

Another use of the C&C pattern is to establish a marketplace. By enabling open communication an industry can move from serving local niches to addressing a much broader audience. While not a mashup, the astonishing growth of eBay demonstrates the many benefits that arise from creating a global community of potential buyers and sellers. A wealth of opportunities for duplicating this company's highly successful model exist; one of which is profiled here.

Reclaimed old-growth timber has become a highly desirable commodity. The wood is extremely attractive and often of higher quality than new wood. This product has an environmentally friendly aspect, too; reclaimed lumber preserves existing timber stock and is one of the simplest forms of recycling. If the industry has a downside it's the lack of a regular pipeline that guarantees a steady supply of material. One local operator might reclaim tight-grained Douglas fir from a barn. Across the country a stock of oak from retired wine-fermenting barrels might be obtained. Yet another company might recover sunken logs from a lake and saw them into new dimensional lumber. Similar events can be staggered over several months and regions. Meanwhile, homeowners who are anxious to obtain this precious commodity hound builders who must locate it and arrange for the material's transportation. The salvage companies do little to facilitate this process other than posting existing and pending inventories on their individual Web sites.

A C&C implementation could collect details on the existing stock, merge together relevant message boards and email addresses, chart aggregated stock by species, and include builders' "wanted" lists. Homeowners and contractors might then plan their work around product availability; salvage companies could in turn plan their recovery projects based on requests for a particular wood or quantity.

C&C mashups built to support a market will generally be created by associations seeking to stimulate their industry. In this example, an environmental organization might finance this mashup as part of its goal to protect existing forests. Similarly, following the example set by eBay, an outside agency might create the platform and extract revenue from fees or advertisements.

Content Aggregation

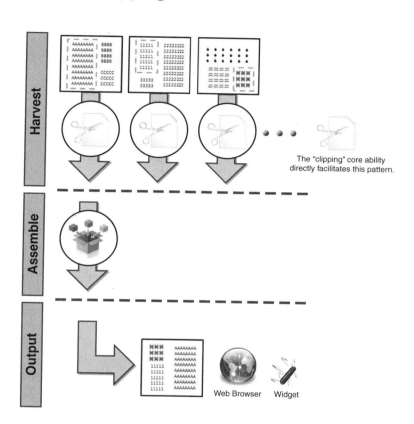

The "clipping" core ability directly facilitates this pattern.

Web Browser   Widget

Core Activities: Action, clipping, data extraction, data entry

Problem

For as long as users have had computers they have wanted to perform multiple tasks at the same time. In the days before multitasking systems were available, text-based productivity applications were created to "pop-up" when a special combination of keys was pressed.[2] The modern computer easily runs dozens of applications at once, organized within rich graphical environments. The quest to increase our productivity has driven advances in both hardware and software

---

2. Most famous was Borland's Sidekick, released in 1983. This tool provided rudimentary application switching for the MS-DOS operating system.

to new levels. We have reached a point where the number of tools concurrently available to us in many cases exceeds our capacity to interact with them simultaneously. This isn't necessarily a case of information overload because the work in itself might be quite manageable. Rather the root of the problem is multitasking—the work of switching between so many applications with different interfaces so as to complete a single job. Studies on the subject show that humans simply aren't capable of multitasking effectively:

> When humans attempt to perform two tasks at once, execution of the first task usually leads to postponement of the second one. Despite the impressive complexity and processing power of the human brain, it exhibits severe capacity limits in information processing. Nowhere is this better illustrated than when we attempt to perform two tasks at once, as such conditions will almost invariably lead to interference between the tasks.[3]

Granted, much of the research conducted in this area concerns completely unrelated activities like driving and talking on a cell phone. It could be argued that using multiple computer systems—particularly to complete a single unit of work—is less disruptive. To date, no studies have been published that have addressed these specific circumstances. In the pre-mashup era there weren't reasonable alternatives to online multitasking; hence there was little point in researching this subject. Nevertheless, the related evidence suggests that switching between visually disparate systems must present a momentary cognitive impediment to the user.

Systems need to be combined in such a way so that the structure itself contributes to decreased complexity and increased productivity. Systems that incorporate more monitors, higher screen resolutions, virtual desktops, and tabbed browsing are conveniences—not solutions. A human operator must still juggle multiple resources at the same time with such schemes. The goal is to create a "single task" from the disjointed operations that are the hallmark of our modern activities.

Solution

New interface paradigms such as RSS (see the Feed Factory pattern), Portals (see the Portal Enabler pattern), and desktop widgets (see the Widget Enabler pattern) are just some of the recent attempts aimed at alleviating our overloaded senses. What differentiates them from the Content Aggregation pattern is that they produce new output artifacts that were not originally provided by the source system. The Content Aggregation pattern consists of the collection of

---

3. Dux, P. E., *et al.* "Isolation of a Central Bottleneck of Information Processing with Time-Resolved fMRI." *Neuron* 2006;52:1109–1120.

visual elements from one of more sites that are then rearranged or recombined within a *common presentation container* with little or no modification. Consider the situation where each part of an overarching task performed by a user requires interactions with subsections of multiple applications. The repackaging of these components onto a single canvas saves the user the inconvenience of switching back and forth between systems.

It is tempting to view all mashups as a variation on this design. This mistake should be avoided! One-off solutions where content is both aggregated and integrated can benefit from mashup technology but this outcome does not indicate the presence of a pattern. The true Content Aggregation pattern is distinguished from other members of the Assemble category by the total absence of interaction between combined resources. Content Aggregation mashups are truly "skin deep." Should aggregated resources undergo any type of integration that goes beyond their visual presentation, the juncture of these activities gives rise to a new class of pattern. For example, combining visual components and subjecting them to common search or display preferences leads us to the Portal Enabler and Dashboard patterns. The classic integration of location data and a map results in the Location Mapping pattern. Multiple communication tools merged into a unified environment wherein messages are correctly routed between components evokes the Communication and Collaboration pattern. Content Aggregation is an activity that operates purely at the presentation level. Its natural complement—integration without any reference to visual artifacts—is the Content Integration pattern.

Related Patterns: Dashboard, Emergency Response, Usability Enhancer

Fragility

The Content Aggregation pattern receives the lowest rating for fragility because it involves only the simplest communication between components. If the presentation of aggregated material is modified by the mashup (for example, providing a chart driven by collected numerical data), a marginal risk exists that the new visualization may introduce inaccuracies. Another risk is that information removed from its natural context may no longer convey its importance. It is possible for a Content Aggregation mashup to include out-of-date material but not provide any indicators that would alert the user to this fact. If your implementations leverage time-sensitive material, you should consider this outcome and take appropriate measures to communicate the relevance and accuracy of harvested content.

Other risks relate to security issues. A Content Aggregation mashup could potentially expose previously secure information in a context that no longer provides appropriate protection mechanisms. Previously innocuous resources, once combined, might reveal highly confidential material similar to how common household products can have an explosive reaction when accidentally mixed. The anti-patterns discuss techniques for tackling these issues without crippling the potential value of enterprise mashups.

Example: *Eliminate Unproductive Task Switching Between Applications and Web Sites*

A common desktop environment (CDE) is a metaphor for providing easy access to the tools that a user requires most often during the course of normal activity. A CDE seeks to directly eliminate the distractions that result when transitioning between steps in a task.

PhotoMark Studios is a commercial film and photography business whose services include leasing studio space, renting photographic equipment, and supplying optional staff ranging from basic assistants to trained photographers. A typical customer inquiry might arrive in a phone message or email that asks a series of questions. "Do you have a kitchen studio? How soon can I rent it? Do you have a food prep area? I require a medium-format camera and a technician, plus a private client lounge. I need these resources for 10 hours. I will be bringing a staff of 20 persons and want a catered lunch. Please provide prices ASAP."

To answer these requests quickly PhotoMark's staff must keep pace with the often-rapid changes in equipment inventory and availability. PhotoMark decides that implementing a service desktop can solve this problem. The system will aggregate material across several internal resources to give employees immediate access to the overall state of the company's products. Additional content from external sources can be included where applicable. In this example, each of the customer's questions is addressed by data that comes from different sources. Once the CDE is in place employees will no longer have to hunt for the answers across systems; all the necessary material will be presented within the aggregated environment.

Table 6.1 shows each question grouped by the section of the CDE that addresses it.

None of the questions listed in Table 6.1 is outside the realm of what potential customers commonly ask. Unfortunately the evolution of PhotoMark's systems for managing its business has made providing timely answers extremely difficult. There is little incentive to redesign the architecture of existing solutions because each resource already achieves its core purpose effectively. For the

Table 6.1 *Components of the PhotoMark CDE Used to Answer Customer Inquiries*

Customer Request	Source of Answer on the CDE
"Do you have a kitchen set?" "Do you have a food prep area?" ". . . plus a private client lounge?"	An annotated floor plan of the PhotoMark studio provides details about the types of studios and their dimensions. Pictures from the firm's Web site may be included in email responses as well.
"How soon can I rent it?" "I need these resources for 10 hours."	The internal scheduling calendar used by PhotoMark is clipped from its native environment for convenient access.
"I require a medium-format camera."	The technical staff uses an online spreadsheet to track equipment availability.
"I will be bringing a staff of 20 persons and want a catered lunch."	External catering menus from corporate partners are present on the CDE. The client is offered several potential cuisine selections.
". . . and a technician."	The relevant portions of the human resources time-tracking system are displayed to show employee availability by job category.
"Please provide prices ASAP."	The corporate rate calculator for staff, studio, and equipment rental is mashed in.

fraction of staff who need to collect information across multiple sources, the proposed CDE will dramatically reduce the amount of time it takes them to complete their work. Figure 6.4 shows the sections that will be clipped from the original systems and the results. Each harvested section is placed on a different tab so that the final interface doesn't become too cluttered.

Some IT professional might call the CDE solution nothing more than a simple portal. In reality, there are some distinctions. The components of a portal, known as *portlets*, are often intended to interoperate;[4] this is not the case with a simple aggregation mashup. And while it is true that portlets aren't required to communicate with one another, they frequently share one trait: They display a summary view of more detailed information. In a Content Aggregation mashup the data in the original system and the mashup correspond on a one-to-one basis.

---

4. Standards such as JSR 168 (http://jcp.org/en/jsr/detail?id=168) have been designed to govern this behavior.

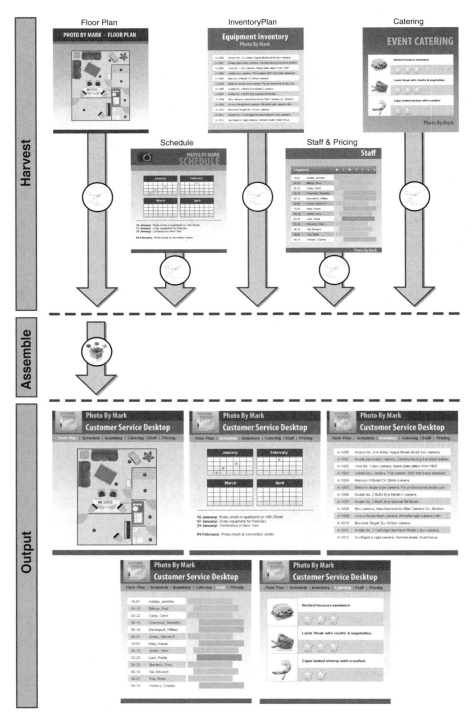

Figure 6.4   *Portions of multiple applications are clipped to produce a service desktop.*

Example: *Stop Using Spreadsheets as Generic Containers for Cut-and-Paste Activities*

Sean is a research analyst at the Victa Hedge Fund. One of his responsibilities is identifying potential investments for further investigation. Sean has developed a variety of closely guarded techniques for sniffing out new opportunities. Once a prospect has been identified his secret methods are put aside and more tedious work begins. Because only a small percentage of the deals he suggests are accepted, Sean must carefully decide which ones merit further investigation. Before performing additional analysis he produces a package of company financials to circulate among his peers. Based on their collective feedback he will decide where he should focus his efforts next.

Sean now performs this task manually. He visits sites such as EDGAR,[5] the SEC's database of fiscal reports and other filings, to collect financial statements. Depending on the industry he might cull information from other government and private repositories as well. He pastes all of the material he collects into spreadsheets. Sean doesn't perform further processing on the spreadsheets; he merely finds them useful as containers for his research. Once he has organized his findings he pastes the sections of the spreadsheet he finds interesting into an email, which he then forwards to his coworkers. Put simply Sean is functioning as a one-man content aggregation machine.

A mashup could be used to eliminate the most boring and tedious parts of this (now manual) work. In fact, the basic activities are so simple that Sean should be capable of creating the solution himself. They key is to create a Content Aggregation implementation that combines all of Sean's data sources into a single view. A spreadsheet is not needed to pull these items together; the mashup itself is the container. This mashup has the further benefit of always presenting the most recent information.

If Sean was content with pasting sections of the mashup into his email messages, this functionality could be the end of the example. But why not eliminate that last burden? Sean can add a small check box next to each section and an Email button. This feature would perform the remaining chore of combining selected content into a message and sending it out. Sean can devote the time he used to waste on cutting and pasting to hunting for new deals.

---

5. http://www.sec.gov/edgar.shtml

Example: *Create an Educational Desktop*

Content Aggregation implementations are especially useful for educational purposes. They can be used to rapidly create integrated learning environments for almost any subject imaginable. Relevant resources from different sites can be gathered together to create a composite view tailored to specific curricula. For example, an organization might pull together internal policies and procedures along with snapshots of the systems that support them to quickly build a targeted training environment. A school or university could pull subsections from various resources to create dynamic instructive platforms that are far superior to outdated textbooks (not this one, of course!). Conflicting viewpoints might be assembled on the same page—a useful approach for illustrating the many different sides of controversial issues. Content Aggregation can help an instructor guide students to specific information rather than subjecting them to the unwieldy process of navigating through levels of irrelevant or distracting material.

Content Integration

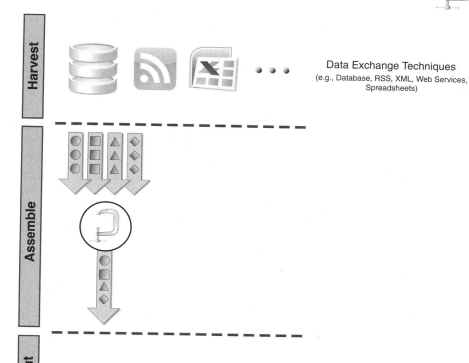

Harvest

Data Exchange Techniques
(e.g., Database, RSS, XML, Web Services, Spreadsheets)

Assemble

Output

Integrated Output via a Single (Nonvisual) Standard*
* Does not need to correspond to one of the harvested formats.

Core Activities: Data extraction, data entry, transformation

Problem

A frequent consequence of mashup creation is the production of new streams of data. Consider the Infinite Monkeys pattern: An implementation can extract data from hundreds or even thousands of Web sites. If the process of visiting so many pages is overwhelming for a single user, the job of combining all the collected material is equally herculean. Nor is this a case of automating simple cut-and-paste operations. Whenever data is extracted from a large number of different sources the likelihood that it will adhere to a common format is low. As we saw in our examination of transformation functionality in Chapter 2, even simple values such as dates and phone numbers can be presented in different formats.

Mashups aside, IT already spends a significant amount of time managing the transparent flow of data to and from applications. As a general rule, new methods for storing and transferring data appear more quickly than old ones can be retired. Today's techniques include relational databases, Web Services, XML, RSS, JSON, and many more. The interoperability of these methods is extremely low. An application designed to ingest XML cannot suddenly consume details from a database without changes to its source code. An RSS reader cannot pull in information from an Excel spreadsheet. Even a system that already understands XML requires additional content adhere to a predetermined schema before it can be used.

The proliferation of so many data storage and transmission methods has created a technological Tower of Babel. In many large-scale organizations dedicated teams exist to serve as what are essentially highly skilled plumbers. They manage the infrastructure and translations that ensure when an application turns on the "information spigot," the correct data flows from the tap.

Whether a project involves creating a new system or enhancing an existing one, data management is an important function. This activity is so widespread that even the smallest of improvements to the process can result in substantial efficiencies.

Solution

The Content Integration pattern provides a quick method for combining data flows from multiple systems into a composite stream. This singular flow can be integrated into existing business processes and applications provided that transformations are applied to create homogeneous output. Unlike implementations of the Content Aggregation pattern, Content Integration implementations do not have a visual component. Of course, neither Content Aggregation nor Content Integration procures the data on which it operates; this is the domain of patterns in the Harvest category (and Feed Factory, which is an Enhance pattern).

A revolutionary characteristic of the Content Integration pattern is that it can be implemented by laypeople outside the domain of the "data plumbers." The same tools that make simple data extraction possible typically allow disparate resources to be easily mixed together or converted to new formats. For example, an application fed by a Web Service would have no ability to understand Excel and RSS data under typical circumstances. An implementation of Content Integration, by contrast, could consume both formats and the Web Service, seamlessly integrate their contents, and repackage the results as a brand-new Web Service ready for deployment. The entire process need not require a new single script or line of code be written.

Content Integration can serve as a stop-gap measure to create new composite data feeds across systems (see the Quick Proof-of-Concept pattern). It can be extremely valuable in handling the technological fallout resulting from corporate mergers and acquisitions. But a word of warning is in order: This pattern must be used cautiously so as not to create system dependencies that are hidden or not well understood (see the discussion of the anti-pattern called Shadow Integration).

Once resources can be combined ad infinitum, the need to remove redundant or unnecessary information naturally follows. The complement to Content Integration that addresses this issue is the Filter pattern.

Fragility

Mashups where data are manipulated result in a higher level of risk. Even the combination of sources that conform to a standard (e.g., RSS) faces potential problems. An error in one of the constituent parts can render the combined resource unusable.

One of the chief benefits of the Content Integration pattern is also its greatest weakness. When the need to use multiple systems to access data is eliminated, so are the checks and balances that those resources provided against one another. Often nothing is left to indicate to the data consumer (whether a user or another application) that information is missing or incomplete. One technique for addressing this issue is to add metadata to the combined resource that points back to the particular systems of origin. This metadata can then be used to track problems back through the mashup to the initial source of material.

Example: *Extend a System to Handle Data Beyond Its Original Design*

Wantage Industries is a manufacturer of replacement parts for *commercial* appliances. When an original equipment manufacturer (OEM) wants to reduce inventory for old or unpopular models, Wantage steps in to provide off-site fabrication and storage services. The OEM can then continue to meet warranty and service requirements across the lifetime of its products. To keep its staff informed about the latest parts they stock, Wantage has developed a series of Web-based training courses. Each class focuses on the products from a particular OEM. The contents are updated regularly based on technical data supplied by each client. Employees are required to audit classes quarterly to keep abreast of the products Wantage will remanufacture.

Wantage has been approached by several of its partners that are anxious to outsource part manufacturing for their *residential* appliance divisions. The work is a welcome opportunity for Wantage. To handle it Wantage is prepared to accept augmented feeds from the vendors for its online catalog and e-learning system. But a potential problem soon comes to light: Data from the new divisions is available only in a format completely different than what is provided in the commercial product feeds. This requires Wantage's IT department to code custom feed parsers for each vendor.

A more efficient solution is to use a Content Integration mashup to move all data to a standard representation. Because the online training system already accepts a feed, the preexisting structure can serve as the blueprint for the new work. Combining the new information into a single conforming source means that the application won't need to be modified to understand the format of the new residential appliance feeds. The main challenge for the feed integrators is that some vendors have duplicate part numbers. To ensure records aren't accidentally dropped, a decision is made to prefix the code of each item in the unified feed with the vendor's name. Once this work is complete, the application is pointed at the mashup as the sole data provider. The new material is seamlessly imported and Wantage avoids having to create and support any new code. Figure 6.5 shows the input streams before and after a Content Integration implementation.

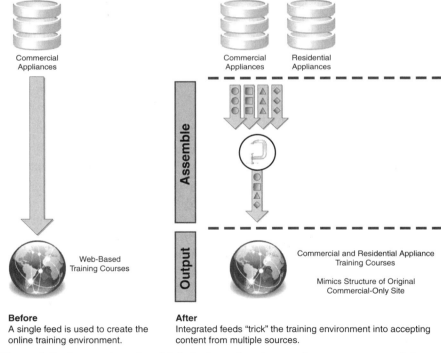

Before
A single feed is used to create the online training environment.

After
Integrated feeds "trick" the training environment into accepting content from multiple sources.

Figure 6.5   *Integration of multiple feeds so that they conform to an expected format and can inject new data into a system without requiring major changes*

Example: *Tie Application Changes to the Proliferation of Products and Services Within a Firm*

Burgeoning Systems (BS) has more than 2,000 internal- and external-facing applications deployed on its network. Each business area has its own designated set of developers and business analysts. Once they've written or purchased a software solution, these employees turn to a Centralized Infrastructure Management (CIM) group to provide hosting environments for testing and production. The CIM team tries to maximize resources by hosting multiple products in a shared environment. Over time this effort has turned into a nightmare because the upgrades or requirements of one application frequently have a negative impact on other programs sharing the same resources. For example, one product might require a database upgrade that causes other applications to suddenly fail.

To manage upcoming changes, the CIM team has installed a change management system. All requests that will affect BS's infrastructure are now entered into this application. The CIM team has already used the Feed Factory pattern to make this information available via RSS. Business areas are expected to check their environments against the change management system for pending events that may affect their team.

Another challenge is to prevent teams from bringing unsupported or unsecure products into BS's environment. A single faulty component can bog down all of the systems on a shared resource or expose them to malicious intent. The CIM team maintains a catalog of disallowed products via a spreadsheet stored on a shared Web server. Pending change requests are manually checked against this list to see if they introduce prohibited technology. In addition, the CIM team tracks its application inventory for product management and charge-back purposes. Each system and the resources it uses (e.g., servers, databases, network attached storage) are recorded in a separate online spreadsheet.

Bringing together these disparate information sources via the Content Integration pattern will offer several benefits. The first step is to RSS-enable the "disallowed products" and "application inventory" spreadsheets. The individual feeds can then be mixed and matched to create several useful new products as shown in Table 6.2.

Table 6.2 *Integrated Feeds Yield Benefits Greater Than Their Constituent Parts*

Resources Combined	Audience	Feed Benefits
Change management system + disallowed products database	CIM team	Indicates changes that should be blocked because they contain unapproved products.

(continued)

Table 6.2   *Integrated Feeds Yield Benefits Greater Than Their Constituent Parts (Continued)*

Resources Combined	Audience	Feed Benefits
Change management system + application inventory	Business teams	Notifies teams of upcoming work that may affect their environment. This is particularly useful for monitoring shared infrastructure.
Application inventory + disallowed products database	All	Provides a dynamic remediation report of products that expose Burgeoning Systems to potential risks.

Distributed Drill-Down

Application Interface

Assemble

Multiple siblings pertaining to unrelated
content may exist at each level of detail

Output

**Implementations
recursively supply
additional detail through
original interface**

Core Activities: Clipping, data extraction, data integration

Problem

A common design metaphor in modern applications is the master/detail view. This user interface technique usually consists of two separate parts. The first part presents a summary view of data known as the master view. The master view displays just enough information so that each item it portrays can be individually identified. The second part of the user interface presents more specific information (known as the detail view). When an item is selected from the master view, the detail view displays additional material for editing or review. Figure 6.6 shows a sample employee directory presented in master/detail form.

Master/detail information can be chained across as many levels as required. That is, the detail record for a particular master item may in turn contain an item (or items) that can be followed to procure even more related data. The process of navigating through multiple master/detail relationships is colloquially referred to as "drilling down." The notion is that with each new step through a master/detail relationship a person is journeying deeper into the details of a specific object.

Figure 6.6   *Simple master/detail functionality is provided by an employee directory application.*

The master/detail concept has served application developers quite well. It provides additional specificity only upon user action; thus it allows large amounts of data to be presented effectively without creating a cluttered presentation. The limitations of this approach stem from the fact that drill-down operations typically occur within the same application. The plain truth is that many useful master/detail relationships exist across different systems but there is no overarching interface to follow them. For example, a firm may use separate contact management and purchasing systems. The master/detail relationship between them is obvious: There is a one-to-many relationship between a customer and the number of orders that customer has placed. But because these applications are stand-alone entities, obtaining this information is an entirely manual operation. This leads to excessive, distracting work similar to the problems encountered during our discussion of the Content Aggregation pattern.

Solution

The Distributed Drill-Down (DDD) pattern provides a master/detail interface across data that is not stored in the same system. Because multiple master/detail relationships can be present, it is not always efficient to collect all of the available material until a user requests it. This behavior stands in contrast to DDD's close counterpart, Content Aggregation; the latter pattern immediately assembles a collection of material. For this reason, the DDD pattern is sometimes referred to as "Content Aggregation with Navigation" (CAN). The new information returned at each step can originate from a variety of external systems— hence the "distributed" nature of the pattern. This term should not be confused with "distributed computing," which refers to the process of splitting a complicated task across multiple computers.

From a usability perspective, it is helpful to indicate when additional details are available. This task requires that a DDD implementation always look "one level down" for each item currently being presented to determine if related materials exist. A user interface could display appropriate icons or links as a mechanism for moving deeper into the information hierarchy when such material is found.

Another difference between Content Aggregation and DDD is that a Content Aggregation implementation may merely collect useful—but unrelated—materials under a unified container. In a DDD implementation, each successive operation is a recursive step into the links between applications that provides incrementally greater detail regarding a specific item. The connections between systems can be actual or purely conceptual, but each subsequent level of detail unmistakably relates in some way to its parent element.

Also Known As: CAN (Content Aggregation with Navigation), Master/Detail, Parent–Child

Related Patterns: Content Aggregation, Usability Enhancer

Fragility

Like its close counterpart Content Aggregation, Distributed Drill-Down receives the lowest fragility score. Assuming an event that breaks the automated connection between systems, it is still possible to perform drill-down operations manually until the mashup is remediated. The chief risk is that an implementation will fail to indicate the presence of additional details where they actually exist.

▼ ——————————————————————————————

Example: *Provide Better Customer Support and Uncover Opportunities for Cross-selling*

CapableCable is a regional cable television provider in North America. Originally, its business consisted of providing basic analog cable services to suburban and rural communities. To support these business operations the company developed some basic systems to manage data related to customer billing, scheduling on-site service and repair, and tracking premium programming and pay-per-view purchases. As time progressed CapableCable branched out into the new realm of digital cable. This brought a myriad of new channel and subscription packages as well as new equipment. Gone was the simple set-top box; it was replaced by a suite of options that included devices with HDTV output and embedded digital video recorders (DVRs). To track these devices across its customer base, CapableCable purchased a new application from a company specializing in equipment rental.

The move to digital media created a variety of other opportunities for Capable-Cable. The company decided to offer high-speed Internet access to customers provided they leased a cable modem. Different packages were made available to provide services such as dedicated IP addresses or increased bandwidth. Not surprisingly the original customer billing system required significant revisions to merge this new service into the existing functionality.

Most recently CapableCable has branched out into the world of voice-over-IP (VOIP) services. VOIP allows the company's customers to make and receive phone calls over their Internet connections. They continue to use their standard touch-tone phones but can make calls at drastically cheaper rates. CapableCable now has a division that functions like a miniature phone company, billing for features including caller ID, call waiting, and voicemail as well as tracking customer issues.

A customer can have numerous contacts with CapableCable as a result of the many services now offered by the company. Each of these services can in turn have multiple subproducts. Figure 6.7 illustrates just a few of these relationships. A large number of the links are currently conceptual, as indicated by the dashed lines in the figure. Thus, if a customer calls CapableCable to request additional services or support, the telephone agent must manually move between resources as the client's questions become more narrowly focused on a particular topic. This was obviously not an intentional situation but merely a consequence of how the company's business evolved. Nevertheless, the lack of a formal structure for providing more detailed information hampers the quality of customer service that Capable can provide.

The decision is made to create a Dynamic Drill-Down implementation to formalize the dashed relationships depicted in Figure 6.7. A solution is designed to begin at the highest level of detail (the customer account record) and provide mechanisms to move farther down the hierarchy of systems and marketing material without requiring employees to switch between a collection of Web pages, internal documentation, and legacy applications. When a customer initiates a call with the support line, staff can now quickly explain the customer's current product selection and efficiently delve into specifics about other packages and services.

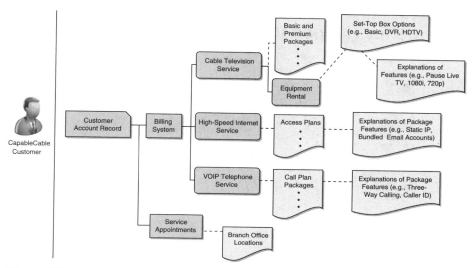

Figure 6.7 *Getting more detail about available products and services requires support agents to drill down through a variety of separate (and sometimes disconnected) resources.*

Emergency Response

 Harvest

Various pattern implementations and data sources used as inputs, depending on the nature of the emergency

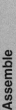 **Assemble**

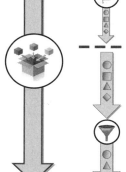

Multiple Aggregation, Integration, and Filtering implementations as mandated by the harvested resources

Output

Web Browser Web Service RSS Report Widget Database

Output may be subject to additional patterns (e.g., Alerter, Translation) as circumstances require

Core Activities: Clipping, data extraction, data integration

Problem

IT departments diligently create work plans for the systems that they will construct. Dozens of popular development methodologies exist, each of which prescribes some amount of up-front effort before the first line of code is written. Basic requirements analysis is a common first step; the design of the overall architecture then follows. Disciplines within the test-driven development and extreme programming families stipulate that developers should create unit tests before implementation finally begins. The ultimate result: a potential lengthening of the time it takes IT to deliver solutions (even though they may be of higher initial quality). As discussed in the introduction to this chapter, sometimes "the right way" is too slow to provide help when it's needed. The Emergency Response pattern addresses these critical situations.

The "unplanned application" is not unheard of in enterprise environments. Sometimes a business opportunity arises that can be exploited only within a brief stretch of time. Or two firms that merge might need to rapidly combine their systems so their customers aren't affected. The "silver lining" to these situations is that the problem has already been scoped, albeit broadly. The applications and data that will participate in the solution are usually identified very quickly. Under these circumstances the "emergency" boils down to an unplanned scheduling of resources and manpower.

Our concern here is emergencies of a more drastic nature where human safety and well-being are at risk. Natural disasters such as earthquakes, floods, hurricanes, tornados, and winter storms are major examples. These events can leave the existing infrastructure in shambles—and create a problem that cannot be addressed by shuffling around headcount. Rather, the solution requires pulling together a menagerie of resources including first responders, charities, corporations, and government agencies whose systems were never designed or intended to interoperate.

Solution

Mashups are a natural solution for the coordination of disparate assets under extreme conditions. But can mashup use in these cases fall under the general classification of a pattern? The randomness of disasters and their specific effects make it impossible to provide more than the most general guidelines for the implementer. When we take the humanitarian impact into account, however, it becomes clear that the benefits of publicizing this pattern take priority over any ideological concerns. If this pattern does nothing more than to raise awareness of the value of mashups in emergency situations, then its inclusion is justified.

Figure 6.8   *Ready America provides useful information to both prepare for and recover from natural and human-made disasters (regardless of your home country).*

The first step in coordinating a response effort is to obtain as much information as possible. The U.S. Federal Emergency Management Agency (FEMA),[6] Occupational Safety and Health Administration (OSHA),[7] and Ready America[8] (see Figure 6.8) are good starting points.

Obtaining information on the most common after-effects for a disaster can help identify which resources will be needed. For example, one of the post-hurricane hazards listed on the FEMA Web site is flooding. An Emergency Response mashup might pull together any or all of the following resources depending on the severity of the incident:

---

6. http://www.fema.gov

7. http://www.osha.gov

8. http://www.ready.gov/america/beinformed/index.html

- Satellite images and weather forecasts to determine when the danger has passed.

- The location of safe sources of drinking water (obtained from area news reports and government Web sites).

- Unsafe bridge and road warnings (from local law enforcement).

- Medical contact and capacity information (obtained from local hospitals and medical centers).

- The location of mobile disaster recovery centers. In the United States, FEMA often establishes on-site offices to assist survivors.

- Contact information for professional water, mold, and sewage clean-up firms (from area yellow pages).

- Available quantity and location of sump pumps (from local retailers' Web sites).

- Travel delays and advisories (from local air and rail resources) that can assist residents wishing to evacuate.

- A wiki or "person directory" to help distant relatives locate loved ones when the traditional communication infrastructure breaks down.

This mashup might then remain in place as an emergency preparedness resource to provide help during future catastrophes. Pulling in sites that compute the local risk of disaster (such as the Flood Risk calculator shown in Figure 6.9) is a good first step in making this transition.

The power of mashups that ensues when they are created cooperatively by multiple individuals is particularly useful during a crisis when no single entity has all the information the public requires. The most important consideration is to remain flexible and allow new resources to be added and removed as the situation evolves.

Related Patterns: Smart Suggestions, Super Search, Quick Proof-of-Concept

Fragility

Deploying an Emergency Response mashup to marshal relief resources is not without some inherent risks. Communication between field agents and agency officials can be disrupted or mishandled. Nowhere was this risk more tragically illustrated than in the aftermath of Hurricane Katrina in the United States in 2005. Tens of thousands of people flocked to the New Orleans Superdome after

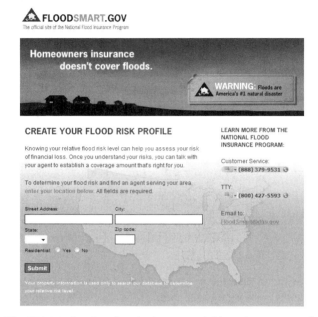

Figure 6.9   *The FEMA Flood Risk calculator, available at http://www.floodsmart.gov, can help U.S. residents learn about the dangers of flooding in their area and take appropriate precautions.*

they were left homeless following the collapse of levees that left much of their city underwater. Part of the city's contingency plan was to use the structure as a temporary shelter. Unfortunately the location was not prepared for the enormous influx of people and FEMA was slow to act on reports that urgent assistance was required.[9] Some citizens ultimately perished due to the lack of an organized response.

The downside of rapidly providing a mashup-based response is that it can have potentially negative consequences. It is just as easy to propagate inaccurate or contradictory information as it is to provide helpful data. Mixing bad information with good can give false credibility to erroneous sources. At a minimum, some type of simple rating or feedback mechanism should be incorporated to leverage the knowledge of people closest to the situation (á la crowdsourcing). Another potential drawback results from an excess of information. The priorities of individuals vary greatly during a crisis: Some will be con-

---

9. "Worker Tells of Response by FEMA." *The New York Times.* October 21, 2005. http://www.nytimes.com/2005/10/21/national/nationalspecial/21response.html

cerned about locating family members; others will need basic shelter. A homeowner may be worried about a lost pet, smell a gas leak, or notice a downed power line. If a mashup attempts to addresses all of these issues on a single screen, the disharmony can render the site useless. Thus a high priority is to provide a clean navigation structure for the mashup. The Smart Suggestions pattern (see Chapter 5) may prove useful in directing user inquiries correctly.

Example: *Issue Emergency Alerts and Locate Volunteering Opportunities*

There is no need to create hypothetical examples for this pattern: It has already been the subject of several high-profile implementations.

VolunteerMatch[10] is a nonprofit organization that has helped coordinate more than 3.7 million volunteer referrals since 1998. One of its focus areas is disaster preparation and relief. A strategic interest in this area is helping volunteers who want to get involved during and after disasters find opportunities that are appropriate to their skills, interest, and location. In 2007 Volunteer-Match launched the first nationwide Disaster Relief Volunteering Map mashup (see Figure 6.10) to help volunteers locate and connect with the communities that need them.

> The Emergency Response Map is a "mash-up" of VolunteerMatch's database of active emergency response opportunities and Google Maps. When VolunteerMatch's nonprofit members post an opportunity in the "Disaster Relief" interest area, the listing instantly appears on the map, where prospective volunteers can zoom into local areas to see needs and eventually click to connect with the nonprofit organization.[11]

In the wake of Hurricane Katrina, a number of mashup sites were created by concerned citizens. Some were intended to help victims obtain more information about the status of specific neighborhoods.[12] Others assisted displaced families in locating temporary shelters.

Public broadcasting affiliate KPBS in San Diego used a Google Maps mashup to show the containment status of area fires in late 2007. The resulting map included nearby emergency services, hospitals, and meeting points for evacuees. The *Los Angeles Times* used mashups to provide similar information (see Figure 6.11). The L.A. map also incorporated micro-blogging service Twitter[13] to provide localized updates and alerts.

---

10. http://www.volunteermatch.org

11. "New VolunteerMatch Service Puts Emergency Preparedness 'on the Map'." VolunteerMatch press release. October 17, 2007.

12. http://www.scipionus.com/

13. http://www.twitter.com

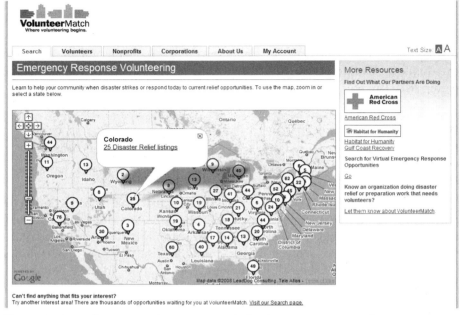

Figure 6.10   *VolunteerMatch's Disaster Relief Volunteering Map mashup connects volunteers and disaster-related volunteer opportunities at http:// www.volunteermatch.org/opportunities/disaster_relief.jsp.*

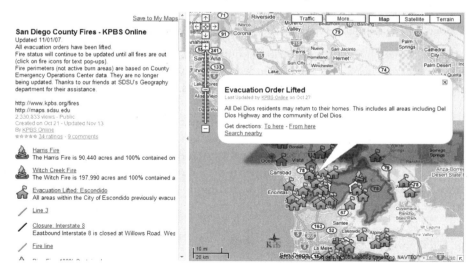

Figure 6.11   *KPBS and the Los Angeles Times used Google Maps as the visualization platform for displaying various information related to wildfires.*

In the United Kingdom, the BBC created a mashup[14] using Google Maps to both plot flood warnings and identify areas that had already been affected. The maps also displayed the locations of neighborhood emergency centers. This mashup was unique because it was not just the creation of a central organization: It also included videos pulled from YouTube and photos mailed by individuals. The BBC effectively turned the public into a massive news force capable of covering a much larger area than its own staff could hope to address. This example demonstrates the ability of crowdsourcing to provide highly localized information within large areas during a crisis.

The nonprofit site SocialActions[15] is using mashups to unite multiple charitable causes under a single searchable interface (as shown in Figure 6.12). Potential donors can explore opportunities based on type, based on location, or with the interactive tag cloud. According to founder Peter Deitz, "This innovation permits prospective donors, individuals, and Web apps to run queries on and map visually the data set as a whole. We see a huge potential in the 29-plus platforms to promote peer-to-peer social change. We're pursuing this work to amplify their impact and to bring about a world in which everyone is a changemaker."[16]

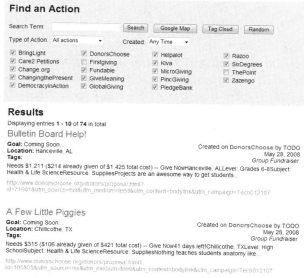

Figure 6.12   *More than 29 independent social platforms (including DonorsChoose.org and Helpalot.org) are mined to create a searchable interface for charities and causes at http://mashup.socialactions.com/.*

14. http://www.bbc.co.uk/berkshire/content/articles/2007/07/23/flood_map_feature.shtml

15. http://www.socialactions.com

16. SocialActions. "A Mashup of 29+ Social Action Platforms." http://www.netsquared.org/2008/conference/projects/mashup-social-actions

Filter

Core Activities: Data entry, data extraction, transformation, action

Problem

The modern world sometimes seems poised to smother us under an ever-increasing burden of alerts, news, facts, and figures. The increased connectivity and complexity of communication has created information overload (IO). We are bombarded by transmissions from so many areas that we spend ever-increasing portions of our time on data management rather than comprehension. According to Osterman Research, the average corporate employee sends and receives a combined total of 149 messages per day. In a 2007 study, 48% of respondents reported feeling overwhelmed by email at least some of the time.[17] At the same time, a typical company's email volume is growing at a rate of nearly 32% per year. The simple act of storing these messages is becoming a huge problem, with capacity requirements expected to increase to almost 82 gigabytes per day by 2010.

Industry research firm Basex named IO as its problem of the year for 2008 based on estimates that unnecessary interruptions are an almost $600 billion drag on the U.S. economy.[18] The Basex study accounts for the cost of lost time by multiplying the numbers of hours by an average hourly rate. If cases of

---

17. Osterman Research. *Results of an End-User Survey on Messaging Issues*. June 2007.

18. Basex. *Information Overload: We Have Met the Enemy and He Is Us*. March 2007.

missed opportunities caused by distractions could be directly measured, the result would most likely show the real cost is much higher.

The Basex study brings another aspect of IO to light: The typical knowledge worker reports spending more than 28% of his or her time dealing with interruptions.[19] These random events can disrupt an employee's work at any point during the day and can lead to a mental state where the anticipation of future distractions makes it hard to focus on the task at hand. Researcher Linda Stone terms this disorder "continuous partial attention" (CPA).

> To pay continuous partial attention is to pay partial attention—continuously. It is motivated by a desire to be a live node on the network. Another way of saying this is that we want to connect and be connected. We want to effectively scan for opportunity and optimize for the best opportunities, activities, and contacts, in any given moment. To be busy, to be connected, is to be alive, to be recognized, and to matter.

> We pay continuous partial attention in an effort not to miss anything. It is an always-on, anywhere, anytime, anyplace behavior that involves an artificial sense of constant crisis. We are always in high alert when we pay continuous partial attention.[20]

In his book *Ambient Findability,* author Peter Morville discusses the consequences of CPA:

> *We pay attention only to messages that find us.* And when we do search, we skim. A keyword or two into Google, a few good hits, and we're done. We satisfice with reckless abandon, waffling back and forth between too much information and not enough. And we make some very bad decisions as individuals, organizations, and societies.[21]

We are presently not very effective at fighting this affliction. Spam filters can block unwanted email messages but they don't prioritize important ones. Search engines provide thousands of results for even the simplest query. RSS feeds provide a constant stream of disruptions, often duplicated from multiple sources. We have solved the technical problems related to knowledge transmission but failed to address the human need for information taxonomy.

Solution

Because they can interact with many of the sources responsible for information creation, mashups are uniquely poised to help deal with the IO issue. By organizing the data that are competing for our attention we regain control over how, when, and where we choose to interact with it. This effort provides "information security," albeit not in the traditional sense of protecting secret

---

19. Basex, *Information Overload.*

20. "Continuous Partial Attention." http://www.lindastone.net

21. O'Reilly, 2005.

passwords or guarding customer details. Rather this term means that we achieve a feeling of personal security when we no longer worry about paying attention to everything at once. The roots of this confidence come from the realization that we are in control of our environment—and not the other way around.

Filter mashups allow complicated *personal* rules to be applied relative to specific circumstances. Possible activities include throwing out bad or irrelevant items, removing duplicate communications, creating and conveying summaries, and even automatically routing messages to different recipients. The goal is to create an information "organizational chart" where the amount of attention a communication receives is directly related to its importance. When combined with good work habits, Filter mashups are a practical weapon in the war on information overload and continuous partial attention.

Related Patterns: Smart Suggestions, Super Search

Fragility

The obvious danger in filtering information is that we might miss something important. That's why we have inflicted IO and CPA upon ourselves—fear can be a great motivator. Yet it should be obvious that our biological processing abilities cannot scale to meet the capacities of our technology. Instead we should set our creations against themselves and let them manage one another for us. The Filter pattern applies equally to the information we both receive *and* create. What can be reduced at the point of creation results in a corresponding decrease at the point of consumption proportional to the total number of recipients. In other words, one way to decrease the risk of missed information is to simply create less information in the first place!

Example: *Sort News Feeds by Importance and Relevancy*

RSS has gained incredible popularity both inside and outside the modern enterprise as a content syndication mechanism. Today there are so many feeds available from multiple sources that subscribing to more than a few can create an overwhelming amount of noise and distraction. A basic Filter implementation can address this problem using a combination of the following techniques:

- *Keyword filtering.* A predefined list of keywords is compared against each headline or message body. This process can be used to exclude stories that match keywords or to include only stories that contain these terms.

- *Author filtering*. Only messages created by specific authors are permitted.

- *Profanity filtering*. Content with inappropriate language is removed.

Many free and commercial products already provide this functionality. If we take advantage of a mashup's ability to harvest additional resources as part of its implementation, we can create even more intelligent RSS filters:

- *Filter by rating*. Many blogs contain a "vote" widget where visitors can rank the value of a post. A mashup can trace an RSS story back to its source and obtain this information. Stories with a low rating can be excluded from the feed; the remaining items can be sorted according to this value. Other indicators (such as popularity or page views) could be mined for similar purposes.

- *Filter by reaction*. If a blog post attracts a large number of comments it may be of particular interest. A mashup can count the number of responses to each post and rank the stories in the feed accordingly. This approach could be paired with a Reputation Management implementation to analyze the posts based on their conversational tone.

The previous approaches focus largely on blogs, which are not the sole source of RSS content. RSS in the enterprise can originate from a variety of sources used to provide alerts on issues:

- Computer virus warnings

- Reported bugs and Help Desk alerts

- System downtime notifications, scheduled maintenance, and system updates

- Low inventory warnings

- Order status

"Filtering" does not mean information should be involuntarily *removed*. The real challenge lies in getting information at the right time. Sometimes the objective is to lift a particular item above the general clamor so that it receives appropriate attention. Here are some steps a mashup author might take to communicate the previous feeds in a more useful format:

1. *Computer virus warnings*. Rather than just alert users, why not take immediate action to prevent the infection's spread? If a mashup has access

to a report indicating users whose antivirus software is out-of-date, it can trigger activity to prevent email attachments from being sent and lock their network drives.

2. *Reported bugs and Help Desk alerts.* By pulling in data from the firm's application inventory, a mashup could determine which team supports the application and send additional notifications via email and SMS.

3. *System downtime notifications, scheduled maintenance, and system updates.* Mashed-in data from the user's calendar would determine if these outages would occur during important work periods.

4. *Low inventory warnings.* A salesperson on the road might not check his or her RSS reader before visiting with clients. Inventory warnings can be repacked as SMS alerts and sent directly to the salesperson's cell phone.

5. *Order status.* Project schedules can be automatically adjusted based on changing delivery dates extracted from an order.

RSS is a natural target for a Filter implementation but is usually not the root cause of IO. Ultimately people *choose* to which feeds they will subscribe. IO is most widespread among the inflows of material that we cannot voluntarily control. The rest of the examples for this pattern provide suggestions for gaining control over this material.

Example: *Combat Information Overload*

Email is far and away the largest source of IO within the enterprise. Market research firm Radicati Group estimates that by 2009 workers will spend 41% of their time reading and responding to email.[22] Even if that figure is off by a few percentage points, it still represents a major drain on time and productivity. A number of tactics for managing our inboxes have been developed but most rely on the discipline of the reader. Fortunately mashups provide an alternative approach. Because most email systems either have an open API or expose a Web interface, users should have little difficulty implementing the following strategies. To get started, create "Respond Now" and one or more "Respond Later" folders. The "Respond Later" folders will group related material that doesn't require immediate action.

---

22. http://www.abcnews.go.com/GMA/TakeControlOfYourLife/story?id=3418958

1. Prioritize messages sent only to you. The mashup can move them to the "Respond Now" folder or some mail systems allow emails to be flagged as "important."

2. Consider auto-filing emails sent to a group account of which you are a member to one of the "Respond Later" folders.

3. Many messages are system generated and are sent from accounts with names like "no-reply." If your mail system doesn't natively offer the ability to categorize these messages, use a mashup.

4. The mashup should periodically examine the contents of the "Respond Later" folders and move old items to the "Respond Now" queue. The determination of what is classified as "old" can be based on a fixed date, the sender's name, or other variables that the mashup pulls from the message body.

5. If your email system allows messages to be color coded, consider using this function to implement a dynamic "heat map" for popular conversations. The mashup can count the number of messages sent and received with a common subject line and "score" the importance of the topic. This value is then conveyed visually by setting the color to red for "hot" topics and blue for less frequent exchanges.

6. Monitor your information sources. A mashup can measure the time it takes you respond to particular users (and the time it takes those users to answer you) by comparing subjects and times in your "Inbox" and "Sent" folders. Consider having the mashup reprioritize messages based on these metrics.

It might be tempting to create a mashup that looks at your calendar and automatically responds to emails when you are booked. If you can provide useful information this is a good idea, but avoid sending replies along the lines of "I'm busy, I'll respond later." Such messages simply generate more noise for everyone else. Once you have some Filter mashups in place, try not to answer emails as soon as they arrive. Instead, set aside dedicated blocks of time for this activity. The nervousness that leads to CPA will vanish once you regain control of your communication environment.

Example: *Pre-search Data for the User*

Any system that incorporates search functionality is a likely candidate for a Filter implementation. This relationship seems counterintuitive. Isn't the point of a search to retrieve only a relevant subset of material from a larger body of information—in other words, to filter it? Yes, but search results are often the first step in an additional screening process. Consider the following examples:

- An inventory system enables searches for specific products but not their dimensions. If the goal is to locate parts of a specific size, each item's details must be examined individually.

- Fuel consumption for the corporate travel fleet is aggregated in a national database that can be searched by sales territory. Regional managers who want to track their local office performance must manually extract relevant line items.

- An online reservation system allows employees to plan corporate travel but the total price of a trip must fall within the firm's guidelines. It's a waste of time to wade through itineraries that are too expensive.

- A timekeeping system allows management to track time spent on a given project by an employee. But if managers want to sort this data based on an associate's location or job function, they must painstakingly look up each person in the firm's corporate directory.

Now the Long Tail discussed in Chapter 1 resurfaces yet again: Wherever search features exist, only the most general functionality is likely to be present. A Filter implementation can act on initial results to limit the scope of data even further. This may entail outright removal of details or an examination of outside sources to determine which data is irrelevant and which should be excluded.

Location Mapping

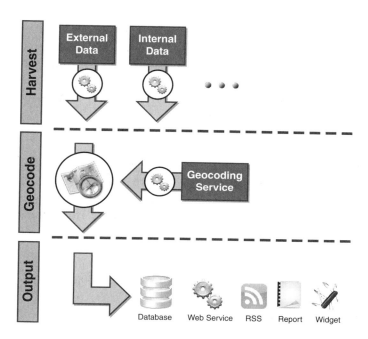

Core Activities: Data entry, data extraction, data visualization, transformation

Problem

Identifying and allocating resources by location was a crucial activity long before the advent of modern technology. Alexander the Great was able to conquer much of the known world in part because he carefully planned for food and supplies to be delivered exactly where and when his armies would need them.[23] Today a large amount of the data that passes through applications likewise has a counterpart in the physical world. For example, employee records represent real people; shipping statements track actual packages. One of the benefits of the digital representation is that we can supplement real-world characteristics like quantity or color with intangible properties such as date-of-hire, job code, or estimated delivery date. Of course, the more attributes we add, the

23. Engels, Donald E. *Alexander the Great and the Logistics of the Macedonian Army.* University of California Press, 1978.

greater the importance of location. Location is valuable because it may be the only attribute shared by dissimilar objects. Positional details allow otherwise unrelated items to be compared based on their distance from a given point or proximity to one another.

Many modern-day systems contain positional information but it is either underutilized or not cast into a useful format. An application may record the home addresses of staff but not calculate their geographical dispersion, even though the latter information could be useful for risk planning purposes. A retail store may offer products for sale but not advertise broadly enough to reach the largest number of potential customers.

The precision of location data can vary widely—from as broad an area as a country down to a specific street address. The ability to display this data on a map is certainly a useful capability; nevertheless, it can be equally important to calculate the relative locations of a basket of items. In situations where a firm has already maximized the value of its internal location data, new opportunities may arise through tying this data to external resources. But before any of these tasks can be accomplished, all geographic information must be collected and converted to a common format.

Applications that collect location data should take steps to verify its accuracy. Failure to do so can facilitate fraud and lead to problems including shipping errors, duplicate mailings, and undeliverable parcels. One study by the U.S. Postal Service found the amount of mail deemed "undeliverable as addressed" totaled 5.4 billion pieces.[24] Approximately 37% of these items (2 billion) ultimately wound up in landfills—waste that's roughly equivalent to the annual emissions from about 180,000 cars.[25]

Solution

The first application of the Location Mapping pattern is to fulfill the need for address verification. Numerous free and commercial products available on the Web can resolve location information with varying degrees of accuracy. A Location Mapping implementation can combine multiple products serving different regions to create a global validation service. The Smart Suggestions, Field Medic,

---

24. http://ribbs.usps.gov/files/UAA/UAASUM.PDF

25. This figure is extrapolated from ForestEthics Group, "Junk Mail's Impact on Global Warming," August 2008, http://forestethics.org/downloads/ClimateReport.pdf. In the report NASA climate scientist James Hansen equates 100 billion pieces of junk mail to the emissions from more than 9 million cars.

and Usability Enhancer patterns suggest different techniques for enhancing applications with this newly acquired capability. Address validation services could also be used against existing databases to flag specific records for further investigation or removal.

The second use of the Location Mapping pattern entails using addresses as a means to establish the relative locations of objects of interest in three-dimensional space. Three values are used to pinpoint any spot on the planet's surface: latitude, longitude, and altitude. In most cases latitude and longitude provide sufficient accuracy for estimating distances.[26] To begin we must focus our attention on geocoding. Geocoding refers to the process of determining latitude and longitude from known physical characteristics. The most common starting point is a street address; alternatively, a computer's network address or a cell phone's proximity to nearby broadcast towers can be used. A Location Mapping mashup can access one of the numerous geocoding services available on the Internet to build a collection of coordinates. Because the surface of the Earth is not a plane, simple Euclidian geometry cannot be used to estimate the distance between the locations except over relatively small areas. Great Circle arithmetic, which pertains to spherical geometry, is more useful in these circumstances. The Haversine formula[27] (shown in the "Calculating Distance Between Two Points" sidebar) is one of several Great Circle calculations that can be used to compute distance more accurately given lat/long values.

The final—and most popular—use of the Location Mapping pattern is to visualize spatial data using a geographic information system (GIS). From the earliest mashup[28] until today, thousands of mashups in both consumer and enterprise settings have been created to collect geographic data with this goal in mind.[29] Harvest mashups are used to collect points of interest and regional statistics than can be mapped to valid locations using the two previously discussed techniques (address verification and geocoding). The results are mashed together with a GIS to support further analysis. Google Maps and Live Maps have been a key enabler for these types of mashups.

Related Patterns: Emergency Response, Reality Mining, Super Search, Widget Enabler

---

26. And it keeps the math simpler!

27. Sinnott, R. W. "Virtues of the Haversine." *Sky and Telescope* 68, no. 2 (1984).

28. http://www.housingmaps.com

29. More than 1,684 as of late 2008, according to http://www.programmableweb.com/tag/mapping

Calculating Distance Between Two Points

Given two points defined as (lat_1, $long_1$) and (lat_2, $long_2$), the distance between them can be calculated by using the Haversine formula:

$$dlon = lon_2 - lon_1$$
$$dlat = lat_2 - lat_1$$
$$a = \sin^2\left(\frac{dlat}{2}\right) + \cos(lat_1) * \cos(lat2) * \sin^2\left(\frac{dlon}{2}\right)$$
$$c = 2 * \arcsin\left(\min\left(1, \sqrt{a}\right)\right)$$
$$distance = R * c$$

When creating a program to solve this equation, it may be necessary to convert the arguments of the trigonometric functions (sin, cos, arcsin) from degrees to radians. If a native function is not available (for example, the toRadians method in Java's Math package), you can accomplish the task by multiplying the degrees by $\frac{\pi}{180}$ (or approximately 0.017453293). The value of R in the equation is the radius of the sphere—in this case the Earth. Unfortunately the Earth is not perfectly spherical so another approximation is required. The value 3,956 miles (6,367 km) is a good starting point. You can learn more about the Haversine formula and discover how to tweak it for increased accuracy via online sources.[30]

An alternative approach is to "cheat." You can use a mashup to supply data to an online mapping product, let it calculate the distance for you, and then extract the distance and driving time. One advantage to this approach is that it can take roads, traffic patterns, construction delays, and driving speed into account rather than providing an "as the crow flies" estimate. The downside is that this technique may not scale to service large volumes of data or provide fast response times.

Fragility

Although the Location Mapping pattern manifests itself in three different flavors (verification, visualization, and localization), geocoding is at the heart of each of these implementations. Risk originates in situations where address

30. "Great Circle Distance Between 2 Points." http://www.movable-type.co.uk/scripts/gis-faq-5.1.html

information cannot be successfully geocoded. This failure can lead to the storage of incorrect information or prevent data points from being successfully plotted on a map. In each of these cases it is a simple task to trap the error condition and notify the user before any harm is done. Location Mapping receives the lowest fragility ranking for this reason.

▼

Example: *Reduce Unnecessary Mailings with Address Validation*

Tangerine Nation (TN) is a retail clothing outlet that has many store locations across the country. It specializes in affordable, stylish clothing for men, women, and children. As part of any customer transaction the company collects the customer's mailing address. It then sends out multiple catalogs during the year. Some catalogs are focused on a particular gender or age group; seasonal issues are generally thicker and targeted at families. Because an entire household may independently shop at TN, the company can easily collect three or more similar customer records that resolve to the same mailing address. Although this duplication causes small problems during TN's focused mailings, the largest overlaps occur for the hefty seasonal issues. Sending double or triple the amount of required catalogs is wasteful from both a fiscal point of view and an environmental perspective. TN has scrubbed its database using basic comparison techniques yet still receive frequent customer complaints about duplicate mailings.

TN decides to use a Location Mapping mashup to resolve each of the addresses for each of its hundreds of thousands of customers. Comparing every single address against each of the others would take hundreds of hours, so checks are limited to records that share the same ZIP code. After processing, TN identifies thousands of duplicate records. Linking these records together not only eliminates unnecessary mailings, but also deepens the demographic data TN has on household purchasing habits. Additionally, the thousands of *invalid* addresses uncovered through this action will be marked for the customer to correct when he or she makes their next purchase.

▼

Example: *Find the Closest Qualified Resources*

Kirby Systems is a professional services firm with more than 200,000 employees scattered across the globe. Senior managers are based in strategic branch offices but a large portion of the workforce operates from their personal residences. When a new project spins up, Kirby flies in associates from all over the globe to temporary office space it has leased. The team disbands just as quickly when the work is finished.

Frequently, once an engagement has been completed, a customer requests additional services. Such requests for assistance can include technical help, training, or enhancements to the solutions Kirby provided. Consider the case where Kirby created a credit derivatives trading system for a firm based in Montreal and the client requests follow-up training for recently hired staff. It's unlikely that Kirby can reassemble the original team because most will have moved on to other assignments or will not have the correct skills. Kirby needs to locate new expertise within its workforce and respond quickly. By mashing together its internal systems the company can locate associates who speak French, have training experience, and understand credit default swaps. Their addresses are geocoded and their proximity to the client is calculated using the Haversine formula. This report—which demonstrates the value of Location Mapping without a visible map—is used to dispatch the closest resource to the customer.

Example: *Spatially Visualize Data*

There is unlimited potential for using Location Mapping and subsequent spatial analysis to help your business. Other ideas include these:

- A corporate sales force may wish to maximize the time agents spend on external sales calls by computing the proximity of potential clients that can be visited on a single trip.

- The political or environmental risk to resources may be mapped based on their location (e.g., airport noise near potential building sites, flood danger to policy holders).

- Company vehicles may be tracked.

- Sales history and forecasts may be organized based on geography.

- Business continuity plans may specify which alternate locations are closest to a particular employee in the event of an emergency.

- A company may establish new marketing strategies based on regional pur-chasing trends.

- A firm may plan bandwidth allotment based on the geocoded IP addresses of network users.

Splinter

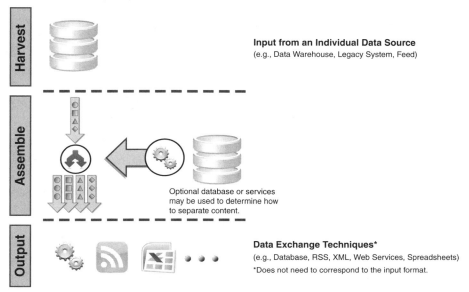

Harvest

Input from an Individual Data Source
(e.g., Data Warehouse, Legacy System, Feed)

Assemble

Optional database or services
may be used to determine how
to separate content.

Output

Data Exchange Techniques*
(e.g., Database, RSS, XML, Web Services, Spreadsheets)
*Does not need to correspond to the input format.

Core Activities: Data extraction, transformation

Also Known As: Content Separation

Problem

Organizations spend considerable time managing the vast amounts of data generated by business activities. To make this information more accessible, many firms have adopted the concept of a data warehouse (DW). Unlike a physical building that is simply a container for various bits of inventory, a DW is an integrated information repository. Data is systematically collected from various heterogeneous sources and transformed to comply with specific formats and semantics before being filed away. The finished environment is intended to allow end users easy access to corporate data. Because of its broad scope, successful DW implementations are expensive and time-consuming endeavors. Consequently some firms choose to focus on aggregating specific business intelligence or supply-chain information.

Many DW efforts fall victim to a number of pitfalls.[31] Postmortem analysis illustrates a handful of the more common culprits:

1. DW activities cannot be completed outside business hours.

2. The costs to capture and clean data are excessive and the DW may be understaffed.

3. Strategic application development is slowed by efforts to negotiate feeds from the DW.

4. End users find it difficult to access the data they require.

The first two items are largely issues of time and money. The Content Integration and Filter mashups discussed earlier in this chapter can help reduce the technical challenges of data collection that lead to cost overruns. Assuming these problems are overcome, that still leaves the last two items on the list. Each stems from a common concern: How can aggregated data be efficiently distributed once it has been collected?

While this dilemma is perhaps more common in a DW environment, this scenario is certainly is not the only place it appears. Mature firms have a tendency to extend existing applications to hold greater amounts of data as their business requirements evolve. This organic approach to growth frequently occurs without being subjected to any long-term architectural planning. When a system eventually threatens to collapse under the weight of poor design, the challenge of moving the intertwined resources to new locations becomes a thorny obstacle.

Solution

We have already observed how enterprise information sources can be combined by applying the Content Integration pattern. This process can be a key step in creating a unified warehouse. We have further discussed techniques for removing redundant or unneeded information by applying the Filter pattern. The final component of our data management triumvirate deals with the separation of data into relevant subsections. The converse of the Content Integration pattern and a close relative of Filter, the Splinter pattern takes a single data source and makes its contents available as separate new streams of data. As the "Problem" section illustrates, this is a common requirement wherever a single data repository is used. A Splinter implementation isn't limited to creating new feeds, however. It can provide alternative means to access them as well. Consider this

---

31. Gartner. *Steer Clear of Common Data Warehousing Pitfalls,* October 27, 2005.

capability to be a variation of the API Enabler pattern (see Chapter 4) brought to bear on the problem of distribution.

Why would a Splinter mashup succeed where the existing dissemination mechanisms failed? The key advantages offered by mashups in this area are their flexibility and ease of use. Whereas developers would previously need to agree on formats and interfaces with a data provider, mashups enable them to accept most sources and transform their data to suit their needs. Similarly many mashup products are intended to be customized by the end user. This removes the burden of employees having to learn complicated data extraction tools because they can interact with DW-fed mashups instead.

The value of the Splinter pattern is not limited to making a DW easy to use. For example, the Dashboard pattern (which we examine in Chapter 7) describes the use of business data to create a console that can monitor a firm's performance. Consider the situation where a single internal system tracks customer order information. If a dashboard is to be constructed for various purchasing activities, those metrics will need to be individually extracted from different portions of the source application's database. In this situation a Splinter implementation can be used to provide each chart or gauge on the dashboard with the unique information required to generate its display.

Splinter is another example of why the term "mashup" is not a good descriptor for the broad functionality provided by this new development model. The inclusion of "separation" functionality might seem misplaced within a category pertaining to assembly; in fact, a similar claim could be made against the Filtering pattern. We assume that the outcome of these operations is the distribution of focused data that will be used to jumpstart new solutions. Furthermore, when multiple resources are aggregated by patterns such as Content Integration, it is a natural consequence that some material needs to be removed or redirected prior to use. As a result it is not uncommon to see all three of these patterns used as part of a single solution.

Related Patterns: Content Integration, Filter

Fragility

Like all mashups that perform direct data manipulation, the Splinter pattern is not without its risks. As with the Content Integration and Filter patterns, chief among these is that something will be unintentionally left out of the final results. There is also the chance that moving data to a different output format will erode some of the intrinsic value it once possessed. While the output of the Integration and Filter implementations is a single product, the goal of the Splinter pattern is to create multiple artifacts whose audience might be a combination of applications and end users. The potential for any discrepancies to be distributed across so broad a range is why this pattern receives a slightly higher fragility score than its closest relatives.

Example: *Create Multiple Data Feeds from a Legacy System*

Snafu Industrial has a legacy mainframe application called OMS that handles all of its account information, orders, and payments. The system was written years ago in COBOL. Each night it outputs an enormous CSV-formatted log file of the day's activities. The system survives in "maintenance mode"; it is extremely important to the business but its code base is so broad, and skilled in-house COBOL developers so few, that Snafu is barely able to keep the OMS application functional. Despite its longevity it serves its original purposes quite well, which is why Snafu hasn't decided to incur the expense and effort of moving to a new platform (perhaps the company will use the Content Migration pattern when it is ready to take this step). But now Snafu employees would like to perform some new operations using OMS data—and IT is considering a mashup to meet their requests.

The traditional solution to this problem would be to write scripts in Perl or Ruby to parse OMS's single output file to create new data streams for other applications. These programs could read in the CSV and dump the subsets of the data to new output sources such as a database or XML file. But there are a few limitations to this approach. Every time someone wants to work with a new slice of data from the OMS output, a new script must be written to create the new extract. Suppose a script already exists but a different output format is needed? Going from CSV to XML can be a nontrivial task. Perhaps other changes to date or currency formats are necessary. Once again, code must be modified. The reliance on hard-coded scripts means that technical resources need to be involved for every change, no matter how trivial; business users cannot perform these actions for themselves.

Snafu doesn't have a DW, but it does have a single canonical data repository that it needs to open up for flexible access. One technique is to create a Web Services interface on the original CSV file using the API Enabler pattern (see Chapter 4). Unfortunately many of the existing downstream tools employees want to use were not engineered to communicate directly with Web Services—not to mention that having multiple requests interrogate the entire source file repeatedly can be highly inefficient. A better approach is to enable highly customizable custom extracts that can be created by anyone with a business case for accessing the data.

Establishing an environment that allows the easy creation of Splinter implementations is one way Snafu can meet this challenge. Many mashup toolsets obviate the need for custom coding to slice and parse the original file. No code is typically necessary to produce a variety of output formats; simple configuration settings control this aspect. Transformation functionality performs any additional massaging to ensure that the results conform to whatever style the new tools and products require for valid input. Ideally each Splinter implementation is available for reuse from a central repository. This allows for further refinement of extracts by other users or even dynamic recombinations (see the Content Integration pattern discussed earlier in this chapter). This is another instance of where "the virtuous circle of mashups" (see Chapter 1) allows each new participant to incrementally increase the value of existing resources. Likewise, a single mashup depot will prevent rework by employees who unnecessarily recreate extracts that have already been developed by others. Having easy access to a variety of data feeds allows employees to perform ad hoc analyses and make rapid decisions instead of struggling to get basic information.

▼

Example: *Split a National Feed to Serve Specific Regions*

One of the markets in which Snafu operates deals with temporary power generation facilities. Sometimes large construction projects require dedicated electrical generation capabilities on-site—especially if they reside in remote locations. At other times an equipment failure or natural disaster may render the existing infrastructure inoperable. In all of these cases, Snafu has an opportunity to sell or lease a solution to the customer. Snafu has a subscription to an external service that issues news alerts about areas affected by extreme weather conditions. Its sales agents routinely scan this data for incidents so that they can call on local government agencies in their respective territories. The company also has a separate service that publishes an RSS feed of recently approved capital projects; agents regularly examine this list in search of new prospects.

It's incredibly inefficient and wasteful for Snafu's sales staff to individually examine each feed. The IT staff recognize that a combination of several patterns can make the organization more effective. First the two external feeds (disaster and capital projects) are combined using the Content Integration pattern. Next the location of each item is determined by an implementation of Location Mapping. Because Snafu operates only within North America, some alerts will be discarded via a Filter implementation. A Splinter implementation then pulls in an internal database of territory codes to create a set of distinct feeds for the individual salespeople (as depicted in Figure 6.13).

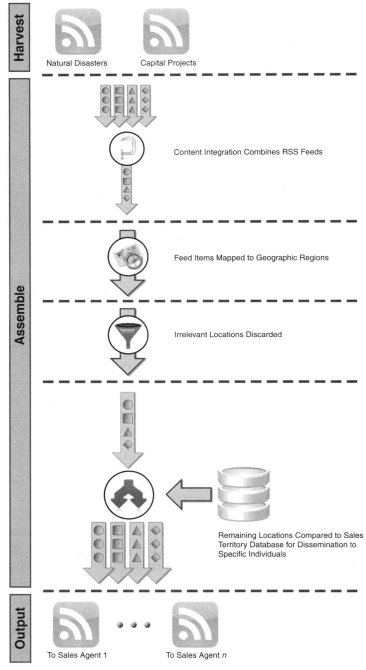

Figure 6.13   *Splintering the output from combined RSS feeds*

Chapter 7

Manage Patterns

Introduction

IT: information technology. It might be more accurately termed information management (IM) because that's why this team *employs* technology in the first place. In fact, before the proliferation of computers in the workplace, many companies had an enterprise IM department that was responsible for maintaining the paper-based records of the firm. When data storage moved online, IM became a discipline within IT; its responsibility changing to supply the information behind emerging software solutions.

Data management is now at the core of every service IT provides. Applications acquire information through user activity or feeds. Network infrastructure carries this data between servers, databases, and other systems that retain or operate on it. Ultimately the output is returned to the user in an endless cycle of collection, calculation, and presentation.

Each previous chapter (and corresponding mashup category) has addressed the activities within these stages. Chapter 4 covered Harvest patterns, examining how mashups can be used to *obtain* data from different sources. Chapter 5 on Enhance patterns looked at how this data could be used to *enrich* existing solutions. Chapter 6 on Assemble patterns showed how harvested content could be *recombined* to present new resources, some of which could in turn be rolled back into new enhancements. Now we've reached a point where it's appropriate to return our focus to the data itself.

Mashups yield vast new supplies of raw material for our systems. Obviously we need to establish the means to process this torrent of information before it becomes overwhelming. This requirement presents technical issues regarding transmission and storage that IT has tackled many times before. The more pressing concern, however, is that humans' personal faculties will not scale to take advantage of this new content or that it may become trapped inside existing methodologies. That's the facet of management that we will tackle in this chapter.

The challenges of data management and its relation to mashups can be separated across a few different topics:

- *Transitioning between systems* (Content Migration, Quick Proof-of-Concept). Sometimes the best way to handle information is to migrate it to new environments that can analyze or process it more efficiently. We briefly addressed the role of mashups as an alternative to enterprise application integration (EAI) and enterprise information integration (EII) solutions in Chapter 1. Products in these categories offer sophisticated features but they are useless when a system is designed to block attempts to access its internal records. Mashups offer unique methods for circumventing these obstructions.

- *Condensing data or processes to align with specific goals* (Dashboard, Portal Enabler, Widget Enabler). Presenting a user with the universe of data and all the possible actions that can be performed on it is a surefire way to create confusion and cause unintentional errors. We examine two approaches—polar opposites—where mashups offer relief. One involves collapsing large quantities of material into high-level summaries that can be quickly understood. The other drills deep into resources to provide highly focused functionality tailored to specific tasks.

- *Securing access to valuable knowledge* (Single Sign-on). If an employee is presented with information outside his or her normal business responsibilities, the risks are greater than mere disorientation. Significant business consequences may arise if trade secrets, customer records, or other confidential material is unwittingly disclosed. Part of proper data management entails protecting these assets so they are not at risk. We have already seen how mashups can help create proprietary knowledge streams; in this chapter we'll see how they can be used to secure those resources.

Another aspect that differentiates this chapter from its predecessors is that most of the Manage patterns typically fall under the jurisdiction of an IT department. By contrast, many of the previous mashups were equally amenable to end-user implementation. This divergence is a result of the bifurcated data management structure within most organizations that can trace its roots back to the days of the separate Information Management division. End users *manipulate* information using the tools that IT provides to store and distribute it. The progression of increased familiarity with data itself resulted in the creation of domain-specific knowledge; this is the realm of the business associate. Meanwhile focus on the technical challenges of administration led to the evolution of the modern enterprise developer. It's not unlike the fictional rift that developed between the Eloi and Morlocks in H.G. Wells' *The Time Machine*.[1] Because the patterns in this chapter are less concerned with content than they are with process and structure, they correspond more closely with the responsibilities of IT personnel.

This distinction should not discourage nondevelopers from exploring this chapter. By now I hope many of the preconceived notions you may have had about application development and mashups have been shattered. A word of caution is in order because some of the issues explored in the following patterns operate at a level below the user interface veneer with which some readers will be most familiar.

---

1. The Eloi lived above-ground in the daylight; the Morlocks labored away in dark tunnels. I'm not saying who's who in this example, though.

Content Migration

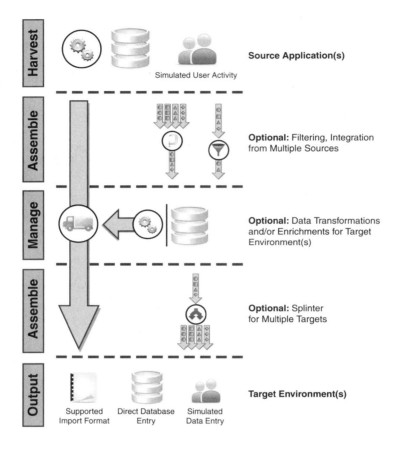

Core Activities: Data extraction, data entry, transformation

Also Known As: Broadcast, Propagation

Problem

When an application or tool that solves a difficult problem first hits the market, it can quickly become very popular. The vendor responsible for the innovation is said to have "first-mover advantage." If the company executes a successful strategy, it can use its initial headstart on potential competitors to establish itself as the dominant force. But marketing a new idea while at the same time supporting customers and financing development is a challenging effort. It's very likely that the effects of these pressures will manifest themselves in the vendor's product. For example, the initial offering might contain bugs, be difficult to use, or be very expensive. When limited solutions are available, organizations will overlook these flaws in light of the greater benefits. But it's often just a matter of time before alternative choices emerge. A profitable niche will attract other vendors that capitalize on the market established by the initial players. Their products enjoy a "second-mover advantage" because as latecomers, they can learn from the mistakes and missteps of their forerunners and use this knowledge to provide superior offerings.

All of this maneuvering leaves the early adopters of new technology in a difficult position. If they have committed a large amount of effort to supply the original system with data, the costs of switching to a new product can be substantial—a quandary known as "vendor lock-in." This circumstance might be unintentional; in its eagerness to pioneer new services a vendor may not focus on adopting open standards for exchanging information with other systems. Of course, the practice may be deliberately competitive and monopolistic: Making it difficult for clients to switch to rivals' products is a technique many firms use to maintain their market share. Sometimes switching between products is inevitable no matter the maturity level of an industry. A supplier may go bankrupt or discontinue a particular product, or the carrying costs of a solution may be so high that a firm is forced to transition to a less expensive or open-source solution.

Assuming a firm has fallen victim to one of these "lock-in" scenarios, how can it escape to an alternative platform without incurring painful switching costs?

Solution

While a vendor can make it difficult to migrate to a competitor's product by withholding export functionality, it can do only so much to lock down its system. An Enterprise Information Integration (EII) tool might be able to extract the required records from an application's back-end database provided it is possible to decipher the structure of the original system. If that approach fails, the data in the original program could be reviewed and rekeyed into the replacement system. Of course, this is a worst-case scenario. This approach requires monumental efforts and has a number of obvious drawbacks. For example, what if the information needs to be changed slightly before the new application can accept it? What about all the possible data-entry errors that could occur? Fortunately mashups offer a better solution.

It doesn't matter if the original system is a blog, document repository, email, version control system, or Web site. No matter what function an application performs, the information it contains must ultimately be accessible to its users.

As author David Linthicum appropriately puts it in his discussion of enterprise application integration (EAI), "In many applications, the user is the only available mechanism for accessing logic and data. In spite of its inefficiency in 'getting into' an application, the user interface has an advantage in that it does not require any changes to the source or target application."[2] The Content Migration pattern seeks to exploit this loophole. The Infinite Monkeys pattern (see Chapter 4) showed that mashups can take normal user activities and scale them to a superhuman level. This action is the key that allows data to be methodically extracted from an otherwise closed environment—but it is not the complete solution to the migration challenge. The chances are reasonably high that the structure and format used by the original and new systems won't match. Mashups' ability to transform data during the handling process can address this problem.

The next step is to copy this content into its new home. If you're lucky, the target system will provide some type of "import" functionality. But if it doesn't, mashups once again provide the answer. Because the new application must naturally *accept* user input, another Infinite Monkeys implementation could masquerade as a group of employees and "manually" enter the extracted resources. Alternatively, the API Enabler pattern could be used to impose custom "import" functionality. This approach is more flexible when the migration isn't a one-time operation and when the replacement system will supplant multiple products. Other mashups (as well as traditional feeds) could leverage this well-defined interface to populate the application with additional data.

The Content Migration pattern doesn't require the original system to disappear after its implementation. This pattern can be used to retain historic material for archival purposes or to provide a sanitized subset of information to a specific group of users. For example, developers could regularly receive a partial dump of production data via a mashup that filters out or obfuscates sensitive customer information. Content Migration can also be combined with application monitoring to provide per-user audit trails (consult the Audit pattern in Chapter 8 for further details).

Migrations aren't restricted to one-time events that are part of some manually triggered "mass relocation" effort. They can be a living, dynamic link between multiple systems used to keep incremental changes to data in sync. Additions, deletions, or modifications made in one application can be automatically propagated behind the scenes to other environments. When disconnected systems require essentially the same information, this pattern can be used to transparently replicate entry tasks in one application to other programs. This strategy eliminates a lot of repetitive work that would otherwise be performed

---

2. Linthicum, David S. *Enterprise Application Integration*. Addison-Wesley, 1999.

by the user. Mashups can even be used to implement transactional capabilities across systems that are otherwise unrelated.

Related Patterns: Infinite Monkeys

Fragility

A primary concern with the Content Migration pattern is that some information will be lost or "mistranslated" along the way. Assuming some sort of error handling is implemented, it is unlikely that information will be dropped without some type of notification being sent. Improper translation is a thornier problem. Depending on the level of transformations applied to migrated data, it's conceivable that some content could be misfiled. A thorough investigation of each environment should be performed post-migration to ensure that the expected information was correctly received at its new home. Because Content Migration is a relatively transparent process with ample opportunities for error reporting and data quality analysis, it receives the second-lowest fragility rating.

▼

Example: *Unify Disparate Knowledge Management Platforms*

Blackbird Aerospace (BA) is a diversified technology company specializing in commercial and military aeronautic and space systems. Not surprisingly the firm employs a large number of technical personnel. Its engineers were quick to recognize the value of wikis for collaboration on large projects and proposals. Unfortunately the same "maverick" corporate culture that has helped BA compete successfully in its sector resulted in a fractured internal environment for knowledge management (KM). Most teams implemented their own wiki platforms without any consultation with other groups. Much of this information is now siloed from the perspective of outside teams (as shown in Figure 7.1). The lack of a single wiki platform also means it is difficult to demonstrate the security and auditability of data—a key requirement for many of BA's government contracts.

Senior management recognizes the value of wikis but has concerns about the fragmented infrastructure. They decide to fund a project to move all of the firm's disparate environments to a unified platform. The result should increase collaboration by exposing more teams to one another's work. The centralization will have another benefit, too: Archiving and searching content should become easier because these tasks will be relegated to a single site.

One of the biggest challenges in creating the unified corporate wiki is consolidating the various data from their current environments. Some wikis are running

Figure 7.1   *Multiple wikis capture content but still leave users isolated.*

on Microsoft Windows servers; others are deployed on Linux or Solaris systems. Some systems store their content on a database; some on the file system. Each product uses similar wiki markup language, but none is identical to the target platform's. Finally, no product provides a standard export/transfer mechanism. Some wikis directly export XML while others offer an open API. A few products offer no interface whatsoever outside of their user-facing Web site.

The Content Migration pattern provides a solution. A mashup can slurp exported content from its native format or API and transform it into a format accepted by the new platform's import functionality. For cases when a legacy wiki has no explicit programmatic hooks, data can be extracted by simulating user activity (see the Infinite Monkeys pattern in Chapter 4). Consolidating a diverse collection of information repositories would have been an almost insurmountable task before mashups. With the Content Migration pattern BA is able to easily obtain and combine the collected knowledge of its employees without excessive cost or effort (see Figure 7.2).

BA's work isn't finished yet: It still has strict auditing requirements to fulfill that are not met by the unified wiki platform alone. For regulatory purposes the company is required to perform a daily archive of all internal content and communications to a "write-once" medium[3] stored at a secure external facility. The organization BA has chosen to provide this utility accepts email threads, instant

---

3. Also known as WORM ("Write Once, Read Many").

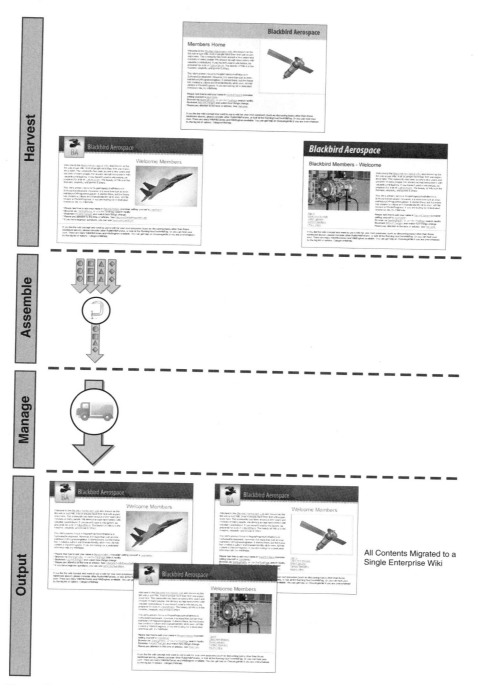

Figure 7.2 *Content from multiple wikis is migrated to a single environment.*

message conversations, and wiki content provided those data are packaged to meet its specific XML import requirements. BA will once again rely on a Content Migration implementation to gather and transform its data for supply to this outside agency.

▼

Example: *Export Data from a Closed, Legacy System to a SaaS Provider*

Chrysoma Property Management has decided to restructure its IT department and retire a number of its internally developed applications. After careful analysis the firm has determined that outsourcing the majority of its systems to a SaaS provider will enable it to better focus on its core business activities. The SaaS vendor can handle the import of customer data in several formats (e.g., CSV, XLS, XML) but the in-house systems were never designed with export features in mind. Most of the original developers have left the firm so it will be difficult and expensive to add this new feature. Yet without some way to extract the existing customer records, Chrysoma is beholden to its legacy systems.

By mimicking user activity the Content Migration pattern is able to liberate captive data. An implementation is created to crawl through the existing software and drill down into customer details similar to how a user browsing through the system would behave. At each step of this "simulated user activity" the mashup collects another portion of the information locked away inside the program. Once the collective data stored by the system has been obtained, a series of operations convert the date and currency values to new formats. The last step is the output of a standard XML file, which is then imported into the new SaaS application. Chrysoma's staff didn't need to write a single line of code to achieve this result.

The replacement system was chosen in part because it provides a content-export feature that should reduce the chances of Chrysoma falling victim to vendor lock-in. The company decides to leverage this feature with another Content Migration implementation to check the success of its previous mashup. Although the SaaS program reports all legacy records have been read successfully, Chrysoma cannot afford to turn off its internal applications until it has verified that no data has been accidentally left behind. Another Content Migration implementation reads the XML exported from the new environment and attempts to verify it using the corresponding record in the legacy system. The first few of attempts uncover some data formatting errors that slipped past the initial import. The original mashup is rerun after a few small modifications and the next check confirms the operation was a complete success.

Dashboard

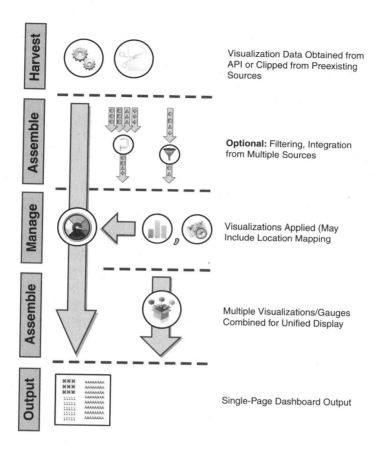

Harvest — Visualization Data Obtained from API or Clipped from Preexisting Sources

Assemble — **Optional:** Filtering, Integration from Multiple Sources

Manage — Visualizations Applied (May Include Location Mapping

Assemble — Multiple Visualizations/Gauges Combined for Unified Display

Output — Single-Page Dashboard Output

Core Activities: Clipping, data extraction, data entry, data visualization, transformation

Also Known As: Cockpit

Problem

As the number of systems within an organization increases, it becomes impossible for any single individual to review the volume of data that is generated on a daily basis—let alone use that information as the basis for analysis of business or IT performance. Yet this reality is at complete opposition to the way most corporations are structured. One look at a typical organizational chart reveals a management structure that starts with a large number of employees in the trenches and retreats to a few senior staff who are expected to set the strategic direction for the firm.

Historically this conflict was resolved by delegating subordinates with the job of reporting only the most relevant information to their superiors. Mid-level managers filtered out irrelevant data so that supervisors could "manage by metrics." Unfortunately the status reports managers received were often static and didn't permit interactively drilling down into particular areas of interest. In other instances the environments being managed were so dynamic that they didn't lend themselves to this approach. For example, when a network is unresponsive or a spike in business activity occurs, a successful organization needs to deal with these issues immediately.

Business dashboards were created to meet the challenges of information management brought about by our technological advances. Stephen Few, author of *Information Dashboard Design,* defines a dashboard as "a visual display of the most important information needed to achieve one or more objectives; consolidated and arranged on a single screen so the information can be monitored at a glance.[4]" These living, dynamic systems are flush with the current activity within a firm. Dashboards aggregate a multitude of data into high-level views that depict the status of particular metrics via simple graphical components such as charts and gauges. Management dashboards show business metrics (e.g., calls processed, orders placed, items returned). IT dashboards describe infrastructure health (e.g., network throughput, server response time). Dashboards can also use historical trends or tolerances to trigger alerts when current observations significantly deviate from expected levels.

How does the data that powers these dashboards make its way from its original home to this overarching monitor? It's a minor task to create a simple interface for displaying summary information but another job altogether to obtain the various measurements that will drive it. You can be certain that most applications were never designed to expose summaries of their internal data for inclusion within a unified real-time monitoring console.

Solution

Like their automotive counterparts, good business dashboards provide a concise view of important information that can be monitored at a glance. As Stephen Few writes:

> To achieve even a single objective often requires access to a collection of information that is not otherwise related, often coming from diverse sources related to various

---

4. Few, Stephen. *Information Dashboard Design.* O'Reilly, January 2006.

business functions. It isn't a specific type of information, but information of whatever type that is needed to do a job. It isn't just information that is needed by executives or even by managers; it can be information that is needed by anyone who has objectives to meet.[5]

The exact content will vary by application but the challenges are clear. The facts that power the dashboard come from a host of potentially unrelated systems. Once obtained, that data must be analyzed, visualized, and incorporated into the final display. Which leads to another important point: A dashboard must be confined to a single screen. No tabs, scrolling, paging, or other navigation shortcuts are allowed. Why? Imagine if the dashboard in your car required you to press a button to view the engine temperature or battery level. You'd probably never bother to check it. Out of sight is definitely out of mind—and the same phenomenon applies when managing the limited real estate of a computer monitor. You can circumvent screen boundaries through user interface slight-of-hand but this will simply result in an ineffective console.

So where do mashups come in? From a general data acquisition perspective, a variety of mashup patterns can be used to obtain the information that is otherwise unobtainable, especially if the dashboard will monitor external resources. The Alerter and Time Series patterns are good candidates for initial collection operations; Competitive Analysis and Reputation Management can provide useful material, too.

The next step is to prepare the information for analysis. A mashup's ability to convert data to a common format makes this job easier. Further processing can be performed by mashing in an analytical product or other sophisticated tools that have been API-enabled. The final step is to create the visualization that will be presented to the user. Some mashup products support this ability natively; others can leverage a third-party resource such as Google Charts[6] or a widget library (see the Widget Enabler pattern later in this chapter).

Another possibility is that one or more of the candidate dashboard participants already provides an acceptable gauge or graph. There's no need to create a new visualization if a perfectly good one already exists. Under these circumstances clipping functionality is highly desirable (see Chapter 3, Core Activities). Clipping can harvest living interface subcomponents from their original locations and redisplay them in an alternative location.

A firm can use mashups to build a collection of canned dashboards tied to specific business roles or goals, but the more exciting prospect is empowering users to create their own information consoles. As Stephen Few intimates in his

---

5. Few, *Information Dashboard Design.*

6. http://code.google.com/apis/chart

previous quote, dashboards can be highly personalized devices. This sounds like another occasion ripe for an appearance by the Long Tail. Rather than presume what users need, consider creating a variety of individual components that can be remixed and rewired on an ad hoc basis. The dashboards they produce will become situational as well as observational.

Related Patterns: Alerter, Content Aggregation, Infinite Monkeys, Time Series, Portal Enabler, Widget Enabler

Fragility

A Dashboard implementation shares many of the same risks associated with a Content Migration instance. After all, what is a dashboard but the transfer of data from a source system to a new visualization environment? For this reason the Dashboard pattern receives the same 2-point rating as the Content Migration pattern.

Another risk inherent to all dashboards should also be noted. If incorrect or inaccurate data is presented that leads to poor decisions or mismanagement, the consequences to a firm can be severe. You might dismiss this warning with the thought that no important actions are solely directed by a dashboard, but understand that the problem can be more subtle. Suppose your organization licensed a particular product on a per-user basis and this information was summarized on a management dashboard. If usage was consistently underreported, you would have little cause to dig deeper. Now suppose it's renewal time—or that a surprise audit is conducted—and the discrepancy is uncovered. Dashboards that incorrectly signal "All is well" can clearly cause serious damage.

Example: *Monitor Customer Experience*

Sloth Hosting is a server collocation facility with data centers outside four metropolitan areas. It specializes in providing managed network services for companies that are too small to manage their own dedicated server environments. The firm's business started more than a decade ago when the only service it offered was hosting static sites for the then-nascent World Wide Web. When that business became more competitive and margins began to shrink, Sloth Hosting branched out and focused on firms that wanted a more dynamic Web presence but couldn't afford to host their own servers.

In the company's early days customer satisfaction was almost a direct reflection of server uptime and response rate. Sloth Hosting could meet customers' expectations using some basic network monitoring tools. As the complexity and geographic dispersion of their hosted environments grew, so did the challenge of keeping those clients happy. Businesses began to stake their entire fortune on Sloth Hosting and its infrastructure.

Customers are increasingly demanding immediate responses to issues such as server restarts and installation of hardware and software upgrades. These "hands-on" tasks aren't addressed by the network health software currently in use. Sloth Hosting needs a way to measure how well it is meeting customer expectations so it can adjust its hiring and budget strategies appropriately.

To obtain more information on each customer's experience interacting with Sloth Hosting, a series of mashups is created to power an operational dashboard (see Figure 7.3).

Data is harvested from a variety of internal systems to create a series of individual displays:

- Total monthly call volume and average problem resolution time are obtained from the support system used by the Help Desk.

- Caller ID information and "dropped call" statistics are pulled in from the corporate PBX. Customer area codes are filtered through a Web service that converts them to a U.S. state abbreviation.

- Call forecast statistics are gathered from a spreadsheet posted on the firm's intranet.

- Customer satisfaction data acquired by automated post-call surveys is mashed in from the back-end database where results are stored.

Each mashup's data is subjected to a particular visualization technique intended to quickly convey emerging trends in the underlying content. Keeping an eye on the various gauges allows Sloth Hosting's managers to spot spikes or dips in customer service requirements as they pertain to particular regions. They can then tactically redirect support issues to underutilized data centers.

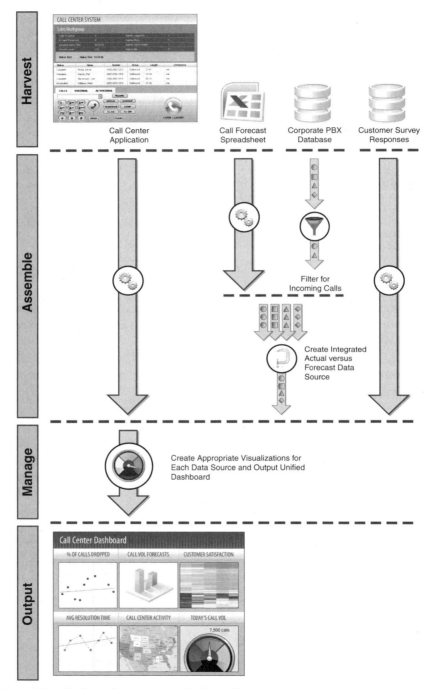

Figure 7.3   *Sloth's call monitoring dashboard*

Example: *Monitor Code-of-Ethics Compliance*

The managers at Ipecac Hospital are concerned by a nationwide trend indicating patients are decreasingly satisfied with the medical care they receive. To determine if their facility is affected they decide to monitor the issue more closely with a dashboard. The hospital already surveys patients upon discharge; one goal with the new system is to make this information more accessible. Managers want to include other "hidden" factors in the dashboard as well. For example, does the number of journal articles published by some of the doctors correspond negatively or positively with successful patient outcomes? Do doctors' prescriptions appear to be influenced by research grants they receive from pharmaceutical companies? Is the hospital understaffed? Has the average time a patient consults with a physician for a similar condition decreased over time? Greater visibility into these topics may influence Ipecac's financial plan and reshape the hospital's "Policies, Procedures, and Ethics" handbook.

Ipecac's staff creates a Dashboard implementation by using mashups to collect both travel records and internal patient data as well as to monitor the Web sites of external publications for staff contributions. The analytical tools incorporated in the dashboard are just one means the hospital will use to investigate quality-of-service issues. As trained medical practitioners the hospital managers are very aware that "Correlation doesn't imply causation"—but they are not ambivalent about issues that may introduce bias into the caregiving process. The Dashboard implementation is their latest diagnostic tool for ensuring world-class performance at their institution.

Portal Enabler

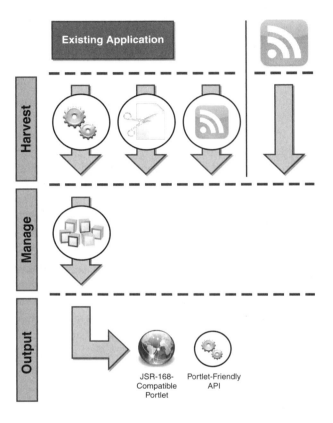

JSR-168-
Compatible
Portlet

Portlet-Friendly
API

Core Activities: Clipping, data entry, data extraction, transformation

Problem

Corporate portals (also known as enterprise information portals [EIPs]) have enjoyed widespread adoption as both internal- and external-facing installations at many organizations. A portal provides a framework for integrating disparate information sources, applications, and communication products under a unified presentation (usually Web-based) model. One benefit of this approach is that it distributes the process of content creation across a firm. No single team or system is responsible for keeping the portal current. Rather, as teams update individual systems, their counterparts on the portal—known as "portlets"—are refreshed in tandem.

A successful Portal implementation faces many challenges, not the least of which is the job of exposing content from an application in a manner that a portal framework will be able to consume. In the past, proprietary solutions for coalescing content from different locations required painstaking work to negotiate common interfaces and data formats for exchanging information. Fortunately those days have largely passed. Now industry standards direct these efforts—most notably, JSR-168,[7] otherwise known as the Java Portlet Specification, and WSRP,[8] the Web Services for Remote Portlets specification defined by international standards body OASIS.

General-purpose portal products that understand these models simplify the process of portal creation. Even so, the time and effort needed to build and test implementations should not be underestimated. Portlets have a design and life cycle all their own that is usually dissimilar from an application's existing architecture. Creating compliant portlets can splinter development resources and require continuous maintenance of multiple code bases.

Solution

The future prospects of corporate portals not withstanding,[9] many firms have already invested significant time and resources building enterprise-wide solutions based on this technology. Before they explore alternative approaches, they'll want to squeeze every ounce of return out of their investment. And if an existing portal fulfills user requirements, there's no reason to change just for change's sake. Mashups can enhance and extend portal functionality by making it possible to incorporate new content that is otherwise inaccessible. While end users might not find that the underlying portal framework is accessible to non-developers, they can still work in partnership with IT staff to develop the mashups that ultimately feed individual portlets.

Several different methods are employed for migrating existing content onto a portal using mashups. One technique involves creating a raw XML or RSS feed against an existing resource (see the Feed Factory pattern in Chapter 5). Many portal frameworks are predisposed to accept these formats and customize their

---

7. The next version of this specification (JSR-286) is currently available for public review at http://jcp.org/aboutJava/communityprocess/edr/jsr286/

8. http://docs.oasis-open.org/wsrp/v2/wsrp-2.0-spec.html

9. Review the Widget Enabler pattern for a discussion of an up-and-coming alternative.

display. Their drawback is that the interactive capacity of a feed-powered port-let is typically limited to embedded hyperlinks. Where mostly static content is concerned, this may be the easiest way to incorporate it.

A second approach relies on the straightforward use of the API Enabler pat-tern to make application data available to IT developers. That team can then create code that conforms to the required portal standard using this interface. JSR-168 is the most likely candidate given that it's already supported both by commer-cial vendors (including BEA, IBM, and Oracle[10]) and by open-source providers such as JBoss (a division of Red Hat) and Apache.[11] Interactivity constraints disappear because IT personnel can use mashups to connect the portlet view back to the underlying system through the self-same API, in effect creating a "miniature" application. While this solution offers the greatest flexibility, it also requires the most work.

A third technique is largely dependent on the capabilities of the particular mashup toolset you have available. As part of their support for open standards and clipping functionality, some mashup products are natively able to generate JSR-168-compliant portlets. This technique can combine the best features of the two previously discussed methods. Both IT personnel and end users can cre-ate mashups that are as easy to deploy as feed-based portlets, yet provide the two-way functionality absent in simple RSS streams. The resulting clipped excerpts should be capable of leveraging whatever authentication or single sign-on functionality the corporate portal provides.

Related Patterns: Content Aggregation, Widget Enabler

Fragility

Mashups can ease the task of portlet creation in several different ways. Each of these solutions has different fragility characteristics.

Clipping When a tool supports first-class clipping, various portions of a site can be directly extracted and integrated into a portal framework. The underlying architecture is a little delicate, however. A server somewhere in the deployment environment runs a mashup agent that impersonates a Web browser; thus the original site thinks it is being visited by an ordinary user. If it requires authenti-

---

10. Oracle's recent acquisition of BEA may signal further consolidation in this area.

11. A more extensive list of vendors can be found online at http://wikipedia.org/wiki/Enterprise_portal

cation, the mashup needs to either directly supply credentials (data entry functionality) or pass along SSO tokens/headers from a "real" user. The server agent continues to interact with the target site until the desired portal content is "displayed." No one ever observes this process because the agent is retrieving and processing the raw HTML without user intervention. Ultimately, the required sections are "snipped" out and fed to the portal framework.

"But wait!" you cry. "What if the returned content has embedded JavaScript, links, or forms that point to the original server? How could those possibly work if only a portion of the page is returned?" That is where the fragility of this approach arises. The URLs of any content on the returned snippet need to be *rewritten* so that they point back to the server agent, which can then execute the request against the original site. Any JavaScript needs to be executed on the server first before the output is returned. Although it appears to the portlet user as if he or she is interacting with the original site, an intermediary mashup layer actually manages all of the requests and responses. A Clipping portlet is not really that different from a Field Medic or Usability Enhancer pattern (see Chapter 5, Enhance Patterns) and therefore receives a fragility score of 4.

Data Entry and Data Extraction A more straightforward approach is to use direct techniques for navigating through resources and harvesting content. We could apply the API Enabler pattern and leave the portlet implementation up to a developer. But in the spirit of empowering the layperson, some mashup products can be instructed to output their content according to industry portlet specifications. This approach does not have the "grab-and-go" ease of a Clipped portlet and is more challenging to construct. Conversely, it does not have the doppelganger aspect of clipping nor its potential problems. Because of its decreased architectural complexity this approach is assigned a fragility score of 2.

Feeds (RSS, XML) Imposing a feed on an existing site uses the same techniques described in the "Data Entry and Data Extraction" subsection, but relies on the portal framework for parsing and presentation services. Because this approach depends on mashups to the least extent, it receives the lowest possible fragility score of 1.

The average of these scores is slightly more than 2, but we'll round that number down to determine the final rating for the Portal Enabler pattern as a whole. When implementing this pattern, keep the different scores in mind and match your requirements to the sturdiest technique of the three.

Example: *Help Customers Make Informed Decisions*

Fountainhead Homebuilding specializes in new construction for the commercial and residential markets. A few years ago the company decided to differentiate itself from its competition by creating an interactive portal that would allow clients to take a more active role in designing their new buildings. The site the firm created lets customers compare floor plans, fixtures, appliances, and other materials and choose the specific designs and products that fit their lifestyle and budget. The outcome was highly successful: Fountainhead received many awards for its work to empower the customer and move away from "cookie-cutter" developments. But keeping the portal content fresh has been a significant challenge. In particular, the site has not been able to keep up with recent trends in eco-friendly ("green") building. Customers want more information about energy use and conservation options available to them.

Looking back at the time and effort required to create its first portal, Fountainhead has no desire to repeat the process—especially given that recent declines in the home-building sector have negatively affected its bottom line. At the same time the company doesn't want to lose the competitive edge its customer-facing portal provides. A quick and inexpensive solution for including more "green" information is highly desired.

Fountainhead's staff discovers that several mashup tools can push content directly to the company's portal. That resolves the technical challenges in publishing the material, but two questions remain: Which new content should be included? and Where it will come from? Mashups provide the answer here as well. They can rewrap a series of useful Web resources for inclusion side-by-side with Fountainhead's existing portlets. This will allow customers to learn more about how their product selections influence their eco-footprint. Two examples include the U.S. government's Energy Star program[12] (Figure 7.4) and the Water Footprint Calculator[13] (Figure 7.5). Each resource can be portal-enabled with minimal development effort to create the customized view illustrated in Figure 7.6. Future plans include creating new portlets that feature alternative building materials and spotlight products such as compact fluorescent bulbs and instant hot-water heaters. Fountainhead is also considering creating a portlet to pull in "green-related" blogs and news stories to round out its coverage on the subject.

---

12. http://www.energystar.gov/

13. http://www.waterfootprint.org

Figure 7.4 *The Energy Star site provides useful data on the environmental impact of consumer habits.*

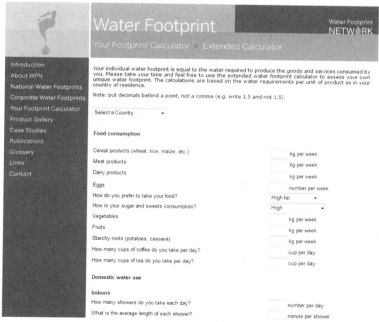

Figure 7.5 *The Water Footprint Network's Calculator educates individuals about the link between consumption and freshwater use.* Credit: www.waterfront.org screenshot used by permission.

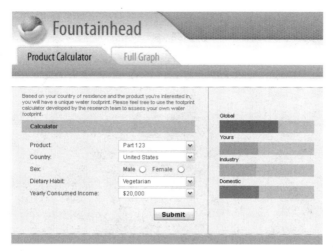

Figure 7.6 *Virtual Water portlet example*

Other Examples

Given the number of portals in existence, there are nearly unlimited cases where the Portal Enabler pattern can prove useful. Here are some other potential applications for this pattern:

- An accounting firm could create portlets for new regulatory and filing requirements. This information could be included on associates' personalized view alongside data on their existing clients.

- An organization could build portlets that feature upcoming corporate events and conferences. The portlets could also include functionality to register attendance or book travel.

- Portlets could be used to pull in external tracking data alongside recent customer orders.

The value of mashups is that they make the creation of portlets easy for developers and end users alike. In the past creating content for a firm's portal almost always required some involvement from corporate IT staff. In contrast, the flexibility and low barriers to entry offered by many mashup products allow a firm to instill a culture of portlet building. Teams or individuals can quickly publish content of direct interest to themselves or their users. This fresh material can renovate existing portals and reinvigorate them as a Mecca for important information.

Quick Proof-of-Concept

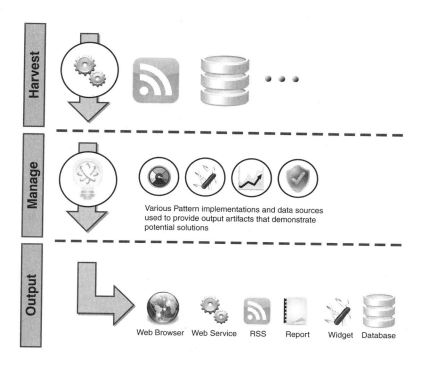

Various Pattern implementations and data sources used to provide output artifacts that demonstrate potential solutions

Web Browser Web Service RSS Report Widget Database

Core Activities: Data entry, data extraction, data visualization, scheduling, clipping, transformation

Also Known As: Prototype

Problem

Unless a firm creates products for sale within the technology sector, its internal IT department will most likely be a cost center: Instead of generating money for an organization, it probably consumes it. Of course, IT support—the systems and infrastructure IT provides—enables revenue centers to maximize their earnings potential. One of the greatest challenges in managing a cost center (or overseeing any business-related expenditures for that matter) is determining how to maximize the return on investment (ROI). It would be nice to know, for example, how much closer the business gets to launching a new product for each additional dollar spent within IT. Yet despite decades of study on the topic, the general consensus is that it is not possible to reliably estimate software development efforts.[14] A cottage publishing industry will vehemently disagree with that statement—but the proliferation of books on the subject should be proof enough that no technique is infallible. We want a solution to this dilemma so badly that we won't let the empirical evidence stand in our way. It's not unlike the perennial search for the perfect weight-loss program.

Software estimates share something else in common with diets: Both are highly individual activities. If you are building a new piece of software identical to one you have already written then you should be able to predict how long it will take. Of course, companies rarely completely rewrite systems they already have. Instead, they incrementally build enhancements on top of existing products. Truly new solutions almost always begin as a journey through uncharted territory where the final destination and cost to get there are only vaguely sensed. We may use our past experience to gauge how much effort we will expend, but ultimately this is an educated guess. Moreover, the larger a project becomes and the more individuals (with varying skill levels) who get involved, the greater the margin of error.

Creating a prototype is one method of addressing the challenges of estimation. Most IT departments (as well as some other groups) have embraced the practice of creating a "throw-away" example to prove-out a design. A rough initial version of a system can provide insight into where potential obstacles will surface and help to refine specifications and estimates. Unfortunately, like most software development tasks, prototyping has chiefly been carried out by trained software professionals. This brings us right back to where we started: Given their finite resources IT departments cannot afford to prototype every potential product. How can the amount of available resources be maximized? How can the business determine which solutions are worthy of initial exploration and subsequent funding?

Solution

In the section entitled "The Fragility Factor" in Chapter 1, we examined the potential weaknesses of mashups and determined they should not be used to support mission-critical operations. The Quick Proof-of-Concept (PoC) pattern adds a small yet crucial degree of clarity to that statement. Mashups should not provide ongoing support for critical tasks but it is perfectly acceptable to use mashups to validate an idea that requires a significant investment to realize. Some examples follow:

---

14. Lewis, J. P. "Large Limits to Software Estimation." ACM *Software Engineering Notes* 2001;26(4).

- Developers create a mashup-powered prototype to obtain user feedback on proposed functionality.

- End users bring mashup-based solutions to IT to demonstrate solution requirements.

- IT uses mashups to gauge the effort involved to formally integrate disparate applications.

- End users test new workflow and business processes by temporarily creating mashup-driven routing agents.

The Quick PoC pattern is related to the Emergency Response (ER) pattern in that neither prescribes a general solution for a specific class of problem. Rather, each describes the use of mashups to rapidly address requirements that vary from one situation to the next. Unlike an ER mashup, however, the Quick PoC implementation is not a final product. Instead, this pattern is used during the discovery and analysis phase of a project because of the flexibility mashups bring to the table. The final deliverable may not use mashups at all, or they may play a more limited role such as transferring data into the new system (see the discussion of the Content Migration pattern earlier in this chapter).

Sometimes the best specification for constructing a new solution is a partially completed product that can be used as a model. IT personnel and users often work together to build that first prototype application. Unfortunately, the authorship of that may take so long and consume so many resources that it morphs into the final product, warts and all. This is an almost inevitable end-state given the divide that has evolved between developers and users. The process usually goes something like this: End users communicate their requirements to IT developers. The IT developers may be fluent in technical topics but not understand business strategies. IT makes its best effort to satisfy the needs of the business users, but those end users are not familiar with the practical considerations and trade-offs that are part of every development project. By the time each side reaches a common understanding, so much effort has been expended that the solution is accepted "as is." Enhancements and rewrites are pushed off to an indeterminate future date—and perhaps never completed.

Mashups can bridge this communications gap. Owing to the mashups' ease of use, business associates can construct their own solutions (or portions thereof) and provide them to IT as a "living" design. IT can then focus on applying its core strengths—creating a final product that is maintainable, reliable, scalable, and secure. Because end users take a more participatory role in shaping the solutions they ultimately receive, higher satisfaction should be expected.

Related Patterns: Content Aggregation, Content Integration, Emergency Response

Fragility

By definition, a proof of concept is not intended to be a fully functioning product or a long-lived solution. The goal could be to test the correctness of a particular design or to confirm that business requirements have been accurately captured. Once a Quick PoC mashup has fulfilled these goals, work can begin on a formal implementation (which may or may not employ mashups). The PoC needn't be abandoned; it can still serve as a reference point for cross-checking the final solution.

Given its intended lifespan, it's tempting to give the Quick PoC the lowest fragility score. But it would be remiss not to recognize outside factors that justify a bump to the next level. Under many circumstances the fragility of a PoC is overshadowed by the excitement created by having a new solution. This infatuation creates a strong temptation to leave the temporary effort in place and soak in clients' appreciation rather than yank the product away and weather disappointment while work on a proper implementation ensues. In fact, the biggest drawback of the Quick PoC pattern is that it might work *too* well. When a PoC perpetuates beyond its intended lifetime, it can morph into a de facto production application. This can cause undesirable consequences down the road if it eventually collapses.[15] The Quick PoC pattern is not at fault in these cases but the attribution of a higher fragility score is an acknowledgment that successful prototypes sometimes stick around longer than they should.

Examples

It would be an injustice to limit the demonstration of this pattern's usefulness to a few hypothetical examples. Every pattern profiled in this book can potentially be implemented under the constraints of a Quick PoC because mashups aren't always built with longevity in mind.

Proof-of-concept instances of the Content Aggregation or Migration pattern could be used to prove the value of a mashup-based approach in comparison to more traditional solutions. A single Leading Indicator example might be used to demonstrate the competitive advantage gained from mining unstructured Web

---

15. In my experience, this event always occurs at the moment it can cause the most harm.

content. Portlet and widget-based mashups (see their respective sections in this chapter) suggest a path to new application interaction models. An end user working in her spare time can use the Quick PoC pattern to propose alternative products and solutions from outside the perspective of the IT department. This is yet another powerful argument for embracing mashups within the enterprise. Mashups don't have to create a completely self-serve user community; simply bridging the communication gap between technical and business-oriented employees is a huge benefit.

In our discussions of the Long Tail, we have learned that many projects go unaddressed for lack of resources. But which issues drain talent away from unmet tasks? The analysis and construction phases of a project are usually responsible for consuming the majority of time and effort. We have already seen how the flexibility of the mashup paradigm surpasses conventional construction techniques in terms of speed. Quick PoC shows how the analysis phase can undergo similar acceleration. The more clearly users are able to articulate their requirements, the quicker and easier it is to craft a working solution.

Single Sign-on

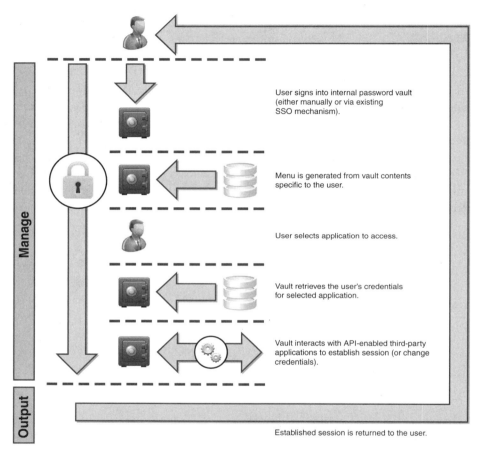

Manage

User signs into internal password vault (either manually or via existing SSO mechanism).

Menu is generated from vault contents specific to the user.

User selects application to access.

Vault retrieves the user's credentials for selected application.

Vault interacts with API-enabled third-party applications to establish session (or change credentials).

Output

Established session is returned to the user.

Core Activities: Clipping, data entry, data extraction, scheduling

Problem

The proliferation of internally developed and vendor-provided solutions within the modern corporation has brought many challenges. A chief concern has been the process of securing these multiple environments so that an enterprise's data and processes are appropriately protected. One line of defense is authentication. Systems that manage proprietary or confidential material should require users to supply appropriate credentials before being granted access to the data. It seems like such a simple prerequisite, but as more applications are added its effectiveness begins to break down.

A user who is frequently required to provide sign-on information may begin to suffer from password fatigue. The symptoms of this ailment include writing down passwords so they won't be forgotten and choosing simple passwords that are easy to remember. Studies have shown that people tend to reuse passwords across systems,[16] thereby decreasing their overall level of protection and exposing both themselves and their firm to unnecessary risk. Suppose a firm uses multiple SaaS providers to manage customer records, track business strategies, and organize the annual summer picnic. The online "party planning" site might be the least secure of the three, making it an attractive target for unscrupulous hacking. If it is compromised and an employee has used a recycled password, the data in the other two systems is then at risk.

Many companies have tried to balance the contradictory forces of password fatigue and secure access by implementing single sign-on (SSO). A variety of protocols and products exist that allow a user to sign on once and have his or her credentials be automatically propagated across multiple systems within the enterprise. Unfortunately this approach does nothing to deal with authentication issues for external products and services, which may actually present the greater risk of being compromised. Password reuse will still occur in this setting, compounded by lenient requirements for password strength and expiration.

A firm can't impose its internal SSO solution on external vendors—but it can't afford to accept weak security either. One approach is to create an internal "password vault" where users can store the various account names and access codes they have created for the different services they use. A password vault may be able to automatically generate strong passwords and remind users to change them frequently.

When a vault isn't integrated with a firm's SSO solution, users will have to remember yet another password. Each incremental sign-on task creates another opportunity for security to be breached due to careless practices. The unfortunate truth is that end users are often the weakest link in providing a secure computing infrastructure.

---

16. "Password Reuse Opens Door to ID theft." PC Pro, March 2007. http://www.pcpro.co.uk/news/106758/password-reuse-opens-door-to-id-theft.html; "Are You Suffering from Password Pressure?" The Guardian, January 17, 2008. http://www.guardian.co.uk/technology/2008/jan/17/security.banks

Solution

Weak passwords can jeopardize confidential data, lead to identity theft or fraud, and cause numerous other troubles that no one wants to encounter. An enterprise can certainly implement SSO to fight internal password fatigue—but how can this approach be extended outside the firm? The answer goes back to the internal "vault" described in the "Problem" statement. Recall that data entry and data extraction capabilities enable mashups to impersonate user activity. If a vault is established, a mashup with the correct password could sign into this repository on behalf of the user and gain access to all of the site-specific credentials it contains. In addition, a mashup could employ a vault's ability to generate new passwords that might be more random (and therefore more secure) than anything users would think up by themselves. Weak user-chosen passwords could be automatically replaced with stronger alternatives. These operations form a blueprint for the steps necessary to provide a secure SSO environment for all applications, regardless of their location:

1. *Establish a password vault.* Externally hosted solutions exist but many firms will consider an internal installation to be the most secure.

2. *Connect the vault to the firm's SSO platform.* This can be done directly or by using a mashup to API-enable it.

3. *Extract the target URL or location for each item in the vault (via API Enabler) and build a custom "applications menu" for end users.* This step is important because it is the key in extending the benefits of SSO externally.

4. *When a menu item is clicked, have an underlying mashup pass the user's SSO credentials to the vault and extract the corresponding user logon and password.*[17] The mashup uses this information to log in on behalf of the user; the application's home screen is returned with the user never having had to manually sign in. This solution assumes that the mashup platform's clipping abilities can seamlessly initiate a session and pass it back to the client.

Although we now have SSO for external systems, there are still weaknesses in this scheme. A user must initially register an application with the vault and the password he or she chooses may not be secure. IT can solve this problem by

---

17. This example is intentionally simplified to highlight the role of mashups. In practice, the vault's internal repository should be encrypted and require two-factor authentication via a security token or biometric identifier.

API-enabling the "change password" functionality on the third-party system. After a user supplies his or her initial credentials, a mashup might then go out to the target site and change the initial password to something completely random and store it back in the vault. This process could be repeated on a regular basis so that passwords are significantly more secure.

The process of registering applications and accessing them can be completely contained within a few mashups so that users aren't even aware the underlying vault exists. As a side benefit, the mashup intermediaries used in this approach introduce the ability to more closely monitor the user of external systems. The discussions of the Reality Mining pattern (Chapter 4, Harvest Patterns) and Audit pattern (Chapter 8, Testing Patterns) suggest possible uses of this data.

There are other instances where mashups can facilitate SSO. For example, if mashups are used as part of a portal or widget strategy (see related patterns in this chapter), they can pass credentials through to the underlying system.

Related Patterns: Field Medic, Usability Enhancer

Fragility

The benefits of a secure authentication environment cannot be understated. Nevertheless, the Single Sign-on pattern takes a nontraditional approach to password management in its attempt to extend security coverage to external systems. This pattern can also be used to address issues related to password strength. This results in the unusual circumstance where users may have no knowledge of their ID or password for a third-party site. If users need access to the system outside the company's network, they won't be able to get it because their credentials are locked away inside the intranet-based corporate vault. But what if a user requests that the "lost" password be emailed to him or her? This presents another potential weakness. If the user recovers a password in this manner and proceeds to change it, the link between the internal vault and the application will have been broken.

Another downside of mashup-managed security occurs when the target environment suddenly changes its layout. Part of the reason these patterns require fragility scores is because not all mashups will be able to seamlessly weather presentation changes. Suppose the "Sign-on ID" and "Password" fields of an application are unexpectedly moved or renamed? A mashup might accidentally enter private authentication data in a public location. An enterprise will have to weigh the potential benefits of the SSO pattern against the drawbacks. One important point to consider is how frequently the external sites are likely to change and whether SSO is a necessity or merely a convenience.

Example: *Provide SSO for Disparate SaaS Applications*

We first encountered Chrysoma Property Management in the "Examples" section for the Content Migration pattern. This firm was using a Content Migration implementation to move data from soon-to-be retired systems to a SaaS provider. As it would happen, Chrysoma ultimately needed to use several different companies to replace the services it once hosted internally. As a consequence the company's users lost the ability to sign into a single site to perform their regular work. Chrysoma associates are now required to keep three distinct login and password combinations—one for each external vendor (see Figure 7.7). This has perpetuated such undesirable practices as choosing simple passwords and writing down login details on a slip of paper next to the computer. Back when all of the applications were internal, Chrysoma tolerated a certain amount of this poor behavior because no remote access to the company's applications was available. Since then things have changed: The SaaS systems are all accessible over the Internet. Anyone who obtains a valid ID/password combination can immediately access all of Chrysoma's sensitive customer data. A threat can now come from a former employee whose access isn't disabled quickly enough, or a hacker or disgruntled member of the SaaS vendor's staff might gain access to account information and use it to sign into other sites. Chrysoma needs a way to boost the security around its hosted software before a breakdown causes the firm irreparable harm.

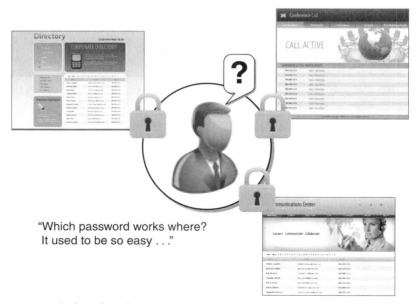

"Which password works where? It used to be so easy . . ."

Figure 7.7   *The benefits of a corporate SSO solution vanished when applications were moved to multiple SaaS providers.*

A decision is made to construct an on-premises password vault based on the design presented in the "Solution" section. A mashup is created for each SaaS vendor to gain access cover sign-on and change password functionality. The legacy SSO solution Chrysoma employed for its internal applications is recycled so that once users log into the corporate network they have immediate access to the vault without being prompted for additional credentials (see Figure 7.8).

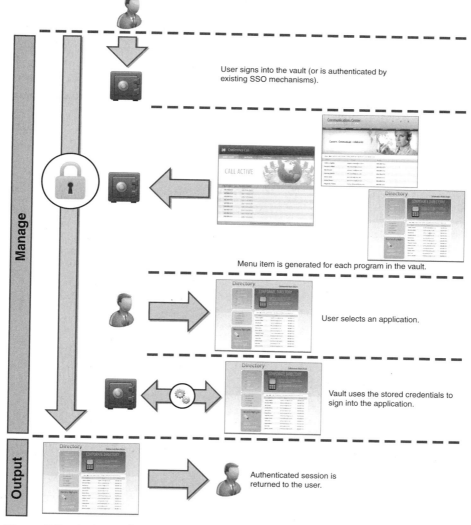

Figure 7.8 *An internal password vault provides SSO and enhanced security for multiple external sites.*

When a user first requests access to one of the external sites, Chrysoma's IT staff create an account and password and enter it into the associate's vault account. To access the application the user selects the desired choice from a menu generated from the vault contents specific to that individual. At predefined intervals the unseen passwords are periodically changed for all available sites, whether they have been accessed recently or not. No two passwords are reused across systems or users. This scheme provides SSO capability with total password obscurity for the SaaS applications.

To prevent malicious conduct by former employees, another mashup is created using the Alerter pattern to monitor Chrysoma's corporate payroll database (which coincidentally has also been moved to a SaaS solution). When any employee is dropped from the rolls due to termination or extended absence, all of that person's passwords are immediately scrambled and the vault access is revoked. This measure prevents associates who temporarily retain remote login privileges from stealing or corrupting Chrysoma's data.

Widget Enabler

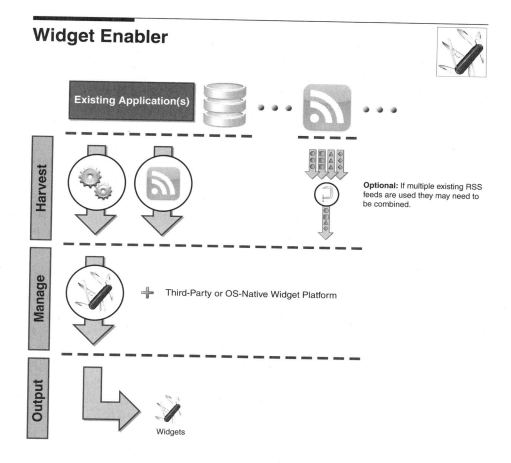

Core Activities: Data entry, data extraction, transformation

Problem

In the Chapter 1 section titled "Mashups and the Corporate Portal," we examined the emergence of a new metaphor for user interaction known as widgets. Widgets can be stand-alone components embedded on Web pages with a few snippets of HTML; alternatively, they can be self-contained "mini-applications" that reside on a user's desktop and provide highly specialized functionality (see Figure 7.9). The benefits of the widget model go beyond simple technical advances. The ability to easily package and disseminate nuggets of functionality means that widgets can leverage network effects and spread virally.

Widgets arrived just as the era of *personal computing* slipped into obsolescence and Web 2.0 emerged with promises of crowdsourcing and social net-

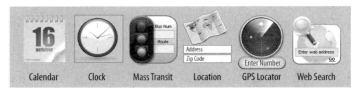

Figure 7.9   *Sample widgets encapsulate focused data or tasks.*

working. Today we openly invite both friends and total strangers into our virtual world via sites such as MySpace and Facebook. Although everyone in this new world is a publisher, not everyone is a creator. To aid in their quest for self-expression, users frequently turn to widget providers for tools they can customize with their personal opinions. Many businesses have discovered that consumers will freely broadcast their relationships with products if the seller in turn makes the user look good by providing trendy content for his or her site. That reciprocal relationship explains why widgets have become the latest method for providing a service while subtly marketing a brand. A bank may provide an ATM-locator widget that turns into free advertising when placed on a customer's personal page. Someone who likes the tool is free to copy it into their own page, which perpetuates its spread. Besides the obvious promotional benefits of this network effect, a widget might generate income for its authors by supplementing content with contextual advertising. At the same time Web-based widgets pose a challenge to their authors. Corporations that want to repackage data and applications under these easily distributable components need to figure out how to connect existing functionality to these new interfaces.

Meanwhile, a simultaneous explosion of widgets on the desktop has occurred thanks to the emergence of platforms such as Apple Dashboard, Google Gadgets, Microsoft Vista Widgets, and Yahoo Widgets. Desktop widgets attract a different audience than their online cousins. Their focus is on fulfilling specific functional needs rather than on providing a means to attract attention. The potential for marketing is still there but the emphasis is on personal concerns like flexibility and ease of use. This is where widgets directly threaten the traditional corporate portal.

An established business probably has a well-established collection of internal systems that support core operations. Reflecting their maturity, these systems are typically the oldest and largest applications within the business. Rather than force users to manually hunt through each system for information relevant to them, many organizations have made significant investments in creating enterprise portals. These systems expose subsections of a firm's overall content to give end users a "bird's-eye" view of which material is available. Unfortunately where most portals fail is in their limited ability to adapt to the diverse needs of their users. "Personalization" was a much-ballyhooed solution to this problem, but in practice it just filters whatever portlets a firm has decided to develop.[18] As you might guess, the Long Tail comes into play once again: Not everyone will see portlets created to meet their specific needs. In other words, you can't "personalize" your requirements into existence.

Rather than maintain the huge infrastructure required to support a portal framework, a firm should consider the value of adopting an enterprise widget platform. This pattern can assist in reusing existing portlets as widgets and in allowing both IT personnel and end users to create new widgets. The unstructured nature of a widget container allows for unprecedented flexibility in creating, connecting, and sharing highly focused computing experiences. Used correctly, widgets can fulfill the unmet promises of portals.

Apart from recognizing their role in a portal replacement strategy, a firm can uncover other value by using widgets. A company that wants to streamline its internal operations should study how its programs' structures affect business activities. For example, it might not make sense to continue supporting monolithic behemoths if only a handful of features are used by different employees. In fact, this policy could be responsible for unwittingly propagating problems related to data quality and information security as users stumble though unnecessary functions and features to accomplish specific tasks. A better approach might be to provide a widget that exposes only the subset of functionality necessary to get a job done.

There is a caveat: Using conventional programming techniques to directly create these kinds widgets is sometimes easier said than done. The removal of seemingly irrelevant or innocuous code during the construction phase might unexpectedly introduce critical errors in the future. Maybe the necessary level of understanding about legacy systems no longer exists internally. Perhaps closed-source vendor packages are involved. Before mashups, we could only dream of an ideal world where none of these barriers existed and programs could be widget-ized without undergoing any changes.

Solution

The "Problem" section described two major widget categories: Web based and desktop based. Both share a common set of challenges but the resolution of these issues varies based on the widget category and the target environment.

- *Acquiring content.* Widgets and their more rigid counterpart, portlets, face a common challenge in acquiring the data they will ultimately display.

---

18. Gartner. *Making Enterprise Portals Healthier.* July 17, 2008.

Two techniques encountered in the Portal Enabler pattern are applicable here as well. The first step is to obtain an XML or RSS feed against the source environment. The Feed Factory pattern (Chapter 5, Enhance Patterns) can create feeds for resources that don't natively expose them. Most widget platforms[19] include the ability to ingest RSS, apply a presentation style, and output a redistributable component.

Another option is to API-enable (Chapter 4, Harvest Patterns) a resource and manually connect (wire up) the interface to the presentation elements that the widget framework makes available. This more technically challenging option opens the door to components that are more interactive. Business should note that savvy external users can enter this picture by repacking existing Web or mobile interfaces into a new widget just as easily as in-house developers can. Such an intrusion can have repercussions for a firm's reputation because users will often mentally associate the widget with the underlying provider regardless of origins of the widget itself.

For internal environments, a firm may be able to tightly manage the widgets made accessible to users, thereby gaining some measure of control over their experience. Of course, once content is available on the Web, it's open season. Outside agencies can repackage public content without the owner's knowledge or consent. All mashups pose this risk, but widgets deserve special attention given their highly transferable nature. We will discuss some strategies to block external mashups in the "Blocking Mashups" section in Chapter 10. One way to mitigate the potential harm from outside widgets begins with recognizing the unfulfilled expectations that sparked their creation in the first place. Delivering a superior, "authorized" solution is often all it takes to redirect customer attention back to the original site.

- *Security.* External widget users require assurances that the personal information and transactions they conduct over a widget platform are protected. A recent report found numerous vulnerabilities across various widget platforms and warned that widgets are "the latest attack vector" for malicious code.[20] Third-party developers could mask malevolent code behind legitimate content obtained from your site (see the preceding section).

---

19. Three examples include Sprout (http://sproutbuilder.com; discussed in Chapter 5), WaveMaker (http://wavemaker.com), and WidgetBox (http://widgetbox.com).

20. Finjan Malicious Code Research Center. *Web Trends Security Report.* Q3 2007. http://finjan.com/GetObject.aspx?ObjId=506&Openform=67

Widgets developed within the enterprise raise another security challenge. Widgets that expose sensitive information need appropriate access controls and auditing to guard against improper dissemination of data. Meanwhile, employees will want the convenience of pre-authentication (Single Sign-on pattern) for any widgets they use. A firm should thoroughly vet any widget platform it deploys internally to make sure these features are implemented properly.

Alternatively, an intermediary mashup layer can supplement widget security by providing additional filtering for malicious payloads, integrating with SSO systems, and providing additional auditing capabilities.

- *Personalization.* Today's users are no longer content to simply accept the products they're given. These "prosumers" frequently want to twist and shape merchandise as a means of expression. In other words, they want to customize a mass-marketed item until it says something unique about *them*. A slick widget design can minimize this desire—users will feel "cool by association"—but it will never eliminate it entirely. The final product should allow some degree of modification without compromising the overall functionality or branding.

Internal users will usually give functional changes a higher priority than simple interface customizations. For example, they may want to see numbers or dates in a certain format, highlight important messages, or sort data in a particular order. Exposing transformation functionality can meet some of this demand.

- *Unified search/inter-widget communication.* This final issue applies primarily to internal widgets used as a replacement for corporate portals. A common feature in enterprise portals is the ability to perform a global search or filter operation that will alter the content of the individual portlets. This feature is facilitated by the fact that the portlets are all running within a common container. A widget platform also provides a container, but usually just for basic presentation and life-cycle management functions. In addition, mixed widget platforms may coexist on a user's desk (for example, Yahoo Widgets and Vista Gadgets). These environments share no common hooks for intercommunication. An intermediary mashup layer can serve as a bridge between platforms by monitoring and retaining specific activities and making them accessible to widgets, portlets, and whatever other applications might benefit from this data. For example, a mashup that provides results for a "search" operation could internally use the Action core ability to instruct other components to perform a similar function.

Whether providing a new product online or on an associate's desktop, the benefits of mashups as part of a widget strategy is clear. In addition to making content accessible, they can enhance and extend these widget platforms with new capabilities. Thanks to mashups, widgets need not stand alone as isolated islands of functionality but can interact with existing thick and thin components to offer a more unified computing experience.

Related Patterns: Portal Enabler

Fragility

Widgets are neither more risky nor less reliable than their more traditionally constructed alternatives such as thick client applications or dynamic Web sites. In fact, the proliferation of commercial and open-source frameworks gives developers a number of proven technologies to employ for widget creation. Built-in accessibility, error handling, and security features often offer an advantage over handcrafted solutions. Thus the main weakness of a mashup-powered widget implementation is the mashup itself. Because API Enabler implementations are the primary agents behind Widget Enabler implementations, their fragility score is carried through to this pattern.

Example: *Help Customers Locate Products and Turn Support Requests into Sales Leads*

As noted in the "Solution" section, widgets are excellent candidates for packaging a specialized activity and distributing it easily. Traditionally, the cost of application development and deployment has been so high that developers have had clear incentives to cram as much functionality into a product as possible. The simplicity of the widget development model means "mini-applications" that focus on specific features can be created quickly. This design aspect should translate into greater usability. One possible use of this approach pertains to specialized retail environments.

MOSFET Semiconductors is an electronics reseller of various electronic components. The company's online catalog lists tens of thousands of items. The specifications for these products are available on individual item pages, but only a fraction of these details are actually searchable. To give some scope to the problem, consider this scenario: Suppose an engineer wants to purchase a microcontroller. MOSFET sells more than 10,000 types of microcontrollers, so browsing through individual entries isn't an option. A simple query engine can be used to attempt to match customer needs to available products—but those searches can still return hundreds of results depending on the details supplied by the user. Ideally customers will answer specific questions that direct them to the most appropriate items.

There is no technical reason why MOSFET needs widgets or mashups to implement a solution to this problem—but there are resource constraints. MOSFET carries thousands of products in hundreds of categories (microcontrollers, microprocessors, transistors, diodes, capacitors, LEDs, lasers, and more). The generic search interface was selected because it was too time-consuming to build specialized wizards for each product category (or subcategory).

Given mashups' ability to quickly impose an API and widgets' capacity for exposing that interface to end users, the creation of a suite of product-chooser widgets could easily be outsourced to off-shore resources for a minimal cost. Figure 7.10 shows some sample widgets for specific components that conduct custom searches against the MOSFET catalog.

Figure 7.10 *Sample widgets for catalog items from MOSFET Semiconductors*

These widgets are not intended to be viral (although there is no reason they couldn't be). The value of the widget platform in this case is that it allows MOSFET customers to quickly locate the items they need, which in turn leads to increased sales for MOSFET. The company could leverage the network effects of this solution by creating "desktop reference" widgets that expose the most granular technical resources of its products (harvested from the internal corporate reference database). When an engineer has questions about a specific part, he or she could use these widgets to examine detailed documentation. Ideally the MOSFET catalog will be mashed in to allow additional units to be ordered easily. If this "instant reference" capability is useful, engineers will send it to their colleagues, which will further increase the pool of potential MOSFET customers (see Figure 7.11).

Figure 7.11 *To achieve viral effects, widgets should provide value first and keep their commercial aspects to a minimum.*

Example: *Reduce "Swivel-Chair" Automation*

Another use of widgets is to reduce or eliminate "swivel-chair automation"—the situation that arises when a user needs to enter and extract data from multiple applications to perform his or her job. This scenario differs somewhat from the problems we discussed in conjunction with the Content Aggregation pattern (covered in Chapter 6, Assemble Patterns). In that pattern, multiple systems participated in a solution only in the sense that each supplied a part of the final result independently. There was no concept of "cutting" information from one system and "pasting" it into another, as there is with the Widget Enabler pattern.

You might wonder how a business process evolves separately from the systems that support it. Perhaps the firm has merged or acquired a new business and needs to enter data across unconnected systems. Or maybe a change in internal workflows reshuffles existing roles and responsibilities. The simplest answer—among the countless causes—is that firms falsely believe it's easier and cheaper to make people change their behavior than it is to modify software. Naturally, these benefits are an illusion.

Swivel-chair automation is fertile territory for mistakes and mishaps. There is no reason for users to suffer through a repetitive task when a mashup can automate it. Mashups and widgets can work together to expose a single, clean interface that masks the host of disparate systems beneath.

Chapter 8

Testing Patterns

What, me worry?

—*Mad Magazine* spokesman Alfred E. Neuman

Introduction

The importance of testing applications simply cannot be understated. Thanks to the ubiquity of computers in our lives, we are more subject than ever before to suffer injury when technology fails. A study by the National Institute of Standards and Technology (NIST) estimated that the cost of software bugs to the U.S. economy is almost $60 billion.[1] "The impact of software errors is enormous because virtually every business in the United States now depends on software for the development, production, distribution, and after-sales support of products and services," says NIST Director Arden Bement.[2]

The irony is that most applications *are* tested in one way or another, yet bugs still survive to plague us. Some software is even shipped with known bugs still present—an issue we addressed with the Field Medic pattern in Chapter 5. Bugs and glitches persist in code that reaches users because of many different reasons. Sometimes a product is deemed so valuable (or marketable) that there is a rush to get it into the hands of willing customers. If the value proposition is great enough, consumers may ignore the occasional hiccup to reap greater rewards. Sound familiar? It's not that different from mashups and their implicit fragility ratings. We *know* mashups can potentially break down, but that doesn't prevent us from enjoying their benefits for as long as we can (and fixing the minor problems when necessary).

---

1. "Software Errors Cost U.S. Economy $59.5 Billion Annually." June 28, 2002. http://www.nist.gov/public_affairs/releases/n02-10.htm
2. "Software Errors Cost U.S. Economy $59.5 Billion Annually."

Known bugs can be a problem—but at least if they're documented, a user might be able to take appropriate precautions to avoid them. The more insidious culprit is the unknown bug. It's been famously said that testing can prove only the presence of bugs, not their absence.[3] Given the complexity of an enterprise infrastructure—multiple operating systems, databases, varying hardware, and so on—it's impossible to completely verify that a program will perform flawlessly under the near-infinite combinations of possible computing environments.

What about the systems created internally by a firm's own IT department? Surely IT's familiarity with the company's various systems should preclude any major problems from cropping up? Of course, this simply isn't the case. Internal developers can face greater time and resource pressures than their commercial counterparts—not to mention that they can inherit maintenance responsibilities for poorly designed systems. Whenever code is changed—even if it's to fix a problem—new bugs can accidentally be introduced. That's why regression testing is so important. It's intended to impose a kind of Hippocratic oath on the development process: "First do no harm." If regression testing is thorough enough, it should guarantee things don't work worse than they did before.

Mashups provide unique value in the field of testing. Traditionally, testing products have focused on technically oriented users. This was a reasonable boundary when application development never ventured beyond the walls of the IT department. But by now we have encountered dozens of cases where mashups permit business users to create their own solutions. Along with this power comes the necessity to test these creations before becoming dependent on them or passing them along to coworkers.

Let's step back for a moment and look at the current landscape for user-initiated development. In many firms Excel is already the definitive tool for the do-it-yourselfer. Some employees spend considerable time tweaking formulas and macros to produce what are essential mini-applications. These spreadsheets may then be passed from person to person and modified a little bit at each stop along the way. This behavior raises a key question: If someone hands you a newer version of a spreadsheet you've been using, how do you know it will work the same way as before? Conscientious users might perform a few manual tests before accepting a new file—but most users will accept the "upgrade" without a second thought. Imagine if they make business decisions based on the new version and it turns out the new application is filled with bugs! Mashups must avoid falling into this pattern of "untested dispersion" if they will be successful as well as popular.

---

3. This quote (in various forms) is generally attributed to the renowned computer scientist, Edsger Dijkstra.

The role of the tester must be completely redefined for the modern firm. When users build their own solutions, they have an implicit obligation to perform some degree of testing. Considering the business ramifications of undetected problems, recipients should strongly consider some type of functional verification as well. One way to encourage this desirable behavior is to make it easier. Mashups provide an uncomplicated platform for testing almost anything with a user interface: End users can build "test" mashups as easily as they can implement the other patterns in this book.

One other point that deserves particular mention relates to how load and regression test plans are constructed. These types of tests demand more than "record and playback" of a user's actions against a system. Although this tactic may reveal problems, truly valuable testing of this nature must be exploratory; it must probe deeply within systems to uncover more serious faults. Once mashups have been used to create an API against an application (API Enabler, Chapter 4), Testing implementations can use that interface as a conduit for verifying all of the combinations of potential actions—whether or not a user has performed them yet. Past activity is definitely a key driver in this process, but mashups can obtain a larger sample of potential input data by hitting additional sources. Obviously any "randomization" of data must be logged during the test process for repeatability.

Testing has become so fundamentally easy that there is little excuse for skipping this crucial stage of software development. And in an era when new systems and solutions can come from multiple sources within the enterprise, accepting an untested product from a coworker without personally performing any validations borders on negligence.

Entire industries have been built around software testing, and the dedicated testing tools in this marketplace currently trump the out-of-the box capabilities of mashups. That said, mashups can be used to perform basic testing functions otherwise limited to products costing enormous sums of money. For example, we've already seen how mashups can facilitate user acceptance testing using the Quick Proof-of-Concept pattern (see Chapter 7).

Many enterprises routinely struggle with the management of a diverse portfolio of applications. A highly functional older system can linger well beyond the popularity of the products on which it's based. Developers must then face the uncomfortable task of using multiple testing products to verify the interaction of legacy systems with new products. This chapter proposes new ways to meet this challenge by leveraging mashups to provide testing functionality across a wide range of platforms and technologies.

Audit

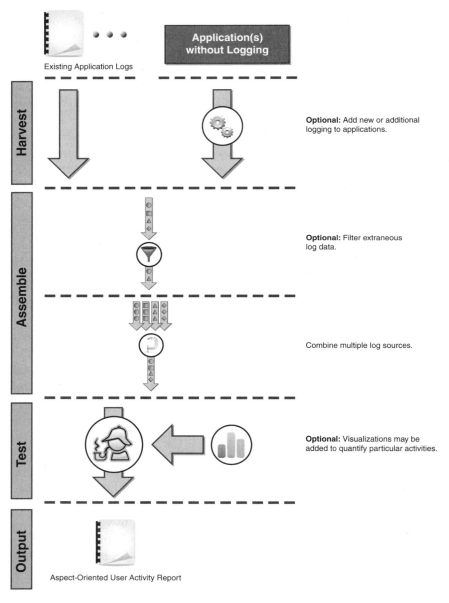

Existing Application Logs

Application(s) without Logging

Harvest

Optional: Add new or additional logging to applications.

Assemble

Optional: Filter extraneous log data.

Combine multiple log sources.

Test

Optional: Visualizations may be added to quantify particular activities.

Output

Aspect-Oriented User Activity Report

Core Activities: Data entry, data extraction, transformation

Also Known As: Aspect-Oriented Mashup (AOM)

Problem

Many bugs are not the result of an obvious defect within a single piece of software but rather occur as the result of the interaction of multiple applications. Looking at individual log files doesn't give the complete picture of what user activity triggered the error. An *audit* seeks to reconstruct the sequence of actions and environmental conditions (such as network or disk constraints) that resulted in an error's manifestation.

To piece together the steps that caused a problem, testers are at the complete mercy of the data made available to them (see Table 8.1). Debugging or error messages reported by the application are naturally the first line of investigation. This material can be either extremely helpful or entirely cryptic depending on whether the original developers anticipated the error. If SaaS or third-party products are involved, there may be no clue whatsoever as to the source of the problem.

The next artifacts consulted are the test results collected by the original developers and testers. These items may reveal known bugs or issues that caused the problem. The final clues come from details provided by the user. User recollections are frustratingly the least valuable asset because employees have firsthand experience with the error but are not trained observers. Nor, it can be argued, should they be. A person focused on performing his or her job shouldn't have to live in fear of the next keystroke or mouse click causing the computer to crash. If a user spends too much time paying attention to a system's behavior, it's probably very buggy or has very low degree of usability.

Table 8.1 *Materials Used for Tracking Down Problems*

Artifact	Usefulness to Testers
System-generated error messages	Value varies. Expected errors are likely to produce more useful error messages than unexpected ones. External applications may "swallow" error details in an attempt to present the user with a more "friendly" message.
Application test results, "known issues" reports	Useful if problem corresponds with a "known error" and can be duplicated. Not useful if the error has never been encountered. Not all external vendors publish a list of known bugs.
User interviews	Stories can be ambiguous and lead testers on a wild goose chase. Users tend to emphasize the activities important to them and to play down or skip minor details. Seemingly insignificant operations that go unreported could be the root cause of the problem.

With evidence like this, it should come as no surprise that even the best-planned applications still have bugs; clearly testing is still part science and part art. Another problem is that none of the elements gets very close to revealing the overall state of the user's environment when the problem occurred. The good news: There is nowhere to go but up. If the value of these artifacts could be enhanced—even if only marginally—the result would be an overall improvement in application reliability.

Likewise, performing audits can add value from a security perspective. An email sent by an employee to a friend or relative to recommend a particular stock trade might seem innocuous enough—but what if an audit revealed the user checked the enterprise's internal trading application beforehand? Suspicion of wrongdoing might be grounds for a company to try and reconstruct past actions from multiple logs, but lack of existing multisystem audit capabilities almost guarantees that some amount of inappropriate, unethical, or illegal activity will go unnoticed until it's too late.

Solution

Aspect-oriented programming (AOP) is a software engineering discipline focused on activities that span both components and applications. AOP arose as a complement to object-oriented development techniques. As programmers worked to encapsulate code and logic into self-contained constructs, the need to capture the broader responsibilities and interactions of the pieces became more important. In the parlance of AOP, a task that occurs within one program is called a *concern,* and tasks that span multiple unconnected systems or modules are called *cross-cutting concerns.* The latter term acknowledges the fact that many of the concerns of a program are scattered in and among the systems that enable it.

For example, the process of opening an account may require a user to interact with one system to perform a credit check and address verification and to interact with a second system for actual data entry. Suppose the data entry system is modified so that it can accept either a five-digit ZIP code or a nine-digit ZIP code (ZIP + 4). The code in the address/credit check system needs to be modified to match this behavior. The problem in this situation is that the data validation code for ZIP codes is duplicated across different systems. A change in one system requires a change in another. AOP attempts to solve this problem by consolidating cross-cutting concerns into external elements known as *aspects.* In this case that means creating a single aspect for address validation and verification. Aspects decrease the overall complexity of applications' architecture and reduce the time and complexity involved in maintaining them. It's good practice to create aspects with future requirements in mind so that they can be leveraged by new solutions.

At the level where traditional AOP takes place, issues such as security and logging are typical cross-cutting concerns. Implementing them as aspects requires an AOP language. One might ask whether business processes that span multiple systems are related to aspects. Conceptually, the answer is "yes." The challenge in the past has been the lack of an easy way to monitor and reshape the flow of these activities. Some firms have begun modeling these processes in an effort to understand (or reengineer) them. But even an optimal process may need to be monitored for auditing, security, or testing purposes. That's where mashups offer an answer: They provide the ability to inject new or enhanced logging features into the multitude of applications with which a user interacts. For example, the same capabilities that allow a mashup to alter an application's behavior via the Field Medic or Usability Enhancer patterns (see Chapter 5) allow supplemental monitoring code to be added as well. The resulting mashups have the ability to track and record all behavior regardless of the systems involved. Such "aspect-oriented mashups" (AOMs) provide unprecedented value for testing and tracking purposes.

AOMs allow two general approaches for reconstructing the process timeline. The first technique involves using patterns such as Content Integration (see Chapter 6) to combine the system logs from multiple applications into a unified view. The value of this information depends largely on what the original developers decided to record. External or third-party applications may not expose any logs whatsoever. The second technique is to employ Usability Enhancer and Field Medic (see Chapter 5) implementations to add new or enhanced logging features. These solutions are AOMs in the purest sense in that they obtain activity and interaction details at a level not possible before mashups existed.

> Envision, for instance, a system in which all kinds of actions and interactions are, with the employees' permission, automatically tagged and fed into a personal "tag cloud"— a visual schematic of the employee's contacts with people, activities, and ideas.[4]

Many of the terminologies used by AOP are equally applicable to AOMs. As the practice of using mashups for testing cross-cutting concerns becomes more popular, firms will likely embrace the nomenclature of AOP.

Related Patterns: Field Medic, Usability Enhancer

Fragility

The aggregation of existing logs is a straightforward task for mashups. Assuming that this data is indexed by a time-stamp, then cross-cutting activities could

---

4. Reeves, Byron, Thomas W. Malone, and Tony O'Driscoll. "Leadership's Online Labs." *Harvard Business Review,* May 2008.

be inferred by examining all records within a given time period. The snag is that applications are notorious for discrepancies in their logging activity. Some track every action; others record only errors. These variations make it difficult to construct an accurate picture of user concerns. Verbose entries need to be filtered out and all records transformed to conform to single standard. The fragility of the implementation under these circumstances is low, but most likely the overall output won't be very useful.

An accurate representation of user activity requires using a consistent approach to collect and store usage-related details. Because not all of a firm's products will have been created by the same developers, the preexistence of uniform material is unlikely. This brings us to mashups as potential providers. The Field Medic and Usability Enhancer patterns describe injecting custom functionality into an application to extend its original functionality. In this instance, basic logging could be added. Although both of these two patterns have high fragility scores in their native category (Enhance patterns), the rating here is lower because they are used strictly for monitoring purposes with the Audit pattern. Nevertheless, this pattern relies on multiple mashups and the failure of any instance will result in only partially logged information. This imperfect data can paint an incomplete picture of the cross-cutting concerns that exist within an enterprise. The fragility score of 2 assigned to this pattern is representative of the balancing act related to it, in which its low functional risk is weighed against its potential to reconstruct inaccurate workflows.

Example: *Add an Audit Trail of Employee Activity*

Excelsior Writers, Inc., offers professional technical writing services for corporate press releases, documentation, and other media. Because the company provides ghost-writing services for major firms, its client list is highly valuable and confidential. During the firm's years in business it has developed numerous specialized templates that allow its employees to quickly turn around content tailored to each customer's specific needs. Lori, an Excelsior employee, decides to defect to a competing firm. But before leaving she attempts to secretly make copies of both the corporate client list and the template library to bring to her new job.

Excelsior management learns of Lori's alleged indiscretions after she resigns. They begin to notice content clearly based on their internal templates being generated by a competitor. As part of research into possible legal action, the managers are determined to discover if Lori is merely working from her memory of the templates or if she has violated her employment agreement by taking proprietary documents off-site.

Because of the private nature of its business, Excelsior implemented audit functionality across most of its internal systems. By reconstructing Lori's activities during her last few weeks on the job, managers hope to uncover evidence of her wrongdoing. The firm will combine four key logs to roll back the clock: the corporate timekeeping system, the CRM[5] system, the enterprise content repository, and the firm's print queue archive. The timekeeping system and print queue had native log features that were deemed adequate when they were purchased, but the content repository and CRM products did not. They're hosted externally by a SaaS provider. Luckily, management decided to implement Usability Enhancer mashups to add logging features before these systems were given to users.

These logs reveal pattern of behavior that appears to be in deliberate conflict with the contract all Excelsior employees sign upon joining the firm. Approximately one month earlier, Lori began accessing records in the CRM database. By itself, this activity was not suspicious; associates often use this data to contact customer representatives about upcoming work. But immediately afterward, the documents in the content repository associated with that client were accessed. Shortly thereafter a series of print jobs was executed corresponding in size with the files that were accessed. According to the timekeeping records, Lori indicated she was writing for a different customer during this period. This audit trail clearly depicts misconduct and will be presented as evidence should Excelsior decide to take legal action against Lori and her new employer.

▼──

Example: *Capture System Usage Trends to Gain Insight into User Behavior*

Soylent Savings is a regional consumer savings bank. Its infrastructure contains numerous applications created in-house and many other products purchased from outside vendors. A number of these systems have been written with audit functionality in mind or had such capabilities added later via mashups. This auditing system helps the bank meet its legal requirements for monitoring employees. Soylent periodically reviews the data it has collected to see how productive its employees are; it also uses the data to spot opportunities to increase efficiency via new systems or business processes. A recent audit uncovers the behavior shown in Table 8.2.

───────────────

5. Customer relationship management.

Table 8.2   *Soylent Issue: Employees Routinely Access System B for Reasons That Are Not Immediately Obvious*

Initial Action	Action Performed Within the Next 10 Minutes
Open new account (System A)	Request replacement ATM card (System B)
Apply for home equity line of credit (System C)	Request replacement ATM card (System B)
Request wire transfer (System D)	Request replacement ATM card (System B)

Initially these actions don't make any sense. No matter which function employees perform, it seems that they almost always access the system for issuing a replacement ATM card. Is some type of illegal activity taking place? Soylent management decides to look into the situation more closely.

As it happens, Soylent recently instituted a policy where all customer interactions were to be viewed as an opportunity to cross-sell other bank products. A number of systems were enhanced (some using the Smart Suggestions pattern from Chapter 5) to display additional offers during a customer transaction. Most employees found the new information distracting and chose instead to open another application to look up these recommendations in a separate window. The system most preferred? "Request replacement ATM card (System B)." Soylent's audit uncovered new information about how its employees work. A decision is made to remove the disparate recommendation engines within each product and create a single, stand-alone system based on the interface created by the System B team. This will also mean that the code base underlying Systems A, C, and D will be easier to maintain going forward.

Load Testing

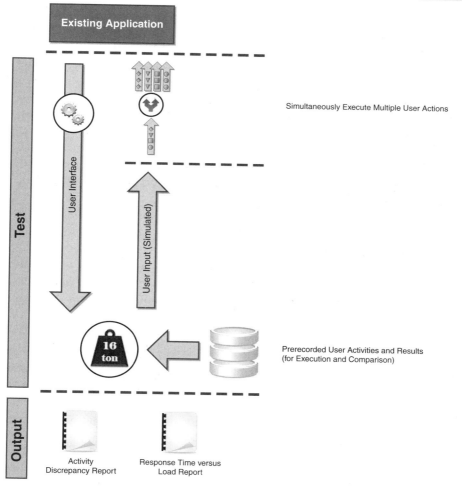

Core Activities: Data entry, data extraction

Problem

One key in planning the deployment of any application is measuring its ability to survive under a heavy or fluctuating load. IT departments sometimes refer to this statistic as *availability*. Of course, many factors can influence availability.

In this instance we are concerned with load related to the activities of a simultaneous group of users. Thus load testing is closely related to two other practices: performance testing and stress testing.

It is one thing to prove that an application can weather a particular volume of users without collapsing, but another job entirely to demonstrate that each user will receive a responsive computing experience during heavy use. Performance measurements made during load tests can uncover the point at which *system stability* overtakes *application usability*. At this crucial point, load testing effectively morphs into stress testing—a gauge of how quickly the scales can be rebalanced so that usability surpasses mere stability.

Load, performance, and stress testing are not new disciplines but rather a common part of any competent software development methodology. What's changed is the scope within which these tests are now applicable and necessary. Mashups have created an explosion of raw ingredients that can serve as the building blocks for new products. Many of these resources were never designed or intended to operate on a broad stage. Even so, they now form the foundation of unique new offerings—which means they must be subjected to the same testing processes applied to traditionally developed applications.

Existing testing tools have some applicability here assuming a mashup exposes an interface that they can understand. Of course, mashups may also create applications or services outside the capabilities of test products contained within an enterprise. Is spending time and money on additional tools and training the only way to deal with this issue?

Solution

Specialized tools remain the preferred method for testing because they have been designed from the ground up to focus on this extremely important facet of software engineering. That said, a firm may be lacking test products for particular languages or platforms. If an enterprise is thinking about adopting mashups to kick-start new development methods, it should recognize the value that mashups bring in closing gaps in test coverage. Mashups are perfectly able to test themselves along with a host of other products.

The Load Testing pattern bears some relation to the Infinite Monkeys pattern discussed in Chapter 4. With that pattern, we examined how a mashup's data extraction abilities could be scaled to acquire information at superhuman levels. Load Testing uses similar techniques to probe system performance repeatedly in an effort to gauge responsiveness and reliability. A key difference between the two patterns is that Infinite Monkeys implementations are generally triggered serially—that is, during the collection of data a single interface is called multiple times successively. This process may even be spread over days or months as part of Time Series or Leading Indicator implementations. One of the important distinctions of the Load Testing pattern is the introduction of an embedded Splinter instance (see Chapter 6). Splinter is used here to take multiple test cases as input and then separate them into individual "action streams" to be executed simultaneously. Tweaking the number of outputs produced by the Splinter effectively determines the number of simulated concurrent users that will hit the product being tested.

Another characteristic of the Load Testing pattern is that it may intentionally scramble the order of user operations or randomize input data with the intention of uncovering application errors. In addition to previously recorded data, new test inputs can be obtained via other mashups or randomly generated. Testing *outside* the range of historical or expected user activities is known as "fuzz testing." Harvest mashups rarely venture down this path because their goal is to observe and collect any variations in output generated in response to a series of unchanged requests.

Mashups and other test tools can enjoy a symbiotic relationship: The transformative capabilities of mashups are used to extend the test tool's reach into other forms of content. For example, a tool designed purely to measure the performance of Web Services could not natively perform load tests on an RSS feed. Conversely, a mashup could repackage the feed as a service for consumption by the testing package.

Mashups can be used to unite multiple test tools to ensure greater ease of use and thoroughness, effectively creating a single "supertester" from the combined abilities of multiple products. A firm might have load and performance test suites intended to simulate specific user activities while at the same time imposing pressure on disk, memory, or network resources. Manually coordinating all of these tools is a difficult and error-prone process that is better left to a mashup; test scenarios that were once thought impossible without a significant investment of time and resources can be constructed quickly with this pattern. A Load Testing implementation could, in effect, take the "load" off the testers and lead to quicker time to market with fewer bugs.

Related Patterns: Audit, Infinite Monkeys

Fragility

Load and stress tests are interesting experiments: On the surface they would seem to have predictable outcomes, yet in reality their results are often unexpected. When a particular function returns a specific answer, logic would seem to dictate that no matter how many times that same function is executed, the result should be the same (assuming all inputs were constant). In fact, load and stress tests expose dependencies and vulnerabilities in the underlying implementation that might not become evident until resources are strained. Under these conditions an application could simply collapse or additional measures put in place to handle the burden could come into play. One of the challenges in executing a successful load or stress test is determining the appropriate definition of "load." For example, should the "load" be measured in terms of system-response time or based on the number of users who can be handled simultaneously (albeit slowly)? If one factor is examined to the exclusion of another, a system may technically pass testing checkpoints yet fail miserably under actual conditions.

The robotic nature of mashups is an advantage if the load test is being conducted against an API or interface designed to serve other systems or modules. Mashups, being essentially code themselves, are adept at simulating the actions of nonhuman clients. In this case their methodical approach to execution corresponds more closely with how the code will actually be exercised.

In other cases the tests' results may be inaccurate. Because mashups are an automated solution, using them to simulate a person's activities carries some risk. A mashup will methodically execute each step of a task, whereas a real-life user might pause between steps to answer the phone or chat with a coworker. Thus, while the mashup may perform perfectly, it isn't necessarily an accurate representation of real-world activity. In some circumstances it may be possible to fine-tune mashup behavior with data captured from end users (see the Reality Mining pattern covered in Chapter 4).

Load and stress tests must be carefully designed to reflect realistic circumstances. Because of their very nature, mashups don't always accomplish this goal where the behavioral nuances of human users is concerned. The fragility score of 2 is awarded to the Load Testing pattern in recognition of this subtle but important discrepancy.

Example: *Measure Web Site Responsiveness*

A Web site's response time is crucial to its success. A recent study[6] reported that users will wait a maximum of 4 seconds before they consider bailing out from an online transaction. The report uncovered some other interesting facts about

6. "Akamai and Jupiter Research Identify '4 Seconds' as the New Threshold of Acceptability for Retail Web Page Response Times." November 6, 2006. http://www.akamai.com/html/about/press/releases/2006/press_110606.html

how site performance affects customer satisfaction. Consumers reported a site's slowness as a leading cause for dissatisfaction, second only to high prices.

> Additional findings in the report show that more than one-third of shoppers with a poor experience abandoned the site entirely, while 75 percent were likely not to shop on that site again. These results demonstrate that a poorly performing website can be damaging to a company's reputation; according to the survey, nearly 30 percent of dissatisfied customers will either develop a negative perception of the company or tell their friends and family about the experience.[7]

For a commercial Web site, failure to perform load and stress tests can clearly be disastrous. Anyone familiar with Web development knows that guaranteeing a specific response time is very difficult because there are so many points in the underlying architecture and infrastructure where a delay can be introduced. Server processing, database response time, network bandwidth, and memory usage are just some of the potential bottlenecks. Each of these resources should be load-tested separately as well as evaluated as a cohesive unit operating to respond to users' requests.

This is a straightforward situation where mashups can clearly help. The scope of the test is "all possible user actions." For retail site, that list is probably limited to a few simple operations such as browsing the catalog, adding an item to the cart, and checking out. A mashup could be implemented for each of these tasks. The success condition (from a performance standpoint) is to receive a response in less than 4 seconds. The mashups could be executed in ever-increasing numbers (Infinite Monkeys) until this benchmark is exceeded. At this point a firm can determine it's comfortable that actual usage will never surpass the tests' parameters or decide that it needs to rearchitect its site to handle more customers.

In other instances, load testing is necessary but the composition of tests is much more complicated. These circumstances tend to involve situations in which either the range of user actions is much broader or the success conditions are more varied, or some combination of the two. Rather than focus on a specific example for this pattern, let's examine some of the basic questions that frame a successful load test:

- *Is the test environment an accurate representation of production?* If it's not the test results do not have real-world relevance.

- *Which conditions are being tested?* It may not be necessary to test the permutations of all possible user actions because some actions may rank higher than others in terms of importance. The performance-critical sections of

---

7. "Akamai and Jupiter Research."

an application should be tested separately. The more granular the tests, the easier it will be to spot problem areas.

- *What are the metrics for success?* Is it an acceptable response time or completing the action without failure while under heavy load? Sometimes a long-running task that executes without interruption is preferable to an immediate response stating, "Please try again later." Spend some time defining the measurements you will make and how they relate to the test conditions.

- *Which load levels will be tested?* Do you have average usage statistics to aim for? Will you test sustained elevated activity or spikes? As load continues to increase, the process eventually morphs into stress testing. If this is not one of your goals you need to determine when this line has been crossed.

- *How will results be reported?* Rather than return a simple pass/fail message, tests should attempt to isolate points of failure to aid with subsequent diagnosis. If database accesses seem to cause problems, the output should reflect this issue.

Once you have explored these questions you are ready to design and perform the actual tests. Because you will probably be executing the test suite multiple times, it's necessary to reset the data to an identical state for consistency. The Content Migration pattern (covered in Chapter 7, Manage Patterns) can be used to prepare an application environment before the start of each run.

Regression Testing

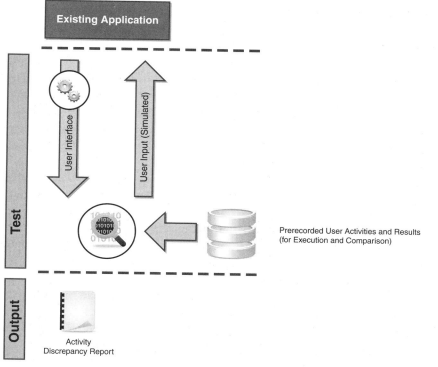

Prerecorded User Activities and Results
(for Execution and Comparison)

Activity
Discrepancy Report

Core Activities: Data entry, data extraction

Problem

Studies of software maintenance have shown that the later a bug is fixed, the more expensive the cost of the remedy. In light of this research, rigorous disciplines have sprung up to influence the development process and push back the time frame for bug detection and correction. For example, the test-driven development (TDD) techniques prescribe creating a test before a single line of code is even written. Naturally, this test will fail when first executed—but the underlying premise is that developers should not begin working on a solution until they understand how to verify its correctness. Other methodologies shift the scheduling of tests around somewhat but never diminish their value.

As important as testing is for new solutions, it is even more critical when work is performed on existing products. A new tool that fails is an annoyance;

in contrast, when bugs appear (or reappear) within established products, it can cause major breakdowns within a firm's processing. To combat this threat, many organizations have set aside dedicated resources for testing. In theory this approach addresses the concern that developers lack the skills or discipline to adequately test their own products. Testers are sometimes viewed as a "checkpoint" for the process of getting a solution into the hands of users. In reality, testing is a complicated endeavor. It requires a thorough understanding of the users' requirements so that they can be reconciled with the developers' creations. Over time a schism has evolved between programmers and end users; by nature testers are required to stride this gap and understand each party's needs and concerns. Because mashups erase the barriers between developer and user, professional testers will likely be disintermediated. If users circumvent developers and use mashup tools to build their own solutions, they'll likely bypass any formal quality assurance (QA) process as well.

If a firm grapples with the ability to control changes that occur internally, what happens when an upgrade to a third-party product is received? Or what if a Web site relied upon by a company is suddenly redesigned? Should it be taken on faith that the providers of these solutions have verified that *none* of their users will be negatively affected? As noted in the introduction to this chapter, the wide variety of computing environments makes it almost impossible for an external provider to guarantee its solution will function properly in all cases. Setting aside the empowering nature of mashups for a moment, it's obvious testers already lose sleep worrying about the impact of external changes on their own applications. Organizations need to ensure that their testing tools are keeping pace with advances in development and that new releases aren't a step *backward* from their predecessors in terms of capability.

Solution

Regression testing is a practice that seeks to uncover instances where application functionality diminishes from one version to the next. Usually these changes result in some type of error, but they can sometimes be more subtle—for example, unintentional interface modifications that impose a different workflow or force users to relearn how to accomplish basic tasks. A thorough regression suite exercises the majority of interactions a user may make with a system. Because all code changes have the potential to introduce (or reintroduce) errors, it's important to test beyond the scope of whatever recent issues have been corrected. This testing could be performed manually. Of course, for an application of any significant size, this process quickly becomes tedious and unwieldy, which is why many commercial and open-source products have been developed to automate this task. As with load testing, when a dedicated test suite is not available, mashups can step in to fill the gap.

The Regression Testing pattern leverages the data extraction and data entry capabilities of mashups to duplicate user behavior. By employing a predefined collection of data, a Regression Testing implementation ensures that input/output results across versions are as expected. Bear in mind that downstream systems may be considered a type of user, as well. Because mashups do not discriminate among applications based on their interfaces or environments, they are equally well suited as test mechanisms for products hosted either internally or externally.

Regression testing is a close companion of integration testing. Whereas regression testing seeks to prove no functional decrease in capability between product versions, integration testing attempts to uncover whether a product negatively affects any "neighbors" in its operating environment. One way to implement integration testing is to execute a suite of regression tests across multiple products even when only a single system has been changed. This kind of integration testing serves as a complement to the Audit pattern. One goal of an audit is to reconstruct the series of cross-application events that led to a problem. By contrast, an integration test seeks to preemptively discover how these relationships might potentially lead to problems. Integration testing is also sometimes used to describe the process of testing multiple modules within a single application—a feat mashups are also capable of achieving.

In the new world brought about by mashups, regression testing is more important than ever. Historically a correct application could not manifest an error that was not somehow the fault of its original design. We know from our examination of mashup fragility, however, that external factors can alter a mashup's behavior. In some cases changes to resources used by mashups will cause outright breakages. This is the preferred behavior to the more dangerous alternative: a mashup that keeps working but returns bad results that go undetected. Regular regression tests against apparently stable mashups can uncover these issues before they cause significant harm.

Consider where the responsibility for creating tests falls when mashups are employed. In the traditional development system, solutions were created and tested by trained professionals within IT departments. When mashups allowed internal developers to be circumvented, they bypassed internal testing and quality assurance teams, too. Business users now find themselves able to create and share their own solutions with passing through any of the internal checkpoints to verify their correctness. An enterprise that implements this democratic model of software creation must take steps to educate its users on the subject of testing. This topic is examined further during the discussion of the One-Hit Wonder anti-pattern in Chapter 9.

Users who accept solutions from their coworkers "on faith" absent of any test results should think carefully about implementing their own regression test plans. As illustrated by the "virtuous circle of mashups" in Chapter 1, mashups have a habit of traveling from person to person and being enhanced along the way. This model is a powerful one for incrementally building solutions, but it creates numerous opportunities for mistakes to be introduced. Each author is likely to be concerned only with his or her specific problems and to ignore how those changes affect features the individual doesn't use. It's like the classic children's game of "telephone"[8] applied to software engineering. For the comfort of any potential consumers, a mashup author should consider publishing an accompanying regression test with his or her creation. Under ideal circumstances the regression test will trickle down and be extended with each new mashup variation. Absent this approach, mashup recipients should strongly consider the value in implementing their own regression tests and periodically reviewing their data for correctness. This is especially important for products created outside the IT department that may have bypassed any established testing procedures.

A key point is that mashups allow the testing process to enlist nontraditional resources. Innovation at many corporations can be hampered by departmental resource constraints that create a testing "log jam." Because *testing* becomes as much a collaborative process as *creation*, new products and features can reach their intended recipients more quickly.

Related Patterns: Content Migration, Infinite Monkeys

Fragility

At first glance it might appear that the Regression Testing pattern does not deserve any fragility score at all. If an implementation breaks, hasn't it accomplished its purpose in clearly demonstrating that the underlying application has changed? Perhaps—but this is not the full story. The first thing we must consider is *what* is being tested. If the pattern is used solely to exercise an API or other nonvisual interface (e.g., XML), then a functional break is a very good indicator that a severe problem has occurred.

Another way that a regression test may be performed is by simulating actions against the "visible" user interface. It's important to keep two potential outcomes in mind:

1. *Significant unplanned interface changes occur between versions but the mashup is able to adjust itself dynamically.* While we normally applaud

---

8. In this game, children line up and the first person is whispered a message. Each child in turn whispers this message to his or her neighbor, and so on down the queue. By the time the last person receives the message, it often bears little resemblance to the original phrase.

this type of resiliency, assuming that users will be able to adapt as flexibly as the mashup is a mistake. A "test failure" *should* be triggered but instead the problem goes undetected. This is the first case where a mashup's *not breaking* obscures the incorrect behavior.

2. *Planned interface changes break existing Regression Testing mashups.* Interface enhancements are a natural part of an application's life cycle. They range from small cosmetic changes to alterations that have a huge effect on a user's experience. In either case, any test mashups need to be retooled so that the interface does not become a barrier to testing deeper functionality.

In the case of unplanned changes, a mashup may not break when it should. Conversely, planned modifications can prevent a mashup from examining more meaningful content. In both of these cases, an outright failure—or lack of one—is not a reliable indicator of consistency across versions. In other words, while the process of testing can be subject to some level of automation, the interpretation of test results should not be completely delegated to mashups. The Regression Testing pattern receives a fragility score of 1 to underscore the risks associated with its potential misuse and to recognize the occasional retooling that implementations will require.

When regression testing occurs under the broad umbrella of integration testing, other systems will likely need to be monitored for unexpected changes. In effect, integration testing constitutes distributed regression testing: Other systems are examined to record inconsistencies that did not exist until a new version of a separate product was released. If mashups are used to implement these assessments, then overall fragility increases with each new system that is added.

Examples

Traditional regression testing is usually limited to a designated QA team. This pattern, when combined with mashups' ease of use, makes it easier than ever to extend good testing practices across the entire enterprise. Some sample usage ideas are highlighted here:

- End users can apply tests to objects they pass among themselves (such as spreadsheets). Before switching to a "new" release mailed by a coworker, an employee can run personal regression tests to double-check that none of the existing calculations has been broken.

- Anyone who is building mashups using a Web site's published API will want to ensure that the mashup's output results match those returned from the site's other interfaces. A regression implementation can verify that a site's Web Services, RSS feeds, and user interfaces produce identical data given the same inputs.

- Moving data from one application to another is discussed in conjunction with the Content Migration pattern (Chapter 7). The next logical step is to make sure that the new system produces identical results. For example, when moving from an internal purchase order system to one provided by a SaaS vendor, it's a good idea to make sure tax and shipping calculations are still accurate. A test against each system should produce matching costs.

- Changes to an application's hosting environment or operating system can have unintended consequences on an application's behavior even if the code hasn't been updated. Regression tests can bring these discrepancies to light before they cause any harm.

- Regression testing user interfaces (UIs) has historically been a thorny problem that is either time-consuming or expensive. Because mashups can simulate a user and interact directly with an application's interface, usability can be regression tested as easily as functionality. A QA team can pinpoint unrequested changes to a program's UI before the system is released to unsuspecting users.

Chapter 9

Anti-patterns

The appearance of right oft leads us wrong.

—Horace (65 B.C.–8 B.C.)

Introduction

If the patterns discussed in the previous chapters represent the bright dawn of mashup use within the enterprise, then anti-patterns are the noisy neighbor who cuts his lawn at 6 A.M. and keeps you from getting any work done. They are the distractions, the shortcuts, and the mistakes to which we're all vulnerable. Like patterns, anti-patterns are not unique to mashups. Just as there are repeatable approaches for tackling many problems, so a variety of pitfalls and traps await the unwary explorer. Although the most common users of anti-patterns are the nontechnical or inexperienced, anyone can venture down the wrong path when decisions are made in haste.

Part of the reason anti-patterns persist at all is because they hide in the dark recesses of application development. When a company focuses exclusively on results and not how those results were achieved, it turns a blind eye to serious consequences that can surface later on. In terms of mashups, these unhappy events could consist of systems that suddenly stop working (Drinking Seawater), create complicated dependencies (Shadow Integration), or violate legal restrictions (Sticky Fingers). Fortunately we can provide a map around these potential obstacles. Just as capturing some common mashup patterns can point people toward solutions, so documenting the "worst practices" of anti-patterns allows trouble spots to be avoided.

Although anti-patterns are the direct opposite of the patterns, we will examine them using a format similar to the one employed in previous chapters. Each section begins with the name of the anti-pattern followed by a brief description of the circumstances where it may arise (the "Problem" section). The next segment corresponds to a pattern's "Solution" section: Although it might seem like an attractive option, it's actually behavior that should be avoided. You'll find this section has been retitled "Sloppy Solution"[1] to underscore this point. The "Related Patterns" citation identifies the patterns to which the anti-patterns are most closely related.[2] You should review the corresponding entries to familiarize yourself with the situations where the anti-pattern might seem like a good fit. The "Appeal" section explains why the Sloppy Solution is both tempting and dangerous. It wouldn't be much of a deterrent to brand a potential course of action as "bad" without providing some justification. Finally, "Remediation" describes an action plan for tackling cases where the Sloppy Solution was followed.

Familiarity with the anti-patterns will help you both avoid them while architecting new solutions and recognize them within current products. Even if you don't immediately remove an entrenched anti-pattern you should document its existence. If you don't, other individuals who stumble across it may form the impression that it's an acceptable or preferred technique. Anti-patterns are replicated through reuse, and mashups are fertile territory for recycling (see Figure 1.5, depicting the virtuous circle of mashups, in Chapter 1). The last thing an enterprise needs is for known defects to be used as the basis for future solutions.

It is a time-honored tradition when describing anti-patterns to give them somewhat humorous names.[3] The purpose behind this nomenclature is two-fold. First, it's important to commit these anti-patterns to memory and the funny names can help in this regard. Second, a little teasing can encourage people to fix their anti-pattern implementations more quickly.

---

1. Shoddy, Slapdash, and Substandard were other contenders.

2. Several anti-patterns relate to multiple patterns and are noted as such.

3. Gas factory, golden hammer, lava flow, and spaghetti code are a few examples.

Skinny Window

Problem

Combining multiple products can result in the reduced availability for the final solution. Mashup implementations frequently rely on more than one system to achieve their goal. In an enterprise environment, each of these underlying products may have different targets for uptime and performance based on specific business requirements. If the overall mashup requires the full participation of each of its constituent parts, there is only a narrow window of time within which it can function properly.

Sloppy Solution

Suppose three systems participate in a mashup:

1. System A is guaranteed to be available 24 hours a day, 7 days a week.

2. System B's Service level agreement (SLA) states it will be available between 8 A.M. and 3 P.M. every day (although it's usually ready by 7 A.M. and overnight processing jobs don't start until after 5 P.M.).

3. System C is generally available from 10 A.M. to 6 P.M. daily. Its SLA obliges it to be up and running only from 12 P.M. to 5 P.M.

Now consider the recovery time of each system in the event of a problem (perhaps when a server crashes or disk space is exhausted):

1. System A advertises failover to a working environment within an hour.

2. System B and System C can recover in less than 20 minutes.

What does this say about the overarching mashup? The answer is to take the intersection of all the SLA data. The mashup is accessible between 12 P.M. and 3 P.M. each day, and in the event of a problem will be unavailable for as long as an hour. Unfortunately an enterprise's staff probably needs more than a three-hour window each day to use the solution.

Because Systems B and C are typically functional outside their stated SLAs, it's tempting to rely on this behavior to increase the mashup's availability without actually doing any work. Based on empirical data the operational window could be extended to encompass the period 10 A.M. to 5 P.M.—an improvement of more than double! And given that 66% of the time an outage will be resolved within 20 minutes, it's tempting to ignore System A's extended recovery time.

Related Patterns: All pattern implementations that rely on multiple sources (e.g., Content Aggregation, Content Integration, and Dashboard)

Appeal

Most anti-patterns share at least one common enticement, and Skinny Windows (conflicting SLAs) is no different. "It's easy" can be a persuasive argument. Ignoring SLAs in favor of using empirical observations to circumvent "weak participants" is one way to deal with the inconvenient availability of particular applications. A mashup developer might not even bother to investigate SLAs in the first place.

SLAs might be sidelined for other reasons as well. If the mashed-up applications are hosted *externally*, fees could be required to establish greater uptime. Because mashup development can occur anywhere within an organization, authors may not have the budget or authority to purchase additional services. Maybe they want to spend money elsewhere. If the source systems are located *internally*, then mashup creators may be reluctant to approach product owners and reveal that their programs are being used to build new systems without their knowledge.

Let's not forget the greatest attraction here: Even though the operational window is small, before mashups came along Systems A, B, and C were separate entities. The mere value of their combined data can overshadow concerns about availability.

Remediation

Building a solution and not taking the limits of its components into consideration is not good practice. Sooner or later a system will fail outside its publicized SLA—and this failure could have severe consequences for any dependent mashups. Rather than hide or ignore these inner limitations, a mashup creator should work backward from the SLA required by users. If Mashup D is powered by Systems A, B, and C and is required to be functional between 9 A.M. and 5 P.M. daily, then its developer must work with teams B and C to extend their programs' operational windows. Likewise, if external systems can be made more reliable at a reasonable cost, then this expense (along with its risks and benefits) should be surfaced through the appropriate channels within the firm.

Drinking Seawater

Problem

Several of the mashup patterns discussed in earlier chapters of this book are able to recombine or repackage existing internal or external resources so that they bear little resemblance to existing systems. The new mashup-powered application may be so well received that business sponsors unknowingly cancel funding for the underlying applications that drive it. What was seen as an independent new product suffers an untimely death as the applications it leverages are switched off one by one.

Sloppy Solution

This anti-pattern's name is inspired by tales of unlucky explorers lost at sea. With no land or hope of rescue in sight, castaways might be tempted to slake their thirst by drinking some of the seawater that surrounds them. Any momentary sense of relief will soon be lost, however. To process the excess salt in the water, a person's body needs to expel more water than it takes in. Persons who drink seawater wind up dehydrating themselves sooner, even though they feel temporarily satisfied.

The Drinking Seawater anti-pattern describes a similar risk for mashup builders. A search for new content to power mashups can be as wasted as efforts to spy land on the open ocean. In desperation a developer might turn to the existing applications and feeds in the surrounding environment. Mashups don't just combine these sources: As the various patterns have demonstrated, they can create *new* products that exceed the capabilities of their predecessors. More importantly in this case, these new solutions don't have to disclose any reliance on their information providers. And why should they? Mashups are tools for harvesting untapped treasure troves of existing content. Let them spread throughout the enterprise! Build mashups without restraint!

Related Patterns: Emergency Response, Dashboard, Portal Enabler, Super Search, Usability Enhancer, Widget Enabler

Appeal

Look at your coworkers. What a sad picture they present—tied to some heavyweight programming language and negotiating with various mainframe and database feeds to produce a product that no one even likes. But don't waste time feeling sorry for them. Instead, point a mashup at their application, pull in some additional sources, and create some new whiz-bang application that everyone loves. You'll become the hero of your firm. What's not appealing about that?

Remediation

If you don't credit your sources, your sense of fulfillment may be as short-lived as our seawater-drinking friends. When management learns of your success, these higher-level personnel may begin to wonder why they are supporting some other projects within the firm that are very expensive and aren't being so well received. Or maybe they'll cancel subscriptions to external services seeing as how you've "reproduced" their features.

As the systems your mashup relies on begin to disappear one by one, you might be able to replace a few from alternative sources. But the decline is inevitable. Eventually a critical component of your mashup will be switched off, and you'll have to explain why your product doesn't work anymore. Dehydration might be a preferable fate.

The Drinking Seawater anti-pattern is an easy situation to avoid. Rather than bask in the success of your creation, go out of your way to recognize the people and products that make it possible. You might even go so far as to advertise system dependencies in your mashup's user interface. Share the spotlight and managers will recognize your initiative, coworkers will thank you for a new solution, and developers will appreciate your drawing attention to the relevance of their work. You may even redirect the focus of your IT department toward creating more mashup-friendly content.

Sticky Fingers

Problem

The Internet is awash in unstructured content. As we observed in Chapter 1 (Figure 1.4), only a small number of sources currently provide access to their data via a public API. Even then, this interface may not be sufficient to extract or manipulate data in the manner desired. These limitations are sometimes intentional. Patterns such as API Enabler (covered in Chapter 4, Harvest Patterns) make it easy to pull content without asking the owner's permission.

Studies have shown that people behave more honestly when they feel they are being watched.[4] It follows that the apparent anonymity of a Web browser deemphasizes the illegality of certain actions. The ephemeral nature of electronic content is surely a contributor to this phenomenon: "Viewing" doesn't seem like stealing.

Sloppy Solution

Once content is available via a public mechanism such as a Web browser, all bets are off in terms of how it will ultimately be used. Even before mashups came onto the scene, most programming languages had some means to load a Web page internally. People wrote applications to scrape sites for a variety of reasons. But it was a time-consuming process to parse the results, and the code was complicated to maintain. As tools eventually improved, one thing didn't change: Development environments remained completely ignorant as to how they were employed. Examining the terms of use for extracted data remained the responsibility of the human operator.

Table 9.1 lists four major targets for content theft and their potential ramifications. The last item, "Subscription/fee-based Web Services," is a particularly interesting situation. Because mashups can repackage existing content, it's possible to create a wrapper around a commercial site to republish its material without permission. This can be a subtle transgression. For example, a developer could create a widget that leverages a firm's single-user subscription at a private site and then distribute that code to thousands. This violation might go unrecognized until the vendor notices peculiar traffic or usage patterns.

---

4. "'Big Brother' Eyes Make Us Act More Honestly." *New Scientist,* June 2006. http://www.newscientist.com/article/dn9424-big-brother-eyes-make-us-act-more-honestly.html

Table 9.1 *Risks Related to Content Reuse*

Content Type	Sample Patterns	Risks
Public content created for open (nonsubscription) blogs and forums. This material is typically not copyrighted.	Alerter, API Enabler, Reputation Management, Feed Factory	Plagiarism, harm to firm's reputation.
Copyrighted content; especially binary files (images, videos, music)	API Enabler, Content Aggregation	Legal action. This content is clearly protected by laws such as the United States' Digital Millennium Copyright Act (DMCA) and the European Union's EU Copyright Directive.
Online shopping applications and corporate Web sites	Competitive Analysis, Leading Indicator, Smart Suggestions, Time Series	Terms-of-use violations, IP addresses being banned.
Subscription/fee-based Web Services	API Enabler, Feed Factory, Smart Suggestions, Portal Enabler, Widget Enabler	Usage violations resulting in legal action.

History has shown that there is little incentive for people to navigate this legal landscape. Many "revolutionary" products have been built on top of intellectual property. Napster and YouTube are two noteworthy examples where intellectual property rights were sidelined during the thrill of creation. In Napster's case its creators' transgressions led to an untimely shutdown.[5] For its part, YouTube has been asked to pull thousands of clips of copyrighted material.[6] "Fair use!" is a frequently heard battle cry. It stems from the portion of U.S. copyright law that allows for limited use of copyrighted material without the owner's consent. Its supporters might be surprised to learn "[t]here is no specific number of words, lines, or notes that may safely be taken without permission."[7] Rulings are made on a case-by-case basis.

The simple fact is that the laws in this area are unclear at best. It doesn't help that laypeople are exposed to seemingly contradictory positions on a regular basis. "How come I'm not allowed to copy a page, but Google's page cache is?"

---

5. "Napster Must Stay Shutdown." *BBC News,* March 26, 2002. http://news.bbc.co.uk/1/hi/entertainment/new_media/1893904.stm

6. "Viacom Asks YouTube to Remove Over 100,000 Unauthorized Video Clips." *USA Today,* February 2, 2007. http://www.usatoday.com/tech/news/2007-02-02-viacom-youtube_x.htm

7. "Fair Use." http://www.copyright.gov/fls/fl102.html

"Why can someone post a news story on YouTube but I can't burn a copy for my friend?" There are no hard statistics on the subject, but it's easy to believe that more theft occurs as a result of simple confusion as opposed to deliberate intent.

Related Patterns: All pattern implementations that obtain data from external sources (e.g., Leading Indicator, Competitive Analysis, and Reputation Management)

Appeal

The allure of using mashups tools for content theft is that it doesn't even seem like stealing. "The information is already on public display on the Web, right?" a person might ask. "What difference does it make if I view it personally or write a small mashup to do it for me?" The World Wide Web has made content more accessible than ever before, and some have confused *ease of access* with *right to access.*

People download movies and songs from the Internet and excuse their behavior by saying, "I never would have paid for that anyway." Or they pirate commercial applications and characterize it as a free trial: "I'll pay for it if it actually turns out to be useful." It's a powerful feeling to be able to assert total control over the relationship between producer and consumer. Can you imagine going out to eat and telling the waiter, "Give me your fanciest meal, and if I like it I'll pay for it"? Or shoplifting some clothes from a store at the mall while thinking, "I'd never actually *pay* to wear this outfit"?

When fee-based services are involved, the appeal is obviously a financial one. It should be obvious to the mashup builder that this sort of activity is illegal, but many still take content anyway. They view themselves as modern-day Robin Hoods—stealing from rich corporations to help the disenfranchised little guy. Cloaked in this warped sense of morality, they allow themselves to feel justified in their actions. The cable and satellite television industry has been fighting a similar battle for years. For this reason many content producers will be interested in the techniques for blocking mashups and other harvesting mechanisms that are discussed in the next chapter.

Remediation

To protect the firm's reputation and assets, mashup creators have a duty to make sure they are not violating any laws or usage agreements in their quest to create the next "killer app." All it takes to get started is a little common sense. Before creating incredible solutions that benefit from mashup-obtained content, it's imperative to check the terms and conditions of the resources being mined.

Public sites usually place a link to any legal details on their home page; for commercial products a little more digging through contracts or other documentation may be necessary.

An enterprise can't rely solely on its employees to justify their own actions—the potential risks are too great. Even the best-intentioned associates can unintentionally violate explicit or implied contracts. This is precisely the reason that many firms regularly perform computer scans to search for pirated software on employee workstations. Network logs can allow a similar scanning process to take place for mashups. Any repeated activity that occurs at regular intervals is one sign that mashups might be at work, especially if it happens on a server instead of a user's desktop. A company might pass this information along to its security or legal teams for further investigation.

Shadow Integration

Problem

Not all enterprise systems rely solely on their own internal content. Many applications depend on a rich tapestry of feeds that shuffle data from one system to another to obtain the information they require. Despite their ubiquity, creating these feeds between systems can be a difficult task. Technical issues such as data mapping and transformation are only a small part of the challenge. Often there is a substantial amount of bureaucracy involved. If a team requires a feed from another system, that application's management may not have any resources to support developing it or they may want to be compensated for their work. The managers could also give the task a low priority and instead focus on issues important to their specific end users. Until these obstacles are overcome, new development efforts can make little progress.

Creating mashup-powered feeds is one possible solution. Of course, once a feed has been constructed its operation needs to be documented and managed properly. Without this formal awareness a firm has no idea how an outage or error in one application will cascade across the enterprise's infrastructure.

Sloppy Solution

The technical process of feed building is fairly straightforward. A rough list of the steps includes these measures:

- Arranging for encoded files or database extracts to be created

- Setting a schedule for the transfer of these files to a temporary location

- Writing batch scripts to detect when the data has arrived (or hasn't)

- Using a scripting language such as Perl or Ruby to manipulate the data

- Reloading the data into new database tables

The recent rise of XML has simplified some of the technical challenges—but it hasn't made it easier to procure network storage, reserve space on a database, or negotiate with other application owners. A development team can avoid many of the hassles of feed development by using mashups. The list of operations then becomes much simpler:

- API-enable the source system (see Chapter 4)

- Define any necessary transformations within the mashup toolset

- Expose the data either as a Web Service (essentially creating a "feed-as-needed") or mine a section of content and write it directly to a database

Two aspects of this process make this approach particularly dangerous:

1. Individual implementations *appear* efficient and benign.

2. The perceived successes from the previous point encourage additional implementations.

Here's the downside: Once mashup-powered feeds have been created, there is little incentive to publicize their existence. After all, if a system known for its reliability is being mined, one would assume the mashup inherits a similar bit of sturdiness. En masse, this type of thinking creates a complicated web of dependencies whose existence can remain a complete mystery.

Sometimes the source system is so slow or holds so much data that a mashup cannot get everything it needs in its allotted execution window. Nevertheless a Feed Factory or Content Integration implementation may be created as part of a Quick Proof-of-Concept scenario. If these patterns somehow remain in place long enough to affect a production environment, then the Shadow Integration anti-pattern still comes into play.

Related Patterns: Content Integration, Feed Factory

Appeal

It can be a huge time saver if a team can procure the data it needs from a system without requiring any outside participation. "It's easier to beg forgiveness than to ask permission."[8] Mashups not only make it easy to create these feeds quickly, but they do so in a way that is almost completely undetectable. A team that's anxious to make progress will always be attracted to the path of least resistance. The immediate gratification of having a working feed easily outweighs concerns about potential downtime.

Another benefit is that mashup-powered feeds don't require their developers have *any* familiarity with the architecture of the source system. After all, the data is usually pulled straight from the user interface. If a huge technical divide separates teams—perhaps because of a merger or a corporate reorganization—it's often easier to create secret layers of integration instead of reconciling these frequently contentious (and often very personal) differences.

---

8. This quote is generally attributed to Grace Hopper, the famous computer scientist and researcher.

Remediation

The easiest way to prevent the Shadow Integration anti-pattern from rearing its ugly head is to avoid creating an environment that encourages it in the first place. Teams should be encouraged to feel a sense of ownership of their applications and data, but at the same time they should not be overprotective and unwilling to share. After all, application developers are ultimately technology-minded humanitarians; their focus is on providing solutions that make business users' lives easier—not on usurping existing applications as part of some imperialistic march through the IT department. In the past, data warehouses sought to accomplish this goal, but they were complicated and expensive efforts that ultimately made it difficult to both contribute and extract data. Mashups make the process easier and they're risky only so long as they remain hidden.

One strategy is to clearly educate users regarding where the data in their applications comes from. This information can be provided by using color coding, on-screen footnotes, or other techniques. Managers may still be unaware of these dependencies (unless they use the products in question) but regular users won't be caught off-guard when one system crashes and several others quickly follow. This is the easiest remedy for mashup builders outside of IT who are secretly connecting applications.

A more formal approach is recommended for feed builders within IT. Errant feeds from undocumented sources create a decentralized system. To create effective failover plans for business resumption or disaster recovery, an enterprise has an absolute necessity to know how its most crucial systems are interconnected. These applications will generally not be architected by end users (although the applications may leverage mashups). At a minimum, most organizations require developers of applications to supply a "run book" or "dependency diagram" before those programs will be admitted into the enterprise's production environment. This document typically contains details such as server and database names, processing windows, expected response times, file locations, and any other information crucial to understanding an application's operational structure. A firm should require that any mashups that reach out to other sites to procure content be described here as well. The group that manages run books can use this data to map the spread of new dependencies. This in turn can inform a discussion about potential consequences and preventive measures for mashup-driven feeds.[9]

---

9. For example, a crucial mashup might be decommissioned in favor of a traditionally architected feed if it will increase reliability.

Dirty Laundry

Problem

One of the main benefits of mashups is their ability to pull together information from multiple sources. In some cases this material is obtained via a public interface. A well-designed API is an important checkpoint for controlling which records can be extracted as well as guaranteeing secure access to data. When an API is desired but not available, a mashup builder can construct their own by using patterns such as API Enabler (discussed in Chapter 4, Harvest Patterns). Implementations typically impersonate a user, which implies that the mashup will have full privileges to whatever data and operations are accessible to a human operator. For convenience (but certainly *not* for security reasons), a developer may embed any sign-on IDs and passwords inside the mashup (see the discussion of the Open Kimono anti-pattern later in this chapter).

Suppose the resulting mashup exposes some of this harvested data to end users without requiring any type of authentication. Now anyone has access to information from one or more systems where—had that individual tried to access the source directly—he or she might have been blocked. The impact of this exposure can range from embarrassment to a full-blown crisis.[10]

Outright exposure of private material is only half of the problem; the importance of data may also increase as part of the mashup process. Consider a financial company with two systems: one for tracking customer details and another for managing client transactions. To protect the clients' confidentiality, the transaction system contains just a customer's identification number. The traders who execute a deal do not know the identity of the customers whom they are serving; the customer name and number are stored in a restricted database that they are not allowed to access. The Trading Desk personnel then build several mashups to monitor orders. Although the main applications they use require a login and password, the mashups do not. Other employees with access to the customer database also create mashups with embedded credentials. Now the secure contact details and support activities are out in the open. This leads a *third* team to the natural conclusion of combining this material to expose the actions of all customers by name. If this wasn't bad enough, those developers proceed to mash in other details such as location (via the Location Mapping pattern, covered in Chapter 6) that shows how certain branch offices provide slower execution times.

---

10. The accidental publication of a company's payroll data is one simple example.

This is all valuable information—but it should not be universally available. What happens when a support agent off-handedly tells a customer he or she is located in a region that historically experiences slow service? The client may decide to move the account to another firm.

Sloppy Solution

The sloppiest of solutions is to ignore the problem completely and openly disseminate data without any security or auditing controls. Although mashups provide the technical capability to free information from its source systems, it does not mean they establish the ethical (or legal!) justification for doing so.

A person who realizes what is at stake may decide to take some precautions. That individual might say, "I will allow the widget I have created to be accessed only by members of my team. Each of them already has access to the underlying applications so no harm is done." This is still not a good idea. For one thing, it circumvents the security and monitoring of the source application because all system access will still occur from a single ID. It also avoids any enterprise-level policies for information protection because the widget owner is now effectively provisioning access every time he or she gives someone else a copy of the widget. What happens when a person changes departments and takes the widget along? That employee's personal ID will be removed from the source application but the one used by the widget is not. The individual therefore retains access when it should be revoked.

The counterpoint to this behavior was hinted at in the discussion of the Shadow Integration anti-pattern. What if the mashup creator is reassigned or leaves the firm? Once his or her account is disabled, the widget will no longer work for anyone.

Related Patterns: All patterns that re-expose any portion of nonpublic data they obtain (e.g., Dashboard, Content Aggregation, and Widget Enabler)

Appeal

As wonderful a convenience as single sign-on is (consult the Single Sign-On pattern in Chapter 7), a mashup creator may believe he or she has provided even greater ease of use by removing the login process altogether. Seasoned developers will immediately recognize the recklessness of this path, but many mashup creators—being new to the development process—are unfamiliar with the risks. Think about this issue from the end users' perspective: Their entire professional lives have been spent struggling with password and authentication issues.[11]

---

11. See Chapter 7 for a discussion of password fatigue.

Now they have the means to banish for themselves and their peers what they view as an annoying, burdensome process.

If a firm's associates do not have a good understanding of the overall organizational structure, then it's easy to ignore the incremental risks as additional systems are mashed together. Application-enforced checks and balances between different departments can be erased by one errant creation. In fact, a developer who is ignorant as to why these barriers exist may feel an unjustified sense of accomplishment in getting around them.

Remediation

By using consistent authentication mechanisms, a firm can mitigate the risk of outright exposure of its confidential material. A mashup that requires any type of authentication to obtain data should never turn around and provide that material without first requiring its consumer to provide some type of credentials. There is one possible exception: If a public account provides basic "view-only" access to material characterized as harmless, a mashup may republish this content.

A core ability of many mashup platforms, publish and promote, was discussed in Chapter 3. The ability to freely obtain and remix mashups is an important part of their value and having a central hub for this activity is indispensable. Not only does a public forum avoid rework by preventing users from reinventing existing solutions, but it also provides a single point for instituting monitoring and other controls over what material can be shared.

Open Kimono

Problem

In the Dirty Laundry anti-pattern we examined the risks of hard-coding security credentials within mashups. The solution was to prompt a user for this information and have a mashup act as a conduit for relaying it to the original application. But like the proverbial weak link in a chain, login information is only as secure as the systems that protect it. Where and how this information is retained and communicated constitute a classic problem of software development that mashups must address.

Sloppy Solution

By now you've probably recognized a trend in the sloppy solutions, which some would call the "ostrich effect." It entails dealing with a problem by burying one's head in the sand to hide from its existence. The Open Kimono anti-pattern is no different. Ignoring security-related issues is akin to strutting around like the fabled emperor who denied his own nakedness.

A mashup creator may solve the problem of Dirty Laundry only to fall victim to this anti-pattern. Whether it involves car locks or building passes, secret passwords or encrypted email, security is part of everyone's life; only the amount varies. The danger in the world of computers is that technologists work diligently to achieve a level of usability that sometimes obscures multiple points of vulnerability. This complexity of the solution leads the layperson to take a certain amount of security for granted when, in fact, none exists.

Imagine you are sitting in a café reading your email. It appears you have established a private channel of communication akin to a traditional analog telephone call[12]—but you are actually sitting at the eye of a tornado of potential malevolence. First, there's your laptop: If it has Bluetooth enabled there's a chance someone could access its contents without your knowledge.[13] The wireless traffic between you and the café's router is also available for public inspection and may not be encrypted. Once you've actually made it to the Internet, your requests and responses could jump through a half-dozen other sites before they reach their target. And let's not forget your latte-drinking neighbor, who might casually glance over your shoulder to see what you are typing.

---

12. These are now extinct, as most communication systems in the world having gone completely digital.

13. This practice is known as Bluetooth snooping.

Because it would be paralyzing to contemplate all the risks to which we're exposed, many people have established their own personal security policies for their daily lives. We arbitrarily address some threats while ignoring others. This individualized approach is fine as an expression of personal choice and priorities, but when it crosses over into the professional environment things get messy.

Related Patterns: Any mashup that communicates credentials over a custom-created API

Appeal

An enterprise cannot allow its employees to make individual decisions about which of the organization's rules to follow and which to ignore. Yet this is exactly what happens when developers take the quickest path and ignore known vulnerabilities. Some examples include using nonsecure network connections, storing passwords in plain text, and leaving personal information in browser-based cookies. To paraphrase John F. Kennedy, we do these things not because they are hard, but because they are easy.

Remediation

Like most of the other anti-patterns, what makes Open Kimono difficult to solve is that it cannot be "coded out of existence" without reducing the value of mashups to essentially nothing. The same freedoms that allow mashups to interact with restricted data sources provide a mechanism for security credentials to be communicated in an unsecure manner or for data to be republished improperly (Dirty Laundry). The scope of this problem extends far beyond the realm of mashups and consequently this text—but that's a good thing because it means ample resources are available to address this issue. Many large enterprises already have a dedicated process for auditing an application's security. They are often engaged during the same productionization process that helps uncover problems related to the Shadow Integration anti-pattern.

The essential point to keep in mind is that the revolutionary capabilities of mashups do not excuse them from the obligations of traditional development practices. Technically oriented individuals should continue to follow their firm's established security policies and procedures. At the same time, an organization's security department should get involved before a mashup platform is released to users outside IT. These personnel can evaluate the situation and create appropriate guidelines to further protect the firm. For example, they could recommend employees complete some online training classes related to basic application security before they are allowed to access the mashup environment.

One-Hit Wonder

Problem

In Chapter 1 we discussed mashups' ability to adapt to changes made in a source system's structure. This flexibility is one of the key features that separates mashups from more traditional harvesting techniques. Because mashups may be used to obtain data without the application owners' knowledge, they must be able to automatically handle any formatting or layout differences when they occur. The lack of a formal contract between information producer and consumer makes this feature a necessity. But there is a downside to this recoverability: While a mashup may be able to detect and accommodate the relocation of a particular field, there is no guarantee that the data it finds there will still be correct. Calculation changes or errors pulled into previously working solutions can unintentionally communicate wrong information, transforming a useful application into a One-Hit Wonder.

Sloppy Solution

It's easy to imagine existing features won't change once a system works correctly. This line of false reasoning presumes that an operation that has already been exercised dozens or hundreds of times will continue to return identical results in the future. But as discussed in Chapter 8, Testing Patterns, no product is immune to potential bugs.

Application developers frequently fall into the trap of assuming that a particular piece of code will always return the same answer when supplied with identical information. For example, all inputs being identical, the calculation of how much storage is required to retain a customer's transaction history should not vary. In practice, we know consistency across results occurs in phases. The storage calculation remains valid only until a new compression technique is introduced, for example. The modification of the underlying arithmetic will produce numbers inconsistent with past results. This marks the beginning of a new "period of repeatability" for future calls to this function.

There is a greater tendency to overlook the possibility of these fluctuations when the functionality is being provided by an unobservable third-party. This can lead to the construction of solutions that are based on *expectations* rather than *understanding,* which leaves those programs vulnerable to breakage after a transition from one stage of consistency to the next. The technology trap laid by mashups is that they require no knowledge about the underlying structure of the products and services on which they rely so heavily. As a consequence, when a low-level change occurs a developer may be caught completely unawares when his or her solution suddenly fails. Even worse, a mashup may continue operations while successfully obtaining *incorrect* data because it has no inherent ability to know when harvested values are wrong.

Related Patterns: All pattern implementations that obtain and act on data from both internal and external sources

Appeal

When a system or process works without modification for a long time, it's tempting to consider this uninterrupted string of successes to be an indication of the application's stability. Were we discussing home-grown solutions completely under the control of a firm's IT department, this would be a reasonable assumption. But where external resources are concerned, past performance absolutely does *not* guarantee future results. Nevertheless, it's human nature to use empirical observations—particularly ones collected over a long period—to create a mental model of how things work. Unfortunately this perception doesn't always reflect reality.[14]

Each of the various mashup patterns has a fragility score that attempts to describe the conditions where an implementation of that pattern may break. Mashups are unique in their ability to recover from some of these situations unaided. Code that can heal itself is especially appealing to developers, who are accustomed to manually fixing code that stops working. They will cheer a mashup that automatically adapts to new situations and perhaps even feel a bit of pride as if they are somehow responsible for this self-repairing behavior.

Remediation

In Chapter 8 we discussed how mashups could participate in testing strategies. Yet even after a mashup's results have been verified, it can still vacillate between merely "working" and "working correctly." This is another distinction between mashups and traditional software development practices: A solution based on a static programming language[15] follows the rigid course of logic laid out by its

---

14. This brand of logic—known as "inductive reasoning"—assumes a consistent outcome given the same sequence of events, but ultimately its "proof" rests solely on a fixed number of previous observations. Philosophers have argued about the validity of this approach for centuries, but any good software developer will tell you to plan for code to break unexpectedly.

15. These languages include C, C++, and Java.

creators. Even dynamic languages[16] depend on general guidelines defined during implementation. Because many mashup tools are targeted toward nontechnical users, these important processing decisions are delegated to the underlying platform in the name of simplicity.

So how do we enjoy the power of mashups without falling victim to hidden errors? Mashups are a new development paradigm, so they require new thoughts about testing. The key is to test more than once and to not assume correctness in the future. Regular regression testing is one possible answer, but keep in mind that these types of tests typically operate on a fixed series of inputs and results. It's just as important to detect discrepancies outside previously observed scenarios. Besides, a full regression test could take quite a bit of time to complete. Even if it was tested each morning a mashup could still be affected by changes that occur during the course of the day.

A more comprehensive plan is to combine regression testing with range testing. Although patterns such as Time Series natively lend themselves to this approach, it can actually be applied almost anywhere. When a mashup receives data from an external resource, the values should be compared to past observations. Any deviation that the developer feels is significant should cause the mashup to signify an error condition. The benefit of this approach over regression testing is that only active functionality is checked. False alarms will inevitably occur, but having too many warnings is far better than having undetected errors.

---

16. Perl, Ruby, PHP, and Python are a few examples.

Malicious Hitchhiker

Problem

Two core abilities can enable a mashup platform to obtain content from otherwise closed resources: data extraction and clipping.

Data extraction works similarly to a user surfing the Web. An internal browser hits a site and renders the page behind the scenes. The finished output is then interrogated for whatever information the mashup creator is after. The primary risk to a data extraction-based solution was discussed in conjunction with the One-Hit Wonder anti-pattern: Values can change either unintentionally or deliberately so a mashup must be hardened against these potential events.

Unlike data extraction, which harvests *rendered* content, clipping obtains the *rendering* for the content. The internal Web browser is still used to pull down raw HTML and JavaScript, but this is where the process concludes. The material is then repurposed for direct inclusion into a user-facing solution. The risks are obvious. It's one thing to return bad values; it's a much more serious problem to return bad code. The consequences could range from the benign (like a "frame-buster" script that breaks the layout of your solution) to the malicious (such as a form that tricks users into revealing their passwords).

Sloppy Solution

The patterns that employ clipping let developers and users outside IT do something they've never been able to before: alter the appearance and behavior of products without accessing (or understanding) the underlying code. It may even be possible to bypass established rollout procedures to redistribute this modified software directly to coworkers. This is clearly the pinnacle of technological user-empowerment, isn't it? If an enterprise establishes this type of environment and users embrace it, shouldn't it be a rousing success?

To a degree, yes. This is part of the thinking behind the popularity of service-oriented architectures (SOAs). Unlike clipping, however, SOAs place strict controls around which services are available and how they interact; clipping has no such restraints. In the rush to create a self-serve platform for creating and sharing new solutions, it's easy to overlook the fact some undesirable sources can hitch a ride during the process. Unfortunately the dangers of outsourcing presentation to external sites are sometimes overshadowed by the convenience of not having to create custom user interfaces for new products.

Related Patterns: Patterns that may employ clipping (e.g., Dashboard, Distributed Drill-Down, Content Aggregation, Emergency Response, Field Medic, Portal Enabler, Quick Proof-of-Concept, Single Sign-on, Usability Enhancer)

Appeal

Technically speaking, there are very few situations where clipping is not replaceable by data extraction. The mashup creator *could* manually duplicate the original site's user interface and wire it up to the source system's functionality by using the API Enabler pattern, but this is not a task for the faint of heart. A fair amount of coding may be needed to create the necessary HTML, JavaScript, CSS, and other resources required. Every time the interface of the source system changes, these custom files will likewise need to be modified to reflect whatever updates were made.

The reason why clipping is a compelling choice is because it eliminates the time and expertise required to undertake this approach. A mashup grabs a "chunk" of the source system's interface and all its supporting artifacts in real time, and pastes it into its new home. Any embedded form controls or JavaScript still works correctly; the mashup acts as an invisible intermediary and funnels updates back and forth between the original and new environments. Anyone who can handle a pair of scissors has the skills needed to become a clipping expert.[17]

Some mashup products allow custom HTML, CSS, and JavaScript to be added or removed from a page during the clipping process. That's how the Usability Enhancer and Field Medic patterns (see Chapter 5) are able to alter an existing program without requiring access to the source code.

Another benefit of clipping is that it is dynamic *and* has all of the regular mashup features related to flexibility. Text on the original site changed? The new text will automatically be included in the next clip. Contents rearranged so that a form has been relocated? A mashup should still be able to find and grab it.

With all of these powers for altering and stitching products together without the burden of programming, it's no wonder clipping is such an attractive option to developers and end users alike.

Remediation

To understand the defenses available, it's necessary to understand the different classes of problems (both detected and not) that can occur during clipping (see

---

17. Okay, that's a bit of hyperbole. But compared to custom-coding Web pages from scratch and connecting them to an API Enabler implementation, clipping is tons easier.

Table 9.2). Possible reasons for these acts are listed in the "Motivation" column of the table.

Table 9.2 *Clipping Operations: Unique Value, But Their Own Set of Risks*

Problem	Motivation	Resolution
A clip fails completely	A site intentionally blocks content when it knows the request is coming from a mashup, or it is randomly deactivated to discourage prospective mashup builders.	A mashup's ability to recover from changes to the source environment is not infallible. Rather than show an ugly "Page not found" message or a blank box, some error handling should be implemented. It may be possible to grab replacement content from an alternative location.
A clip displays incorrect or inappropriate information	Rather than simply withhold information, displaying wrong results or unbecoming content can inflict serious damage on the business and the reputation of the clip authors.	It is very difficult to automatically detect when a site purposely defaces itself to hurt any surrounding clips. Crucial sections of a clipping-based solution could use a companion API Enabler implementation to perform regular regression or range tests (see the One-Hit Wonder anti-pattern). Assuming the tests pass, the clipping operation should be allowed to proceed.
A clip attempts to obtain private user credentials	If a site knows it is being clipped, it may include instructions or form elements that trick users into revealing their IDs or passwords.	Removing all form elements is one option if a clip doesn't need them. Injected auditing functionality could track which data a user is providing a clip and where it is being submitted.
JavaScript that breaks the overall presentation of a solution is included in the clip	This might be an intentional defense against clipping that doesn't surface until content is redisplayed outside its original home. Alternatively, the scripts might intentionally modify other clips to introduce problems.	Disabling JavaScript for clips is one option, but that could render a clip unusable. Placing clips in an embedded frame offers a little more protection. Disabling JavaScript functions and including a local copy of any required functions is a tedious but thorough solution. Some mashup products pass clips through an external server that prevents JavaScript errors but not presentation tricks.

The overarching guideline here is "know who you are clipping." A mashup's success is ultimately determined by the company it keeps. When internal resources within an enterprise are involved, there should be little cause for concern. As soon as external sites become involved, however, some prudence is necessary. A reputable firm may take steps to block clipping[18]; the firm is completely within its rights to enforce its terms of use and protect its intellectual property. One would *not* expect a company in good standing to spite potential customers by inflicting deliberate damage. Conversely, if an untrustworthy or undependable system is pulled into a clipping solution, then let the masher beware.

---

18. Some techniques for blocking clipping operations are discussed in Chapter 10.

Chapter 10

Final Thoughts

Introduction

The patterns we have examined in this book provide some powerful techniques for using mashups to seize business opportunities and tackle previously abandoned or ignored issues. Yet this text would be incomplete if these solutions were recommended without discussing the challenges inherent in establishing an enterprise mashup environment. As we begin to wrap up our discussion, we will step back from the patterns themselves and address a few of the surrounding issues that can help further mashups' adoption and usefulness.

One primary area of concern is technical capability. A common misconception regarding mashups is that they can harvest only Web-based content. While a wealth of information can certainly be mined there, many sites have equally large amounts of data locked away in proprietary formats such as XLS and PDF. In the section "Mashing Up Binary Types" later in this chapter, we will examine how this content can be made accessible to mashups.

The revolutionary capabilities of mashups do not excuse them from rules regarding monitoring and control. Mashups that spread unchecked within an enterprise can create as many problems as benefits. Solutions that violate corporate policies yet still pass freely between users might escape the notice of existing governance mechanisms. The coverage of anti-patterns such as Dirty Laundry and Open Kimono touched on a few of the potential dangers in this area. The "Security" section in this chapter discusses techniques for *blocking* mashups from accessing sensitive material so that a firm can cultivate collaboration without suffering unnecessary risk.

The technology behind enterprise mashups is real and it is here today. As further evidence of the proliferation of this technology, a collection of vendor case studies has been included as an appendix in this book. These stories are not intended to endorse a particular product or to act as a substitute for conducting your own due diligence in choosing a platform, but they do demonstrate how several firms have used the patterns in this book to resolve longstanding problems and to create new business opportunities. I encourage you to explore this section while considering any similarities to your own workplace.

Mashing Up Binary Types

If we were to create a list of the many different types of content available on the Web, the first few items would probably be something like "Web pages," "blogs," and "news stories." All of these are essentially the same thing: plain unstructured text with a few presentation instructions (HTML) mixed in. If we thought about it a little more, the next thing we might write down could have something to do with all of the dynamic sites out there—for example, the ones that let you book a trip or search a catalog. These sites expose a small interface that acts as a gateway to a huge database of information stored behind the scenes. Finally, we might remember to include the many public APIs available on the net.

The ability for a mashup to leverage these sources depends on the particular product being used. For example, depending on the core abilities supported by the platform, a mashup may be capable of calling a Web Service but not be able to simulate user actions for browsing a catalog and extracting product descriptions.

Although a lot of raw material is available through this means, it's probably just the tip of the iceberg. It would be crazy to imagine a firm where every computer didn't have a Web browser, but it would be equally surprising to discover end-user desktops with *only* that application. In most corporate settings, only a small amount of content authored is targeted specifically for the Web or intranet. Much of the generated knowledge is stored within generic office applications such as word processors and spreadsheets. And there it sits—locked away on a local drive or network file system in a format understood only by the program that created it. Even if this information does somehow make it to the Web, a browser won't understand it. A user will have to either download the file for local viewing or use some third-party plugin to access its contents.

Some mashup vendors have attempted to create platforms that understand a range of these types of files. Rather than be limited to a particular product this section provides an approach for allowing any mashup to access proprietary formats. A word of warning, though: This solution does require some coding. If you are a nontechnical associate you'll probably want to pass this section along to someone in your IT department.

The first task is to locate an open-source or commercial product that understands the format in question. Table 10.1 lists a few common examples.

Table 10.1 *Common Binary Types and the Programming Libraries That Understand Them*

File Type	Library/Product
XLS, XLSX (Microsoft Excel)	Apache POI[a] (Java), Actuate eSpreadsheet[b] (Java), Sunflower Excel[c] (.NET)
DOC, DOCX (Microsoft Word)	Apache POI (Java, DOC only), Aspose.words[d] (Java, .NET)
PDF (Abode Acrobat)	iText[e] (Java), PDF Clown[f] (.NET)

a. http://poi.apache.org/
b. http://www.actuate.com/products/rich-internet-applications/spreadsheets/index.asp
c. http://www.duodimension.com/component_convert_excel_xls_spreadsheet_html_net/
   excel_xls_html_overview.htm
d. http://www.aspose.com/categories/file-format-components/aspose.words-for-.net-and-java/
   default.aspx
e. http://www.lowagie.com/iText/
f. http://sourceforge.net/projects/clown

Once you've obtained the appropriate library, the next step is to examine the capabilities of your mashup toolset. Can it harvest raw Web pages? Does it need to interact with a SOAP API? Can it download a binary file and store it internally, or is it able to extract hypertext links from a page? The answers to these questions are important because you will be constructing a small application to convert the file into a format the mashup can understand.

For example, consider a Web page that has a link to an XLS (Microsoft Excel) file. Imagine you are using a mashup tool that can mine a Web page directly. The following steps would make the XLS available for mashing:

1. The URL of the file is extracted from the page.

2. The URL is sent to the Web application you constructed.

3. The application retrieves the XLS from the given location.

4. The application parses the XLS and spits out plain HTML.

5. The mashup retrieves the necessary details from the resulting page.

In this case, the mashup told the "converter" application where to download the file by supplying it with the URL. Alternatively, it could have downloaded the file itself and sent it directly to the converter if (1) the mashup platform supported this feature and (2) the converter was written to accept binary uploads.

What if the mashup platform can communicate only with a SOAP or REST API? The solution isn't much different. Instead of writing the content to plain

HTML in step 4, the converter application is created to expose an interface using whatever protocols are required. For an XLS spreadsheet, it's easy to imagine needing functions like `getValueAt(tab,row,column)`.

The exact implementation of the converter application will vary based on the file type, library, development language, and mashup product being used. The general approach of the solution does not vary, however. You need not be limited by what a mashup vendor provides to reach other content sources. A series of small applications can act as intermediaries for unlocking new streams of information. It's foreseeable that as the popularity of mashups increases, both commercial and free services for converting content into mashup-friendly formats will begin to appear.

Security

A final important topic regarding mashups in the enterprise focuses on *control*. Few firms will completely abandon their existing development methodologies on the assumption that mashups provide some magical panacea to all of IT's historical woes. Left unchecked, mashups can actually create entirely new classes of problems. As powerful and useful as the patterns in this book can be, they require some overarching supervision to reach their full potential.

This section is also for the enterprise that is completely opposed to mashups. How can they be stopped (or at least slowed)? Which mechanisms are available to help a company protect the content it puts online?

Blocking Mashups

If a site exposes a public API, then it must be assumed externally developed solutions are welcome. We won't concern ourselves with how mashups behave in these situations. The real challenge lies in protecting content intended for use only by legitimate users. Some mashup products can impersonate a Web browser so successfully that they're able to extract data at levels unachievable by humans. So if a site has been counting on the physical limitations of a person's time or attention as a constraining mechanism, it might be overwhelmed when a mashup zooms in and starts grabbing everything it can find.

Of course, this issue isn't limited solely to the need to maintain a particular level of performance. A company may not want external agents to access its site for purposes that have nothing to do with why the product exists in the first place. Consider the example in the Competitive Analysis pattern where one firm completely traversed the online catalog of another firm in an effort to detect any large price gaps between similar merchandise. The "target" of this operation has every reason to want to block this behavior because it simply helps its rival.

Mashups weren't the first tools to scan the Web. Search engines routinely dispatch agents (also known as crawlers, spiders, robots, or simply "bots") to collect information to build their indexes. Less reputable sites sometimes use crawlers to harvest email addresses displayed on a site as a prelude to massive spam campaigns. Well-behaved bots observe a few guidelines. First, they usually declare their identity in the "user-agent" field of an HTTP request. Site owners then know when their sites are being visited by a nonhuman entity. Second, robots should obey the contents of robots.txt, a special file that contains instructions on pages that are off limits.

If a mashup product complies with these conventions, it's a simple task for Webmasters to turn them away at the front door. More typically, mashups' purpose is to mimic users as accurately as possible, which means not revealing their identity or restricting their actions. In this sense they bear a greater similarity to spambots—and that means many of the same defensive measures designed to thwart spammers can also block mashups.

One technique commonly used for this purpose a CAPTCHA. A CAPTCHA is a deliberately distorted image that a computer cannot recognize but a person can (see Figure 10.1 for an example). As image processing and recognition software has grown more powerful, an all-out arms race has erupted between CAPTCHA creators and their would-be circumventors. They're a good first line of defense, but they suffer from several drawbacks:

- A CAPTCHA may not be solvable by someone with a visual disability.

- CAPTCHAs decrease the usability of a site proportionate to their frequency of use.

- Clipping functionality can be used to grab a CAPTCHA and present it to a user in a different context. For example, one could imagine grabbing a CAPTCHA from Site A and displaying it on Site B. Perhaps visitors to Site B

Figure 10.1   *A simple CAPTCHA. Credit: CAPTCHA sample provided by Meghan Ogrinz.*

get to play a game after solving the CAPTCHA. Meanwhile the results are communicated back to Site A. Thus Site B's users have become unwitting accomplices in facilitating the breach of Site A. One famous example of this approach went so far as to reward users with a series of pornographic images for their efforts.[1]

Another tactic is to convert crucial pieces of text-based information into images. Spambots may be sophisticated enough to apply OCR[2] to defeat this approach but most mashup tools haven't incorporated this functionality (yet). It's not necessary to convert every bit of content into a picture; a few key values will suffice. An online store might shield its prices in this manner. Data extraction operations will be stopped, but clipping will proceed unhindered. The difference between text and images means nothing to a clipping agent because clips are concerned with only presentation—not the raw values underneath.

Purposely malformed HTML can work as a mashup deterrent. Commercial Web browsers are very adept at handling disordered or missing tags while still rendering the presentation the designer expected. By comparison, mashup tools generally lack this level of sophistication. Although a data extraction operation will grab content under the guise of a user, it never directly redisplays what it has captured. Instead, the structure of the document is parsed to remove the information of interest. An intentionally incorrect or confusing layout might trip up this operation. The disadvantage is that there is no way to know how effective this countermeasure is without testing it against a variety of potential harvesters—an expensive and time-consuming task.

The remaining methods try to stop mashups before they even reach a site, or at least limit the length of their stay. By blocking access from a particular IP address or a range of addresses, mashups originating from known sources can be prohibited entry. Mashups could also be blocked by monitoring for excess traffic from a specific "user" and then denying access. Alternatively, users could be limited to a fixed number of requests per day, which would hamper a mashup's ability to harvest data in one fell swoop.

One thing is for certain: Once content is available on the Web, it will be examined by a host of visitors. There is no single fail-safe approach for creating content visible only to humans. After all, Web pages must expose themselves to user-facing browsers to be seen at all. Clipping and data extraction piggyback

---

1. Catone, Josh. "Spammers Use Striptease to Crack CAPTCHAs." November 1, 2007. http://www.readwriteweb.com/archives/captcha_striptease.php

2. Optical character recognition; the process of converting an image into machine-readable text.

on this architecture, which is why they are so hard to stop. The best defense is to use a combination of the methods presented and to supplement your site's terms of use with specific language against mashups; at least if technical solutions fail you'll have possible legal avenues to explore.

Securing Mashups

In his article "'Mashup' Websites Are a Hacker's Dream Come True,"[3] Paul Marks touches on some of the privacy and security risks inherent in mashups:

> A hacker could feed false data to a crime location mashup, for example, perhaps to help raise property prices in a particular area by making it appear crime-free. A prankster could create bogus traffic jams on a mashup map, diverting traffic in such a way that queues are actually made worse.

Mashups are a new technology that poses security challenges yet to be considered by many firms.[4] One reason the field is particularly vulnerable is because it attracts so many followers from outside the realm of traditional software engineering.

IBM has entered the picture with SMASH[5] (short for Secure Mashup), which it donated to the OpenAjax Alliance.[6] SMASH doesn't address all of the potential trouble spots; its chief advantage is to validate components to make sure they originate from trusted sources and to isolate malicious code. Even so, it's a valuable first step that recognizes the importance of mashups within the enterprise.

The developer-facing Dojo JavaScript toolkit is poised to introduce similar control mechanisms into its latest release:

> With dojox.secure, untrusted scripts and widgets can be safely loaded directly into a web page with fine grained sandboxing of their capabilities, while still allowing them to access a controlled subset of the DOM and JavaScript environment.[7]

Not to be outdone, Microsoft has been exploring this issue with its MashupOS project, which seeks to extend Web browsers with "a set of abstractions that

---

3. May 2006. http://technology.newscientist.com/article/mg19025516.400

4. Smetters, Diana. "Building Secure Mashups." http://www.parc.com/research/publications/details.php?id=6462

5. "IBM Cracks Web 2.0 Security Concerns with 'SMash'." Press release, March 13, 2008. http://www-03.ibm.com/press/us/en/pressrelease/23676.wss

6. The OpenAjax Alliance is a consortium devoted to encouraging the adoption of AJAX and associated best-practices. http://www.openajax.org/index.php

7. Zyp, Kris. "Secure Mashups with dojox.secure." August 1, 2008. http://www.sitepen.com/blog/2008/08/01/secure-mashups-with-dojoxsecure/

isolate mutually-untrusting web services within the browser, while allowing safe forms of communication."[8]

It's clear that mashup security is still a developing science. IBM and Microsoft have their own particular products and ideas in this space; Dojo is targeted squarely at programmers. The lack of a uniform approach for creating and securing mashups leaves the field ripe for possible exploitation. Firms need to weigh the potential risks and benefits before deciding which content should be mashable. One course of action is to restrict mashups so that they operate only on internal sites or those of trusted corporate partners. Keep in mind that malevolence doesn't have to manifest itself through code. It can be just as damaging to mash in bad data.

Conclusion

> Nothing is as powerful as an idea whose time has come.
>
> —Victor Hugo

The quote at the beginning of the section contains an important truth. Throughout history, only a few inventions have been celebrated as accomplishments in themselves; rather, it's the changes that they portend that capture our imagination. Time is something whose shortage many of us lament, yet until the invention of the mechanical clock there was no common standard. Longitudinal timepieces opened the world to exploration[9] and created a universal frame of reference for humankind. The telephone was revolutionary, but its technical achievement was surpassed by the notion that people would be able to communicate with one another instantly over vast distances. The automobile shepherded in an age of personal freedom where people could lead lives beyond their traditional neighborhoods. The personal media player (PMP) gave owners the freedom to choose when, where, and which music and videos to experience and defined new publishing and marketing industries in the process.

The truth is that the technology behind mashup products isn't radical; if anything, it's evolutionary, not revolutionary. With ever-increasing volumes of

---

8. "MashupOS: Operating System Abstractions for Client Mashups." http://research. microsoft.com/~helenw/papers/mashupOSHotOS.pdf

9. In her book *Longitude: The True Story of a Lone Genius Who Solved the Greatest Scientific Problem of His Time* (Walker & Company, 2007), author Dava Sobel provides a fascinating recount of how and why this invention came about. It is surpassed only by the BBC's production based on the text, which is available on DVD.

unstructured information moving online, it seemed inevitable that some way to mechanically process this data was necessary. Mashup tools exploit the advances made by products such as search engines and in fields including syntactic analysis, artificial intelligence, and usability. The real value of mashups lies in their ability to act as agents of creation. They are the means of transforming mere thoughts into concrete implementations. By incorporating and extending the inherent usability of the Web, mashups destroy the barriers that isolate consumers from producers. We are all empowered to build solutions, regardless of our technical abilities.

Now we are free to have ideas. Some may be worthless, but others will be as unstoppably powerful as Victor Hugo suggests. The key change that mashups bring about is not the ability to scrape Web pages or create widgets, but rather freedom from the bonds of self-censorship.

In 2001, Tim Berners-Lee and his coauthors imagined the promise of the Semantic Web as being able to "open up the knowledge and workings of humankind to meaningful analysis by software agents, providing a new class of tools by which we can live, work and learn together."[10] The vision of many was that specifications such as RDF (Resource Description Framework) and SPARQL[11] (the language for querying it) would serve as the gateway to this new era. In light of mashups' success, history may portray the ongoing work on SPARQL and RDF similarly to the crazy flapping contraptions that attempted to challenge the Wright Brothers. The Semantic Web is *already* here, and mashups are responsible for creating it. To continue with our flight analogy, firms can either accept it with its current features and limitations, or they can flap their metaphorical wings and hope for other solutions to get off the ground.

The patterns discussed in this book are not imaginary.[12] They can be adapted to your firm's needs and implemented with any number of currently available products.[13] No doubt in exploring this content you have imagined other uses of the technology. I encourage you to embrace your inspirations. The one obstacle mashups are powerless to remove is the restraints you've place on yourself. Don't renounce the benefits of your own creativity by imagining you don't have the necessary skills or resources to get started. If you hit a roadblock, you can always try to mash together part of a solution created by someone else.

---

10. Berners-Lee, Tim, James Hendler, and Ora Lassila, "The Semantic Web." *Scientific American,* May 17, 2001. http://www.sciam.com/article.cfm?id=the-semantic-web

11. SPARQL is a recursive acronym that stands for "SPARQL Protocol and RDF Query Language." Engineers can be so clever.

12. Hypothetical examples notwithstanding

13. Consult the case studies in the appendix for some examples.

Like any new product, mashups are currently on the fringe of many corporations' radars. Although they are popular in the consumer space, these successes have created the incorrect preconception that mashups have little to offer to the modern enterprise. People are inclined to characterize mashups by what they see, not by what they do. "Cheap gas near me? Closest ATM? Cute but not practical for my workplace." Nothing creates legitimacy and respect like a directly applicable implementation. Look around your firm for simple instances where the patterns can be applied and tackle them first. Once you have created a few solutions, the viability of mashups will be well established and you should easily find supporters for more complicated endeavors.

No one could have imagined the explosive growth of the Internet, the World Wide Web, or dozens of other related technologies. But people did recognize opportunities at singular points in time. Those who seized them enjoyed valuable advantages; latecomers were left playing catch-up. We stand poised at the edge of another great expansion thanks to mashups. Will your firm ride the crest of this latest wave, or will it tread water until it has no choice but to move forward?

Appendix

Corporate Case Studies

Introduction

While the growth of mashups within the enterprise has been a relatively recent phenomenon, this approach to development has already enjoyed some prominent successes. The case studies presented in this appendix provide unique insights into how commercial firms have seized upon this new technology to offer unprecedented solutions while simultaneously realizing significant savings in development time and expense.

As mentioned in Chapter 1, providing implementation code for the patterns is currently impractical owing to the general lack of standards in this emerging industry. For this reason, the inclusion of these stories is a crucial element in demonstrating that the examples discussed throughout the main text are achievable via the variety of products available today. The following case studies were written in cooperation with several prominent vendors in this space.[1] Naturally, the purveyors of these tools have a vested interest in expanding the marketplace for mashups, but I strongly encourage you to focus on the quantifiable business benefits that have been achieved as opposed to the specific products that were used. Keep in mind that the subjects of the case studies all have unique corporate policies guiding the information they can release to the public. For those companies that allowed their names to be included, I am especially grateful. Where identities were withheld for competitive or legal reasons, there is nevertheless significant value in learning more about the use of mashups under real-world conditions.

You will note variations in how return on investment (ROI) for mashups is reported. This is to be expected given the broad applicability of mashups in an

---

1. Supplemental reading related to the products used in the case studies is available on this book's companion Web site, http://mashuppatterns.com

enterprise setting as well as their penchant for solving Long Tail problems (refer to Chapter 1 for a more detailed examination of this topic). Taken individually, Long Tail issues generally do not produce huge savings relative to their required labor, which is why they linger unaddressed in so many organizations. Mashups allow many of these previously unaddressed issues to be solved with lower cost and labor requirements. And what might initially appear to be a relatively small accomplishment can have large effects on productivity, savings, and employee satisfaction once it spreads horizontally across a firm. New mashups might even emerge that incrementally add value by building upon these previous successes.

As a bit of final guidance, let me strongly recommend that any efforts to introduce mashups into your workplace begin with a thorough vetting of the problem domain to determine which mashup patterns may apply. From there, you can work backward to uncover the core activities (see Chapter 3) that are required. Only after this process has been completed should you begin the due-diligence process to pick an appropriate mashup tool. While the following case studies illustrate the inherent value in mashups, the fact that considerable upfront analysis and planning preceded their implementation should not go unnoticed.

Afni

Summary

Afni is a leading outsourcer of customer service, insurance services, and receivables management operating 12 call centers across the United States and employing more than 3,000 call center agents. The company built a series of mashups to simplify agent desktops, improve productivity, and reduce average handling times for customer support calls.

Value Proposition	Reduce average handling times, increase first call resolution rates, and reduce performance and compliance penalties
Mashup Content Sources	Wide range of applications across multiple customers, including host/mainframe, Web, Windows, and custom-designed applications
Mashup Output	XML, Web Services
Mashup Developers	Afni IT developers
Target Audience	Afni contact center agents
Vendor Product Used	OpenSpan
Mashup Patterns	Accessibility, Content Aggregation, Usability Enhancer, Distributed Drill-Down, Content Migration, Integration, Workflow

Problem Statement

Afni provides call center functions to many *Fortune 500* enterprises, each of which has a unique set of applications and business processes that Afni agents must learn and follow. In the contact center industry, it is very common for customer data to be scattered across multiple applications; agents must then waste time navigating through applications and constantly toggle back and forth between applications to resolve customer issues. In Afni's case, the challenges were even greater because most applications are owned and controlled by the company's clients. Afni's IT organization has little or no control over the applications and no access to their source code.

Afni's primary goals were to simplify agent desktops to improve productivity, reduce average handling times, increase first call resolution rates, simplify agent training, and ensure compliance with customer requirements.

Solution

Afni chose the OpenSpan Platform to build a series of mashups for its contact center agents. Each mashup—or "buddy" application according to Afni terminology—

auto-populates customer data for each customer support call. This provides agents with a 360-degree view of the customer and eliminates the need for them to navigate through a series of applications. The user interfaces generated by the mashups were constructed to match the desired call flow (business process). In other words, an agent simply needs to follow the natural flow of the screen from top to bottom. Input fields are color coordinated to alert agents if they need to collect additional information or complete a particular workflow. If agents require additional data not directly accessible from the current screen, they can click on a link in the mashup and open up the underlying application responsible. A mashup will automatically navigate to the appropriate screen, further saving agents' time. At each step along the way, the overarching mashup tracks and logs agent activity to ensure compliance with client requirements and to help identify performance bottlenecks.

Mashup Patterns Used

Afni's usage revolves around several mashup patterns:

- *Accessibility.* Numerous third-party (client) applications participate in Afni's mashups. This collaboration is extremely important because Afni does not have access to client applications' source code and does not have the right to directly modify the applications in any way. Without mashups, Afni agents would be forced to learn and interact with a wide range of client and Afni applications directly.

- *Content Aggregation.* Mashups pull customer data from multiple applications and present it to agents in a unified customer view. This allows Afni agents to spend less time navigating and toggling between applications and more time servicing customers.

- *Usability Enhancer.* Afni mashups provide agents with a streamlined, unified view of the customer. In addition, the mashup-generated user interfaces are designed in such a way as to walk agents through the desired customer support call flow. Agents simply need to follow the flow, working from top to bottom of the screen. Fields are color coordinated (green and red) to inform agents which steps need to be completed.

- *Distributed Drill-Down.* Afni mashups limit the direct interaction between agents and client applications. Although client applications are active on agents' desktops, the primary user interface is the mashup. If an agent requires additional customer information beyond what is provided by the mashup, he or she can simply click on a link in the mashup, which triggers a separate automation to bring forward the client application and navigate to the appropriate page view— further saving the agent time and effort.

- *Content Migration.* While there is tremendous value in limiting the number of applications that an Afni agent must access directly, it is still necessary to update client applications with new or updated customer information. Mashups automations address this issue directly. Any customer fields that are changed in the Afni mashup are automatically applied to relevant client applications behind the scenes and without any direct involvement by the agent.

- *Integration.* Not only does Afni automate processes (e.g., data entry) across applications, but the company now logs call notes automatically to capture agent activities and customer data. This step provides Afni with an audit trail and helps to prove that the company is compliant with client requirements. In addition, it helps to identify bottlenecks that can be addressed by Afni's quality teams.

- *Workflow.* One advantage of mashups is their ability to quickly add or change agent workflows when mandated by a client policy change. Even if a client application cannot be quickly modified, Afni can modify the mashup's user interface or the underlying processing to support new client policies, all without affecting the client application.

Benefits

Afni's mashup implementations deliver a number of important benefits to its staff and customers:

- Afni contact center agents can now spend more time resolving customer issues instead of navigating to and toggling between applications. They are able to resolve customer issues more quickly and have improved the company's first-call resolution rates.

- Customer satisfaction is improved when support call times are reduced and when a higher percentage of support cases are resolved on the first call.

- Afni's clients benefit because their customers receive a better overall quality of service and because they are assured that mandated policy and compliance requirements are being achieved in a timely and efficient manner.

- Afni, as a company, has benefited from improved agent productivity and first-call resolution rates, simplified agent training, and reduction of performance and compliance penalties. Afni has also improved its ability to respond quickly to its clients' needs (e.g., policy changes). A company manager's own words say it best:

"Afni has achieved a number of important benefits by building mashups with OpenSpan technology," says Jeff Badger, ITS Director. "By speeding access to customer data and eliminating a number of cumbersome manual processes, we have been able to improve productivity and reduce average handling times for customer support calls. We're also much better prepared to support the needs of our *Fortune* 500 clients. OpenSpan enables us to apply changes to our mashups and supporting workflows in a very timely manner as our clients' business policies change."

Associated Press

Summary

The Associated Press (AP) made a huge leap forward in aggregating content from a host of technologically dissimilar news sites. The information was transformed into a new product that led to a new revenue stream for the AP.

Value Proposition	Achieve superior content aggregation and generate new revenue, both for the company itself and for its 1,500 member newspapers in the United States
Mashup Content Sources	Web sites and RSS feeds
Location of Processing	In-house server
Mashup Output	XML output is provided for the customer's internal processing flow, which feeds into a centralized repository
Mashup Developers	End users
Target Audience	End users
Vendor Product Used	Agent Community GEN2 (Connotate)
Mashup Patterns	Content Integration, Folksonomy Enabler

Problem Statement

The Associated Press is the oldest and largest news organization in the world. It has thrived through the era of the pony express, telegraph, and computer.

The AP relies on two main sources of content. The first source is the company's own 3,000 writers and photographers around the world, all of whom deliver content in a form dictated by the AP. The second source of content is more challenging: 1,500 member newspapers around the country generate, produce, and transmit their own content using a variety of technologies. As a news-sharing service, the AP faced several dilemmas:

- How could the AP pull all this information into a centralized Web repository?

- How could the AP enhance this information and develop new sources of revenue for the company and its members?

- How could the AP accomplish the preceding goals efficiently, without placing additional burdens on member newspapers that are already grappling with financial pressures?

Newspaper Web sites often lack effective metadata for searchability and targeted advertising. When the AP began investigating how to standardize this information, it found that less than 1% of these sites met the required standards for enriched Web feeds that facilitate Web advertising sales. The member newspapers were frequently engaged with their own business challenges and could not spare the technical resources to retool their systems—especially to meet standards imposed by an outside party. The AP sought a win-win solution: the ability to collect, enrich, and distribute the content of its members that would enable a new set of business offerings, while requiring minimal effort from its partners.

The challenge was not a matter of figuring out how to quickly throw text on the Web. Issues related to large-scale content ingestion, aggregation, and enrichment needed to be solved.

Solution

The AP was able to automate its content ingestion and aggregation processes and create a new source of revenue. More than 75% of the Digital Cooperative content now comes through solutions provided by the Agent Community GEN2 product from Connotate. Its Intelligent Agents collect information and metadata, apply contextual information, and send it to a database where it is normalized and indexed. This information then becomes a source of new revenue and content for the AP and its member newspapers.

The software-based Agents were trained to pull information from newspaper feeds and Web sites. Computer-literate users—not programmers—created the mashups in the Agent Studio's point-and-click environment. These Intelligent Agents log into sites, navigate many layers deep, and read numerous formats including HTML, RSS, and databases. For example, one Agent might be trained to pull content from the numerous RSS feeds on the Web site of the *Atlanta Journal Constitution* and then go deeper into the Web site to bring back the complete story details and metadata not included in the RSS feeds (Figure A.1). The Agent ultimately provides the complete story and metadata in a standardized schema for consumption by the AP's existing infrastructure.

To speed up the payoff from the new offerings, the AP needed to enlist its member community. The AP accomplished this feat by providing business incentives for members. Just as importantly, the Intelligent Agents allow the AP to respect the technical diversity of its members' Web sites. This flexibility kept the barriers to entry into the Digital Cooperative low and helped enlist nontechnical resources to contribute to the solution.

Mashup Patterns Used

- *Content Integration.* The AP case study is a classic example of the Content Integration pattern, taking all the content of the member newspaper sites and combining it without inflicting technological anxiety on the 1,500 individual resources that supply the material. This creates a resource that is indeed greater than the sum of its parts.

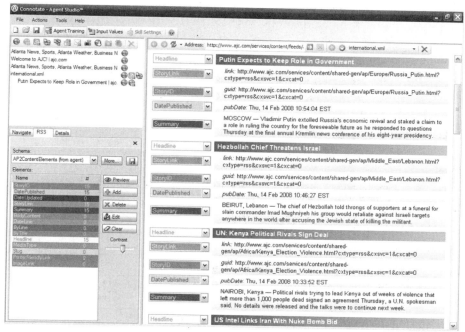

Figure A.1 *The AP used the Connotate mashup platform to enrich RSS feeds.*

- *Folksonomy Enabler.* Member content is now taggable with a robust set of custom metadata—including subject categories and entities (people, places, and things). For example, a story might be tagged with the keywords "business," "interest rates," "Federal Reserve," and "Ben Bernanke."

Benefits

The Content Enrichment service—the first within the AP's Digital Cooperative—is already providing strong business benefits:

- It triggers more hits from search engines that index content using keywords and metadata (previously these artifacts did not exist).

- It allows for customizing content around a specific subject area and targeting stories for specific markets.

- It supports contextual advertising with links in relevant subject-area categories and classifications.

- It groups related content items even if they don't share the same keywords.

- It powers widgets that distribute content and reach audiences in their preferred location.

Audi

Summary

Audi's information technology group used mashups to drive its self-service IT initiatives and to speed application delivery.

Value Proposition	Enable end-user portal application development without IT support
Mashup Content Sources	IBM Websphere Portal
Location of Processing	In-house Portal Integration server
Mashup Output	JSR-168-compliant portal services
Mashup Developers	All Audi employees
Target Audience	All Audi employees
Vendor Product Used	Kapow (Kapow Technologies)
Mashup Patterns	Aggregate, Translation, Portal Enabler, Quick Proof-of-Concept, Splinter

Problem Statement

Part of Audi's business strategy is to double in size without increasing IT costs. To meet this goal Audi's IT team took an aggressive approach to self-service development that leverages the company's existing portal infrastructure.

Solution

Audi has a business-to-employee (B2E) portal for every employee in the company including the Volkswagen group. In leveraging this portal, the IT group developed a strategy to "let our customers do our work" via a "process portal." Kapow's Portal Content Edition is used to build new services and portlets, and business process management tools from jCOM1 are used to assemble the application flow. This combination allows any employee to generate "codeless" portals without IT support.

Mashup Patterns Used

- The ability to directly generate JSR-168 portlets for Audi's IBM WebSphere Portal infrastructure is a robust application of the *Portal Enabler* pattern.

- Virtually every employee was empowered to innovate using the *Quick Proof-of-Concept* pattern against departmental data.

- *Language Translation,* when necessary, was an important part of the mashup development process to engage the broadest audience.

- The resulting mashups both *Aggregate* and *Splinter* data for easy reuse by other users.

Benefits

Mashups, according to Audi, are valuable for their role in "practical new application generation" and the ease of integrating different platforms. These benefits were recognized in several areas:

- Application deployment was observed to be both faster and cheaper, without the need to replace existing systems.

- Employees no longer had to wait for IT support.

- Departmental data was effectively repurposed across the enterprise for marketing, sales, transportation and logistics optimization.

- Many intranet and sales applications were mobilized and translated.

Mashups also enabled Audi to repurpose dedicated external Web applications for internal use. This capability has proved extremely valuable because the company does not allow its employees to access content outside the firewall in a normal browser.

Audi's product managers used to check each of the 20 sources individually and copy the results into spreadsheets. While the task was time consuming and inconvenient, Audi's information-technology department didn't want to pay as much as $500,000 to combine all of the data into one application using traditional software-integration techniques, says Anton Hermann Kramm, a member of Audi's IT management team. But using a mashup tool from Kapow Technologies Inc., one developer was able to build the new application in just four days for a fraction of that cost. Mr. Kramm says developers at Audi have built about 30 mashups, using data from nearly 100 sources.[2]

---

2. "'Mashups' Sew Data Together." *The Wall Street Journal,* July 31, 2007. http://online.wsj.com/article/SB118584045835882843.html

Defense Intelligence Agency

Summary

The Defense Intelligence Agency (DIA) implemented mashups to improve the speed, timeliness, and accuracy of the organization's situational awareness.

Value Proposition	The DIA wanted to improve the timeliness of analyses by leveraging emerging data service standards without violating agency's strict standards for security, governance, and monitoring.
Mashup Content Sources	Web sites
Location of Processing	In-house server
Mashup Output	XML
Mashup Developers	End users
Target Audience	End users
Vendor Product Used	Presto (JackBe)
Mashup Patterns	Alerter, API Enabler, Dashboard, Filter, Leading Indicator, Location Mapping, Reality Mining, Time Series, Super Search

Problem Statement

The DIA's[3] stated vision is the "integration of highly skilled intelligence professionals with leading edge technology to discover information and create knowledge that provides warning, identifies opportunities, and delivers overwhelming advantage to our warfighters, defense planners, and defense and national security policymakers."[4] With more than 12,000 military and civilian employees worldwide, DIA is a major producer and manager of foreign military intelligence. It provides military intelligence to the Department of Defense and the intelligence community in support of U.S. military planning and operations and weapon systems acquisition.[5] One of the agency's major challenges is to isolate potentially significant information from a vast array of sources.

Solution

The DIA has applied mashups to the problem of military intelligence gathering in an effort described as "one of the most successful Web 2.0 projects in govern-

---

3. http://www.dia.mil

4. http://www.dia.mil/thisisdia/mission.htm

5. http://www.dia.mil/thisisdia/intro/index.htm

ment to date."[6] The DIA's mashup effort, called Overwatch, is a dashboard application that acts as a "virtual operating center," integrating a wide range of intelligence sources into a single browser-based situation-awareness dashboard (see Figure A.2). JackBe's Presto product was selected to create this implementation. In addition to integrating with the DIA's public-key infrastructure (PKI) framework, the DIA mashup solution required Presto connect to many services within DIA's network. Presto acts as an intermediary between analysts and services. This approach provides a platform that lets analysts mash "normalized" data sources regardless of their implementation type (SOA, RSS, SQL, or otherwise).

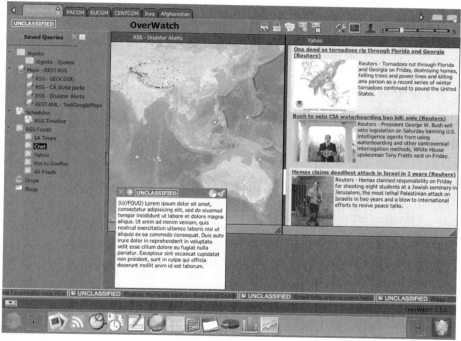

Figure A.2 *Overwatch Dashboard (Unclassified)*

Mashup Patterns Used

- *Alerter.* Analysts receive alerts based on custom conditions.

- *Filter.* Analysts can apply personalized criteria to isolate important information from the pool of available content.

---

6. Intelligent Enterprise, May 12, 2008

- *Leading Indicator.* Analysts monitor multiple message feeds to make situational assessments.

- *Reality Mining.* Analyst actions can be fed into context analyzers to detect common usage patterns.

- *Time Series.* Analysts take a snapshot of the mashup data to provide intuitive time-based analysis.

- *API Enabler.* Analysts share mashup data so others can consume and customize the data.

- *Super Search.* Analysts interact with search engines and mashup results to other internal and external data.

- *Dashboard.* Analysts are provided with a dashboard of mashlets, which are easily consumable.

- *Location Mapping.* Analysts feed mashup data to geospatial engines for rapid geospatial tagging.

Benefits

- The Overwatch program has become an important tool that allows analysts to track information resources around the world in real time.

- A number of project members went on to win awards for their work on Overwatch.

- Overwatch continues its evolution today with continued integration of existing and emerging technologies within the DIA, including the DIA's security and services infrastructures.

MICROS Systems

Summary

MICROS Systems provides enterprise software applications for the hospitality and retail industries. The fast-growing company has more than 220,000 software installations in restaurants, hotels, casinos, and leisure properties in over 130 countries. When MICROS noticed an increase in issues related to software quality, the company took a close look at its application development process. The recommendations that resulted were twofold: (1) The company needed to change and improve its development process and (2) it needed a way to capture metrics related to project delivery timelines, costs, defect ratios, and other data.

Value Proposition	MICROS improved customer satisfaction and saved more than $4 million by providing better-quality products on a timely basis.
Mashup Content Sources	Databases
Location of Processing	In-house servers
Mashup Output	HTML
Mashup Developers	IT personnel
Target Audience	Internal users, IT personnel, management
Vendor Product Used	Business Mashups, Serena Mashup Composer (Serena Software)
Mashup Patterns	Content Migration, Workflow

Problem Statement

When MICROS noticed an increase in challenges customers encountered were related to software quality, the company took a close look at its application development process. "We created an internal task force to review our development process, and also hired external consultants to provide recommendations," says Jos Schaap, Vice President of Hotel Product Development for MICROS Systems. The recommendations that came back were twofold: (1) The company needed to change and improve its development process and (2) it needed a way to capture metrics related to project delivery timelines, costs, defect ratios, and other data. "We had no way of evaluating or measuring the effectiveness of our application development process," says Schaap. The task force came up with an improved development process with new checks and balances, but Schaap realized it would be too costly to manage and enforce manually. Schaap was determined to improve software quality but needed a system that could enforce new development processes while providing metrics and reporting to gauge progress.

Solution

With Serena Business Mashups, MICROS found an advanced workflow-based solution to standardize, track, automate, and enforce a new and improved development process. The company selected Mashup Composer for its highly flexible, advanced capabilities for IT process management.

Mashup Patterns Used

- *Content Migration.* Duplicate data entry was avoided by the use of mashups to automatically update an existing customer service application.

- *Workflow.* MICROS was able to save an enormous amount of money because the enforceable workflow ensured adherence to its sanctioned best practices. With solid, previously designed best practices adopted from various industry development best practices including CMMI,[7] MICROS was able to obtain reliable data to make management decisions.

Benefits

Serena Business Mashups has enabled a rapid increase in MICROS's product quality while significantly reducing the company's costs. "With Business Mashups, we have seen an 85% reduction in critical defects, amounting to $4 million in annual cost savings related to reduced customer troubleshooting as well as time and resources spent developing new releases and service packs," says Schaap. Business Mashups has brought about a dramatic improvement in software quality by automating enforceable, repeatable processes for developers. "It ensures developers are going through the necessary checks and balances," he adds.

In addition, Business Mashups has provided another missing link: data, metrics, and reporting for improved decision making. Schaap can now report on the history of actual work, including when projects are completed and by whom. He can measure defect ratios and on-time application deliveries, for example, and send reports to the MICROS regional distribution network and executive management team, proving to the company that he is getting a handle on quality. Similarly, the sales department can use these measurable results in the sales process to lure new business prospects. "I send Business Mashup

---

7. Capability Maturity Model Integration (CMMI) is a framework for improving business processes.

reports to our management team every month, and every month we are able to show a decrease in the number of defects," he says.

Business Mashups have also helped Schaap and his eight development teams improve their planning and estimating activities. "We now can predict how long various projects take and provide accurate estimates around software delivery time frames," says Schaap. Armed with this historical information, Schaap can schedule the right people to work on the right projects at the right time. Other statistics, such as percentage of on-time, early, or late deliveries, have enabled Schaap to benchmark and set new goals for improving upon those figures and measuring progress. "We are using the data to work toward a more lean development organization," says Schaap. The company has saved $60,000—the cost of one employee—by integrating Mashup Composer with the company's customer service application, thereby eliminating duplicative data entry. The integration has also led to improved customer service, as customer change requests are updated instantly within the customer-facing application.

With mashups and Schaap's astute leadership of the application development team, MICROS is delivering high-quality applications to its customers, improving customer satisfaction, and enhancing its image in the marketplace. Looking ahead, MICROS hopes to build on its initial success with further improvements in product quality and on-time delivery ratios.

Philadelphia Stock Exchange

Summary

The Philadelphia Stock Exchange (PHLX), recently acquired by the New York Stock Exchange (NYSE), is one of the most diverse exchanges in the world, offering equities, options, currencies, indexes, and futures. The regional exchange serves as a "wholesaler" for large financial services firms such as Goldman Sachs and Merrill Lynch. PHLX is audited every year by both internal and external auditors. With six to seven signatures required for every change request, the legacy paper-based request process could take several days to successfully navigate. When it came time for audits, IT personnel spent days wading through thousands of documents to find specific items for auditors.

A new mashup-powered process-management solution has transformed IT operations at PHLX. Approximately 2,500 hours of administrative work has been saved per year; the change approval process has been significantly reduced due to automation; uptime for all mission-critical systems is 100%; and IT is handling more change requests without hiring additional employees.

Value Proposition	The Philadelphia Stock Exchange needed to streamline the time and effort spent creating audit reports
Mashup Content Sources	Databases, Web Services
Location of Processing	In-house servers
Mashup Output	HTML
Mashup Developers	IT personnel
Target Audience	Internal users, IT personnel, auditors, management
Vendor Product Used	Business Mashups, Serena Mashup Composer (Serena Software)
Mashup Patterns	Audit, Content Aggregation, Workflow

Problem Statement

Working in a complex IT environment and highly regulated industry, Bernie Donnelly, Vice President of Quality Assurance for PHLX, says that the biggest challenge he's faced over the years is managing and tracking application changes. Additionally, the U.S. Securities and Exchange Commission (SEC), Commodities Futures Trading Commission (CFTC), and internal and external auditors audit PHLX every year.

Using a purely manual approach where every change required six to seven signatures, paper-based requests could take several days to get approved. "We had to carefully document all application changes and approvals on paper. Every year we'd fill up an average of 10 boxes full of change control documents," says Donnelly. When it came time for audits, Donnelly's team spent days wading through thousands of documents to find specific items for auditors. "We also had very limited visibility into what projects were going on across departments," says Donnelly. With automated, enforceable change control processes, PHLX could deliver new application changes faster to keep up with market demands.

Solution

PHLX determined that mashups provided the flexibility it required. "We could tailor the workflow processor to meet our specific business needs," says Donnelly. PHLX chose tools from Serena Software to implement the necessary enhancements. "Making an electronic copy of a change request or authorization only solves part of the problem," says Donnelly. "Mashup Composer solved our core problems by giving us a centralized platform with enforceable processes for controlling change. We could track all of the data related to any given change request including signatures, approvals, test results, time-stamps, and attach documents for improved accountability, reporting, visibility, and traceability."

Mashup Patterns Used

- *Audit.* Previously manual processes were automated with full traceability for complete, quick, and easy auditing.

- *Workflow.* Change management processes were enforced to ensure proper approvals and accountability.

- *Content Aggregation.* Multiple audit and workflow trails were pulled together to create reports for external auditors.

Benefits

Mashups have transformed IT operations at PHLX. "We now have clear audit trails from cradle to grave," says Donnelly. For a recent CFTC audit, the company used Mashup Composer to deliver 60,000 electronic pages to auditors within 10 days of the request. "The auditors were blown away. We've set a new standard for the futures industry," says Donnelly. Previously, it took "a small army" of team members one full month to collect the boxes, go through the documents, index papers, and make photocopies. With electronic files, PHLX has eliminated paper and storage fees, resulting in significant cost savings.

Donnelly estimates that the automated signature and approval process saves the company 2,500 person-hours per year alone, equating to cost savings of more than $160,000. With mashups, the overall change approval process has been reduced. "The authorization process is electronic and fully automated. Mashup Composer workflows route signatures around the organization for approval, which means we are much more productive and responsive as a department. We're not running around the building anymore trying to get a piece of paper signed by someone," says Donnelly.

Donnelly is proud that the company's uptime for all mission-critical systems is 100%, which he attributes in part to the Serena products. "With Business Mashups, we have an enforceable process in place to guide developers through change requests. It's a major enhancement to the change authorization process," says Donnelly.

Mashups have served as a magnet, bringing department teams together to work more effectively. "Mashup Composer reports give everyone the big picture. Everyone gets visibility into all of the projects in the pipeline and target dates. We can coordinate with other groups several weeks in advance to head off potential conflicts."

Simply Hired

Summary

Simply Hired is a Web 2.0 company that uses mashup tools to aggregate and update millions of jobs listings on a daily basis. These job listings drive a vibrant advertising network.

Value Proposition	Initially, aggregate 1 million job listings in 90 days. Ultimately, aggregate job information from thousands of sites.
Mashup Content Sources	Public and partner Web sites
Location of Processing	In-house server
Mashup Output	SQL database
Mashup Developers	A small development team
Target Audience	Millions of Web job seekers and sellers of job intelligence
Vendor Product Used	Kapow (Kapow Technologies)
Mashup Patterns	Alerter, API Enabler, Infinite Monkeys, Quick Proof of Concept, Time Series

Problem Statement

Simply Hired's business model is predicated on harvesting millions of job listings on a daily basis. The company's development team picked Kapow's Data Collection Edition after determining this approach would be up to 10 times faster than a "do-it-yourself" approach.

Key requirements included the following considerations:

- Ability to harvest 1 million job listing within the first 90 days of the project

- Easy access to all sites, including those with complex JavaScript and AJAX scripts

- High availability and scaling based on a stateless server technology

- Transformation of Web data originating in thousands of different unstructured formats into a standard format that could be directly written to a commercial database management system through a JDBC interface

- Avoiding data duplication at collection time

Solution

The Simply Hired engineering team considered several custom-coding alternatives such as Python, PHP, and JavaScript. These approaches were found to be extremely intolerant of Web site changes and therefore difficult and time-consuming for development and maintenance.

The Kapow Data Collection Edition met the key selection criteria and avoided the problems associated with a scripted do-it-yourself approach. Simply Hired now collects job postings from a wide variety of Web-based sources from its business partners, including *Fortune* 1000 Web sites and large commercial job posting boards.

Mashup Patterns Used

Simply Hired's use of mashups was an effective demonstration of the following patterns:

- *Alerter.* When page content shifts so dramatically that a mashup cannot automatically adjust its collection activities, a notification is sent to developers that maintenance is required.

- *Infinite Monkeys.* Thousands of Web sites are harvested programmatically for their underlying content

- *Time Series.* By recognizing and harvesting only information that changes, the response time of the underlying systems (including those with complex JavaScript and AJAX scripts) remains unaffected. Keeping a time series of previously collected data makes this optimization possible.

- *API Enabler.* Web Services were created for sites where no public interface existed, thereby allowing for the filtering and reformatting of data at collection time.

- *Quick Proof-of-Concept.* With more than 1 million jobs being aggregated in 90 days along with integration of an existing SQL database infrastructure, Simply Hired demonstrated how mashups can not only provide unique new solutions, but also deliver them quickly.

Benefits

"When we deployed the Kapow Mashup Server, we immediately realized up to a 10× productivity increase, depending on the task," said Peter Weck, CTO at Simply Hired. "We could not have reached critical mass as quickly as it did without Kapow Technologies. We highly recommend this solution to anyone whose business depends on integrating internet content, either for internal enterprise mashups or for innovative business models that serve customers through a Web site."[8]

Thanks to mashup technology, Simply Hired created the largest jobs database on the Web within 90 days, and developer productivity was 10 times higher than could be achieved with traditional methods.

8. "Simply Hired Sets New Industry Records with the Kapow Mashup Server." Press release. http://www.simplyhired.com/press/archives/2007/06/simply_hired_se.php

Thomson Financial

Summary

Thomson Financial, a subsidiary of Thomson Corporation, now Thomson Reuters, employs 8,700 employees delivering integrated information, technology, and applications to the financial services industry. A few years ago, the company analyzed its business processes and found common business challenges: issues of accountability and visibility, as well as "hand-off" or workflow breakdowns between people, departments, and systems.

With a focus on streamlining sales, services, and operational processes, the company deployed mashups as a front-office solution to engage employees, eliminate hand-offs, and lock down processes. As a result, Thomson Financial has seen a double-digit increase in employee productivity gains along with many other benefits. Today, 34% of its workforce uses mashups to manage day-to-day activities.

Value Proposition	Streamline business processes for in-house staff and provide faster service to new and prospective customers
Mashup Content Sources	Databases, Web Services
Location of Processing	In-house servers
Mashup Output	HTML
Mashup Developers	End users, IT personnel
Target Audience	Internal users, IT personnel, management
Vendor Product Used	Business Mashups, Serena Mashup Composer (Serena Software)
Mashup Patterns	Content Aggregation, Communication and Collaboration, Workflow

Problem Statement

Thomson Financial analyzed its sales and related processes across the company and found common business challenges: issues of accountability, visibility, and "hand-off" or workflow breakdowns between people, departments, and IT systems. There were significant challenges in the sales organizations, for example. The company's sales and services departments were operating independently as silos, were not communicating with one another, and were bogged down with time-consuming administrative work.

Thomson Financial needed to streamline its business processes to gain advantages of scale and efficiency—as well as nimbleness and speed. "We took significant steps to improve and streamline our sales and support processes, but we still had 'hand-off' breakdowns. There was a lot of opportunity to improve adherence to our new processes," explains Warren Breakstone, Executive Vice President and Chief Operations Officer for Global Sales, Marketing, and Services at Thomson Financial. "We had accountability issues as well. People didn't know what they were responsible for—or when. And all levels of management lacked visibility into the key projects, initiatives, and metrics that were important to them." The company spent "lots of time and money" on reengineering efforts, applying patchwork solutions that did not ultimately solve its long-term business problems.

Says Breakstone, "We needed a solution that would make it easy for people to engage and a mechanism to lock down workflow between people, departments, and systems. We also needed to motivate people to adhere to new processes. Employees needed to get something in return for adopting our new processes."

Solution

In the face of these commonplace challenges, which are all too familiar to most large companies, Thomson Financial found an uncommon solution for solving critical challenges. "We took a traditional 'back-office' tool—Serena Mashup Composer—and transformed it into a front-office solution to address critical visibility, accountability, and handoff issues," says Breakstone. Mashups have become the central nervous system—and the glue—of the company's new, streamlined global business operations. The company originally selected Mashup Composer for internal Help Desk incident management, but soon extended it to many other aspects of the business to bridge silos, eliminate paper-based processes, improve communications, secure hand-offs, improve visibility, and lock down processes.

"Mashup Composer is simple to use and apply to different business problems since you don't need someone writing lines and lines of code all the time. It's unique because it's configuration based rather than code based," explains John Hastings-Kimball, Vice President of Workflow Solutions for Thomson Financial. "The result is minimal time and effort spent administering the system, wide employee adoption, and the ability to apply the application to solve unique business challenges."

Thomson Financial has not only standardized and enforced sales, services, and related operational processes to reap efficiency gains, but is also providing executives and managers with business intelligence metrics through dashboards for improved decision making and performance on a global scale. "Most of our core sales and services processes are now tied together by Serena Business

Mashups," says Breakstone. The company has applied mashups to improve processes, collaboration, and accountability in key areas including the customer-facing Help Desk, sales proposal development, customer enhancement requests, and product trial management.

Breakstone explains, "A sales manager can open his Business Mashups dashboard and find out, 'What are my action items today?' He may see a number of different tasks that require action—sales orders to review, commission payments to approve, product trial extensions to authorize. All of these tasks can be acted upon within Mashup Composer, which triggers workflow routing to the next individual or department." Primary mashup users are sales personnel, but the implementation is also used regularly by sales operations, contract managers, billing representatives, product managers, and call center agents.

"Our employees love it," says Breakstone. "They like the improved visibility and control that they achieve by having access to reliable, accurate information. Instant dashboard access to business intelligence and reports enables them to better manage their teams and achieve improved results for their parts of the business. They really like knowing the status of issues and who needs to take the next action."

Mashup Patterns Used

- *Content Aggregation.* Information was pulled from various sources to create complete sales proposals in a short amount of time.

- *Communication and Collaboration.* Employees communicated across departments to engage appropriate resources and provide faster customer support.

- *Workflow.* The process of product trials was managed to ensure nothing fell through the cracks. All trial customers were contacted as part of the process to close the "last mile" and create an increased revenue stream.

Benefits

Thomson Financial is an efficient, healthy, fleet-footed, customer-centric company—a result of its innovative use of mashups. The company has seen a double-digit increase in employee productivity since the implementation of its mashups. "We have also reduced errors, improved customer service levels, and become a more responsive company, which is critical in the financial services industry," says Breakstone. The results are in:

- Thomson Financial has overhauled its sales proposal process with mashup-powered solution. "It used to take about five days to pull together a sales proposal. Now it takes three minutes," says Hastings-Kimball. "Our sales teams now spend more time with their customers and prospects to increase revenue."

- Product trial management has been transformed thanks to mashups. "Signing up a customer for a product trial, managing it, and enforcing an expiration date used to be a burden on sales. It took about four days to get paperwork through sales, the contracts group, and billing," says Hastings-Kimball. "A trial can now be set up in an instant—literally."

- Mashups have helped Thomson Financial become more responsive. "Managing customer enhancement requests used to be a clunky process of email and phone calls. Requests are now pushed from the customer service agent deep into the company to the product manager who specializes in a particular area. Once the request has been addressed by the product manager, Mashup Composer closes the loop with a communication back to the customer stating that the issue has been addressed," says Breakstone. "Everyone in the company is responsible for providing excellent customer service and Business Mashups helps ensure that we deliver it."

- More than 3,000 employees—or 34% of the company's workforce—use mashups to manage their day-to-day job functions for improved productivity, collaboration, and accountability.

Thomson Reuters

Summary

The Scientific business division of Thomson Reuters implemented mashups that enhance the collaborative community's value to its community members by providing them with a self-service "Badge" representing professional research that can be easily syndicated to independent blogs, Web sites, and wikis.

Value Proposition	The Scientific business division of Thomson Reuters wanted to extend the reach of its professional collaborative community, adding value for its research-oriented members and thereby creating greater member loyalty.
Mashup Content Sources	Web sites
Location of Processing	In-house server
Mashup Output	Mashup-driven widgets
Mashup Developers	Community developers
Target Audience	End users
Vendor Product Used	Presto (JackBe)
Mashup Patterns	Location Mapping, Reality Mining, Time Series, Usability Enhancer, Widget Enabler

Problem

Many applications of mashups are applicable to researchers, whether the type of research they conduct involves the scientific, medical, financial, or other fields. With more than $12.4 billion in annual revenues, Thomson Reuters[9] is one of the world's largest information brokers. In 2007, approximately 88% of the company's pro forma revenues were derived from electronic products, software, and services.[10] Thomson wished to broaden the reach of one of its scientific community portals, ResearcherID,[11] which functions as a "gateway to researchers and their published works" for "accurate author and publication identification." ResearcherID provides first-person author profiles, publication lists, and citation metrics, thereby creating a source for research collaboration.

9. http://www.thomsonreuters.com

10. http://www.thomsonreuters.com/about/

11. http://www.researcherid.com

Solution

Dynamic mashups associated with specific users (who are typically researchers in fields such as physics or medicine) were developed using the Presto product from vendor JackBe. These mashups, also referred to as "Badges," include users' published research and demographic citation views. In addition, ResearcherID Badges were designed to be easily embedded in a user's personal blog or Web site and to be emailed to peers. Each Badge, when embedded in a personal blog or portal, gives a dynamic preview of the researcher's data to the community. Clicking on the Badge takes the visitor directly to that researcher's page within the ResearcherID site. Thomson Reuters also included two other mashup-based widgets for the members of ResearcherID: the Collaboration Network, a graphical cross-reference of the researcher's professional collaborators, and the Citing Articles Network, a map-based view of independent references to the researcher's publications.

The new, broader dissemination of Thomson Reuters' scientific-oriented mashup information elicited some concerns about the new potential uses of that information. ResearcherID mashups are freely distributable by the community's users. Once the Web at large was exposed to the company's ResearcherID information, a key question arose: Would the existing terms of service that ResearcherID guarantees apply to this new information in a manner that matched Thomson Reuters' business goals? Answering this question necessitated a policy review of those commitments and, more importantly, led to all security requirements being embedded within the mashup.

Mashup Patterns Used

- *Widget Enabler.* Badges can be easily embedded in a third-party blog, wiki, Web site, or email.

- *Usability Enhancer.* Badges simplify user access to mashups and include click-through access to functionality to the underlying ResearcherID Web site.

- *Location Mapping.* Badges display a researcher's citation distribution on a Yahoo map. View is created by a mashup that passes researcher data through a geocoding service.

- *Time Series.* Badges deliver aggregated data that represent a researcher's publication profile. The usage information can be viewed historically or geographically.

- *Reality Mining.* All usage of Badges result in activity log entries that can be mashed together with environmental sensors to provide new and unique data visualizations.

Benefits

Mashups were a successful addition to the ResearcherID community. Within weeks and with little direct promotion or advertising to its community, hundreds of independent professional blogs and Web sites had Badges in them, all linking back to ResearcherID. The mashup-driven Badges allowed the community members to become the extended "sales team" that pushed the community's reach well beyond the formal boundaries of the community portal.

A European Credit Union

Summary

Mashups eliminated a manual account creation process and enabled mobile device access to key account information.

Value Proposition	Streamline new account creation processes on mobile devices without duplicating existing infrastructure
Mashup Content Sources	Existing credit union Web sites
Location of Processing	In-house server
Mashup Output	Integration of existing portals with customer mobile devices
Mashup Developers	IT mobilization team
Target Audience	More than 100,000 customers and their mobile phones
Vendor Product Used	Kapow (Kapow Technologies)
Mashup Patterns	Accessibility, Usability Enhancer, Workflow

Problem Statement

A Europe-based credit union wanted to streamline its complex account creation process, eliminate manual data transcription, and enable mobile devices without duplicating the existing IT infrastructure. Under the existing process, a customer would input information via a Web application and a special team would transcribe the information into another back-end system to create or update the account.

Solution

The firm executed a comprehensive mashup-powered integration effort using products from Kapow Technologies. The new solution collects data directly from the existing Web form, transforms the information, creates a new data stream, and then directly loads it into the existing back-end system.

The credit union's account creation, updating, and account inquiry processes were then mobilized using a similar integration approach. Mobile device communication with the existing Web applications was developed with a new set of integration mashups. These mashups translated the existing Web interface into a format suitable for the mobile experience without requiring the existing code base to be modified.

Mashup Patterns Used

- This credit union demonstrated a unique approach to *Accessibility* by providing a mobile interface driven from the existing code base. In the past, a separate development team would have been required to support this additional platform.

- *Usability Enhancer* was leveraged to simplify a costly and error-prone manual transcription process.

- The *Workflow* pattern made sure account transactions flowed through an appropriate approval process.

Benefits

Several important benefits arose as a result of this effort:

- The new-account creation time was reduced from 10 minutes to 1 minute.

- The transcription team was reassigned to other areas, and overall quality improved because manual processing was eliminated and data was automatically transformed at collection time.

- The second set of mobile device integration mashups enabled more than 100,000 customers to use their mobile devices to create accounts, access information, and transact business. This was done without any duplication of the existing Web infrastructure, saving both development and maintenance costs.

A Financial Publisher

Summary

One of the world's leading financial publishers made a quantum leap in data collection using mashups. Clients are now able to apply specific criteria to searches and obtain results from multiple sites. Through their implementation of mashups, the firm was able to stake out a dominant position in a competitive industry.

Value Proposition	Stay ahead of the competition and deliver measurable business value to subscribers by automating the process of gathering and publishing key information.
Mashup Content Sources	Web sites
Location of Processing	In-house server
Mashup Output	XML
Mashup Developers	End users
Target Audience	End users
Vendor Product Used	Agent Community GEN2 (Connotate)
Mashup Patterns	Alerter, Super Search, Workflow

Problem Statement

A financial publishing company faced the daunting task of navigating the abundance of information on the Web. How could it capture relevant information from the rapidly changing base of available content and distribute it to the company's users?

Capturing large quantities of Web-based information posed both technological and human challenges:

- *Quality and quantity:* Just downloading the quarterly earnings release of *Fortune 500* companies represents a huge volume of information. The structures of the Web sites where this content is made accessible can vary greatly.

- *Scheduling:* During quarterly filing season, performing manual data collection tasks becomes extremely time-consuming. An employee would have to repeatedly check the company Web site to see if a new file has been posted. If an existing file is updated, the user has no way of knowing that fact unless he or she opens the file and checks its contents.

- *Analysis:* Once a new file is identified and downloaded, manual intervention is required to extract the meaningful information.

The publisher needed to automate these tasks for greater efficiency and speed. This firm operates in a competitive niche where every minute matters; beating a competitor to the punch by even a few minutes is a major scoop. The objective was to automate these repetitive processes and perform them many times a day, every day.

The publisher had the following requirements for any solution:

- *Enterprise grade:* Scan tens of thousands of sites with specific frequency on a 24 × 7 basis.

- *Workflow:* Support the customer's process workflow, which continues to evolve.

- *Business users as experts:* Enable business users to train Agents using the tool rather than relying on programmers.

- *Downstream automation:* Download documents as well as metadata to facilitate automated processing in successive steps in the customer's workflow.

- *Language independence:* Work with Web sites in any language and using any programming method.

Solution

The company hired several dozen temporary workers to build mashups using the Agent Community GEN2 product from vendor Connotate (the technical qualification to be hired was simply "the ability to browse the Web"). Because Connotate's Agents (the vendor's terminology for a mashup implementation) do not require programming, the temporary workers were able to create a critical mass of tens of thousands of mashups in a very short period of time. The Agents visit millions of Web pages daily.

Using these Agents the company can extract corporate financial filings from thousands of sites around the world within one hour after they are posted. Some Web sites are visited as frequently as every minute. Quarterly filing season became much more manageable through the implementation of these mashups. Employees no longer have to click repeatedly on a corporate Web site while waiting for reports to be posted. An Agent is able to detect any new files—even revisions to existing files—and download them and deliver them to the appropriate person.

Today the company is able to monitor thousands of company Web sites and instantly be alerted to new press releases, financial reports, or news stories wherever they appear. For example, mashups help this client monitor companies in Eastern Europe and Asia, which are not subject to the same financial reporting requirements as U.S. companies. Instead of relying on a human to repeatedly check these sites, the company uses mashups to monitor them and bring back any new documents.

Mashup Patterns Used

- *Alerter.* Users are automatically notified of new or relevant changes to information sources.

- *Super Search.* The latest information is at users' fingertips faster than they can find it anywhere else and indexed according to the publisher's standards.

- *Workflow.* Data is provided directly to those who need it based on embedded analysis. The mashup has elevated staff focus to analyzing relevant information while decreasing time spent finding and extracting data.

Benefits

At the time these mashups were developed, no one in the industry had been harvesting the Web in this fashion. The mashups put the financial publisher in a position to knock out potential competitors before they posed a significant challenge. The manager who led the implementation project earned a promotion because previously impractical business offerings were now possible due to the functionality enabled by mashups.

A Government Aerospace Contractor

Summary

Mashups allow this firm to manage the delivery of supplies via large aircraft into emergency areas. Many of these aircraft have special airport runway requirements. Thus it is crucial to mine any available source to determine if landing sites are both suitable and undamaged before assistance can be provided

Value Proposition	Quickly bring together disparate public and private data and services to build an application useful in emergency situations
Mashup Content Sources	SQL database and Web Service content converted into Atom feeds
Location of Processing	On the client
Mashup Output	Mashup-driven widgets
Mashup Developers	Tech-savvy end users
Target Audience	End users
Vendor Product Used	IBM Mashup Center
Mashup Patterns	Distributed Drill-Down, Emergency Response, Feed Factory, Location Mapping, Usability Enhancer, Super Search

Problem Statement

This contractor faced the challenge of managing the delivery of relief supplies into areas experiencing emergencies via large aircraft. These large aircraft frequently have special airport runway requirements, such as needing a certain minimum length of runway for safe landing and departure. Such criteria immediately limit the selection of usable locations. Further, depending on the nature of the emergency, many airports in the affected region may be damaged and unacceptable for landing planes even if the runways are long enough.

Solution

In the aftermath of the Hurricane Katrina disaster, many businesses and organizations have actively sought ways to more quickly and effectively respond to unforeseen events. Given that often little is known about the event before it occurs, it should come as no surprise that situational application capabilities provided by mashups is viewed by these groups as a natural tool to help provide a prompt response in the event of an emergency.

The Emergency Response mashup helps manage logistics for large aircraft by detailing which airfields are open, which of those airfields can land planes with a given set of requirements, and what other data is available to assist staff in organizing and coordinating the relief effort. The mashup provides a search box in which the user can select location and runway length requirements. Once the search button is clicked, messages are sent to other widgets to filter their data based on the specified values and results are displayed. Color-coded points are then plotted on a map to represent airports. These push-pins fire events when clicked, which cause tables of other data to be updated based on the selected airport. The final interface is depicted in Figure A.3.

Figure A.3 *The Emergency Response mashup constructed to provide up-to-date airfield information for large aircraft.*

Mashup Patterns Used

- *Emergency Response.* The union of the patterns used in this solution demonstrates the capacity of mashups to provide a quick method for constructing situational solutions when response time is critical.

- *Feed Factory.* Numerous feeds were created against a variety of data sources. Basic airport characteristics were obtained via a direct database query. Another database provided airport identifiers and status information. A third feed was created to provide instant access to Notice to Airmen (NOTAM) data; NOTAM reports are issued by government agencies to alert pilots of any hazardous conditions.[12] The resulting Atom feeds are used by a Super Search implementation.

- *Super Search.* An otherwise static collection of airport characteristics was search-enabled so that locations suitable to specific aircraft could be located easily.

- *Usability Enhancer.* In their original disconnected state, none of the participatory applications cooperated to provide the quick response time needed in an emergency situation. By combining the multiple content sources under the unified widget environment provided by the vendor, the incongruity between sites vanished and a single useful platform emerged.

- *Location Mapping.* Airport status and runway location data resulting from user search activities is periodically published to a map indicating the location and status of available airports. Airports that are open with usable runways are presented with green icons; open airports without a suitable runway are colored yellow; closed airports are colored red. Weather data is received from a separate Feed Factory implementation and overlaid on the map

- *Distributed Drill-Down.* After a particular airport has been selected from the map, detailed information on available runways is presented.

Benefits

In an emergency situation, time is a critical asset that cannot be squandered. However, swift action can lead to greater problems if it is not properly informed. The final solution provides two key benefits by linking a variety of public and private resources: Responders not only have access to data that helps inform their decisions, but they also receive that information from a single, easy-to-use environment. By leveraging the power of mashups this firm is able to assure its employer of its capability to act tactically without putting pilots, support staff, or equipment at unnecessary risk.

---

12. One sample source is the FAA's NOTAM page at https://pilotweb.nas.faa.gov

An Investment Bank

Summary

A major investment bank used the power of mashups to harvest data and uncover leading indicators from a sea of information. This research can suggest new trading opportunities.

Value Proposition	A sell-side financial services firm provides its clients with innovative sources of information, enabling better-informed trading decisions.
Mashup Content Sources	Web sites
Location of Processing	In-house server
Mashup Output	This customer uses email, spreadsheets, Blackberry alerts, and database delivery.
Mashup Developers	Developers and end users
Target Audience	End users
Vendor Product Used	Agent Community GEN2 (Connotate)
Mashup Patterns	Alerter, Competitive Analysis, Infinite Monkeys, Leading Indicator, Time Series

Problem Statement

Investment management firms must deliver proprietary trading insights ahead of their competitors and anticipate market trends. In the fiercely competitive world of investment management, uncovering and delivering innovative research is vital to an investment bank's success. One of the world's largest diversified financial services companies sought a better solution to the problem common to many modern businesses: how to mine and manage the mind-boggling sea of data that fuels unique ideas.

This firm manages more than $600 billion in assets and maintains offices in more than 30 countries. Investment banks have traditionally encouraged investment activity by offering insightful research, but producing unique research has grown more challenging with the explosion of data on the Web. There are now more than a trillion Web pages on the Internet. Employees commonly reported spending a quarter or more of their time just gathering information—surfing the Web and cutting, pasting, and reformatting the data found there. Some members of this company's staff—such as junior analysts who were hired for their analytical abilities—spent the majority of their time performing these tedious activities.

Consider an analyst tasked with monitoring the number of homes for sale on a particular home builder's Web site. The analyst would have to visit the site every day and gather hundreds or thousands of data points to check inventory and sales activity. Even if the analyst focused on just one home builder rather than undertaking a comprehensive view across a set of home builders, the manual effort would be overwhelming. Soon meetings and other duties would make it almost impossible to maintain this mundane routine on a regular schedule. Even the best minds in the business can't perform up to their full potential if they spend a disproportionate amount of time sifting through data. Clearly, a better solution was needed.

The client identified two main objectives:

1. Automate the erratic Web data-gathering efforts being performed by analysts

2. Expose regularly collected data in a manner that stimulates new research and analysis, which would in turn help to differentiate the firm from its competitors

Solution

The firm selected the vendor Connotate to automate its data collection process. Deploying automated mashups freed analysts to expand their research efforts and spend more of their time making the sorts of decisions and judgments that only humans are capable of.

At the core of the solution lie Connotate's intelligent Agents (the vendor's terminology for its specific implementation of mashup technology). These Agents are activated at the same time every day and gather thousands of data points from a single Web site and compile it in whatever format desired. The Agents allow the investment bank to automate complicated tasks such as monitoring online consumer marketplaces in several countries. This task that would have been extremely difficult to complete manually, but the Agents give the client an advantage over competitors that haven't figured out a way to see through the blinding snowstorm of data on the Web.

The Agents regularly harvest data on a variety of topics:

- *Job postings.* Job postings have been a public resource since the early days of the Web, but until recently they have not been fully exploited as valuable sources of information. A cluster of postings for a certain type of qualifications might suggest that a company is undertaking some kind of new initiative. A time-series analysis of this data may reveal trend lines illustrating how many software developers a company is hiring or how much the company is expanding in Asia or Europe. Similarly, an increase in job postings might indicate that management is confident that future prospects are good. Conversely, job posting data could foretell bad news before it becomes public: The sudden removal of job postings may be an early warning that a company expects poor quarterly earnings. Armed with such insight, a trader might take a very profitable position.

Of course, even the best information does little good unless it reaches the right person. Intelligent Agents can be programmed to automatically monitor conditions around the clock and send alerts via email, to a mobile device, or in whatever format the client chooses.

- *Currency markets.* Currency markets are an area of obvious interest for financial institutions. Agents can pick up news that normally wouldn't make it into the mainstream newswires. For example, Agents were able to pick up warnings of a coup in Fiji from local newspapers before the news circulated among the mainstream newswires. The investment bank was then able to take advantage of this information in its business dealings.

- *Travel pricing.* Price fluctuations can be monitored by checking travel pricing for multiple trip scenarios several times each week. This provides a window into consumer trends, the health of the travel industry, and many other interesting points for analysis. Such a task would be all but impossible manually but mashups enables the firm to provide innovative research in this area.

Mashup Patterns Used

- *Alerter.* Users can receive research notifications at the devices of their choosing via instances of the Alerter pattern.

- *Infinite Monkeys.* Repetitive tasks occur at frequencies unachievable by humans. The Agents do their job perfectly all day, every day. For example, an analyst for the travel industry can employ Connotate's Agents to monitor airline ticket prices, cruise line packages, and other indicators around the clock.

- *Time Series, Leading Indicator.* The case study further illustrates the ability to harvest data, including prices, in a Time Series implementation as well as the ability to examine data in new ways, thereby enabling the implementation of the Leading Indicator pattern.

- *Competitive Analysis.* Monitoring the job postings of various firms provides insight into corporate initiatives or impending troubles.

Benefits

This firm achieved substantial results within one year. Financial institutions are characteristically unwilling to publicly share their results, but some metrics can be highlighted. The firm expanded its use of mashups from North America to Europe and Asia. The managers who oversaw the project were promoted. And one manager said, "We cannot operate without it."

A Telecommunications Provider

Summary

Mashups offer a creative mechanism to repurpose and combine content (e.g., city search information) with traditional network-based services such as location and presence that can provide added value to customers.

Value Proposition	Provide a custom experience for mobile service users by mashing together personal content with Web-based telecommunications products and services
Mashup Content Sources	Telecommunication Web Services, personal contact data
Location of Processing	On the client
Mashup Output	Mashup-driven widgets drive network services
Mashup Developers	Tech-savvy end users
Target Audience	End users
Vendor Product Used	IBM Mashup Center
Mashup Patterns	Accessibility, Communication and Collaboration, Feed Factory, Location Mapping, Super Search, Widget Enabler

Problem Statement

Telecommunication companies constantly seek to gain a competitive advantage through differentiation of their content and services. At this particular firm, this overarching business goal was frequently not supported by the internal methods used for developing and deploying new products. The typical approach was to negotiate contracts for content, create new products based on this material, and roll out the offering to the entire customer base. Given the resource investments required by this process, the firm was hesitant to experiment with new offerings because of the high costs required to support new market-wide offerings with unknown returns.

Solution

In this particular scenario, the prospective business opportunity was developed by producing a mashup that could locate and contact available "buddies" by combining mashable content with network-based services. To accomplish this goal, the mashup allows the user to query a list of contacts and either send an SMS message or initiate a third-party call with a chosen contact. In addition, the mashup uses visual color cues to indicate the presence status of the contacts

Figure A.4   *The final output uses the Lotus Widget Factory to display the mashup-powered feeds and services.*

in the contacts list. When the user clicks on a contact in the list, the last known location of the contact is displayed on the map. The resulting interface is shown in Figure A.4.

Mashup Patterns Used

- *Accessibility.* Existing content sources were modified to provide suitable interfaces for a mobile environment.

- *Communication and Collaboration.* Various Web Services were used to handle the tasks of sending SMS messages, initiating phone calls, and determining the presence information for a given user.

- *Feed Factory.* An Atom-based feed of contact information is produced against a back-end database and used to provide a filtered list of users to the Communication and Collaboration implementation.

- *Super Search.* Once presence information was linked to a user's address book, the ability to search on this additional indicator was added to the previous methods for locating contacts.

- *Location Mapping.* An existing Web Service capable of reporting the latitude and longitude coordinates for a user was combined with the native mapping features of the generic map widget to display presence and location information via pin points on a map.

- *Widget Enabler.* The new feeds, services, and presence information are fed to the Lotus Widget platform, where their display can be further formatted and customized.

Benefits

With mashup technologies, new products are much less expensive to develop and deploy. This company was able to adopt a "Long Tail" approach—offering many applications and services, each of which may be used by only a small percentage of its customer base. These offerings can be a combination of traditionally offered services (such as network-based services), presence information, partner services (e.g., city search information), and user-generated content.

Index

The First How-To Guide for Developers Who Want to Create Enterprise-Quality Web 2.0 Mashups

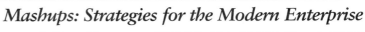

Mashups: Strategies for the Modern Enterprise
J. Jeffrey Hanson • ISBN 0-321-59181-X • © 2009

Discover how to build successful enterprise mashups—one of today's fastest-growing areas of software development. This book

- Walks enterprise developers step-by-step through designing, coding, and debugging their first mashup
- Surveys all of today's leading technologies and standards for rapidly constructing high-quality mashups
- Provides extensive code examples throughout

Mashups offer great potential for businesses seeking faster, better ways to leverage today's immense public and private data resources for competitive advantage. In many cases, however, developers and managers are still trying to understand the best ways to successfully create mashups for their own environments.

Mashups: Strategies for the Modern Enterprise brings together all the insights and techniques they'll need. Author J. Jeffrey Hanson walks readers through every step of creating a working enterprise mashup, including design, implementation, and debugging, illuminating each stage with detailed sample code. Along the way, Hanson surveys the broad spectrum of technologies and standards that have recently become available to simplify mashup development, helping enterprise developers choose the best options for themselves.

This book covers comparing and selecting the right mashup implementation styles, preparing to implement mashups, overcoming technical and business concerns associated with mashups, applying today's best mashup patterns, and much more.

informit.com/title/9780321591814
safari.informit.com

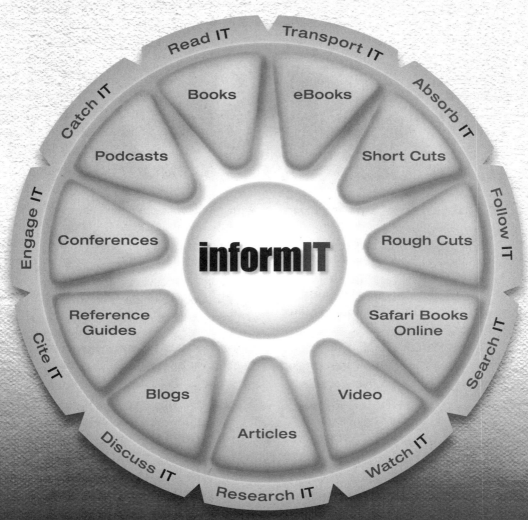

MASHUP PATTERNS
Designs and Examples for the Modern Enterprise

MICHAEL OGRINZ

FREE Online Edition

Your purchase of **Mashup Patterns** includes access to a free online edition for 45 days through the Safari Books Online subscription service. Nearly every Addison-Wesley Professional book is available online through Safari Books Online, along with more than 5,000 other technical books and videos from publishers such as Cisco Press, Exam Cram, IBM Press, O'Reilly, Prentice Hall, Que, and Sams.

SAFARI BOOKS ONLINE allows you to search for a specific answer, cut and paste code, download chapters, and stay current with emerging technologies.

Activate your FREE Online Edition at www.informit.com/safarifree

> **STEP 1:** Enter the coupon code: ZHGMPWA.

> **STEP 2:** New Safari users, complete the brief registration form.
> Safari subscribers, just log in.

If you have difficulty registering on Safari or accessing the online edition, please e-mail customer-service@safaribooksonline.com